E PLURIBUS UNUM

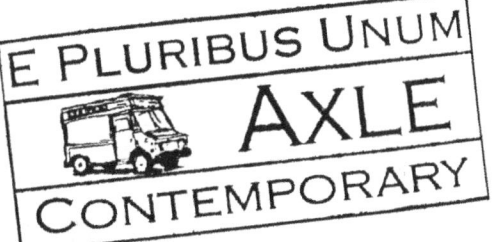

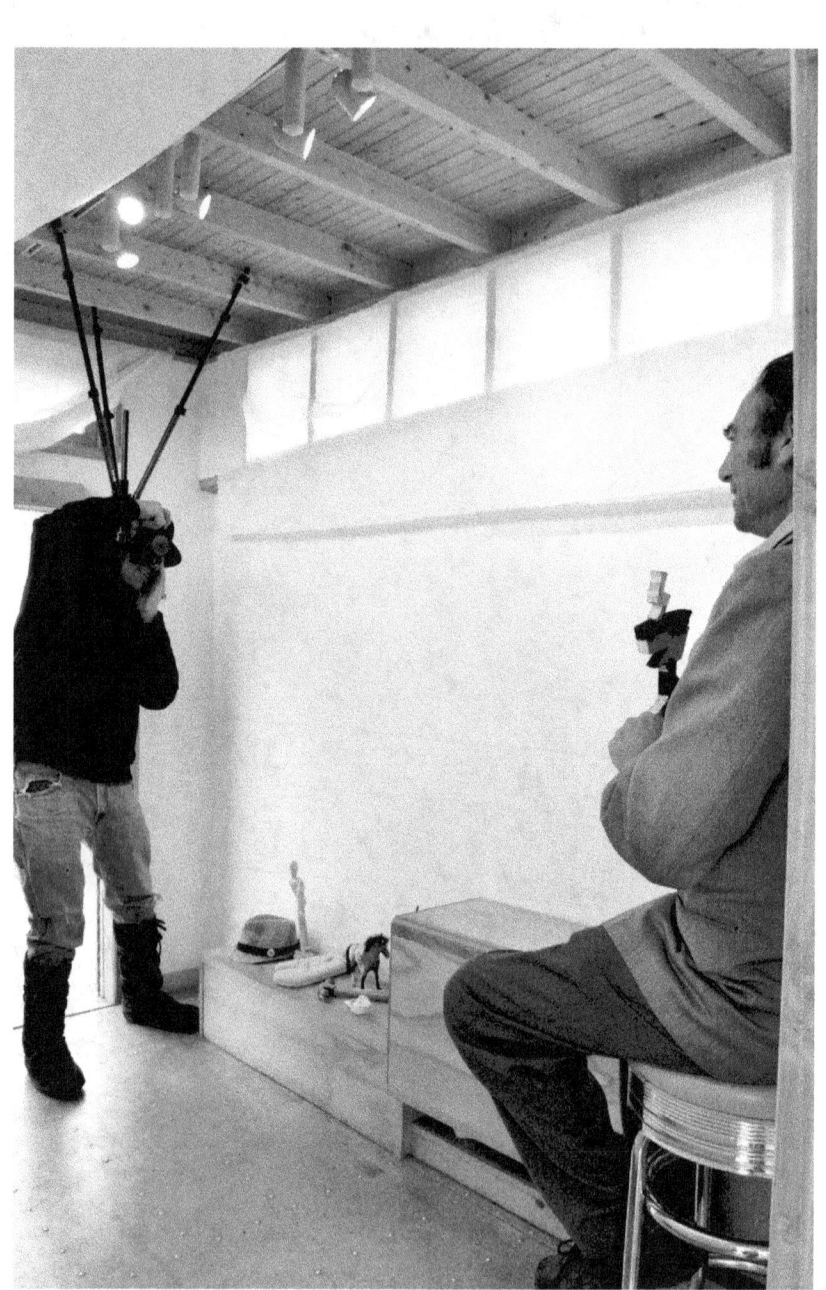

E PLURIBUS UNUM

a citywide art project

by

Axle Contemporary

March 2-11, 2012

Santa Fe, New Mexico

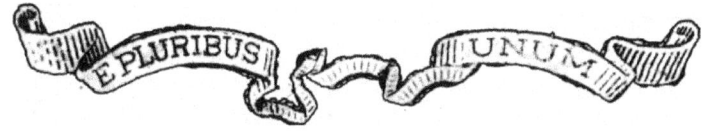

Axle Contemporary Press, Santa Fe, New Mexico

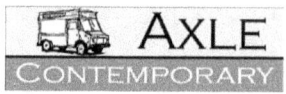

Published by Axle Contemporary
P.O. Box 22095
Santa Fe, New Mexico 87502
www.axlepress.com

ISBN:
978-0615628820
0615628826

Axle Contemporary would like to thank Janet Dees and Irene Hoffman at SITE Santa Fe for inviting us to participate in MARCH 2012 which served as an inspiration for this project. We would also like to thank our location partners for their warm embrace of the project with enthusiasm, publicity, and electricity. Partners are: SITE Santa Fe, The Railyard Art Project, The New Mexico Museum of Art, La Montañita Co-op Market, The Santa Fe University of Art & Design, The Santa Fe Community College, Sunflower Market, Counter Culture, Harry's Roadhouse, The Genoveva Chavez Community Center, and The Santa Fe Children's Museum.

Table of Contents

Introduction

Since its inception in 2010 Axle Contemporary has been a welcome addition to the Santa Fe art scene. They have devised interesting exhibitions that have taken advantage of the unique format of their mobile gallery by either making inventive use of the interior of the truck or conceiving of projects that are conceptually motivated by the mobility of their art space. *E Pluribus Unum* represents the latter approach.

For ten days in March 2012 Axle turned their gallery into a traveling photo booth that they situated at eleven different locations throughout Santa Fe. Willing citizens were asked to take a photo with an object that held some meaning for them. They could bring their own or choose from those provided by the gallery. Sitters chose objects from the sentimental to the silly. Several people sat with their children or their pets on their laps, embracing what they loved the most. I chose an enigmatic statue of a silver-spray-painted couple, a gag gift from a staff holiday party. The items ranged from passports, cell phones, paint brushes, wedding rings, cameras, teapots, books, art objects, and musical instruments, reflecting the diversity of participants' sensibilities.

The sitter was given a copy of their photograph. A copy was also pasted to the side of the Axle Contemporary truck and uploaded to a slide show on their website to create a continuously increasing archive. Additionally, the photos were superimposed onto one another to create an evolving composite image that was presented as a short film. The aim was to create a collective portrait of a diverse cross-section of the "City Different."

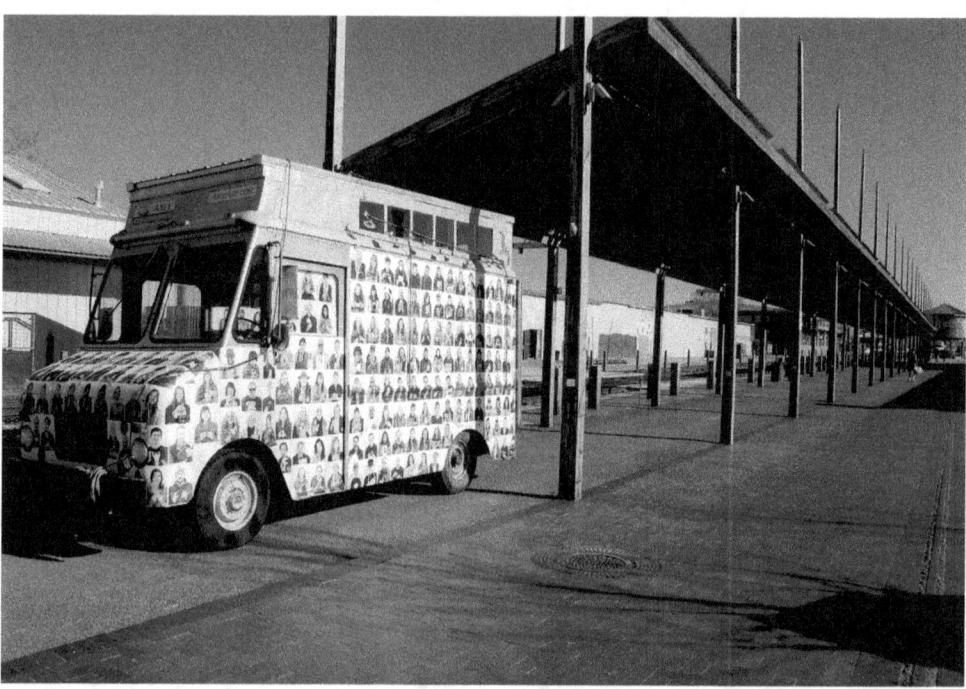

E Pluribus Unum was community building in several ways. It presented an opportunity for people to come together, drawn by their desire to participate in a novel project. On the first day at SITE Santa Fe almost 100 people had their portraits taken, and over 560 individuals had their portraits taken over the ten days of the project. Waiting to have my portrait taken in front of SITE on Friday March 2, I had the opportunity to chat with some Santa Feans that I had not met before; I know that others had the same experience. As the days progressed, the archive of images grew, on the side of the Axle truck and online, creating a roving and virtual portrait gallery. Looking at all of these portraits, it was great to see many familiar faces. This fostered a great sense of connection to this community that I have been apart of for only 3 ½ years. It was also great to see the portraits of people that I did not know, individuals who contribute to the uniqueness of Santa Fe.

E Pluribus Unum was instigated by an invitation to participate in SITE 's *March 2012* online exhibition project, which featured a different artwork by a different artist each day in the month of March and was inspired by Seth Siegelaub's notable conceptual exhibition *March 1969 (a.k.a. One Month.) E Pluribus Unum* was featured live on the March 2012 website on March 2nd, and all of the portraits taken that day are apart of a slide-show archive on view in SITE's galleries. *March 2012* is set within the larger exhibition *Time-Lapse*, which was curated by myself and Irene Hofmann, and takes the theme of art that changes over time as its organizing premise. With *E Pluribus Unum* Axle took up the idea of a continually evolving artwork to create a compelling and captivating portrait of a slice of the Santa Fe community.

-Janet Dees, SITE Santa Fe

People, Objects, and Time: From Many One

In the time of colonial America itinerant painters, folk artists, would travel from community to community on horseback, to paint portraits of families. Post millennial America offers new opportunities to capture portraits of the people. Digital photography, portable printers and a mobile stepvan offer ever more accessible ways to reach community, and perhaps even more empowering, reveal the depth of community to itself.

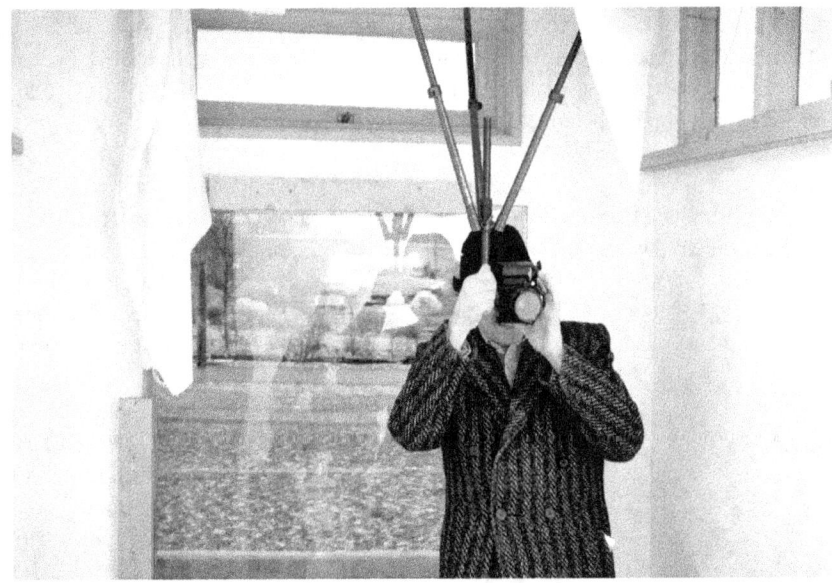

In each portrait an object is held. The object was brought in by the individual, or was chosen from a large group of random objects set up in the van. The object by its' very material nature gathers significance in the portrait. The significance may have existed for the person long before the portrait was taken or may have been chosen in the spur of the moment allowing for a synchronous generation of meaning. Objects that were brought in ranged from childhood and now antique toys to the ashes of the dear and departed. Objects available in the gallery varied from a globe to power tools and wooden spoons to teddy bears. The objects serve to catalog the many aspects of our life in 2012. They exhibit our psyche, our collection of goods, the antiques, and ephemera that will define us 50 years hence.

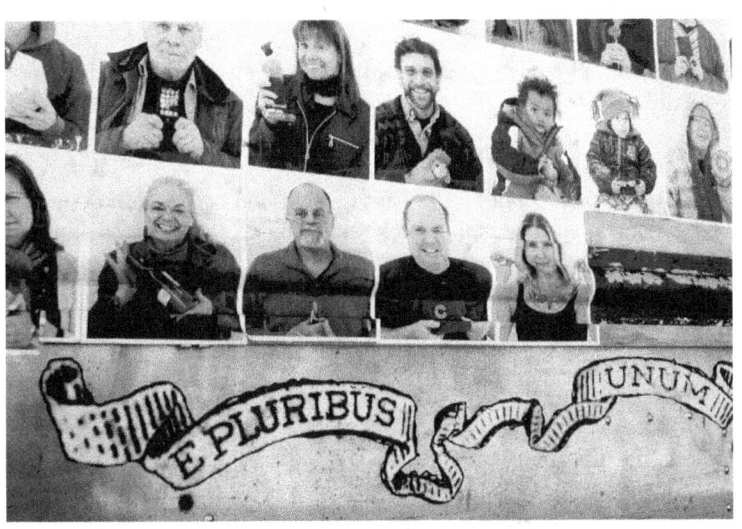

The digital mechanics of compiling and compositing the 566 portraits into one, result in the eyes and face of a transcendant vision of a female form, her eyes alternatingly peaceful and wise, the archetype of the feminine, worshiped and revered across cultures, and history. And all the objects, held in the hands of all the participating people reveal the transient instability of any item. In the end, the material object appears as a wispy vague shape, fleeting and ephemeral.

The 10 day collection of photo portraits, wheat pasted on the side of a stepvan, show an engaging group of people, earnest, sincere, and ready to add their aspect to the mix. One can't help but extrapolate that the same quality seen in these portraits would be captured in any community across America, or for that matter across the globe. Images of self assurance, humor, curiousity, hopefulness, and intelligence.

In 1776, the time of the itinerant portrait painter, the first Great Seal committee of the United States suggested a motto for a nation inventing itself; The latin phrase E Pluribus Unum; from many one. Then and now any community has the great potentials that become evident through the power generated by co-operation and collaboration. In that spirit we hope to reveal a portrait of cohesiveness that represents the trust and co-operation at the heart of any working community.

-Jerry Wellman, Axle Contemporary

Process and Inspiration

When we were invited to create a work of art as Axle Contemporary for SITE Santa Fe's MARCH 2012 show, we were both pleased and challenged. We had created Axle as a collaborative work of art (as well as an art gallery), but what SITE was looking for was something that could live for a day on the web (virtual mayfly?), and as a video projection in SITE's gallery and also be alive in the Axle Contemporary mobile gallery.

We certainly enjoy using "new media" to expound, expand, and promote our ideas and projects, but haven't used the web as the primary place to exhibit a work of art. We tend to appreciate and produce projects that take an "Old-School/New-School approach: Using outdated technologies in conjunction with the latest technologies. Our Haiku Roadsign Project

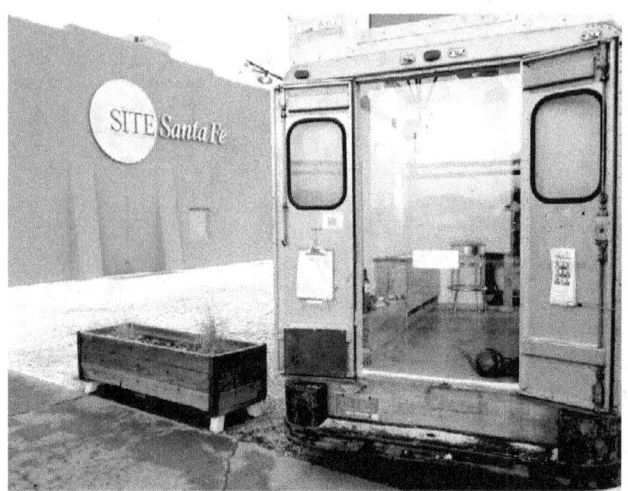

used a faded highway sign to display contemporary Haiku, but had a QR code on top, to allow people to watch the project unfurl on a blog via smartphone).

So, around Christmastime, Jerry drove to Indiana with his family and I drove to L.A. with mine, and we both promised to think freely and write down any and all ideas independently, hone them into workable projects, and meet in January to show each other our lists and pitch each other ideas. We came up with a total of 14 ideas by our January 5th meeting, and they were all good (well maybe not the two of us sitting in our underwear in the van on the street filled with 100 chickens for 24 hours with a live video feed). In editing our list, we realized that there were very tight parameters that we needed to follow (works online, works as a short video or slide projection, works in and with the mobile gallery, works in a day). For me, tight constraints are a great source of inspiration. Creativity can be fueled by limitations. At Axle we like to work with limitations and conventions and boundaries and parameters. We like to play with them, challenge them, tickle them, cross them and then jump back over, walk the line, cross the line, draw the line, or erase the line.

So, we asked ourselves: What boundaries do we want to engage with this opportunity at SITE, beyond the limitations of the mobile gallery and the timeframe and the web? What is the perception of SITE's identity and persona, and how does it compare and contrast with our own? We arrived at questions surrounding exclusivity and democracy, and around hierarchical selection and self-organizing principles. SITE has often been perceived in our community as exclusive and impenetrable, a far western outpost of an exclusive secret society of art cognoscenti based in New York, London and Berlin (although we believe that this is neither true, nor how they would like to be seen). And Axle? We are perceived as a democratizing force, waging battles against the dominant hierarchies, empowering the people, and tilting at wind-

mills on the potholed and dusty streets of New Mexico (although we believe that this is neither true, nor how we would like to be thought of (We'd like a MacArthur grant, a pavilion at the Venice Biennale, and houses by the beach on the Vineyard)).

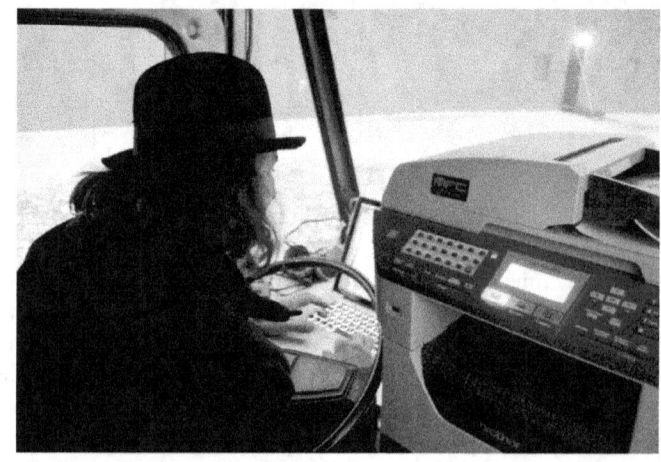

E PLURIBUS UNUM (from many one), is the fruit of our collaboration. A ten-day, city-wide project, it invites the entire community to participate, to engage with their creativity, to express themselves in images. To move from the public spaces of the city to the halls of SITE Santa Fe, to the world wide web, to be collected and disseminated for any and all to see, virtually, and in a fat and weighty old-fashioned book.

In 1969, Seth Siegelaub curated MARCH 1969 (aka One Month). 31 artists each were invited to make a piece of art, one on each day of the month. The results were collected in a book rather than hung in an art gallery. Irene Hoffman and

Janet Dees created MARCH 2012 as an homage to Siegelaub and an updated version of his idea for our times, using the internet as the tool for dissemination of the work. The March 2012, exhibition at SITE is a show within a show, being a subset of the encompassing Time-Lapse exhibition. E Pluribus Unum is playful within this context. We asked all members of our community to create works of art (through expressions, identity, drawings, or object selection). These are part of our exhibition which is part of March 2012, which is part of Time-Lapse. Contemporary technology has not only moved the "book" to the web, but also moved the book from the exclusive domain of publishing houses, into the hands of independent operators. We are presenting our exhibition as a book as Siegelaub did, although we are but one of the 31 artists in SITE's March 2012.

The project: We transformed our mobile gallery into a small portrait studio with a system of moveable translucent and opaque drapes to control the natural lighting depending on time of day and orientation, as well as an electric lighting system for the evenings. The studio was left bare except for a couple of low shelves with our collection of random small objects for people to choose their item to hold, although we encouraged everyone to bring something special of their own. As our objects were selected and used in the portraits, we would retire them and replace them with new items on the shelves.

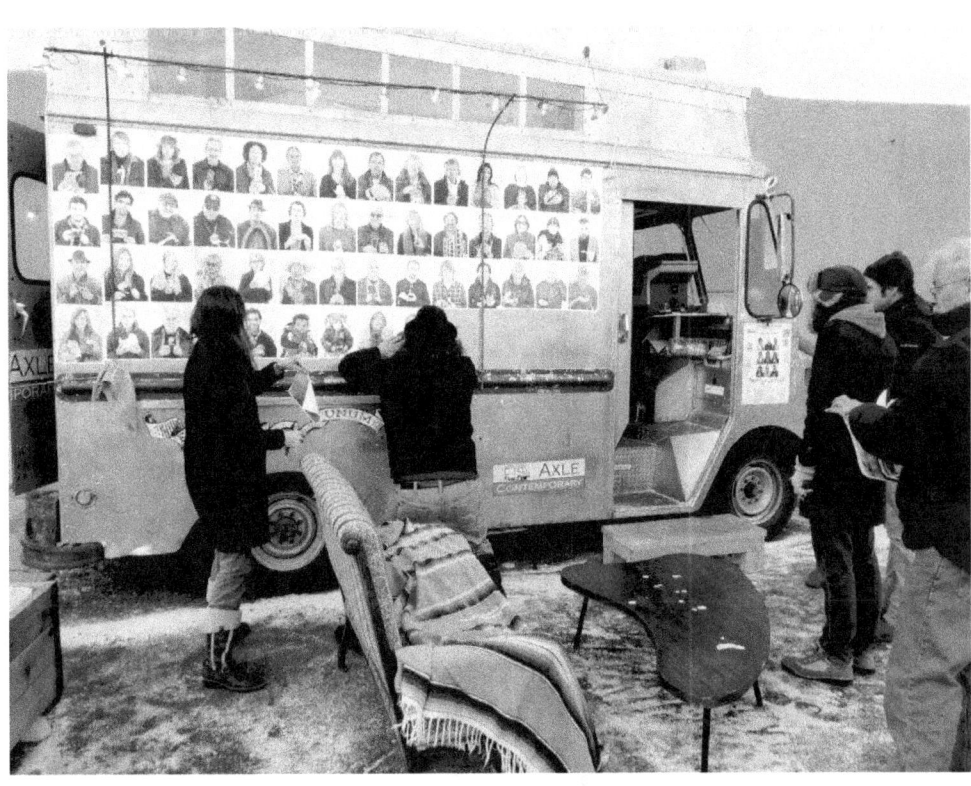

We publicized the project and locations through the local newspapers, on the radio, via social media, and e-mail. We chose locations across a broad range of Santa Fe, including art and tourist destinations, grocery stores, restaurants, swimming pools, colleges, and the farmers market. Everyone was welcomed inside for a brief portrait session, holding a special object. Within minutes, a 8x10 print was generated from our onboard printer with one copy distributed to the participant, and another pasted to the exterior of the vehicle. Our online site was also regularly updated with the growing collection of images.

Over the course of the ten day project we captured images of 566 people. Day by day, and for the entire project we have created images that incorporate equal parts of all the images. This is an image that we conceived of before we began the project, but have only seen as the work has taken place of layering one image onto another in the long series. What has emerged is a soft image of a beautiful woman with a light emanating from her heart chakra. Would this image look different if it was a blending of portraits from elsewhere? Is this an image of Nuestra Señora de Santa Fe, or a more universal spirit? This can only be answered as we continue our explorations, perhaps bringing this project beyond Santa Fe, and capturing people, rooted in time and place, in other communities. Forward!

-Matthew Chase-Daniel, Axle Contemporary

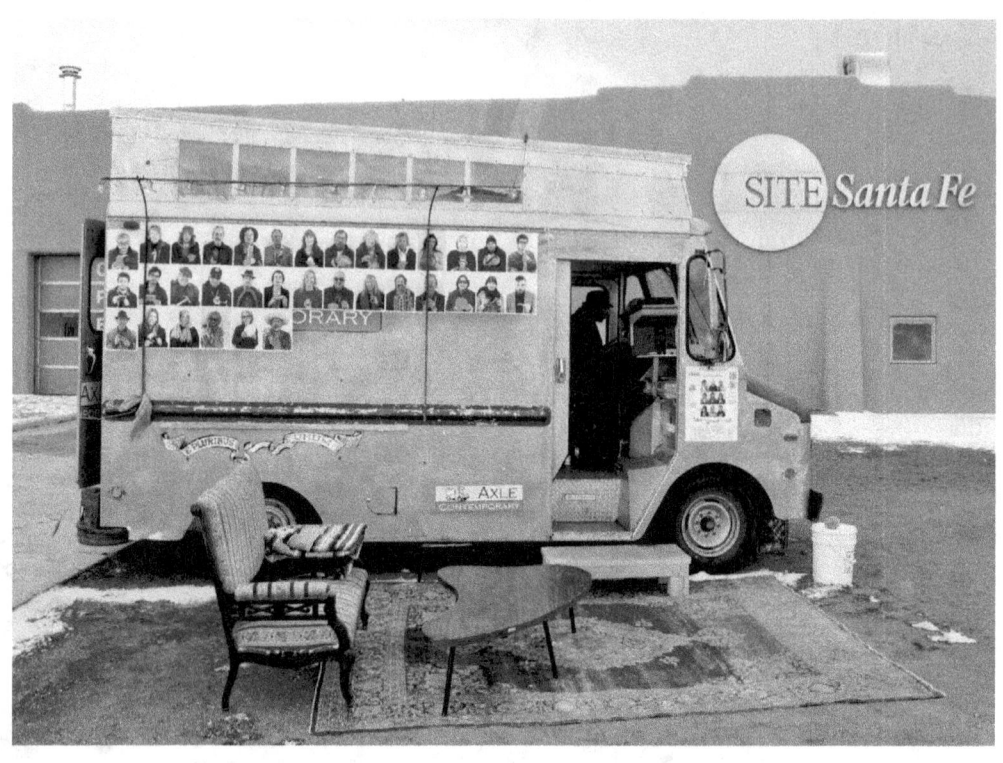

SITE Santa Fe

1606 Paseo de Peralta

Friday

March 2

10am-7pm

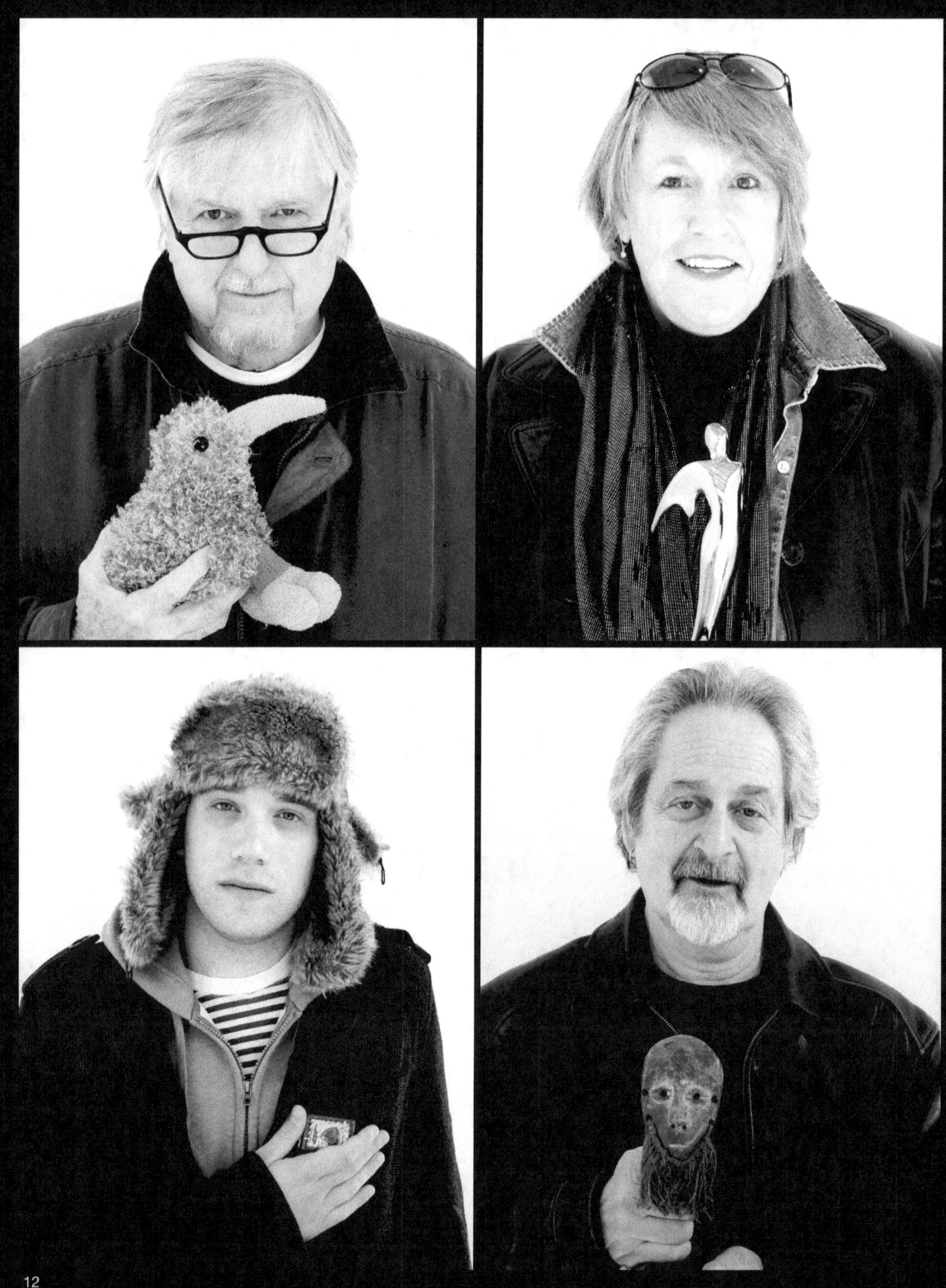

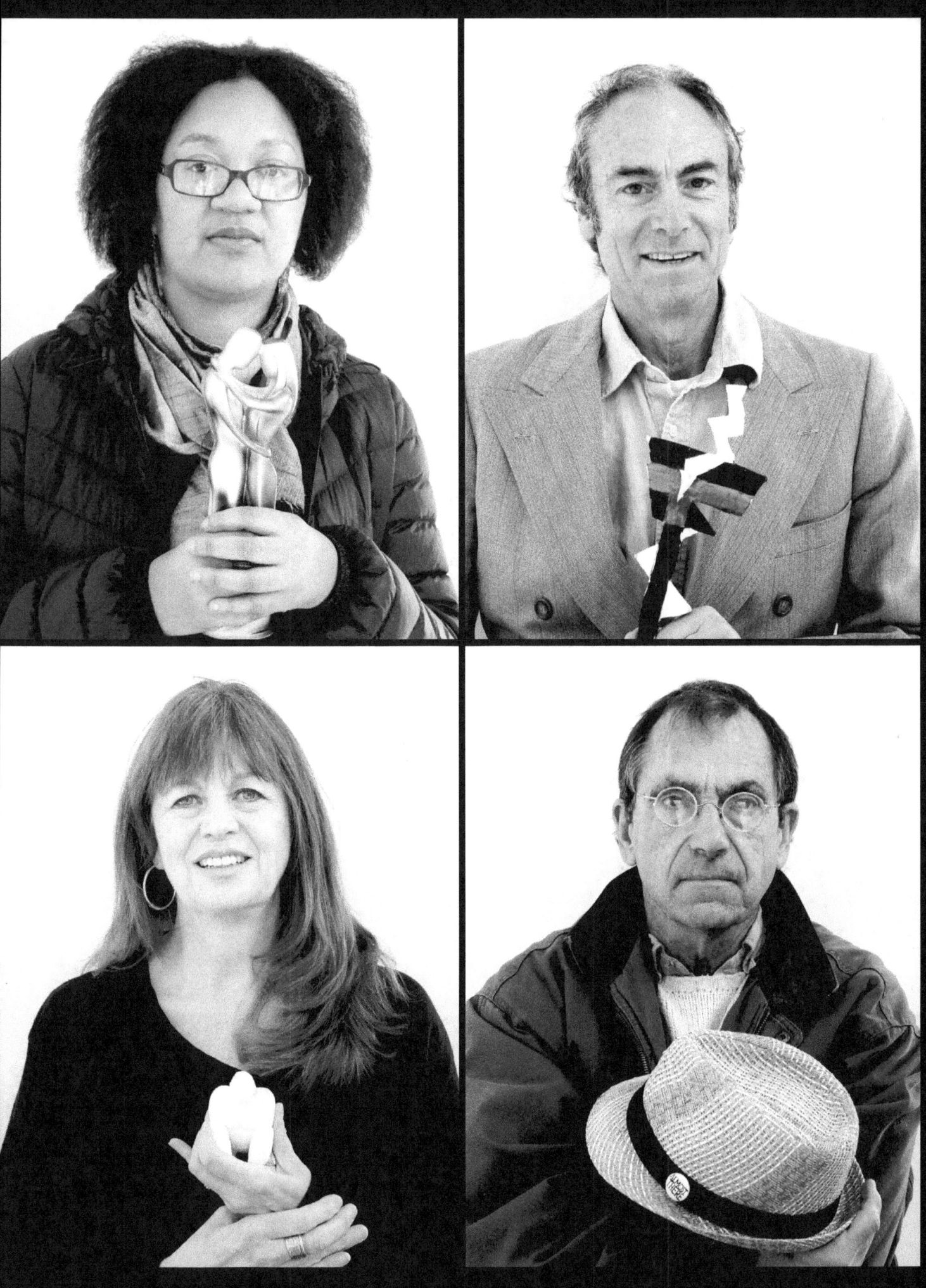

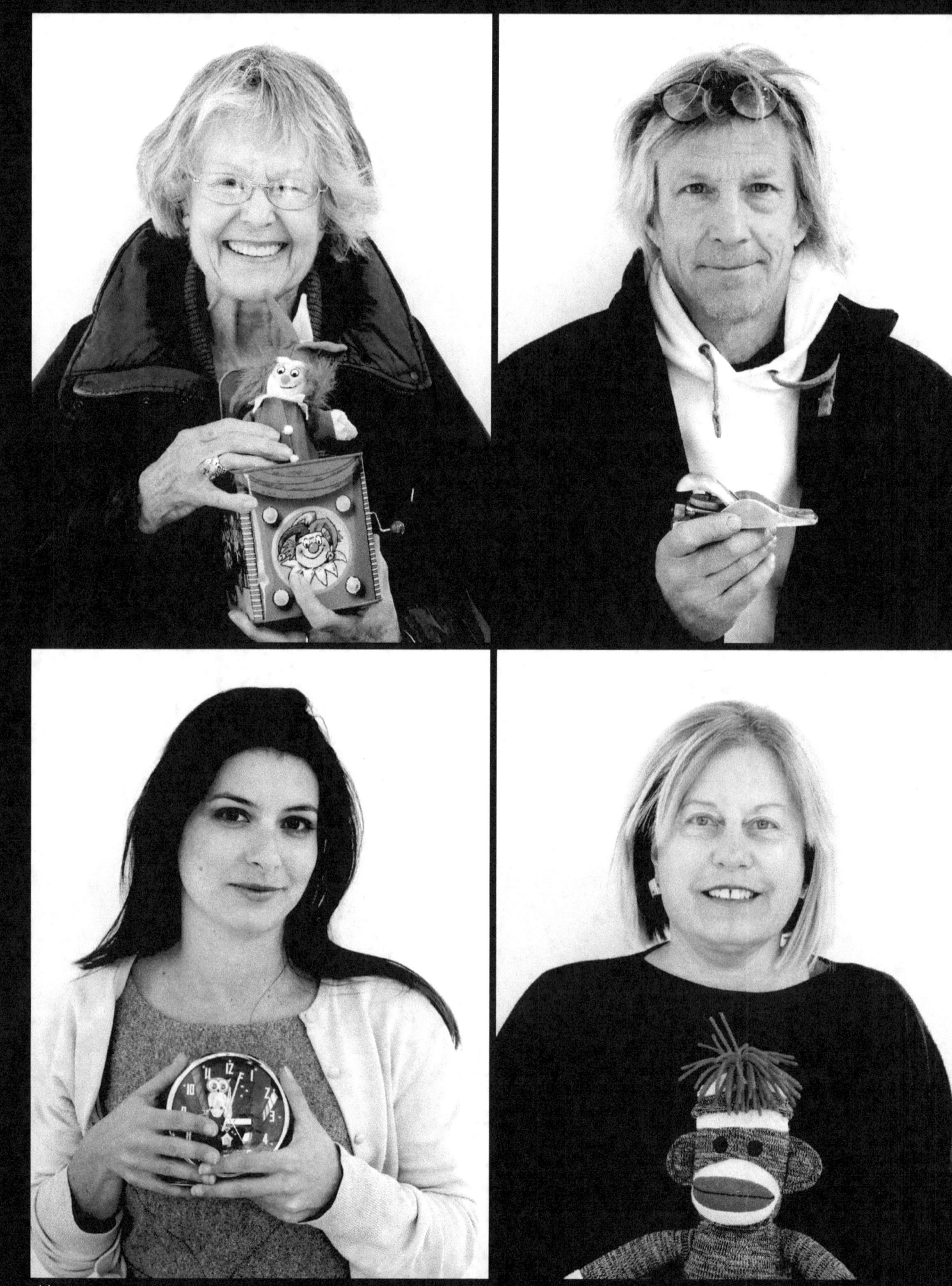

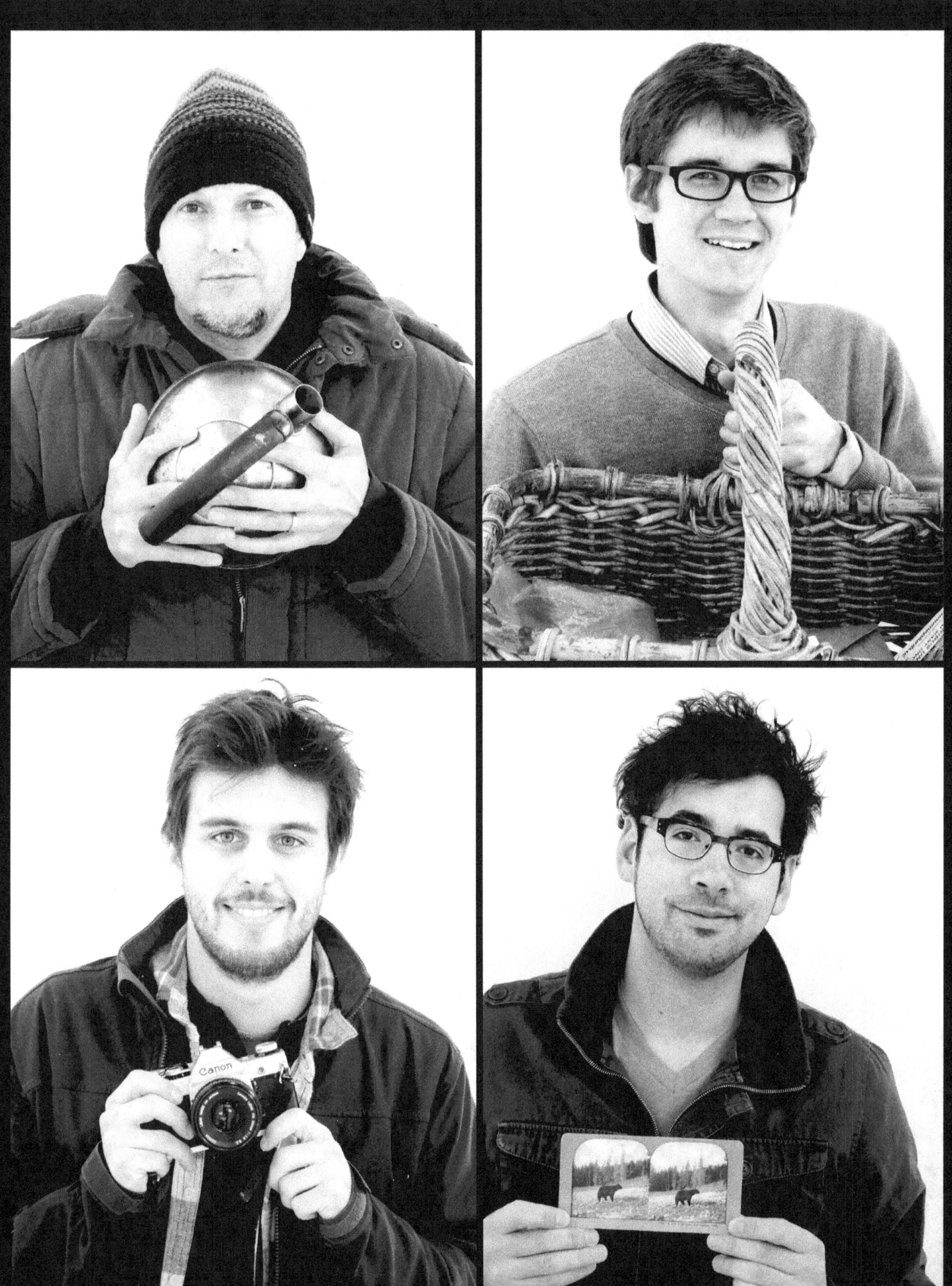

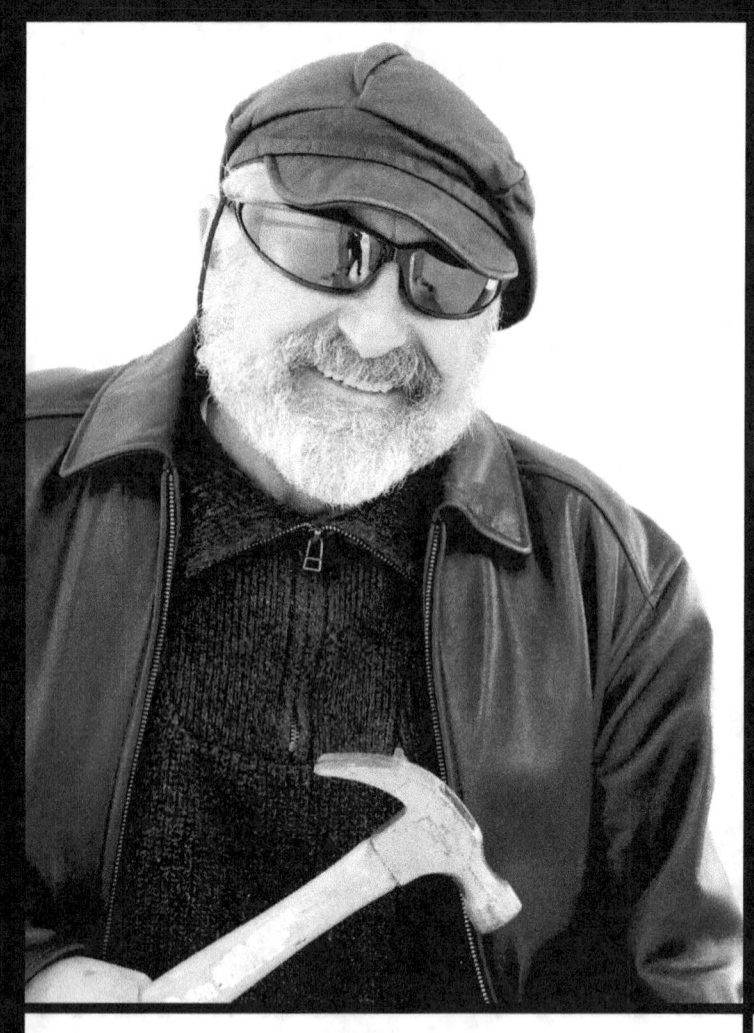
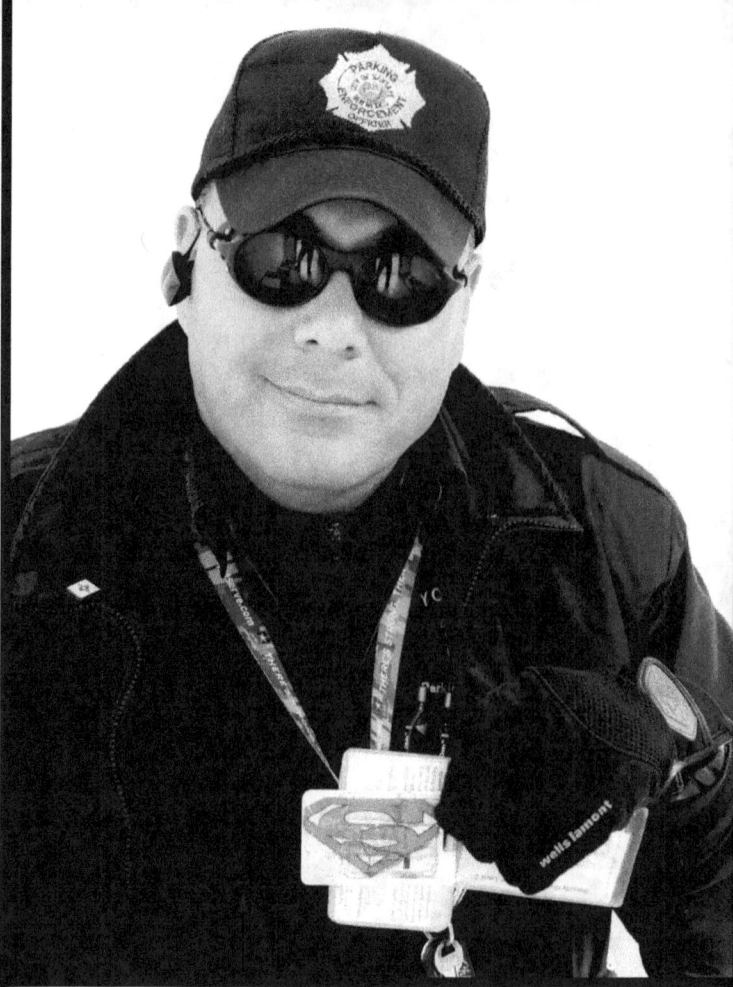
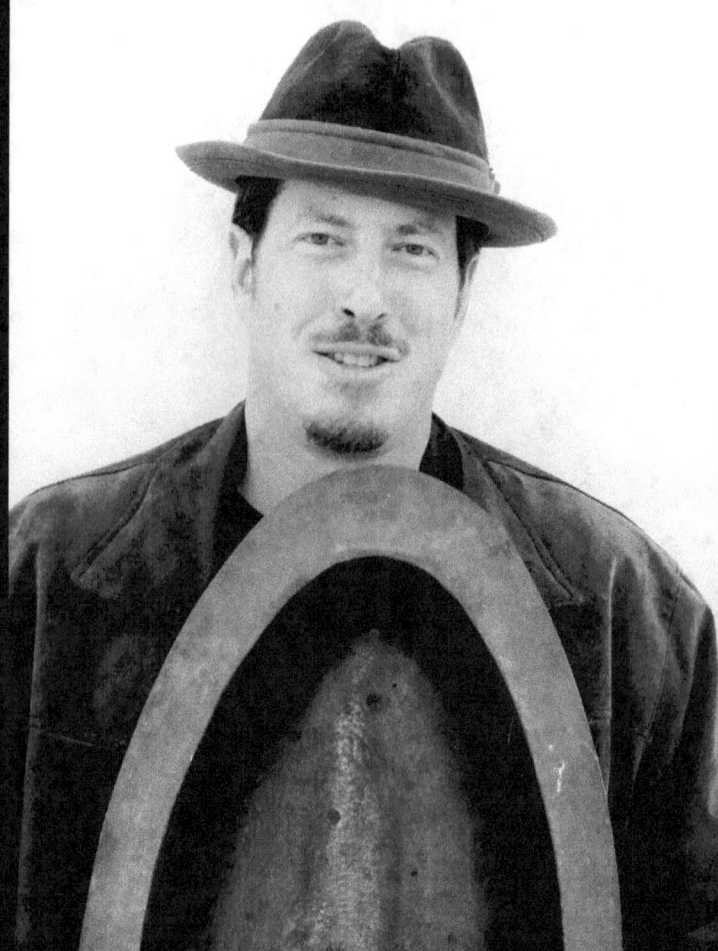
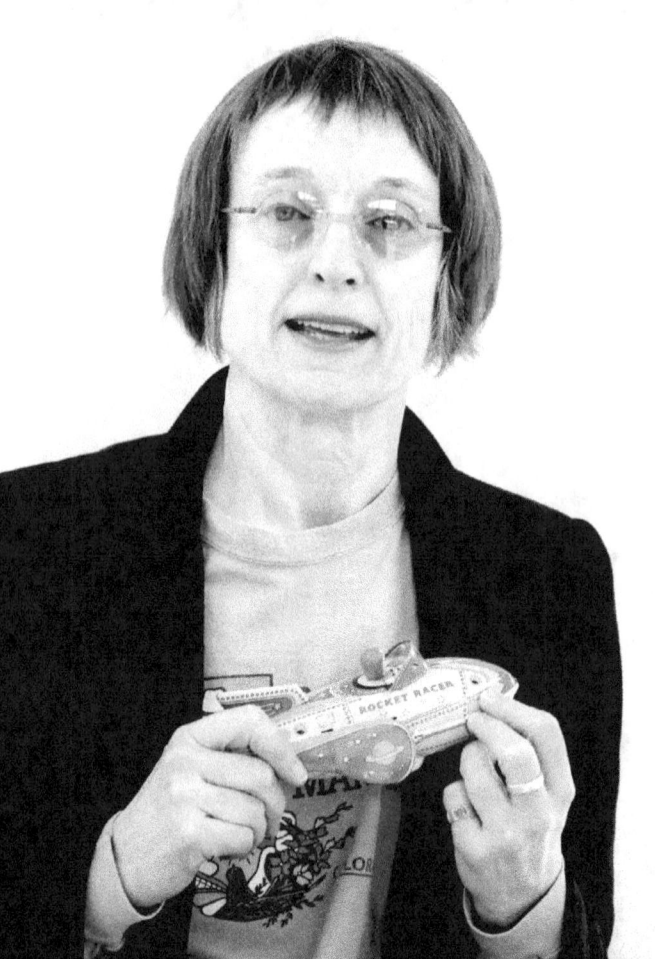

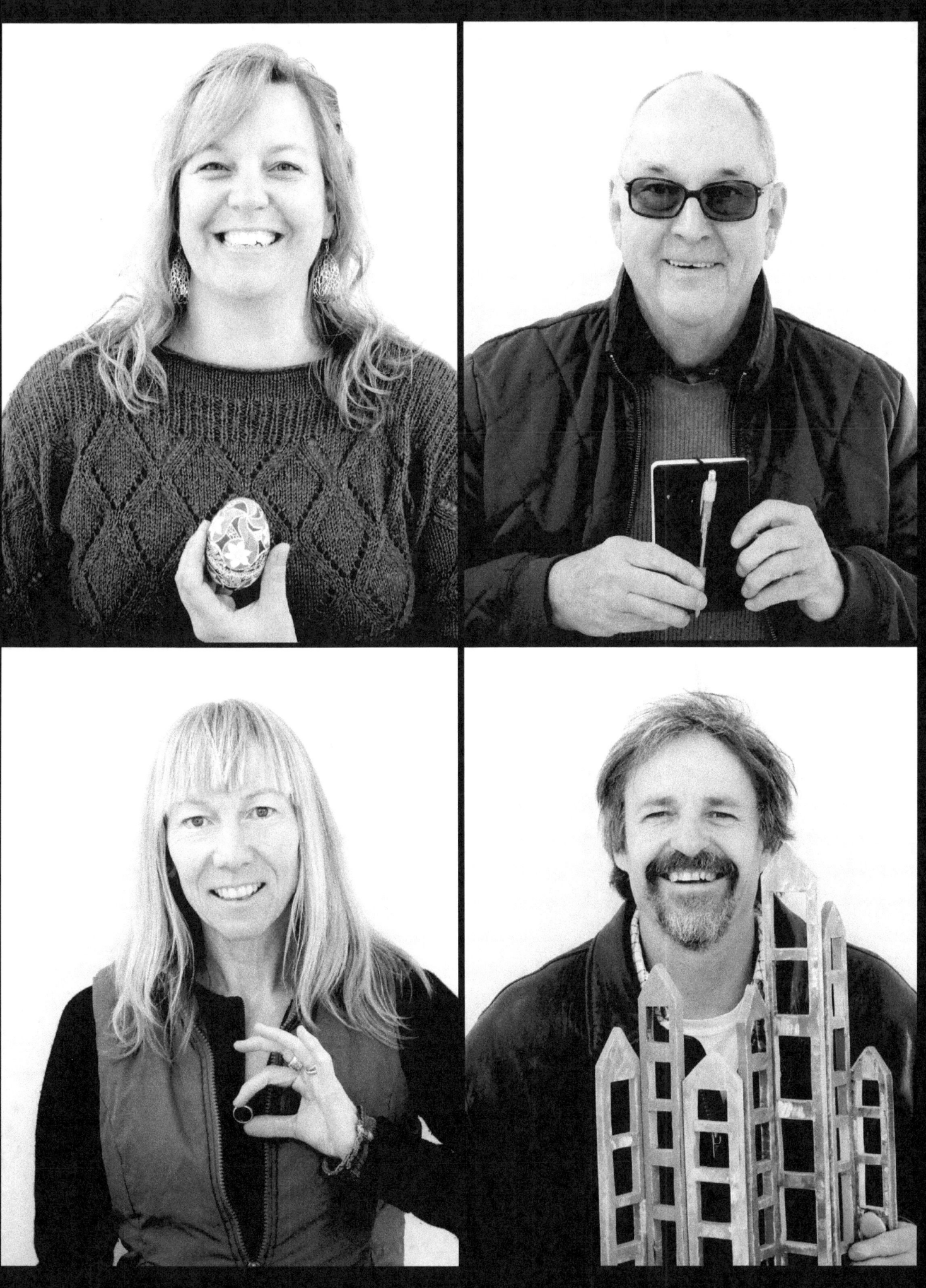

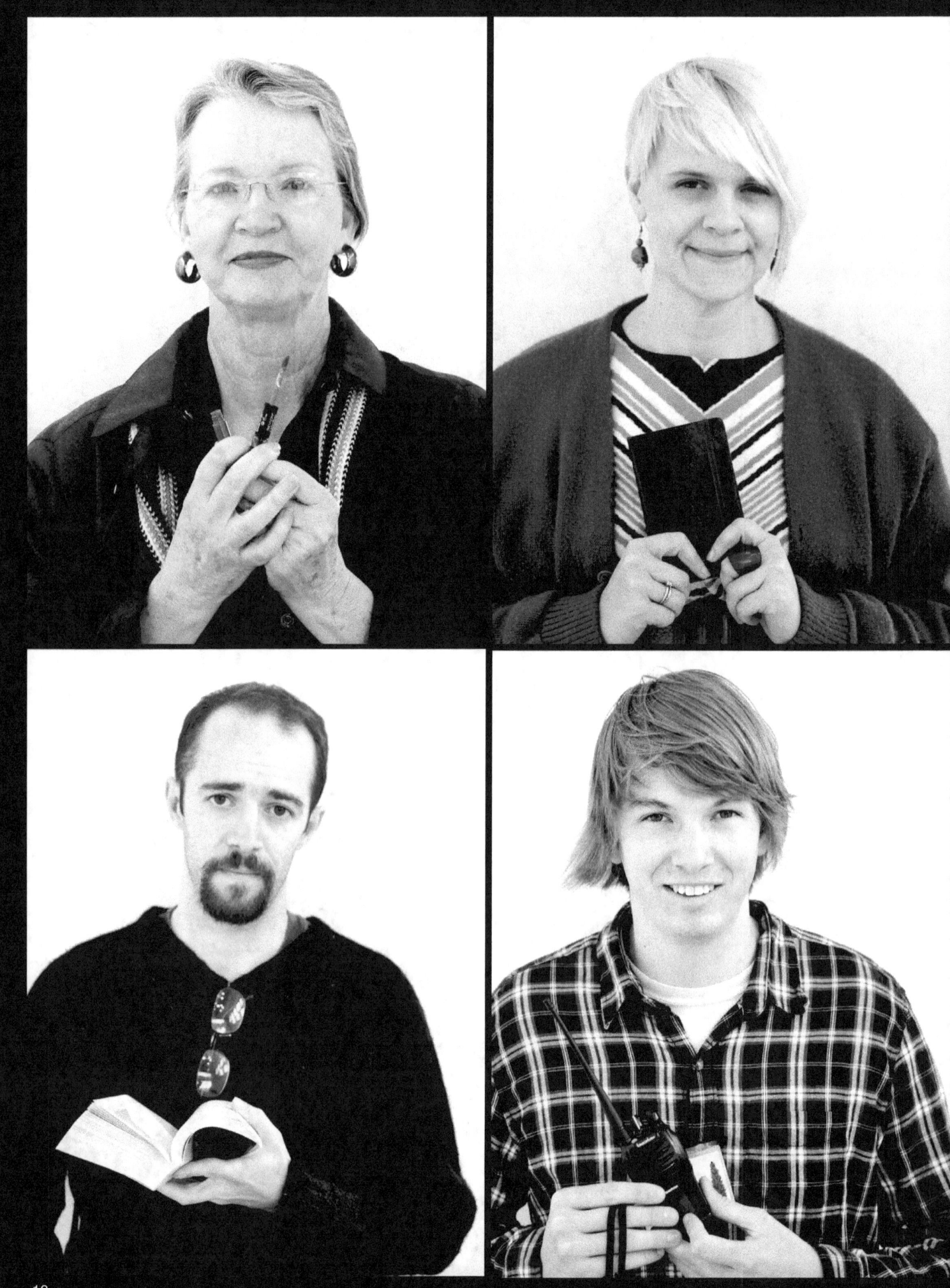

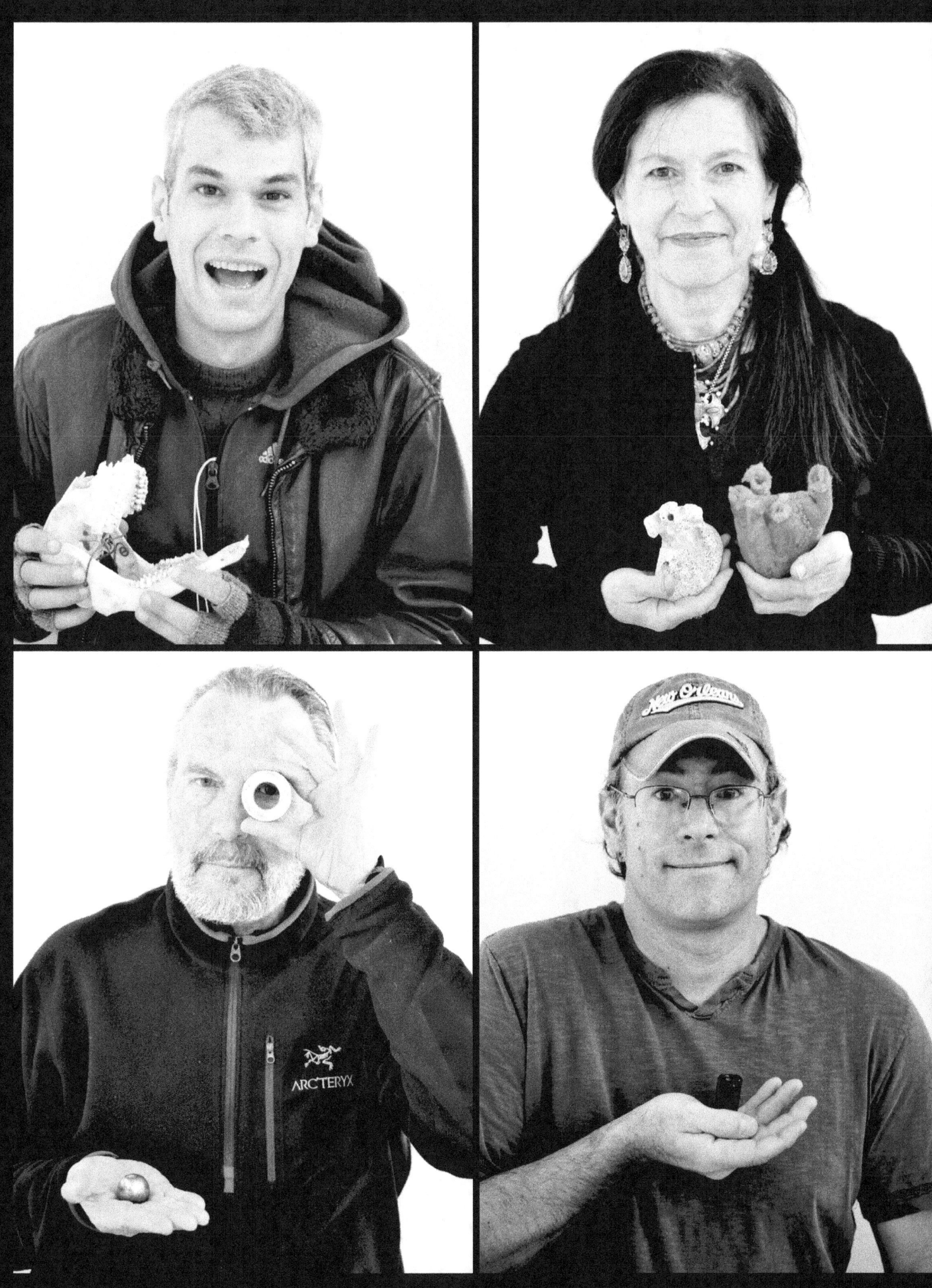

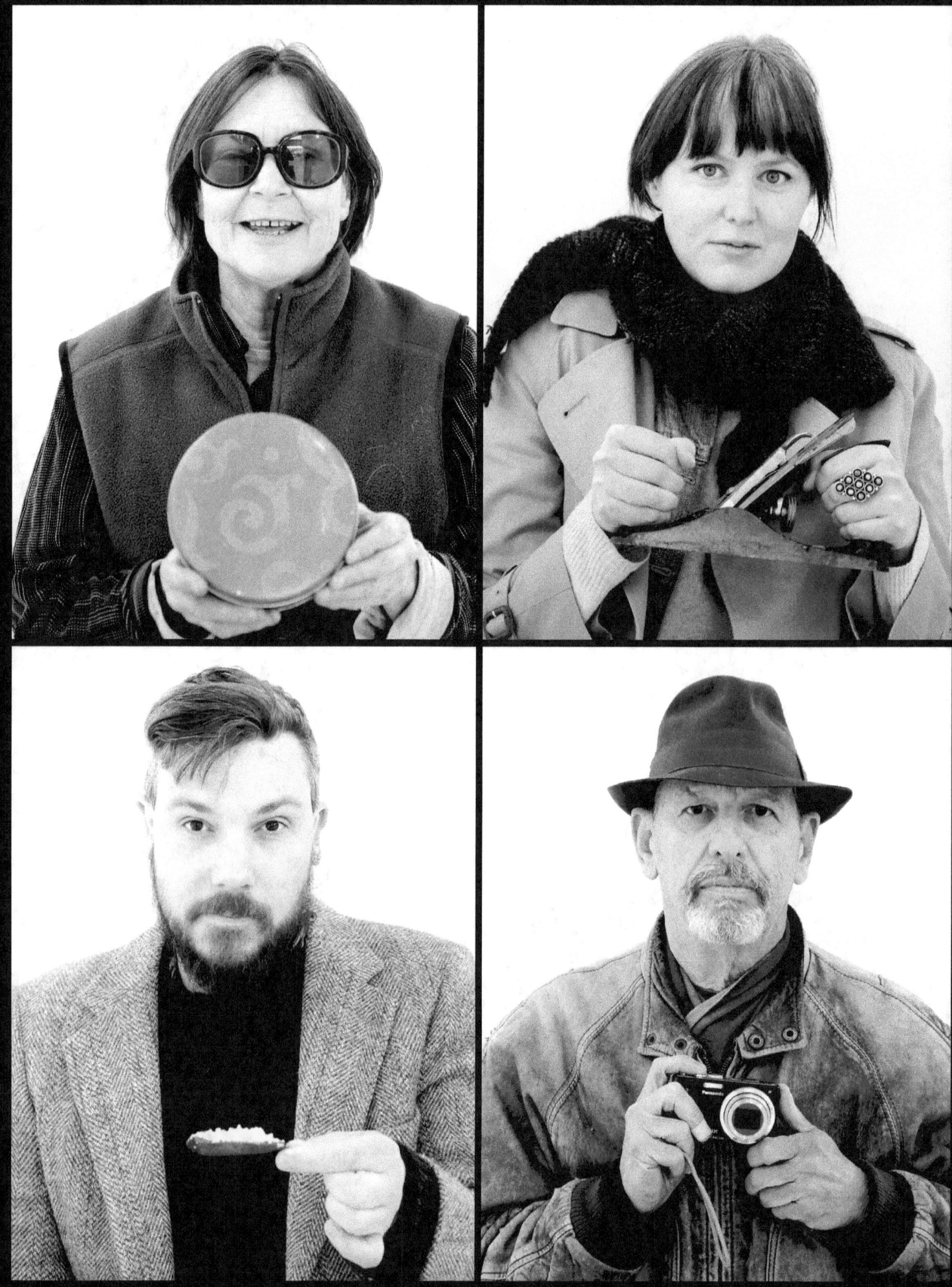

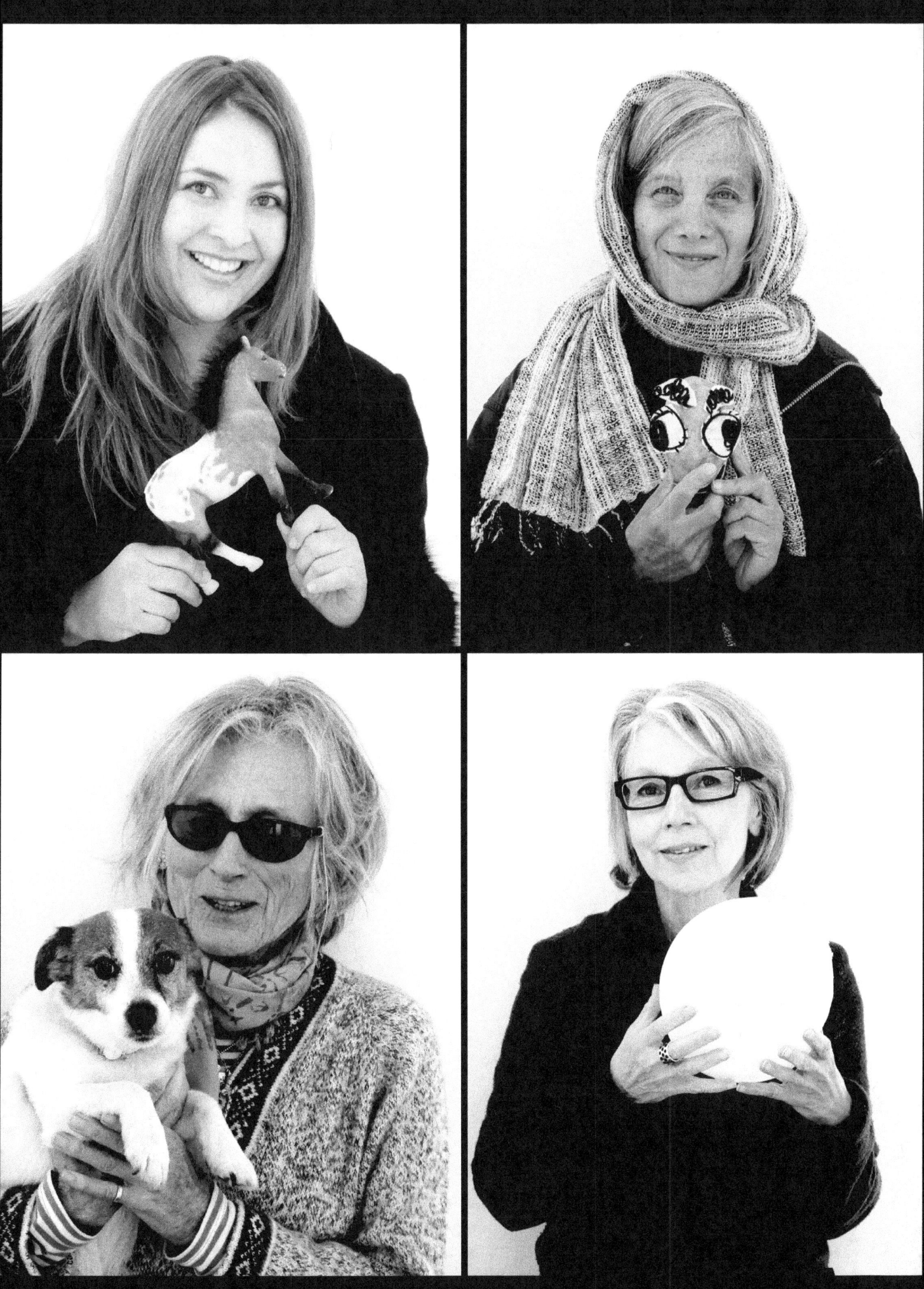

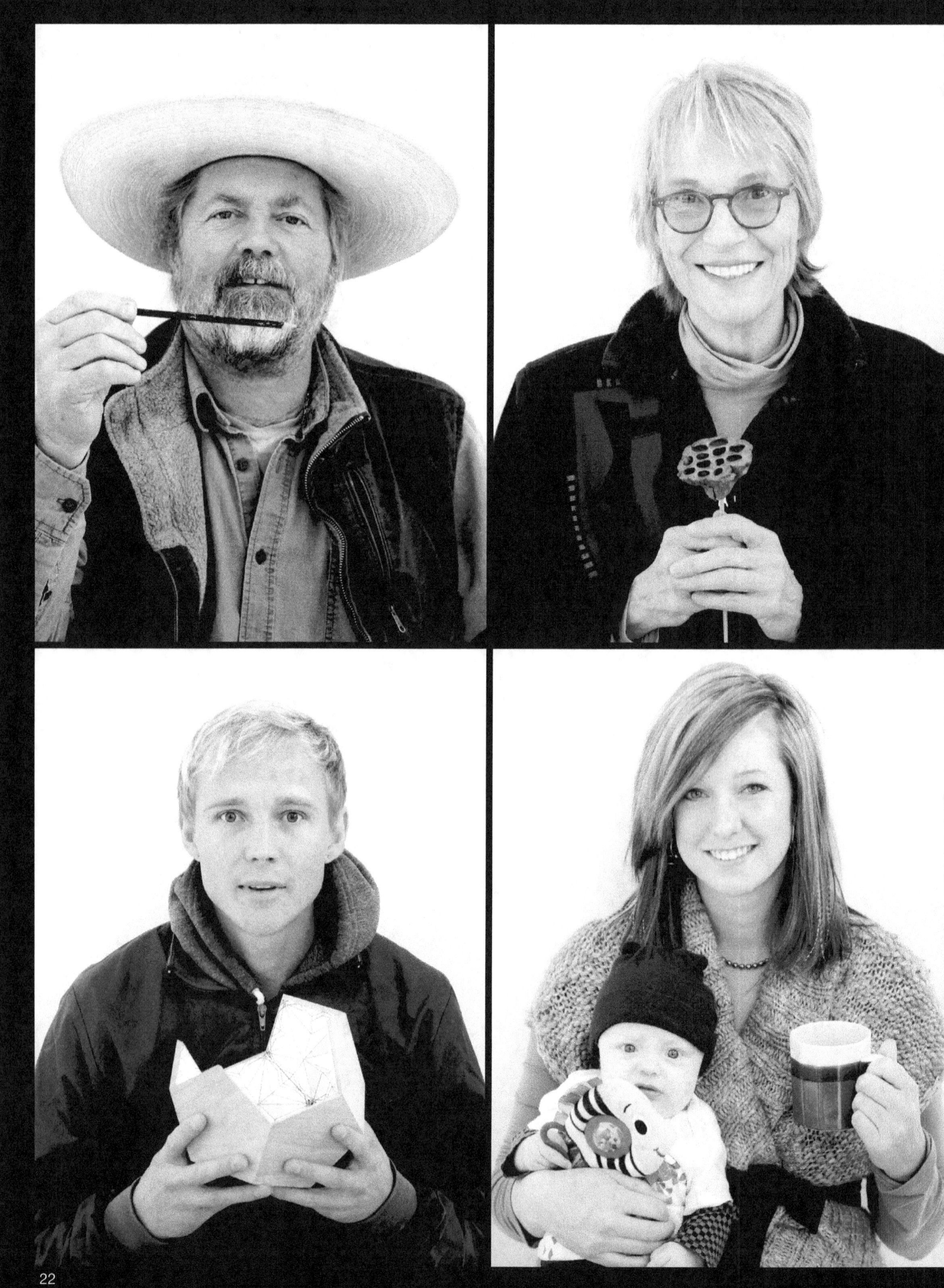

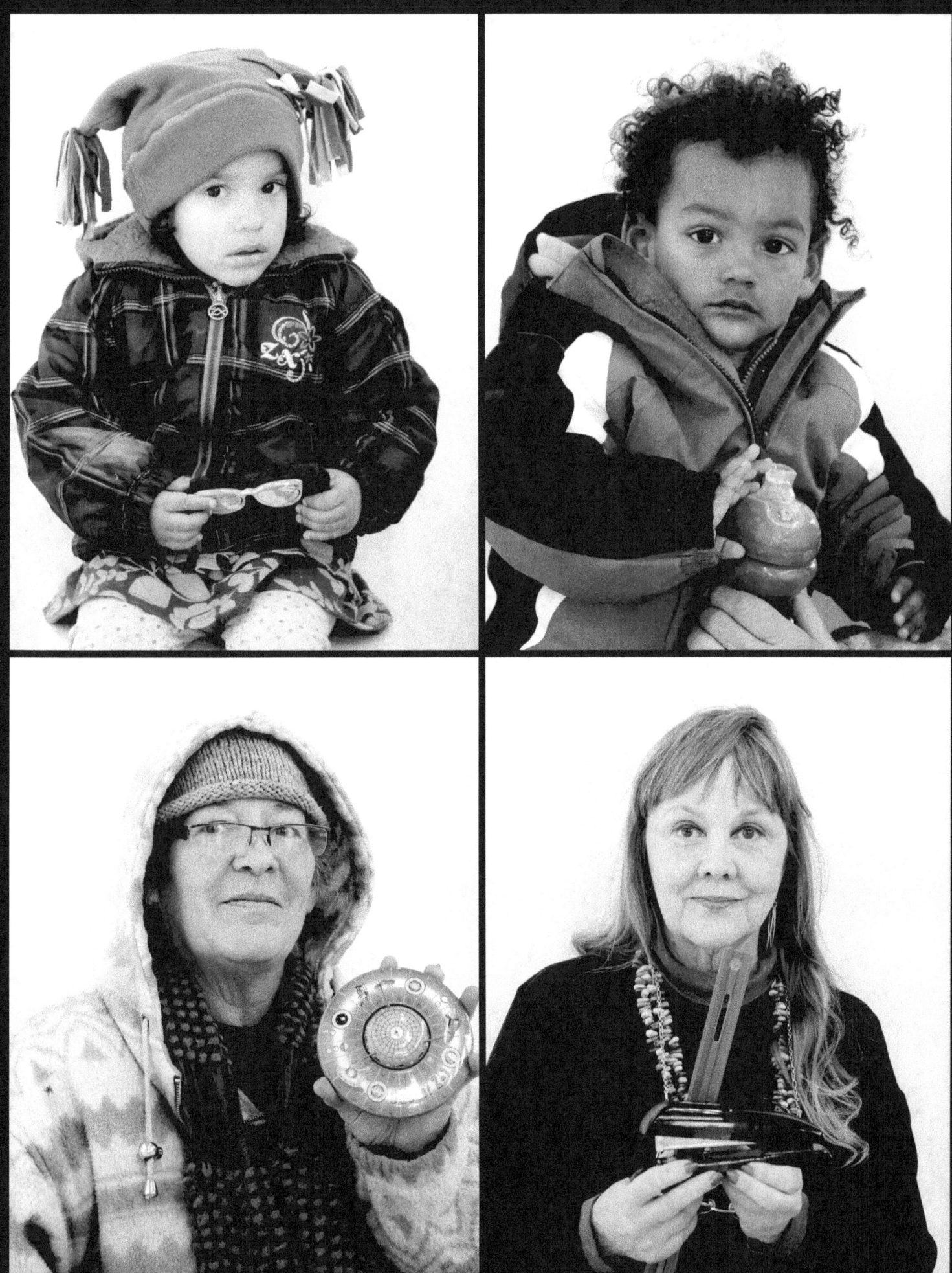

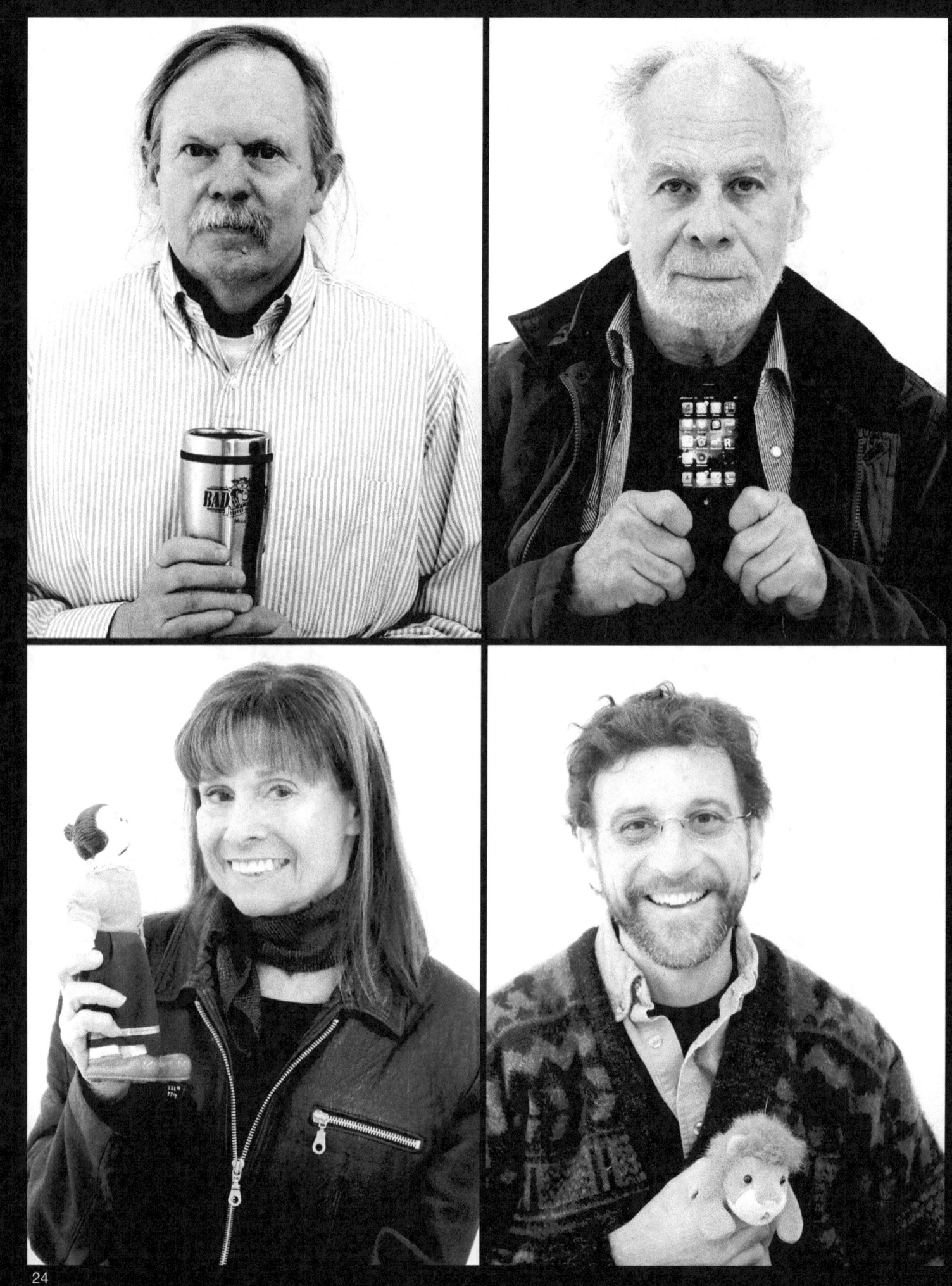

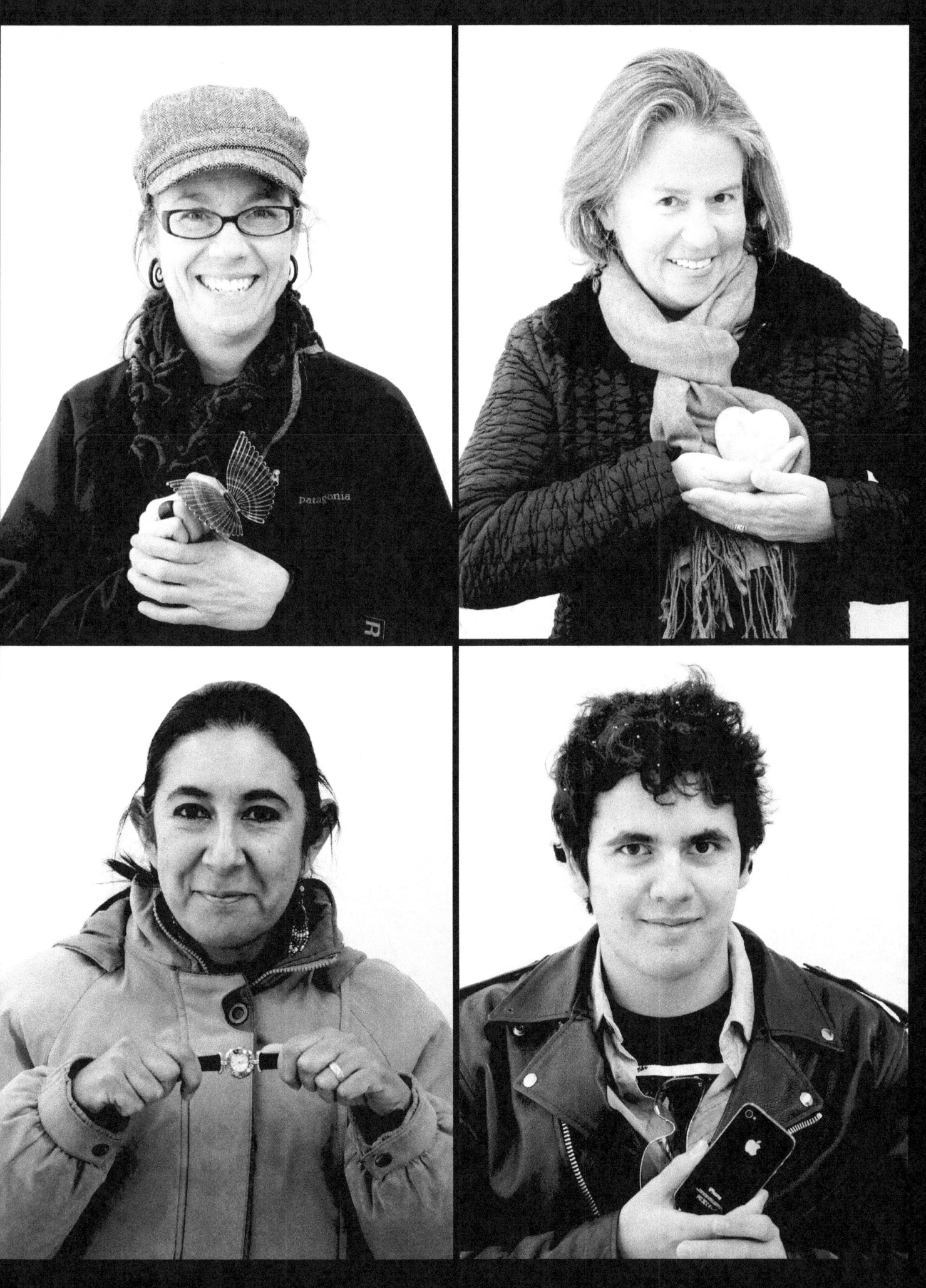

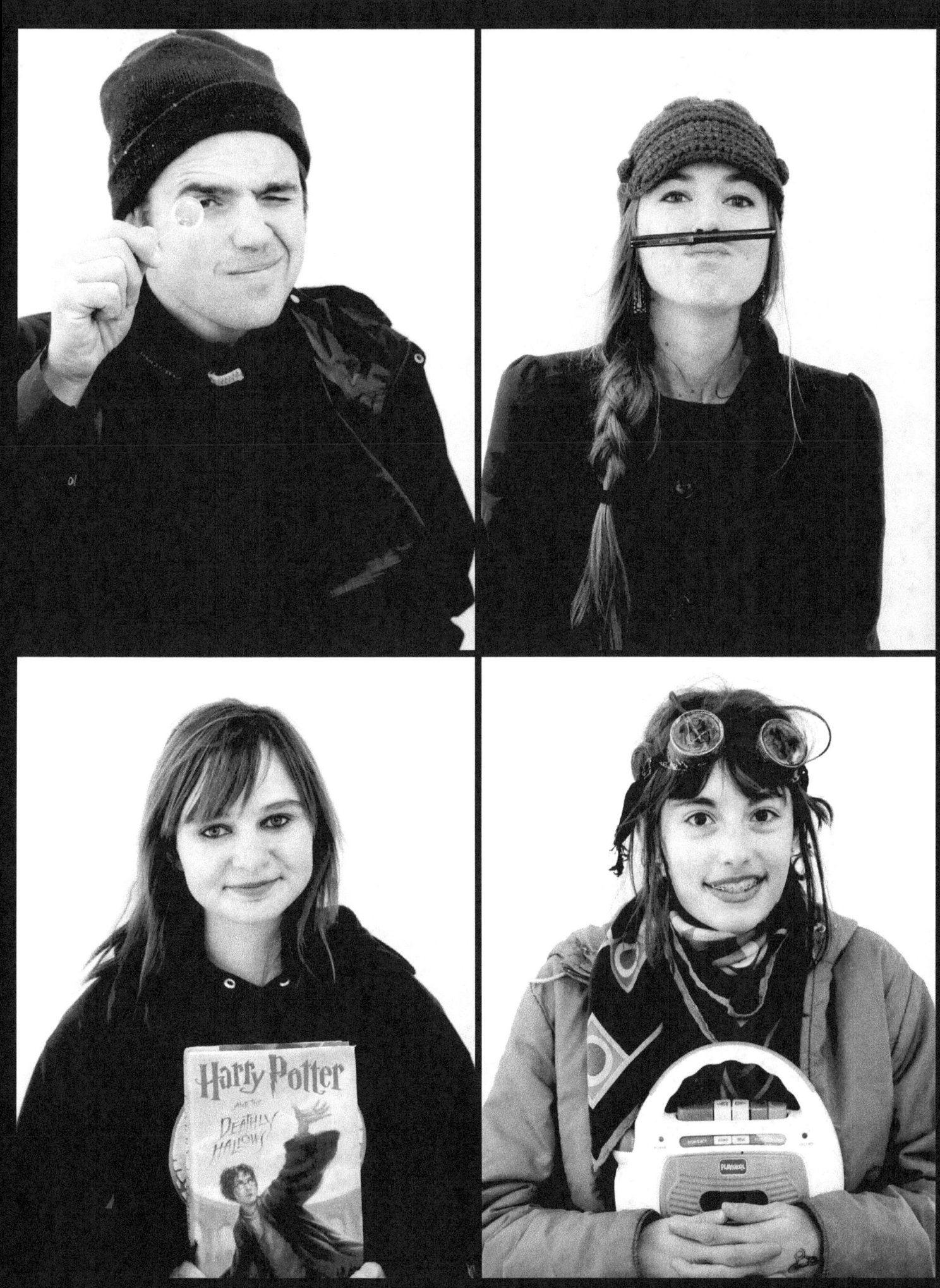

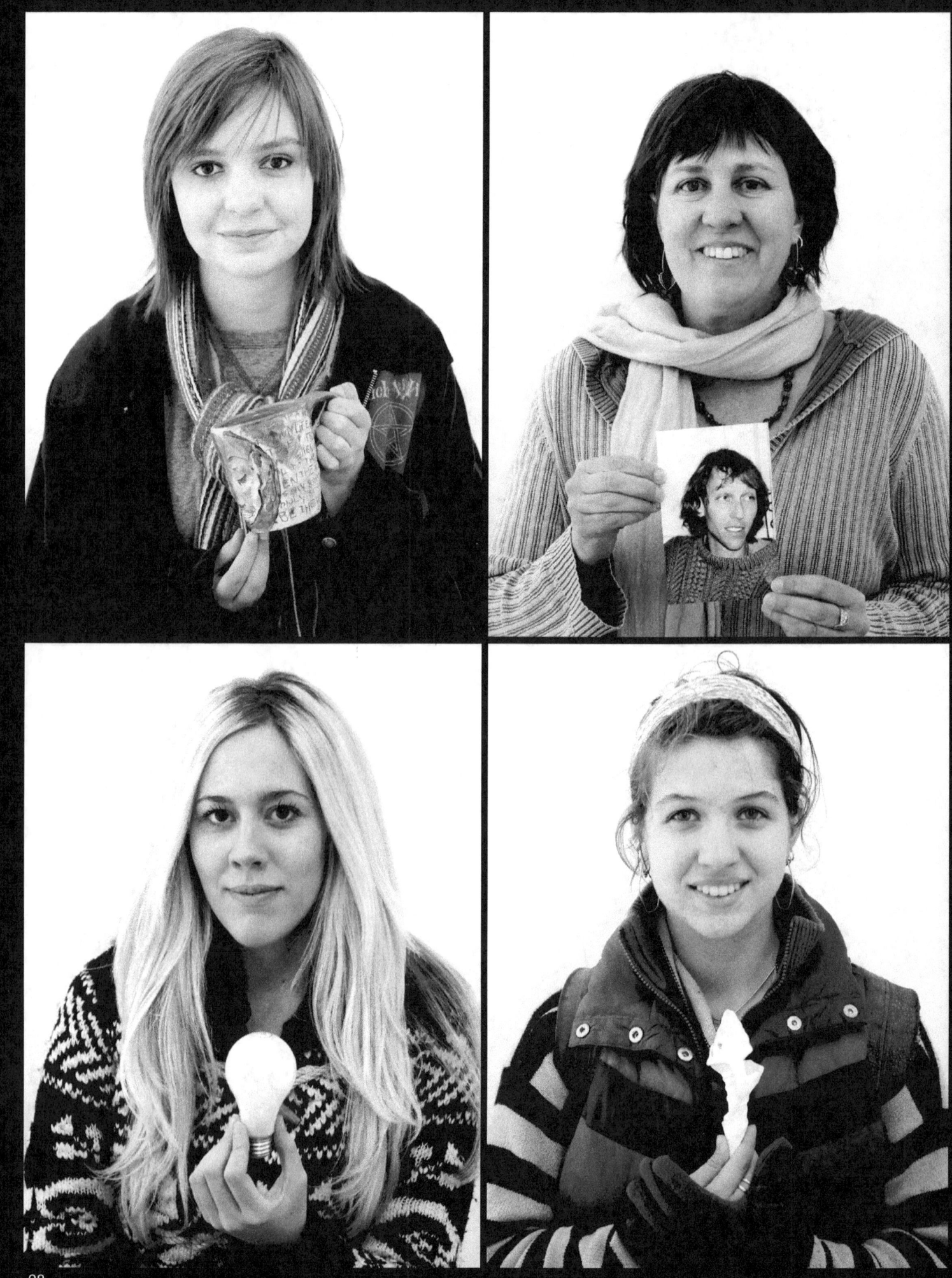

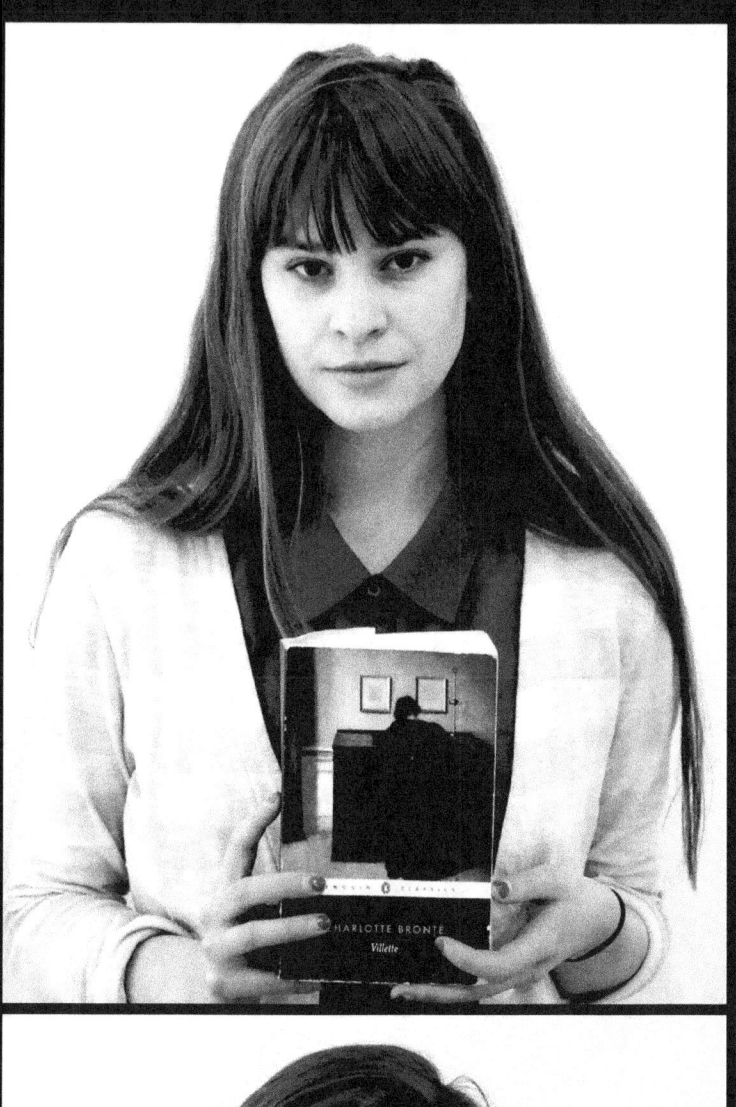
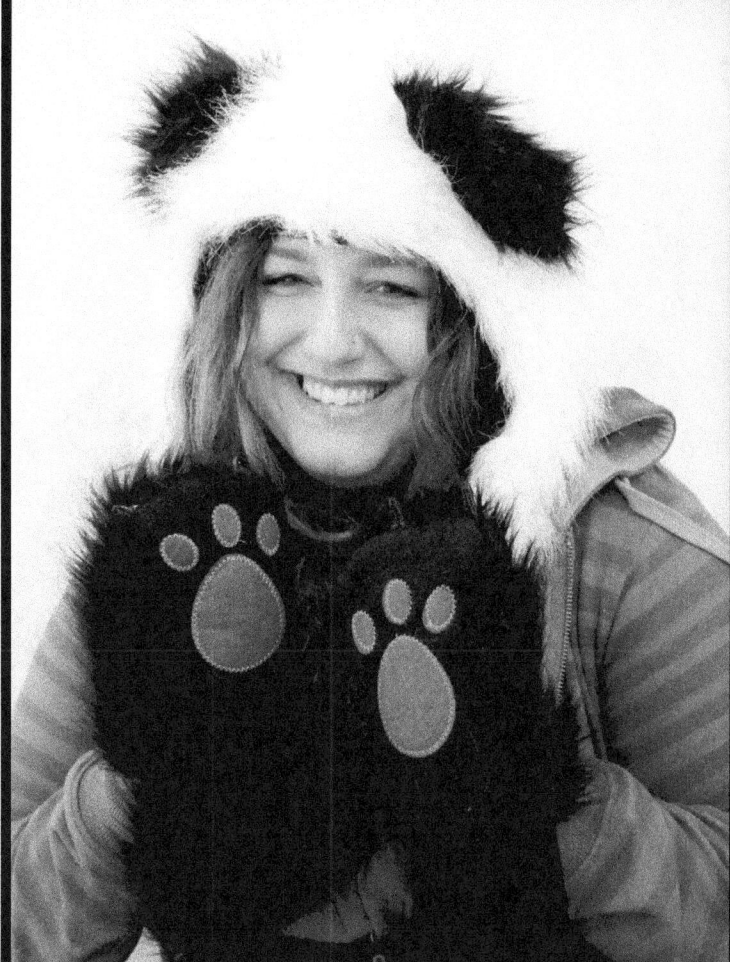
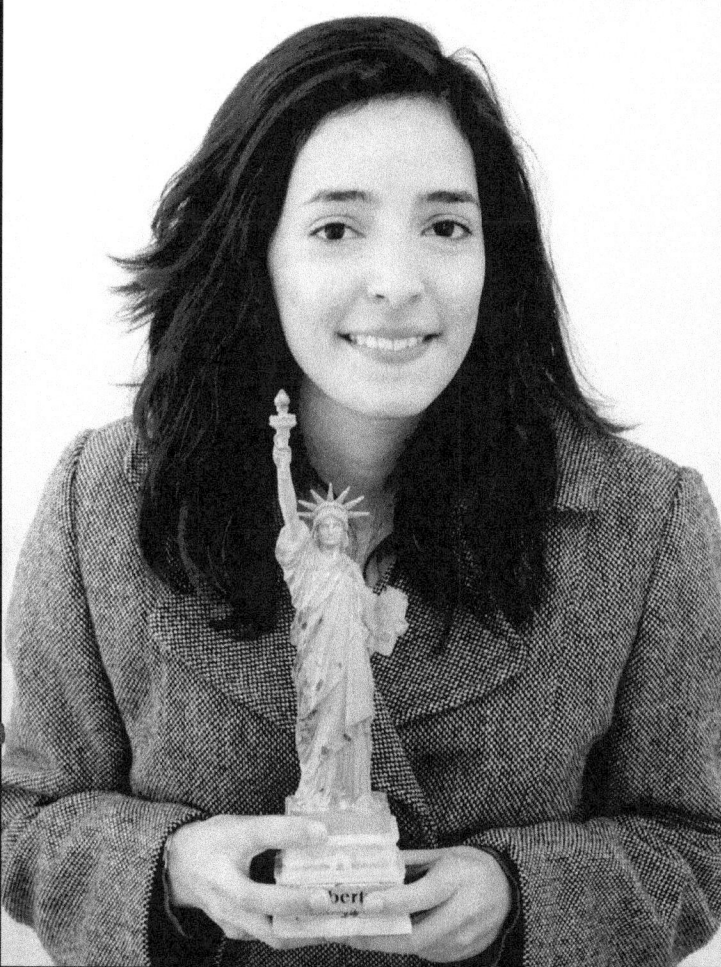
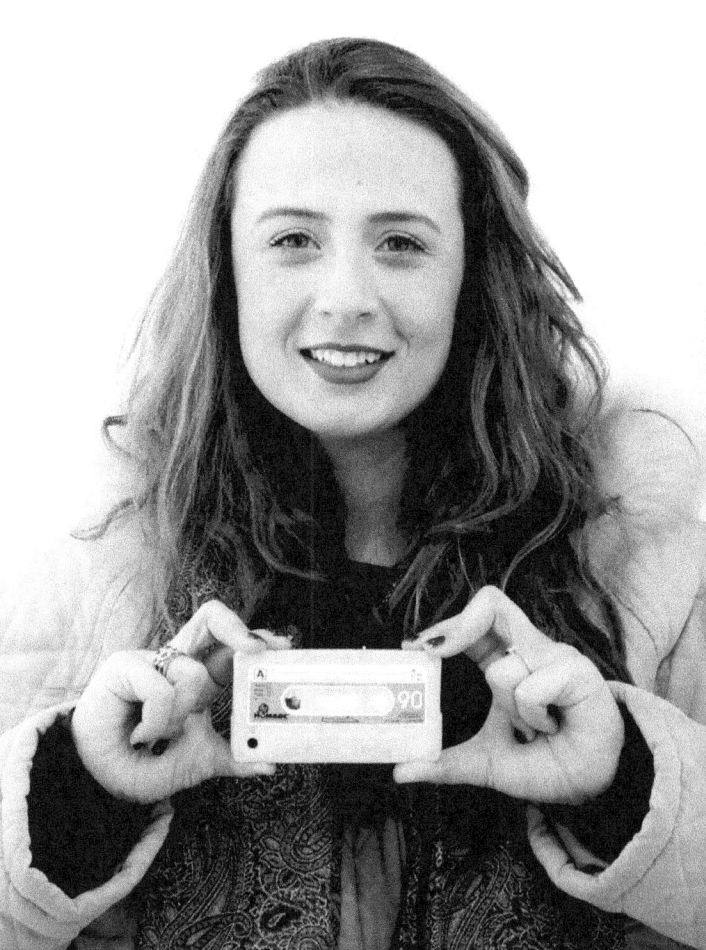

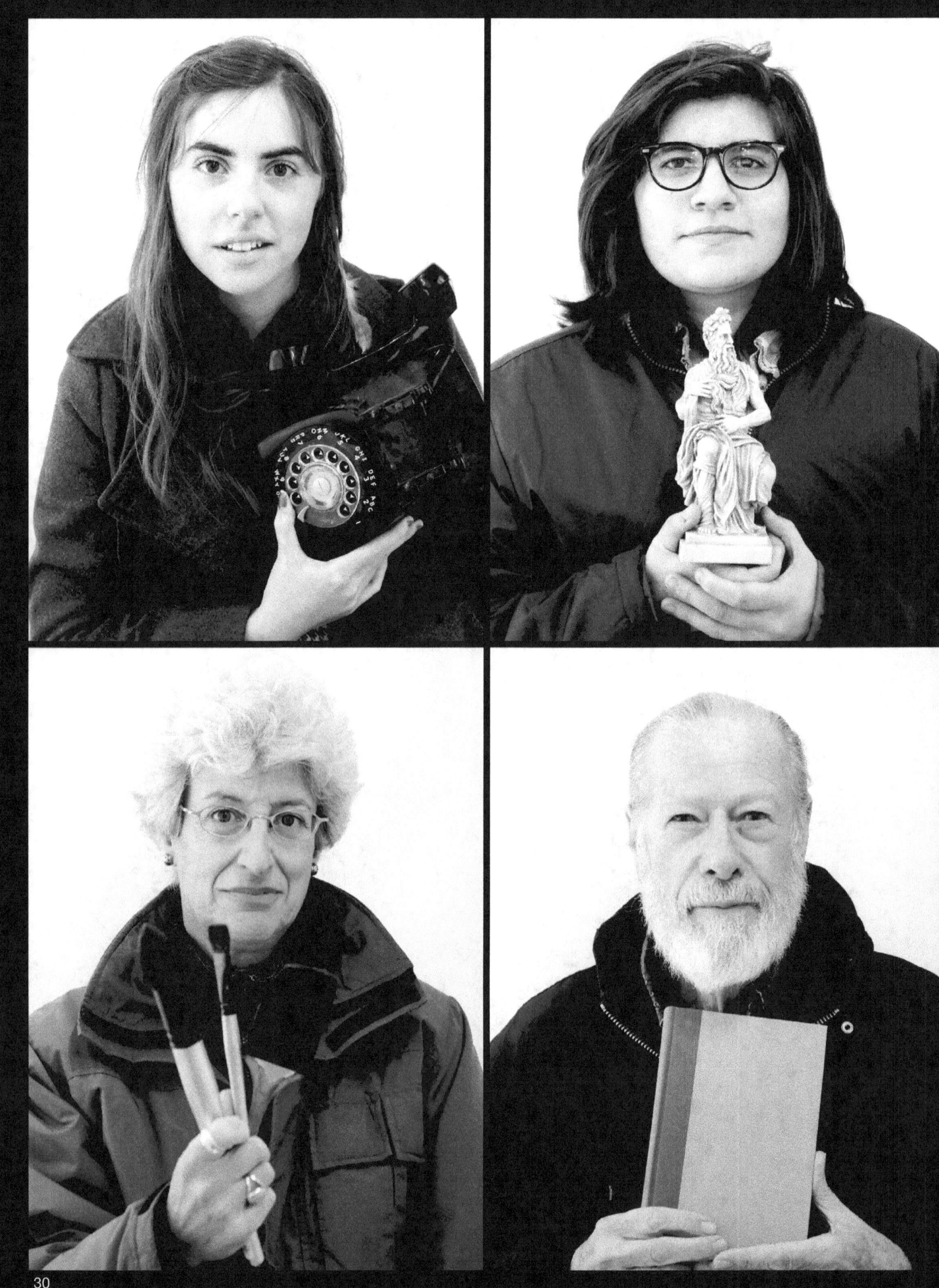

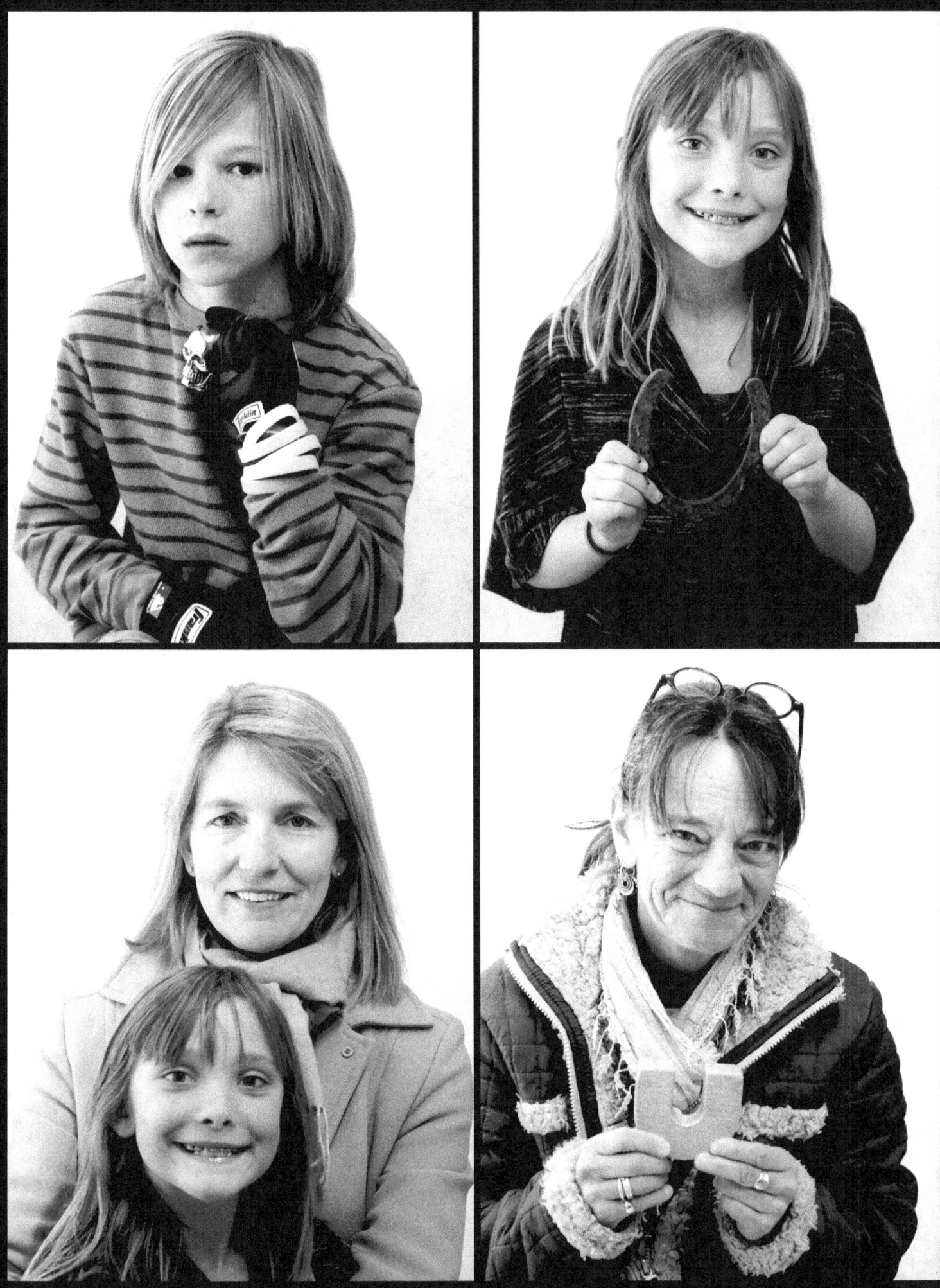

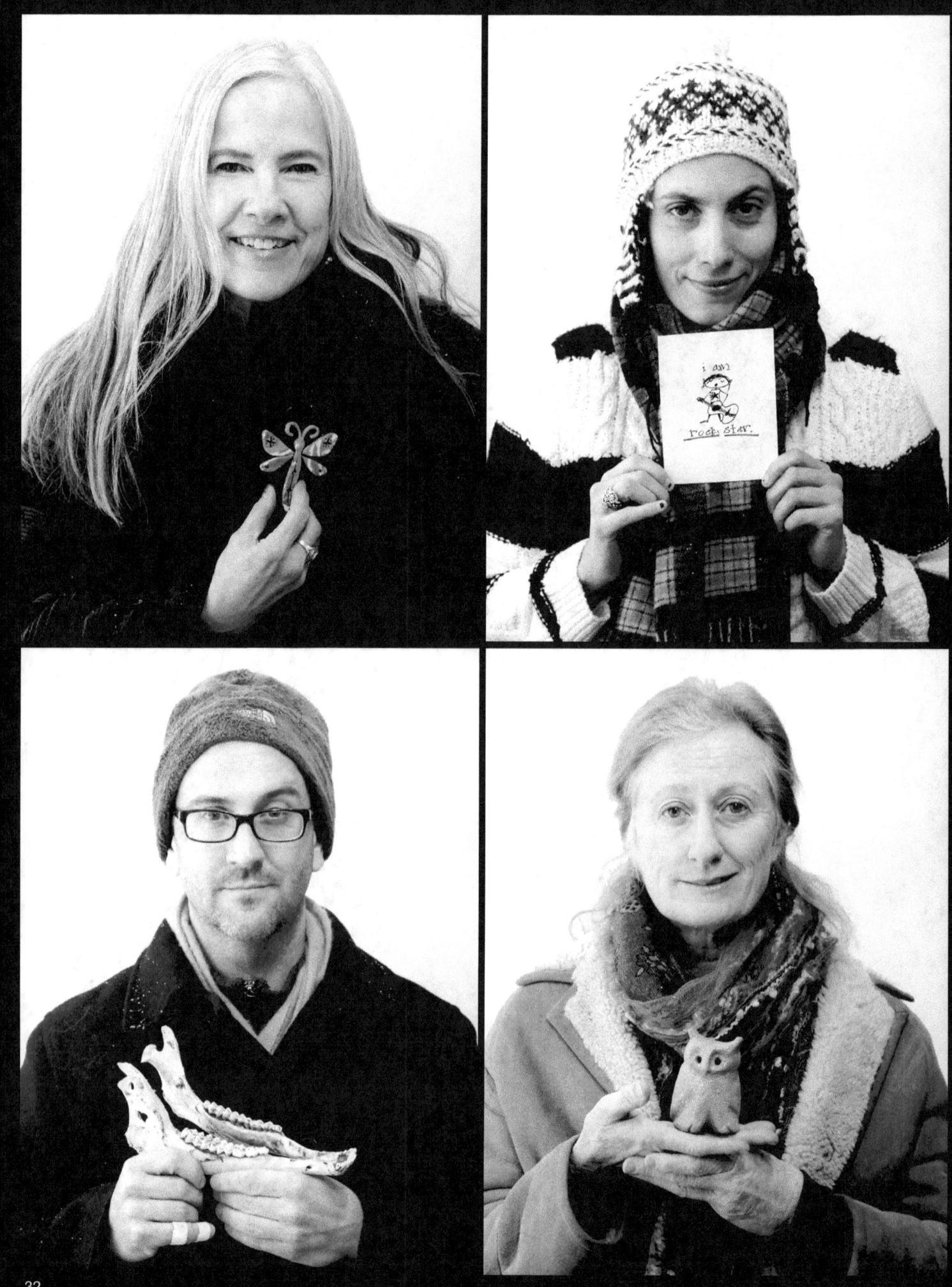

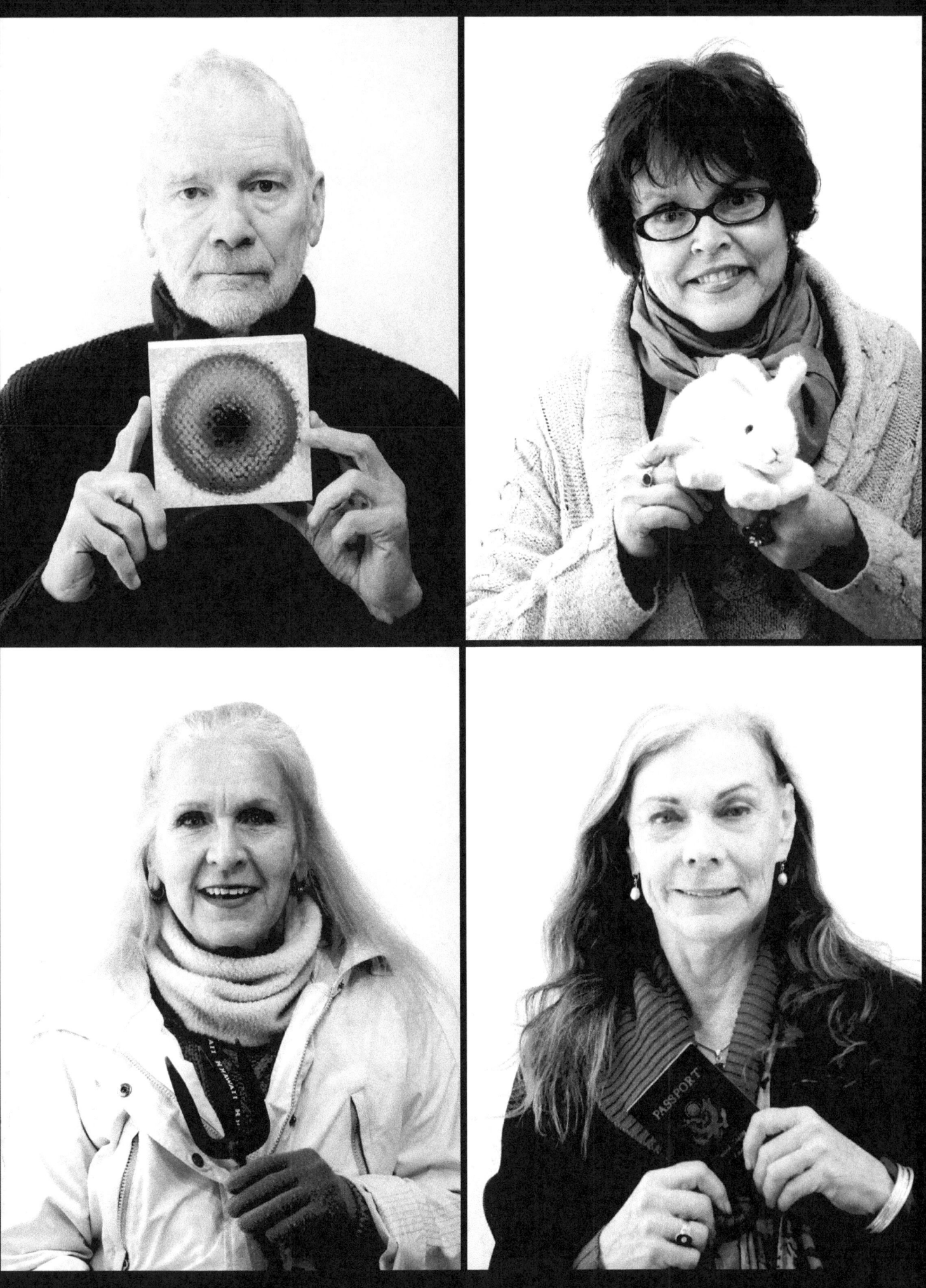

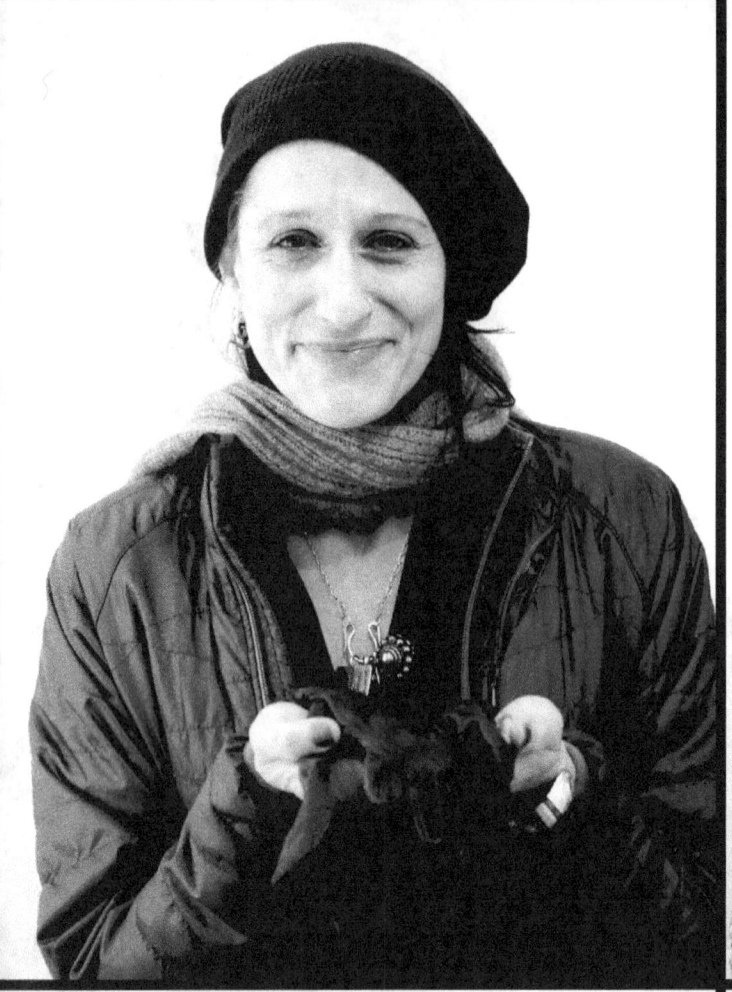
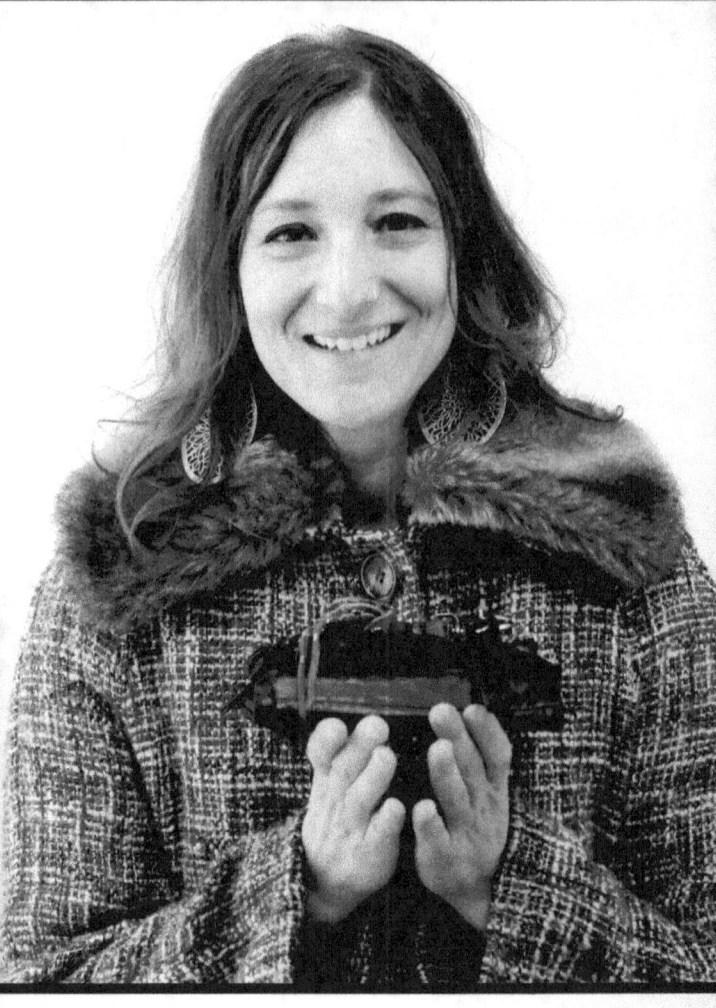
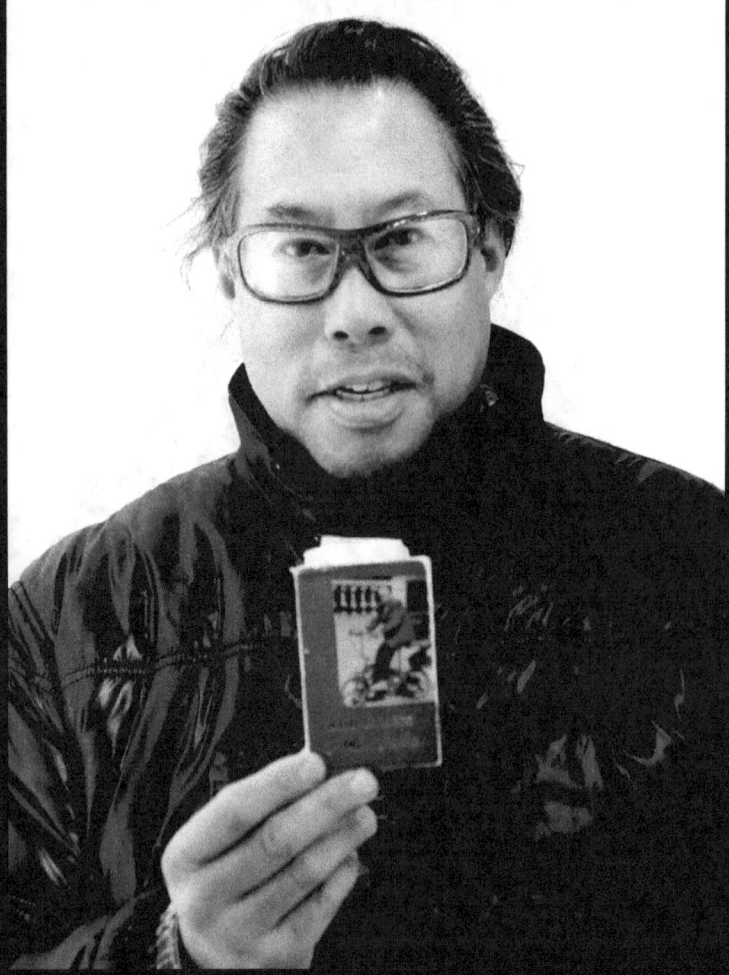
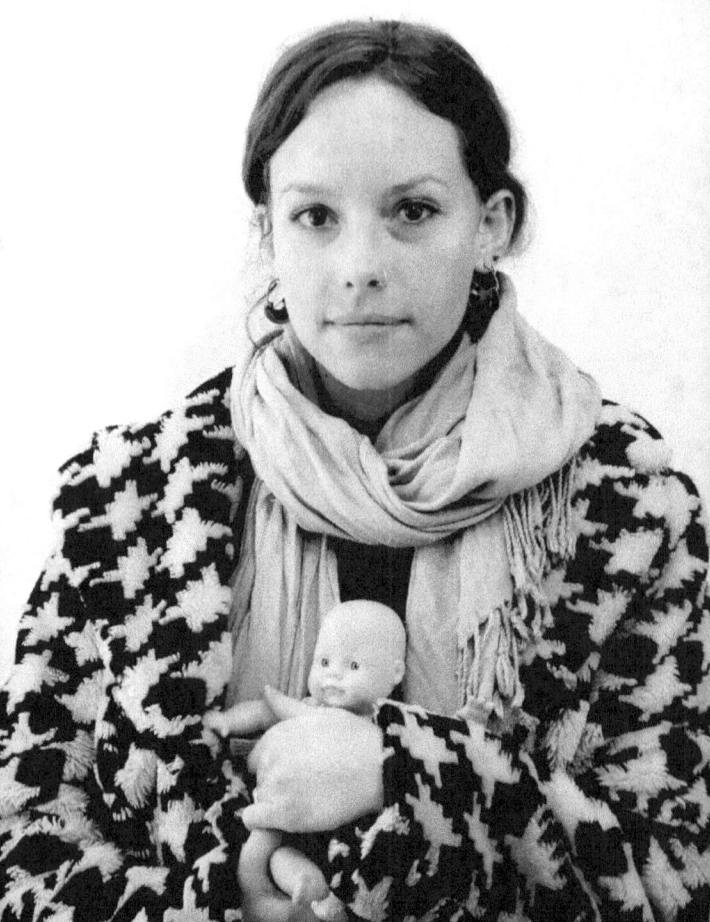

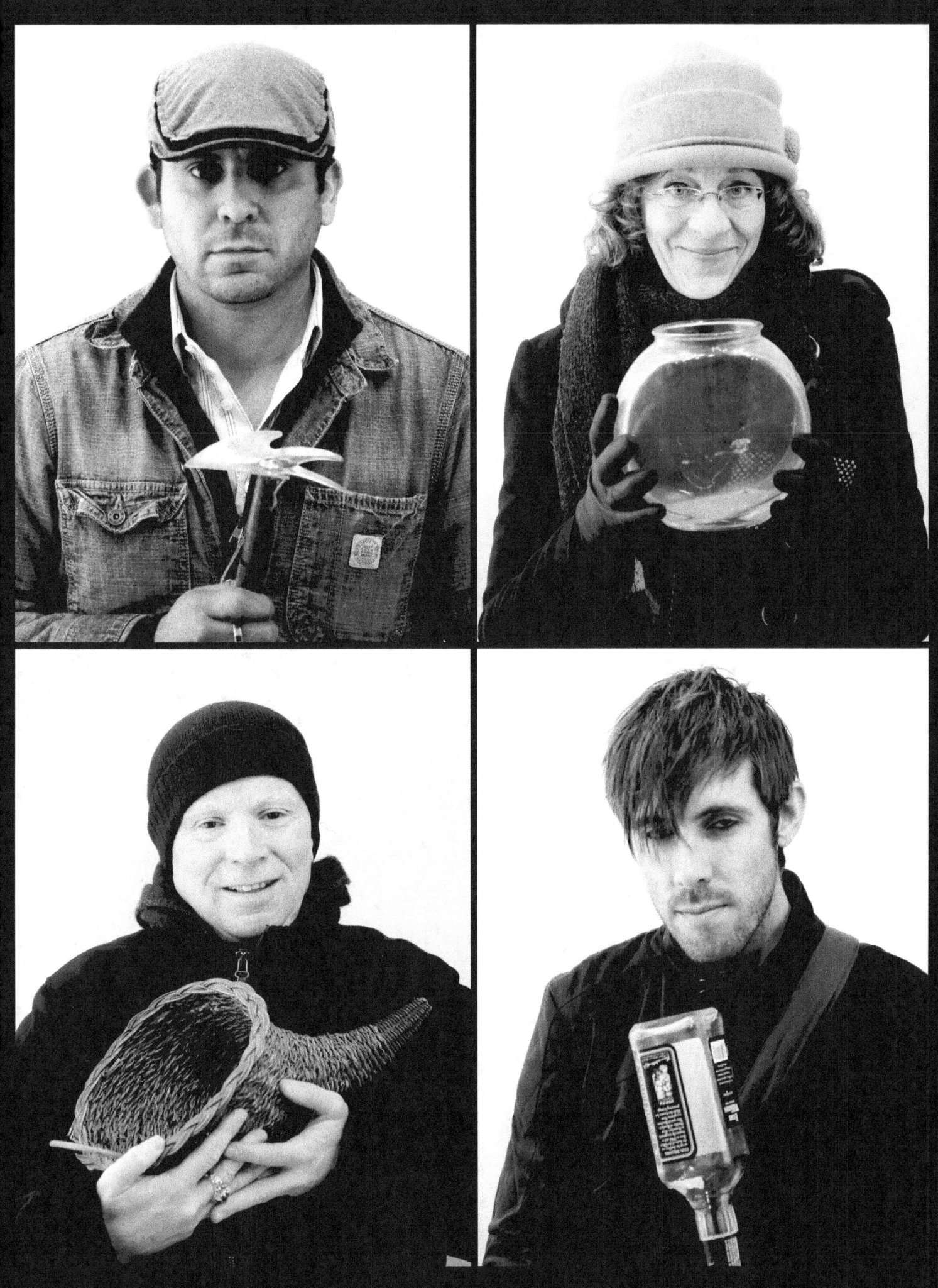

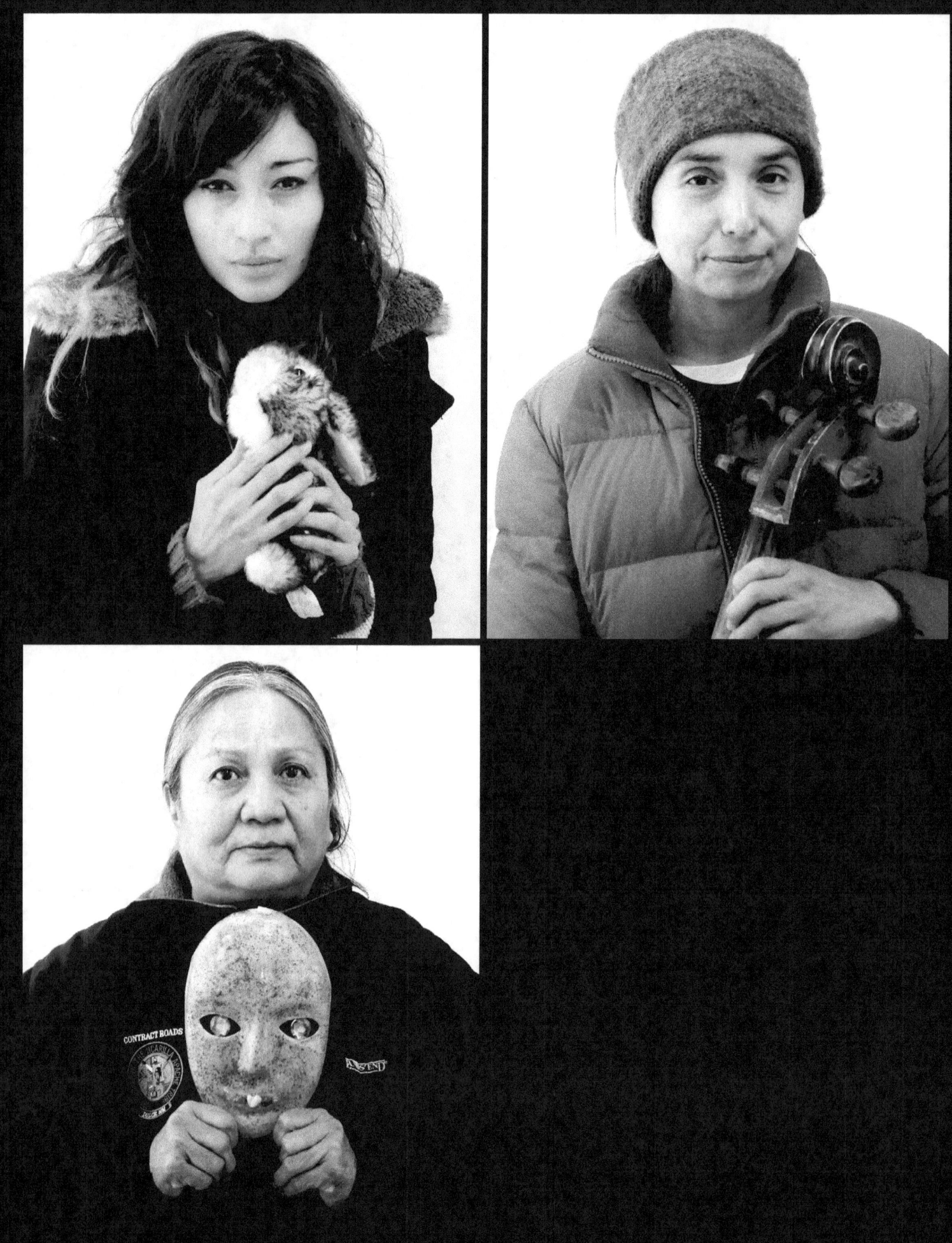

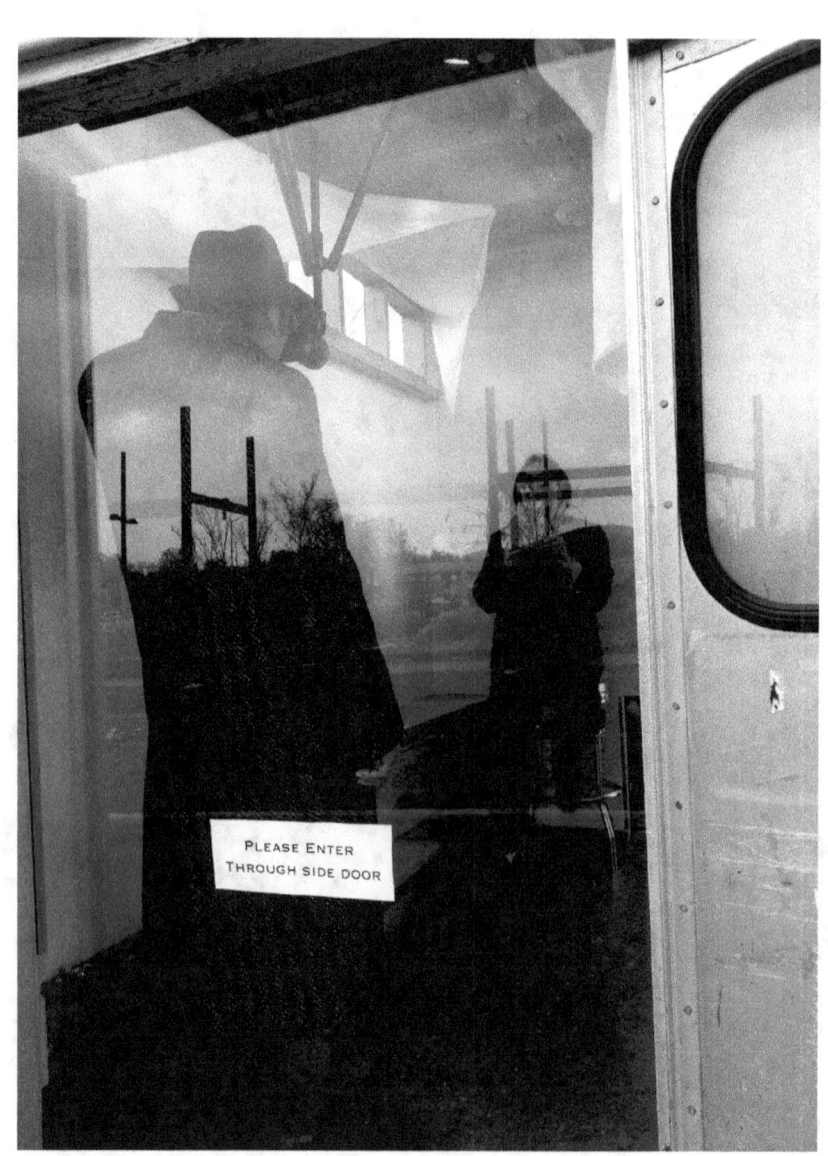

PLEASE ENTER
THROUGH SIDE DOOR

The Railyard

1607 Paseo de Peralta

Saturday

March 3

8am-1pm

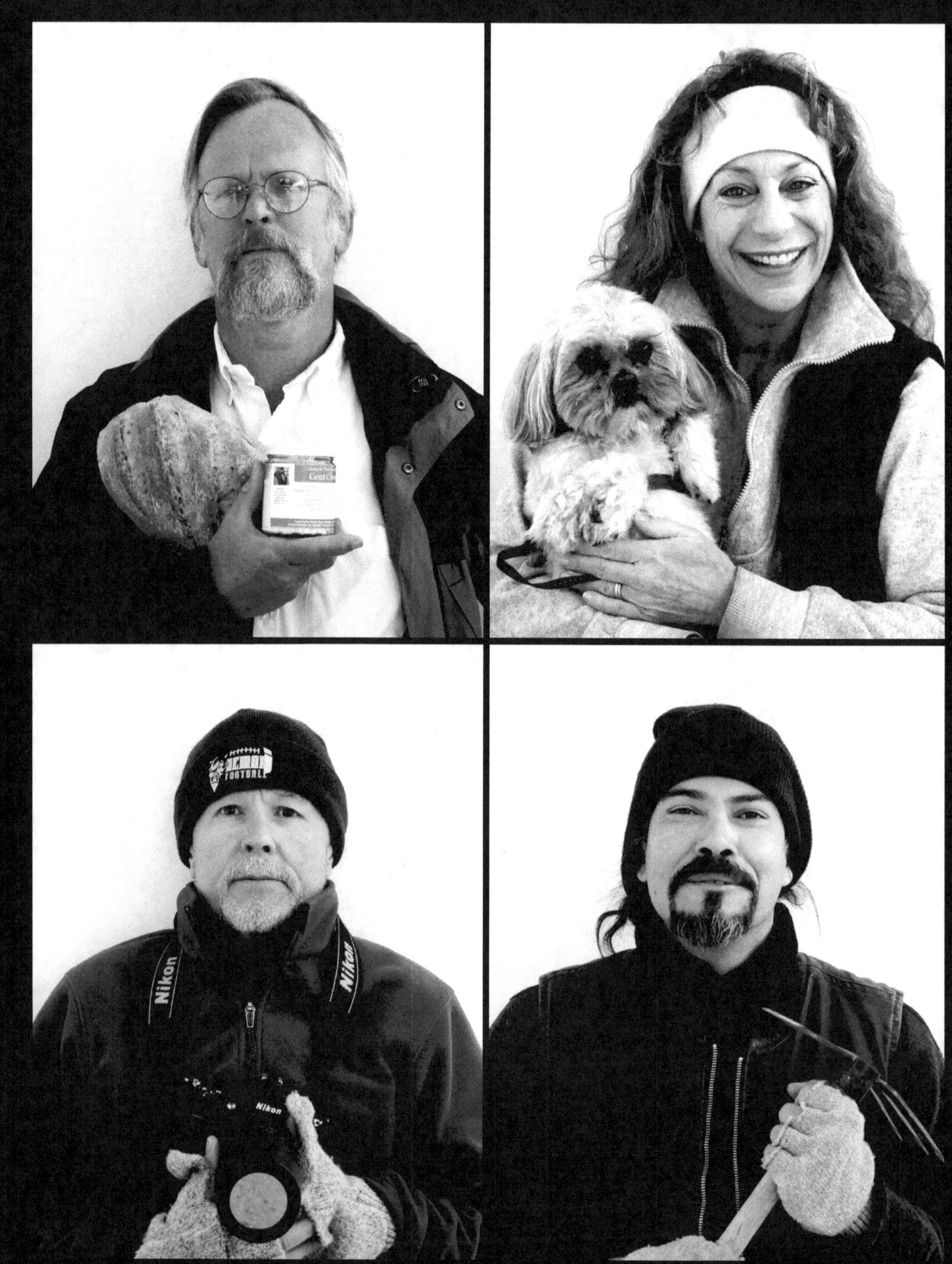

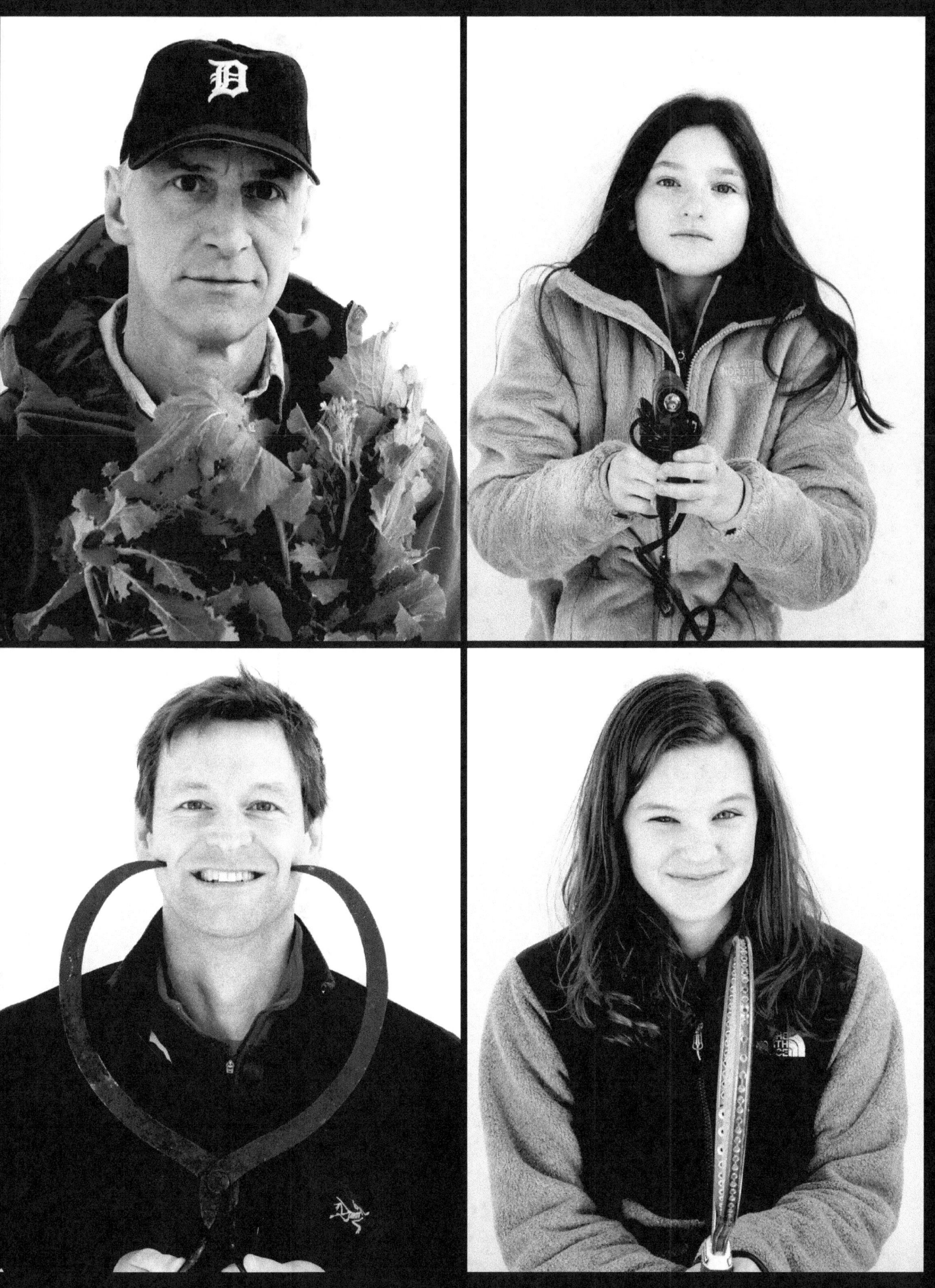

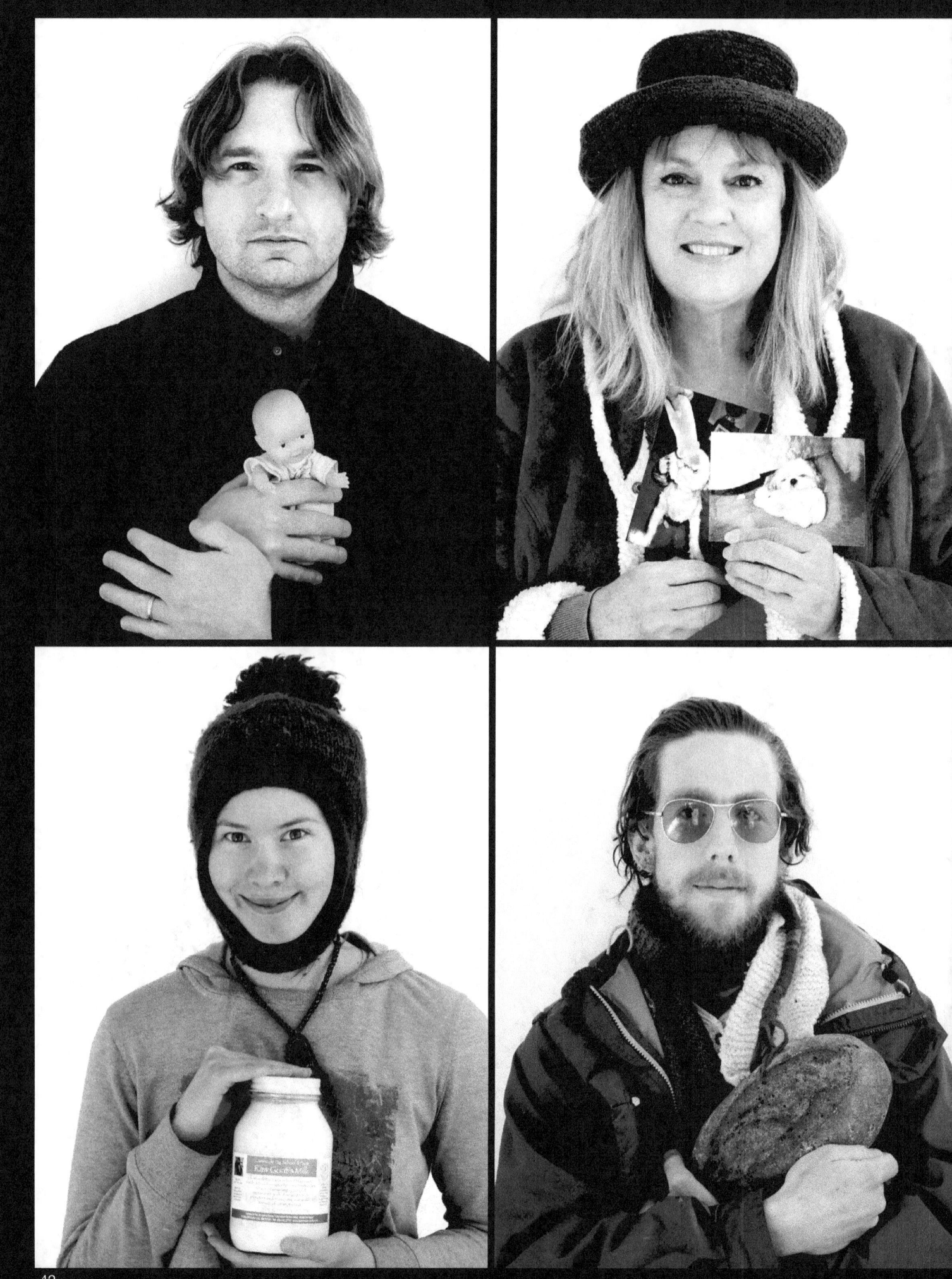

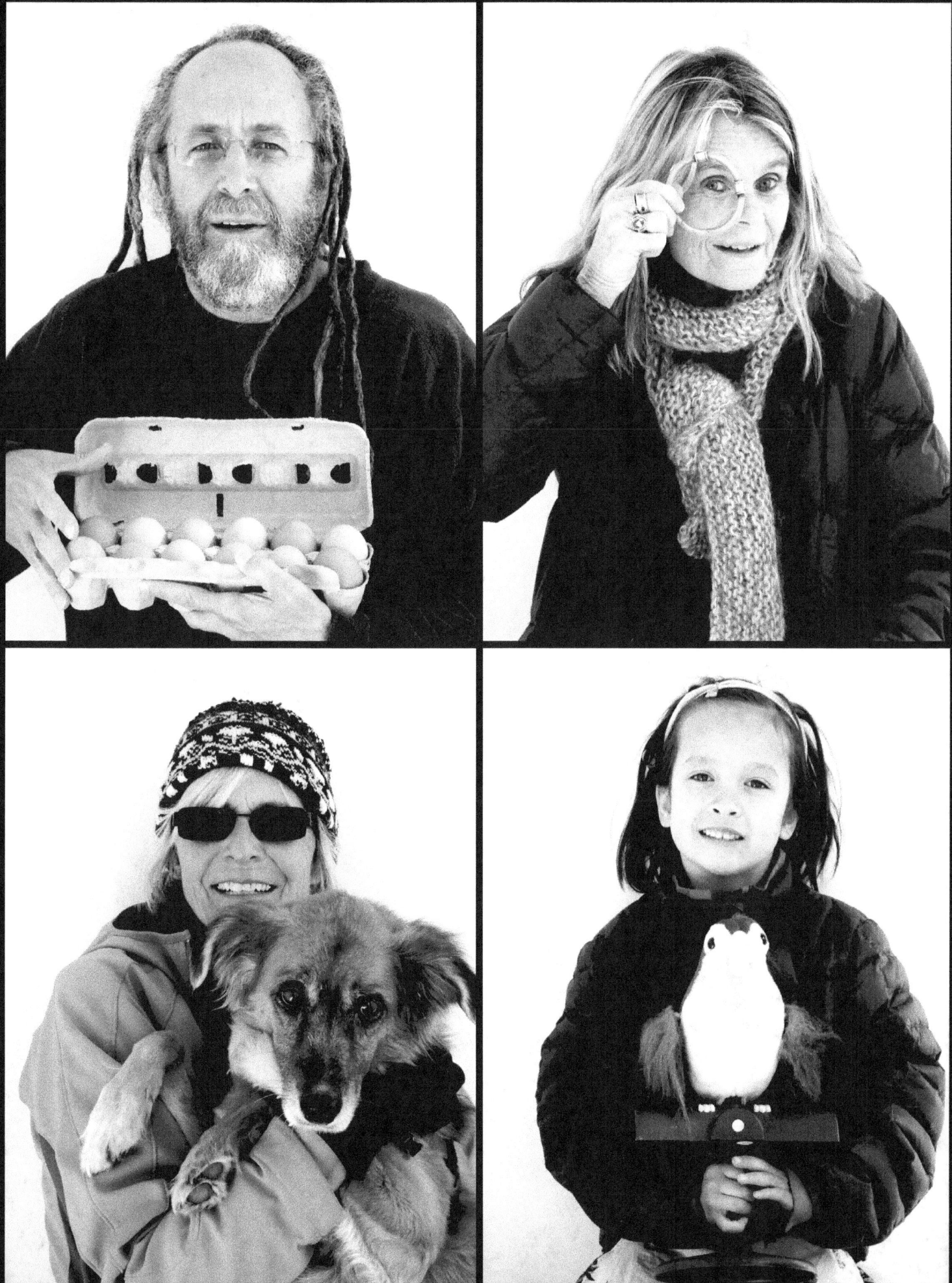

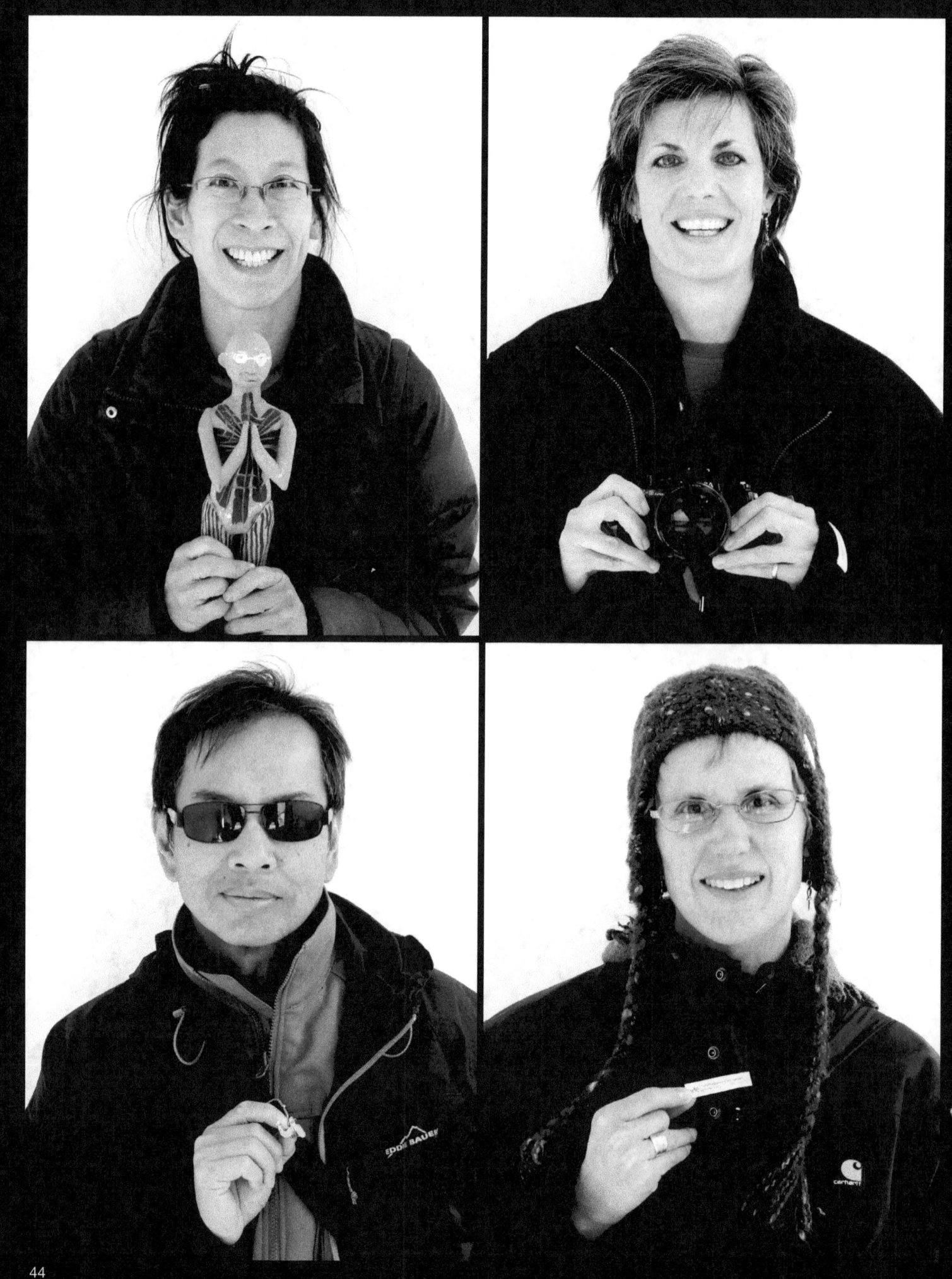

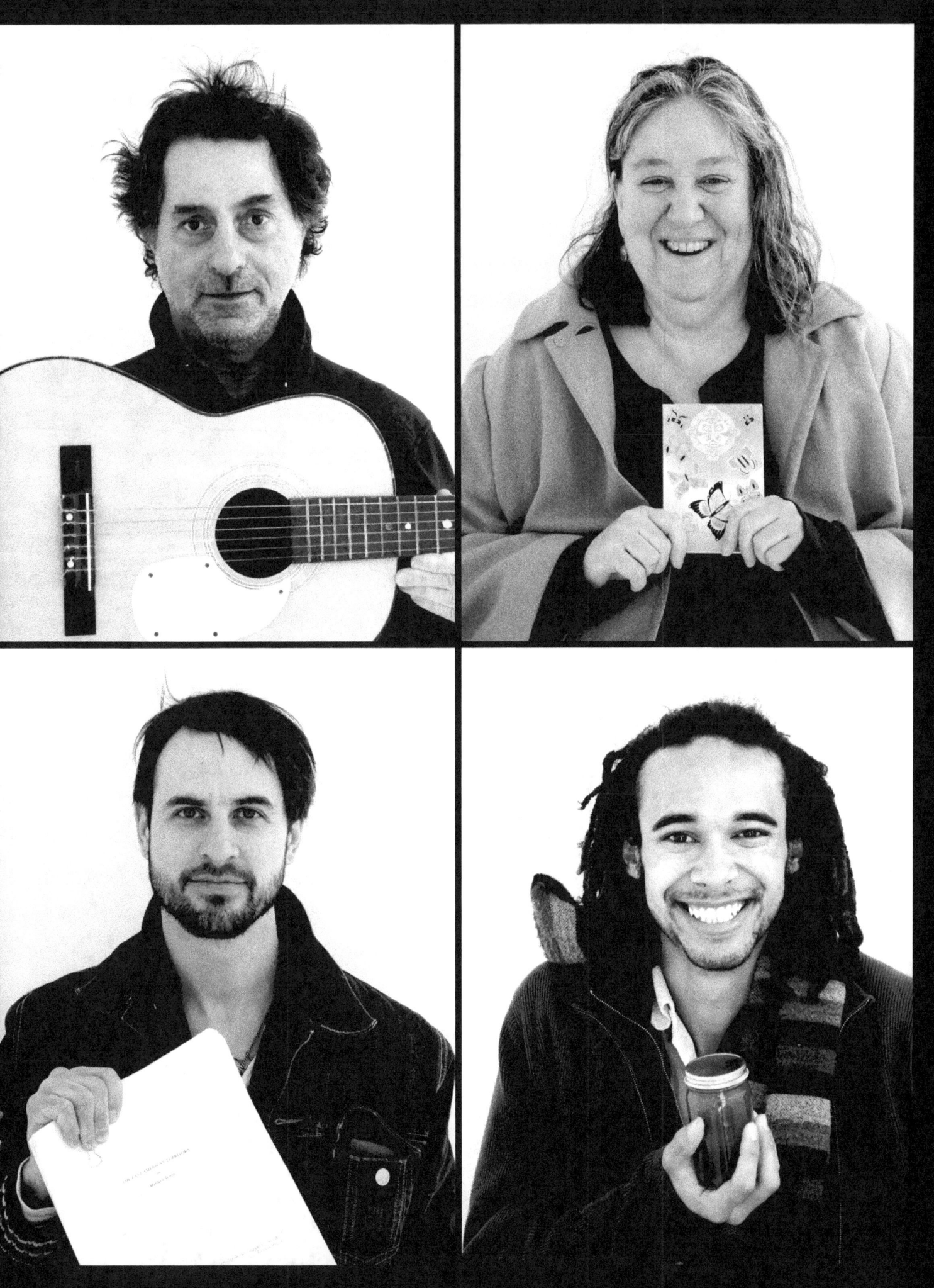

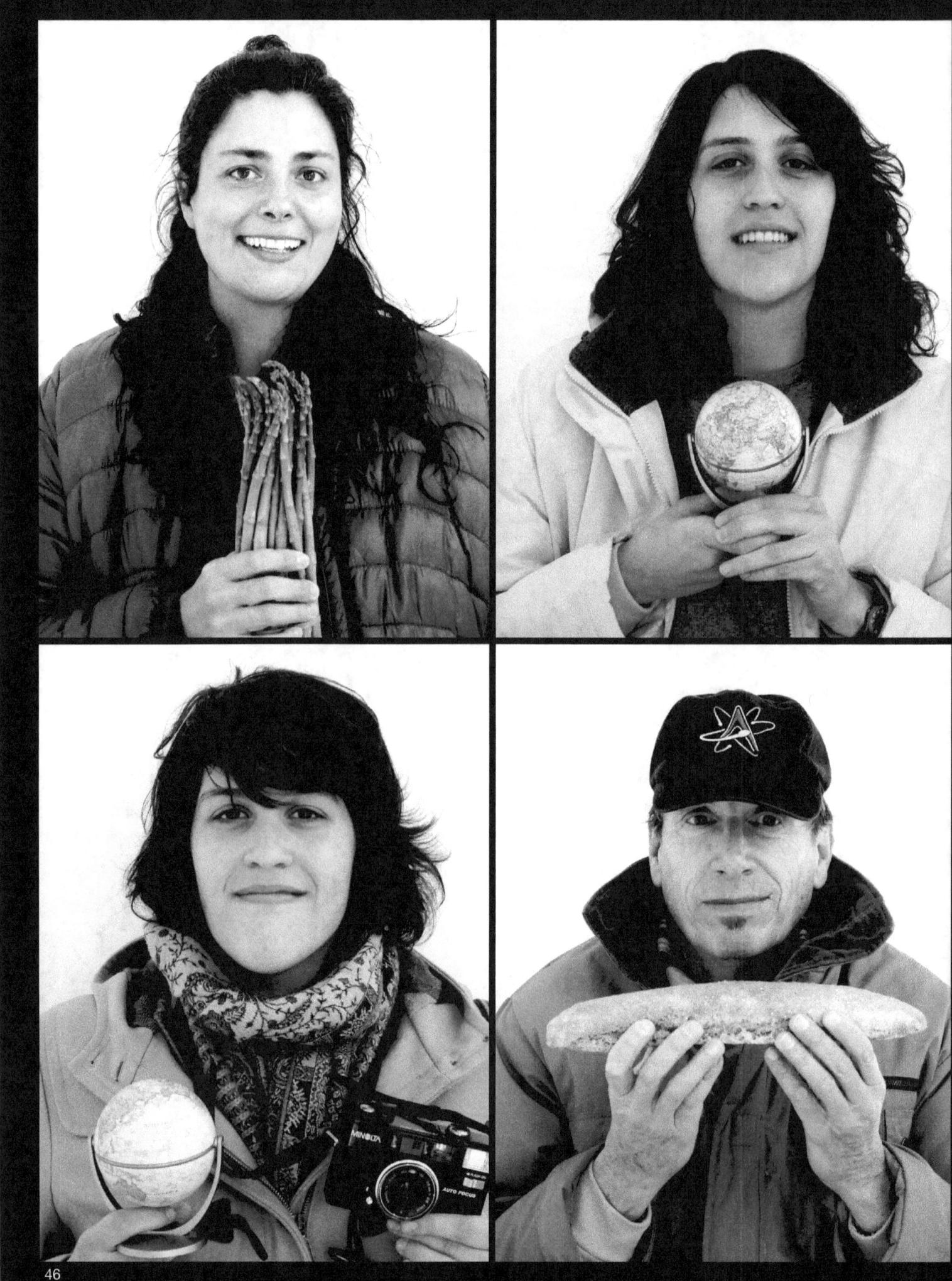

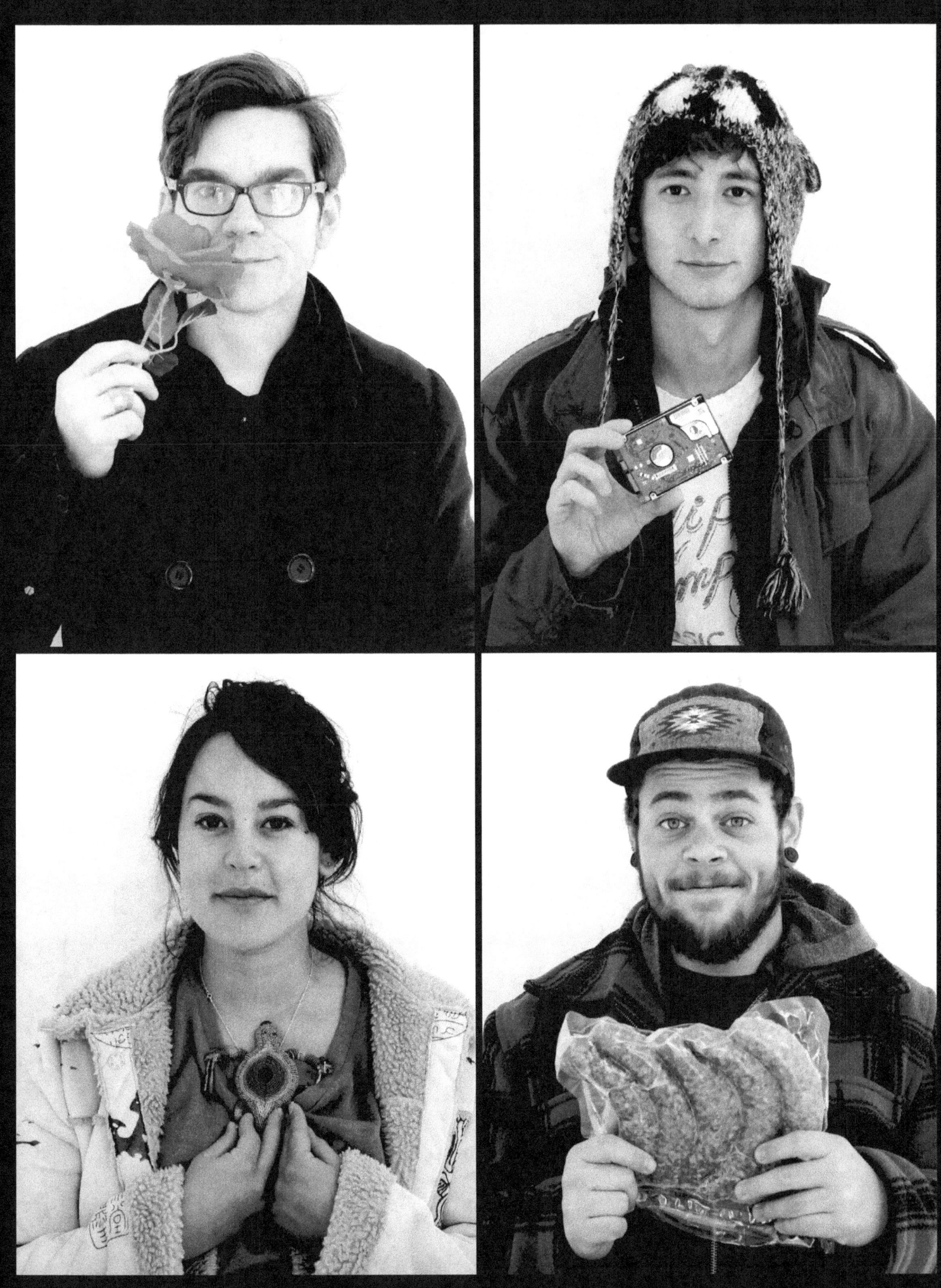

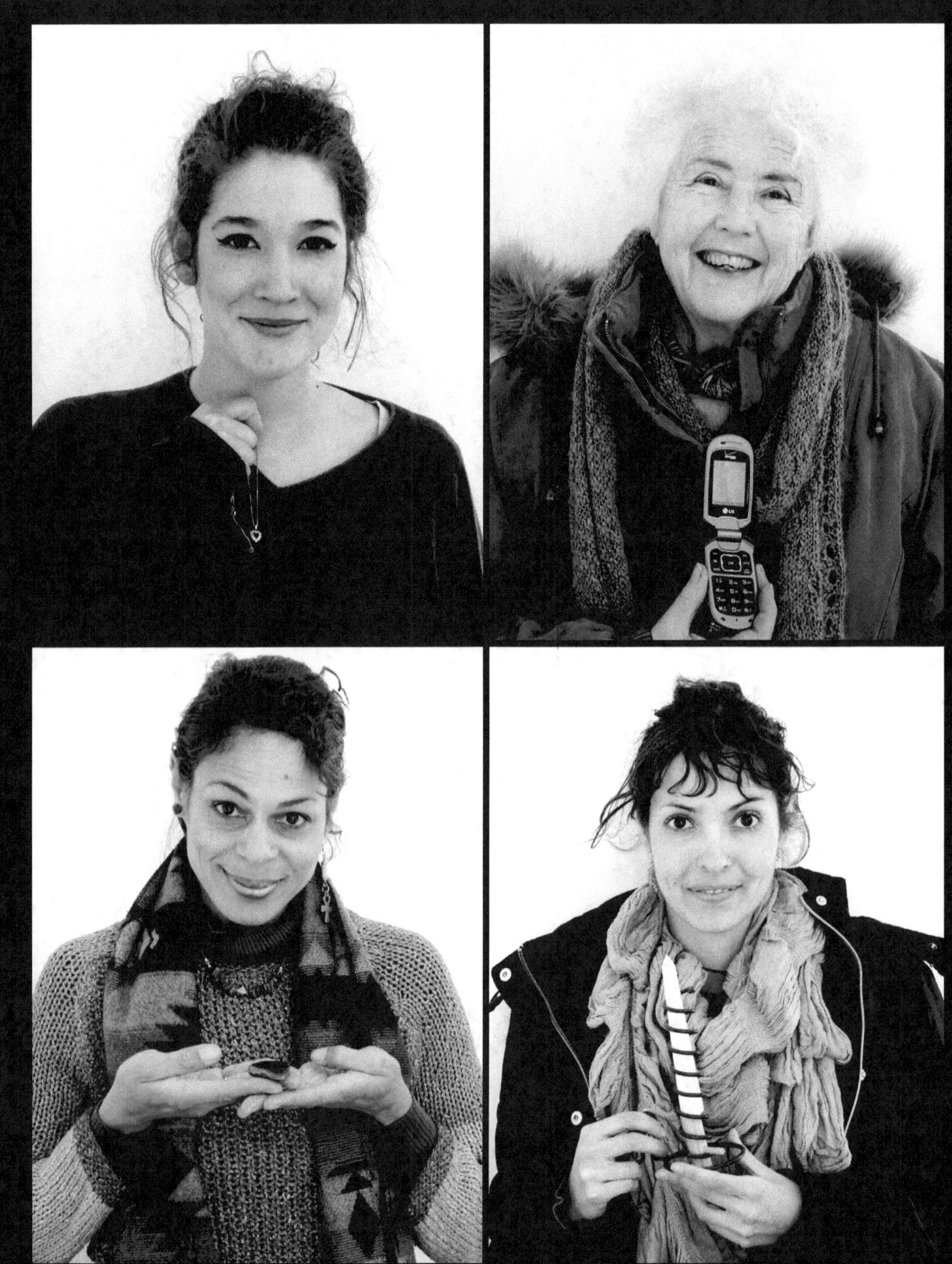

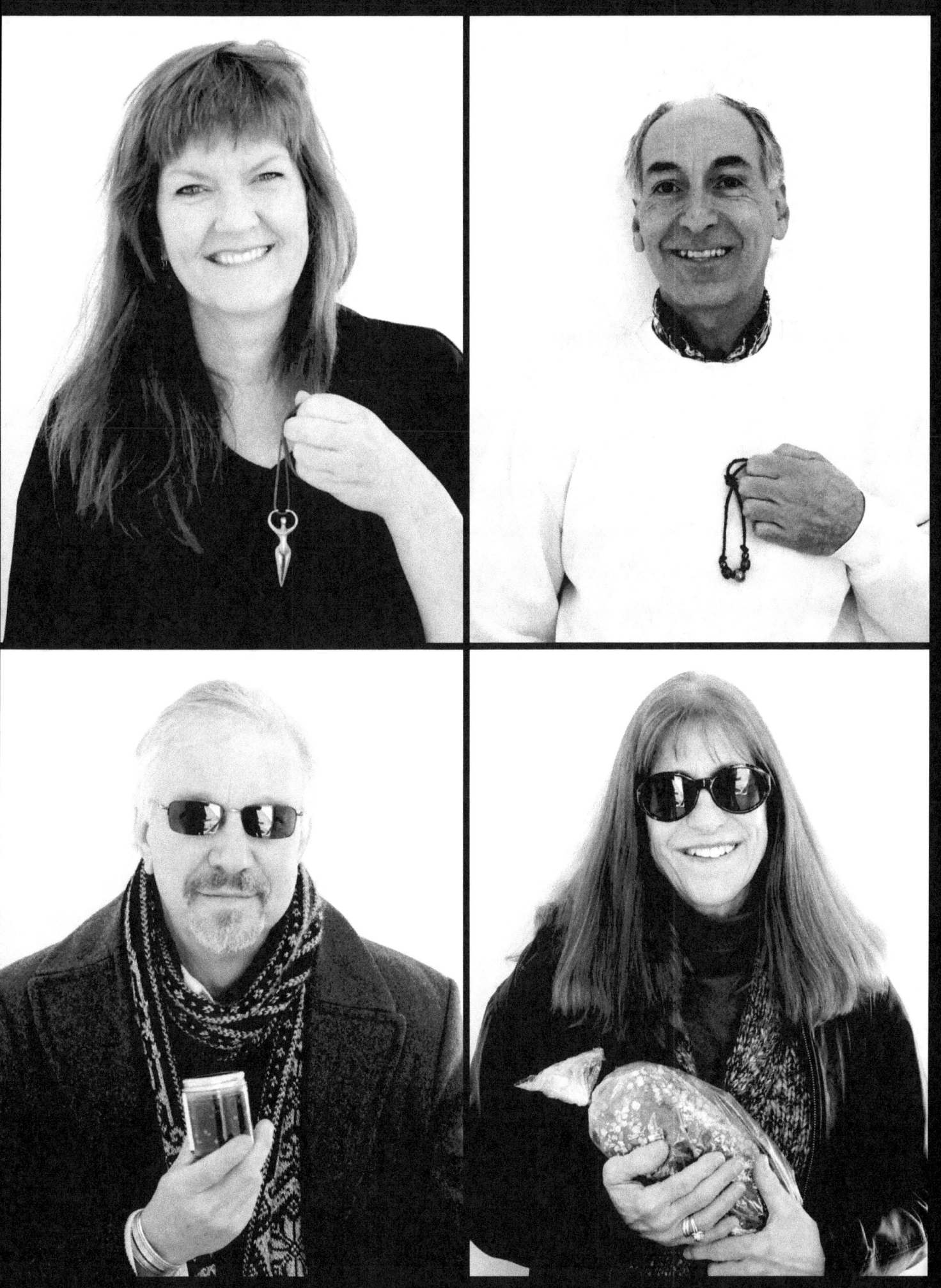

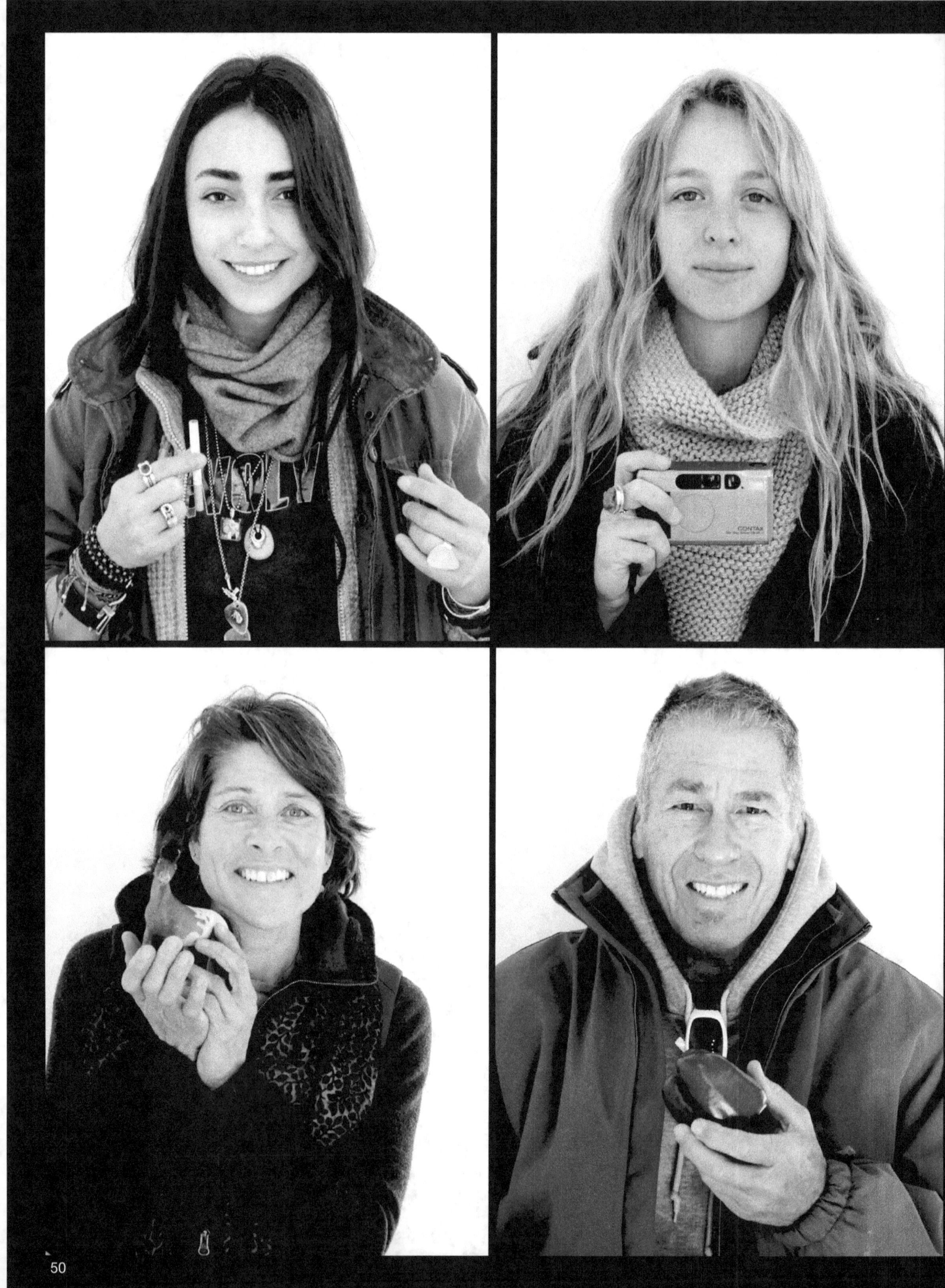

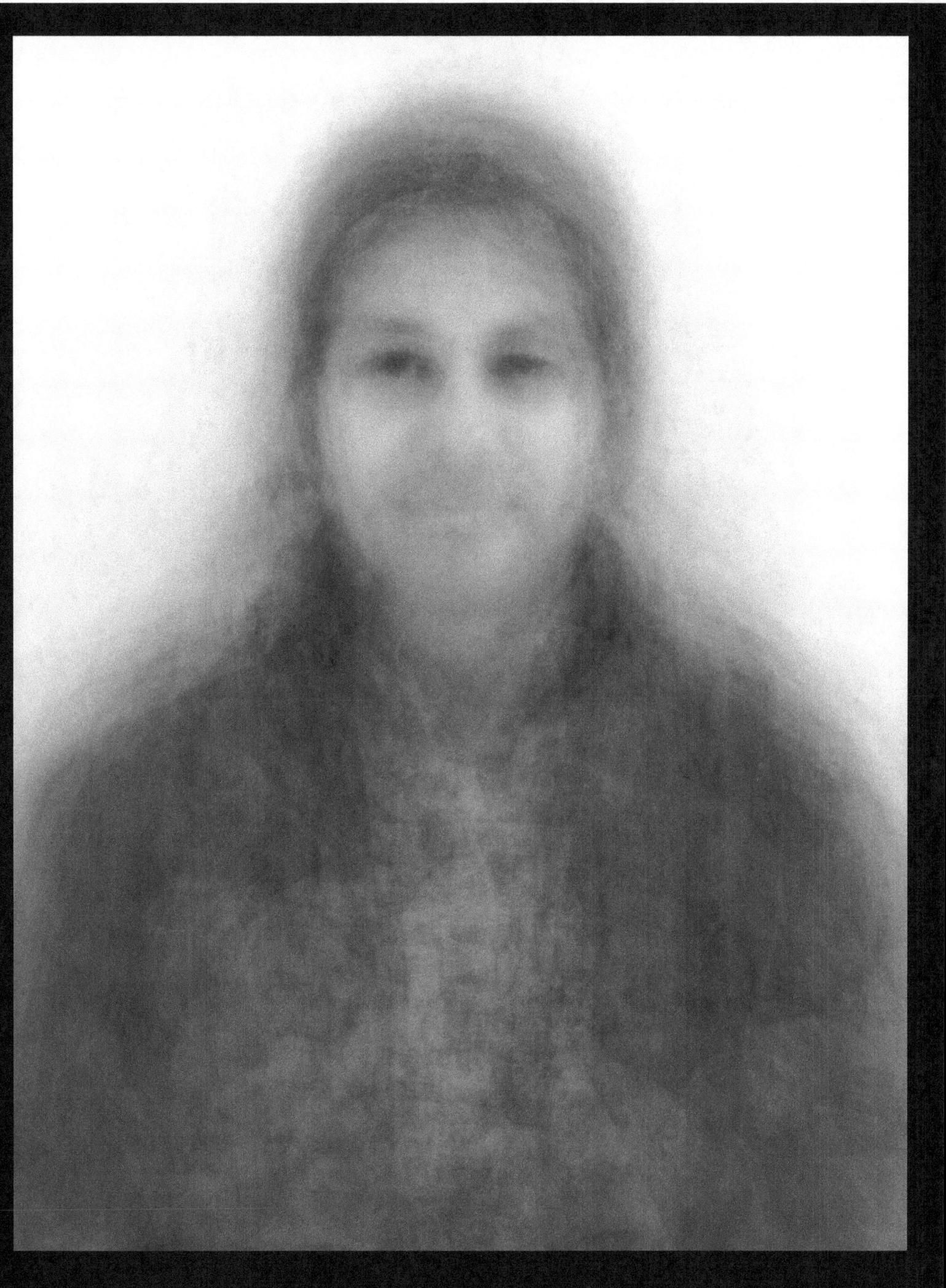

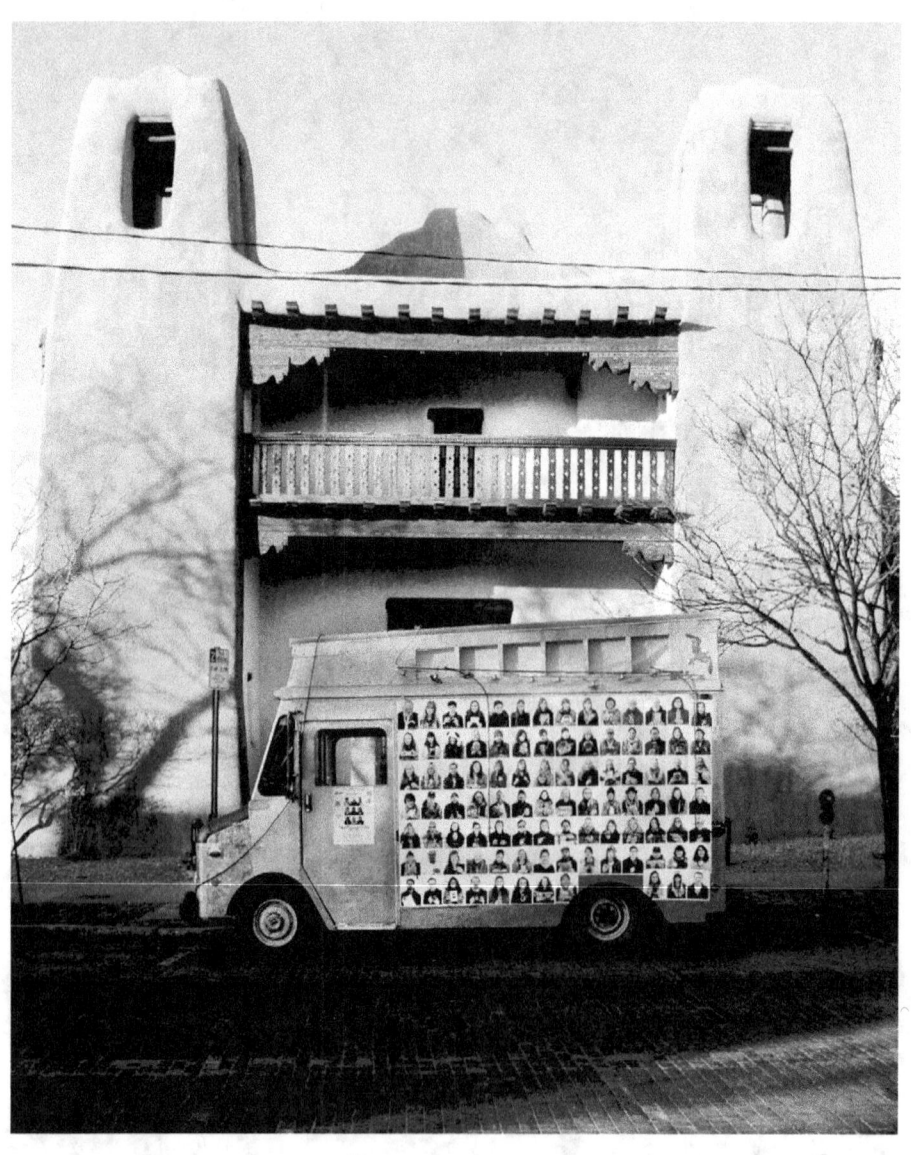

The New Mexico Museum of Art

107 West Palace Avenue

Sunday

March 4

10am-5pm

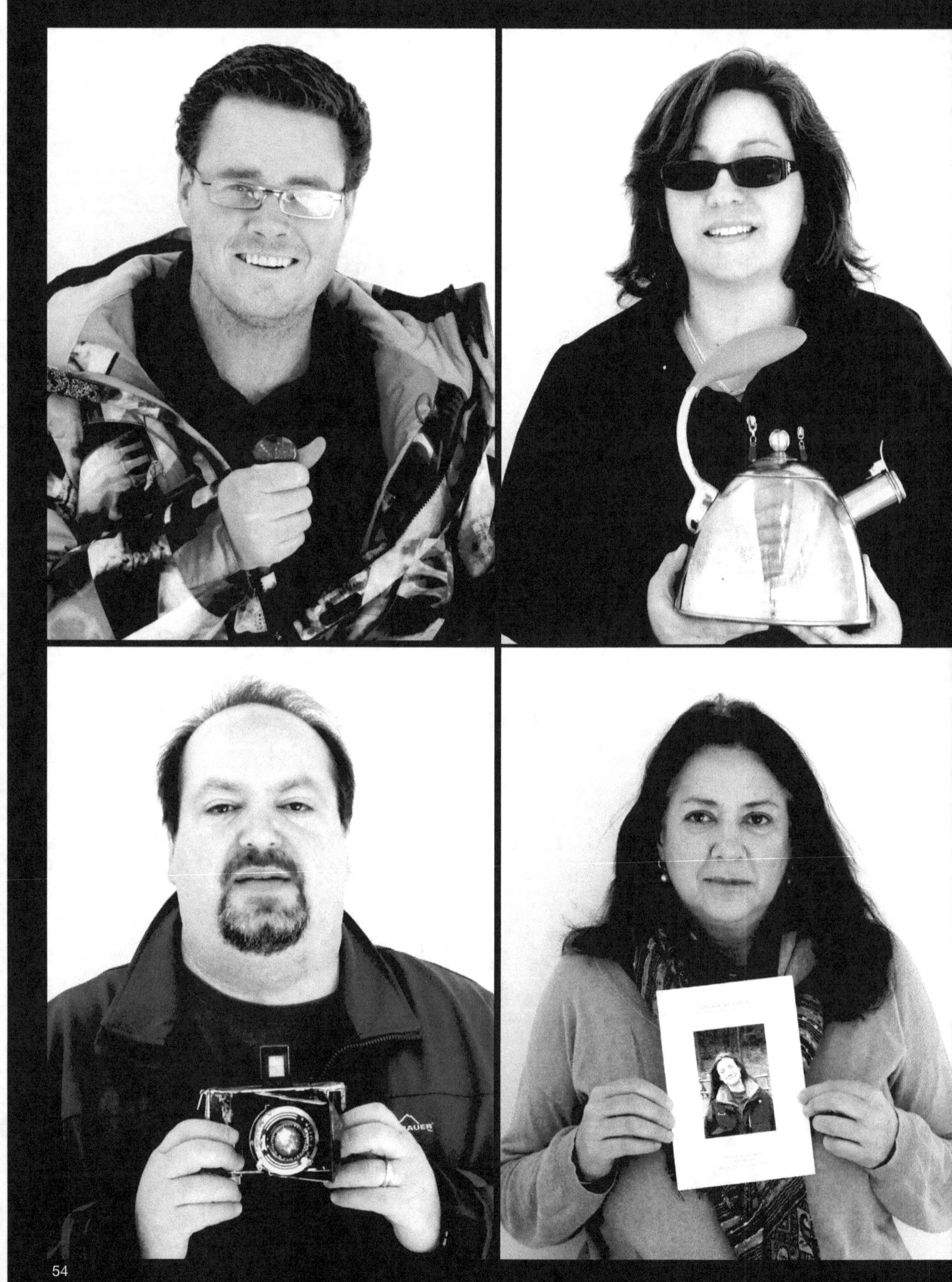

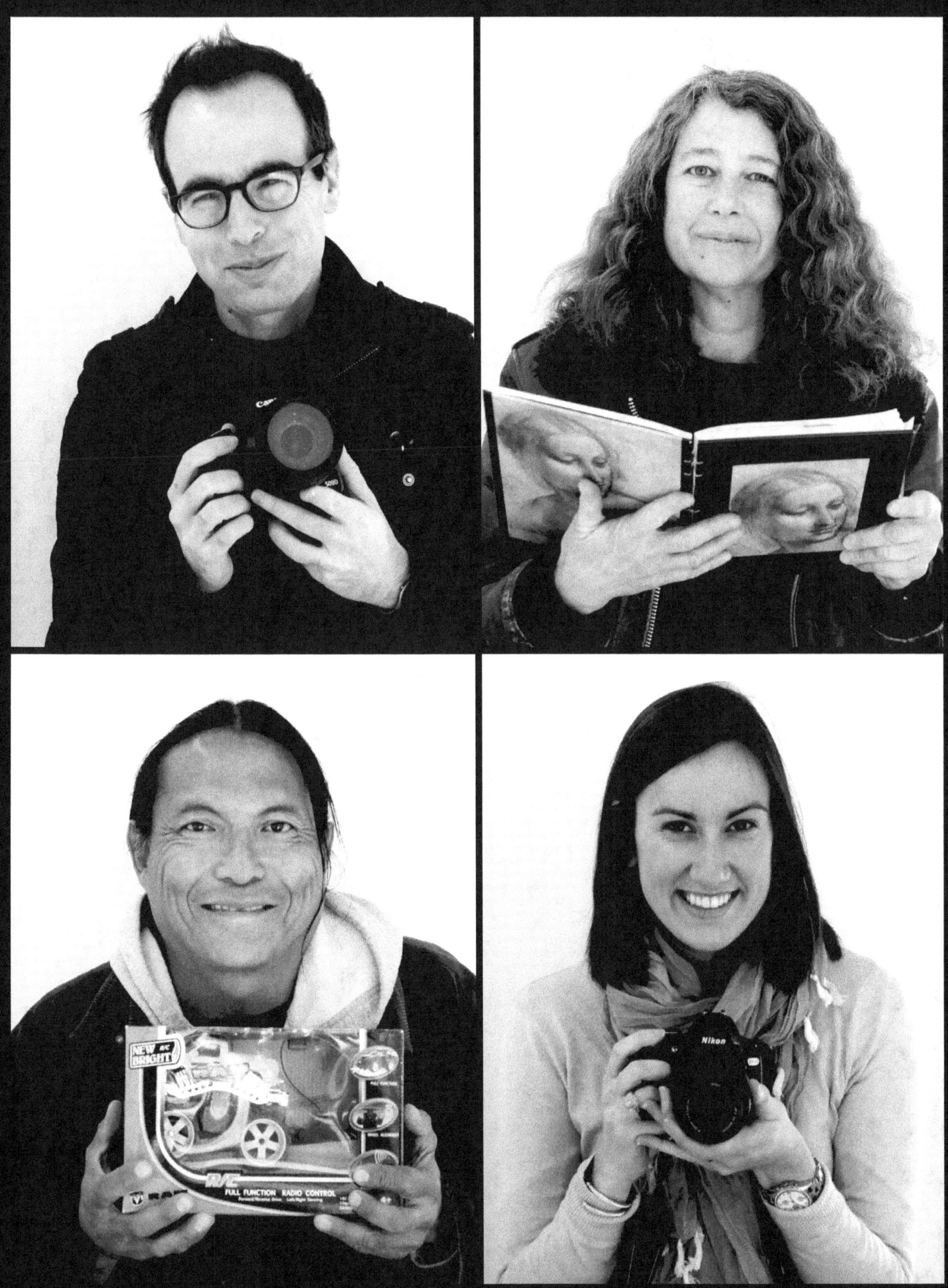

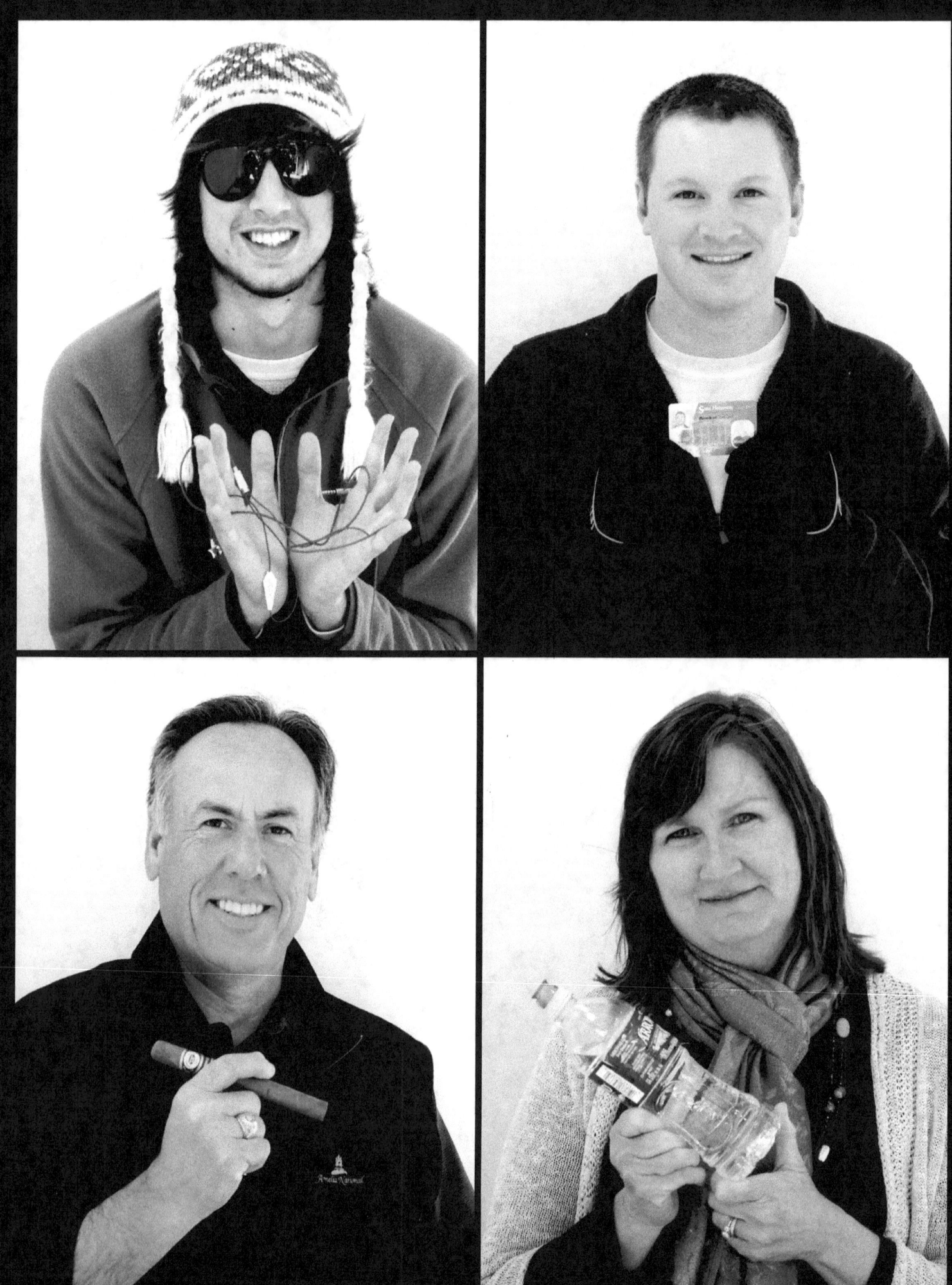

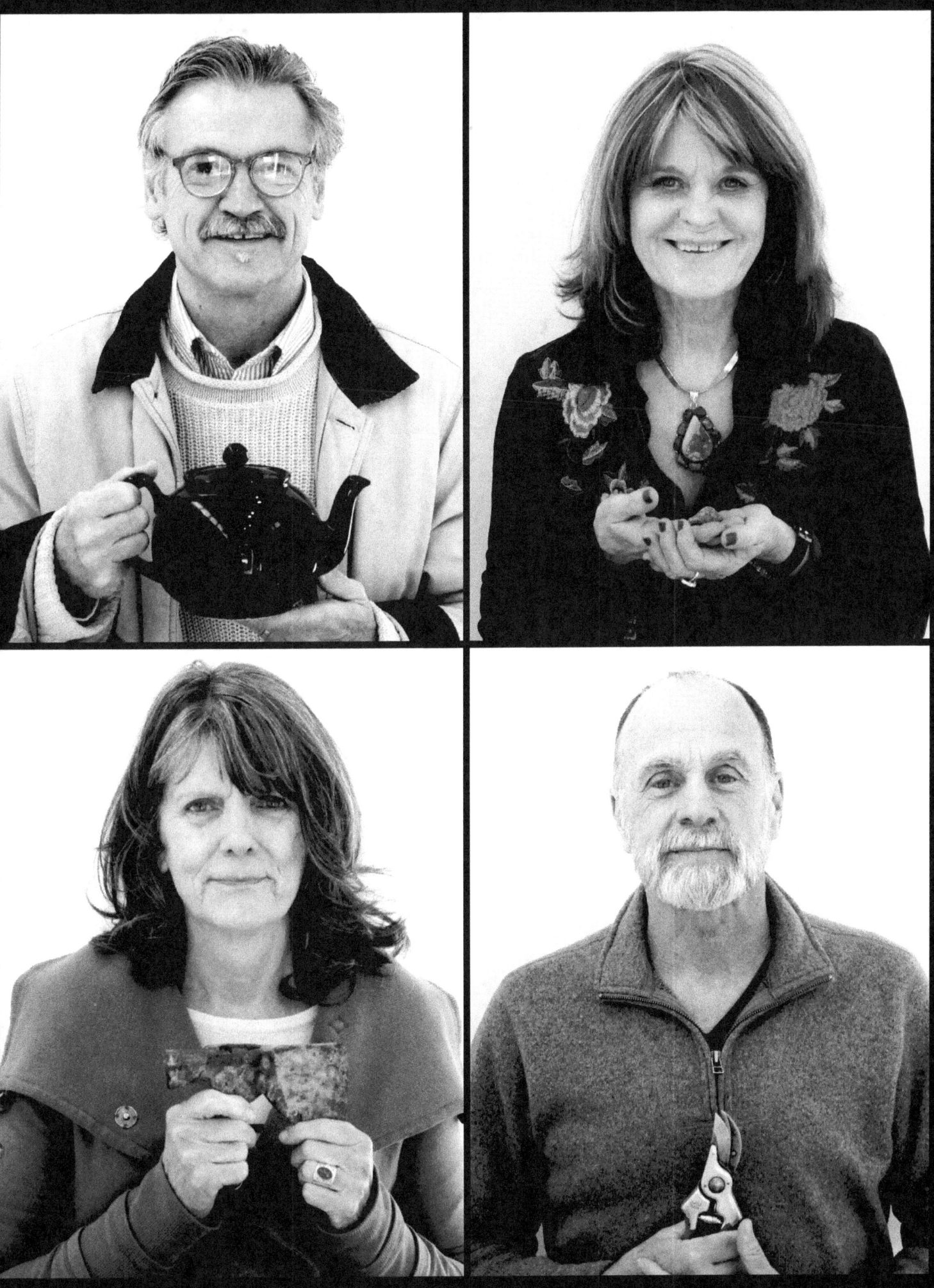

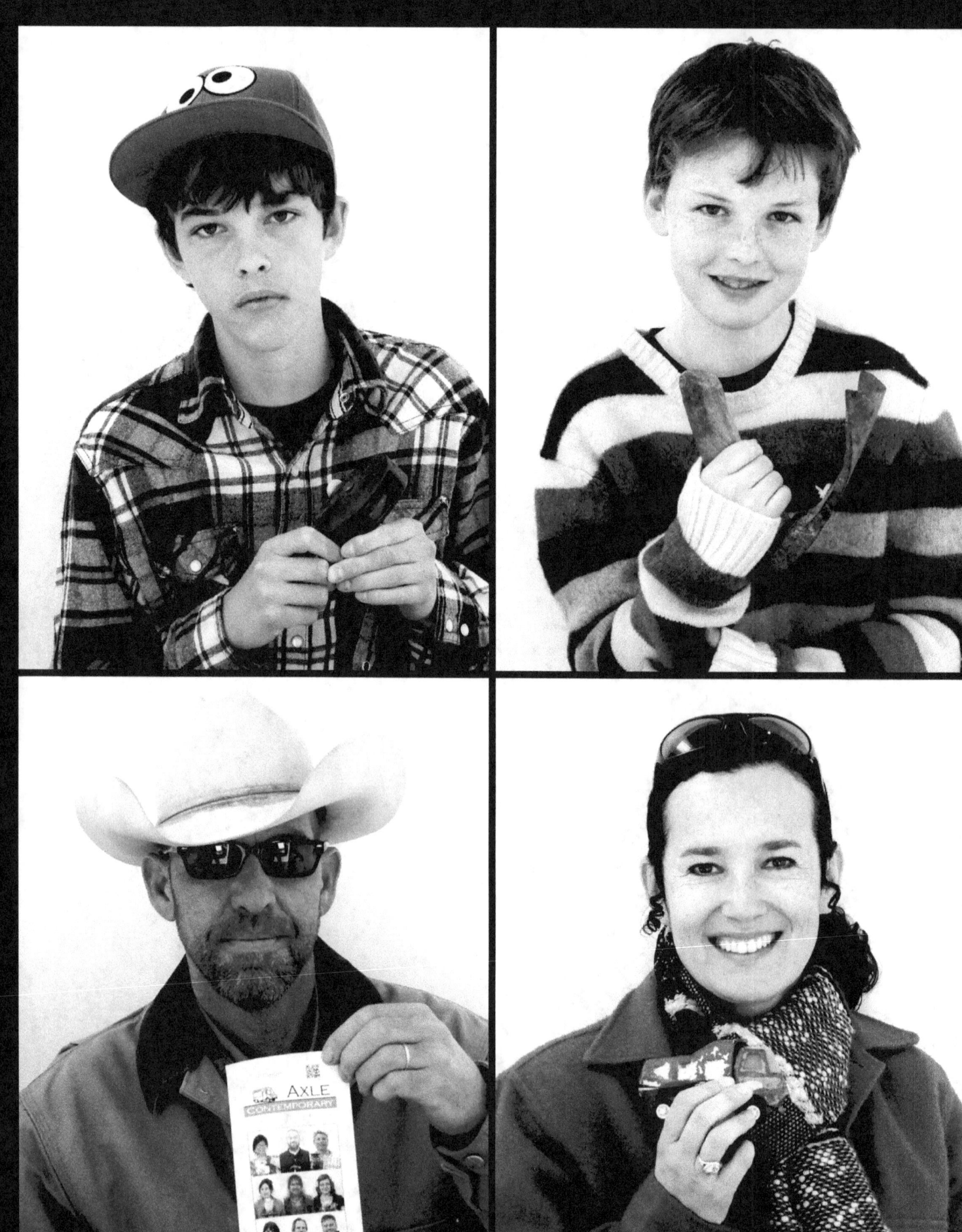

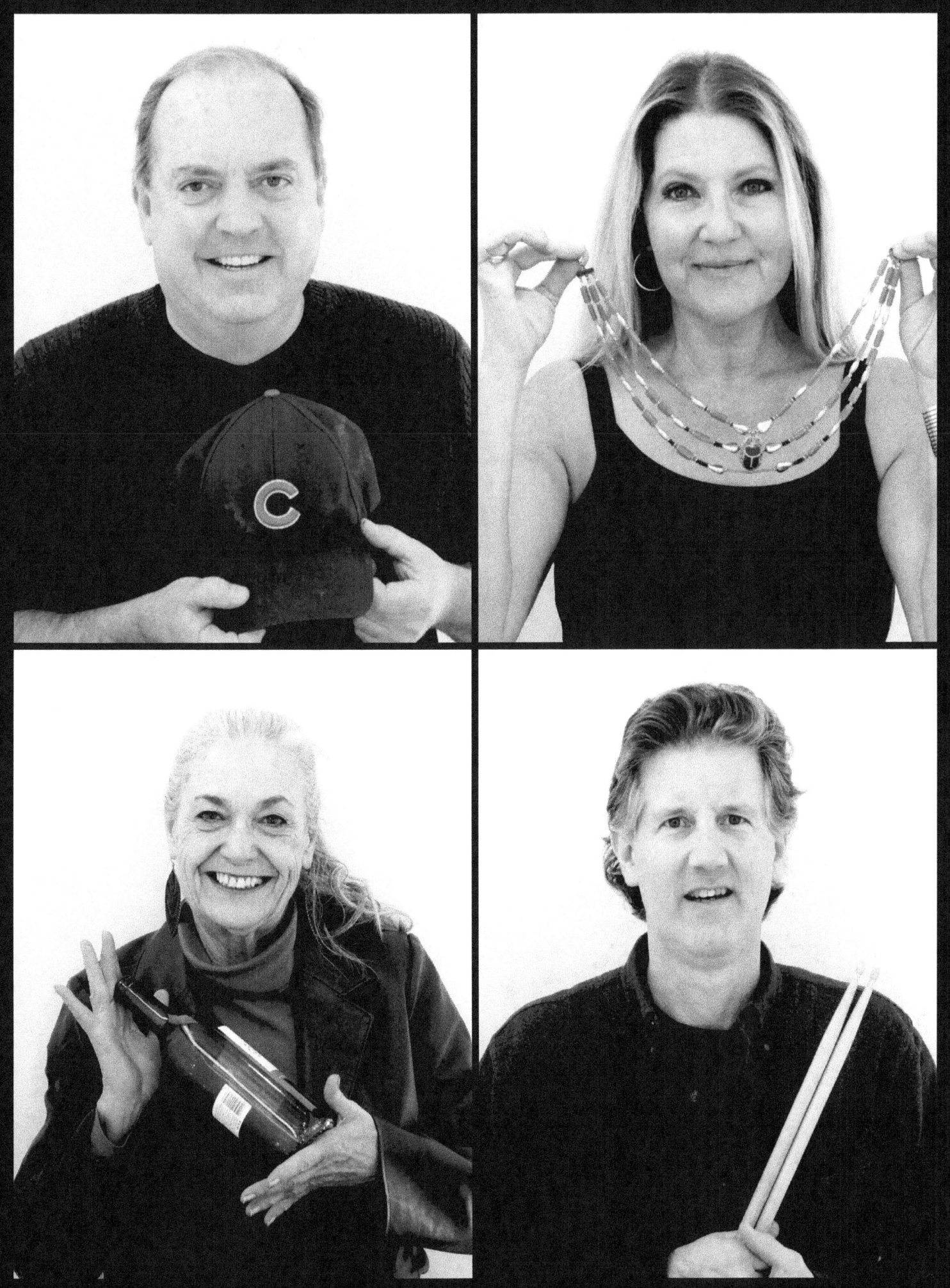

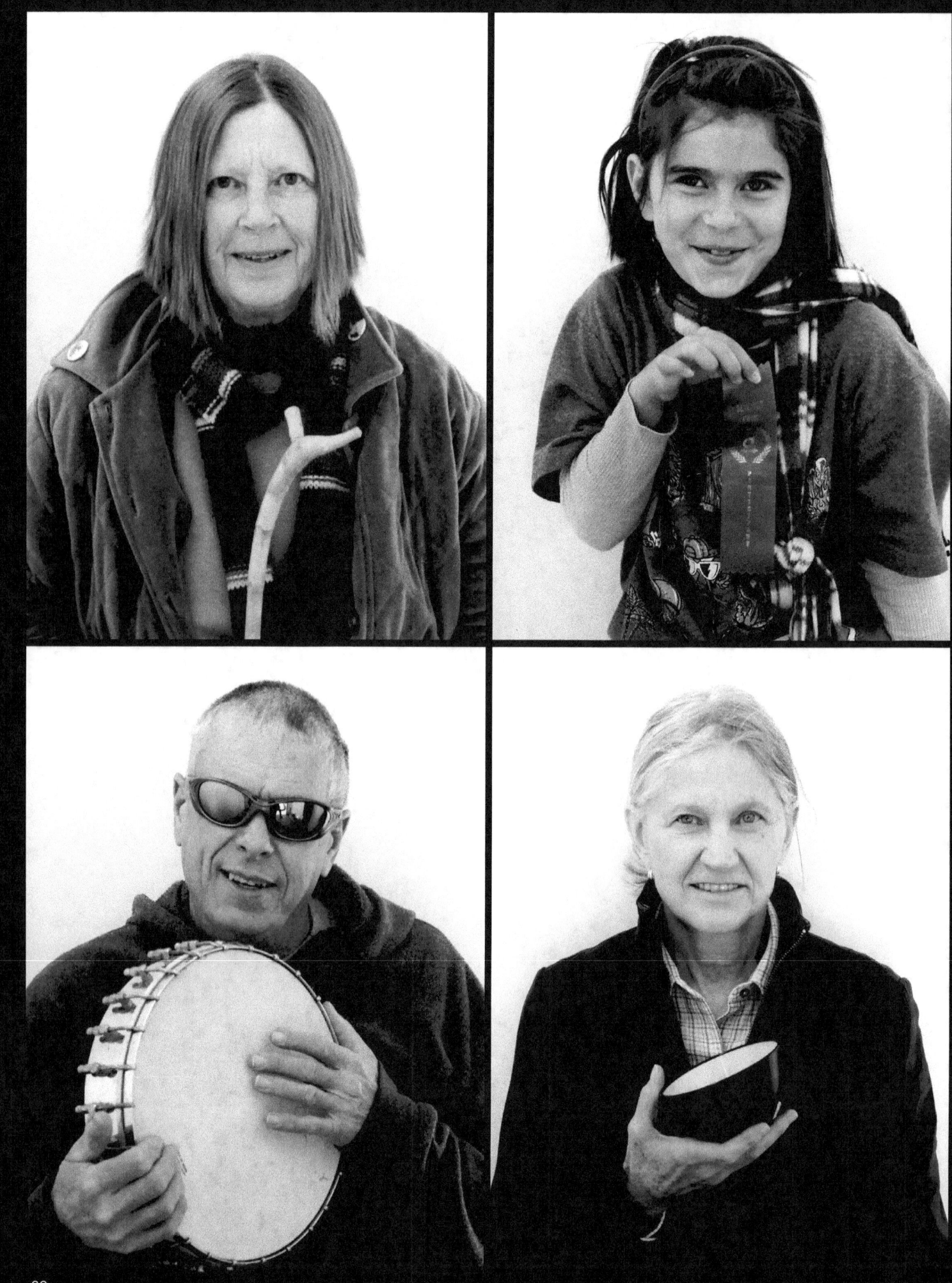

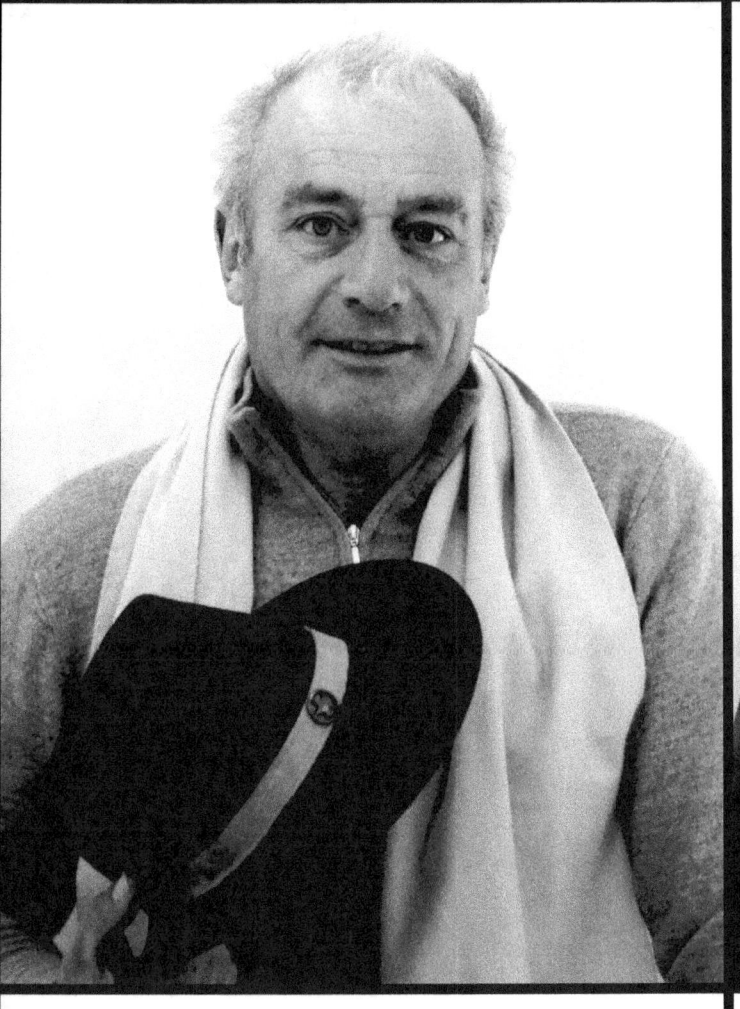
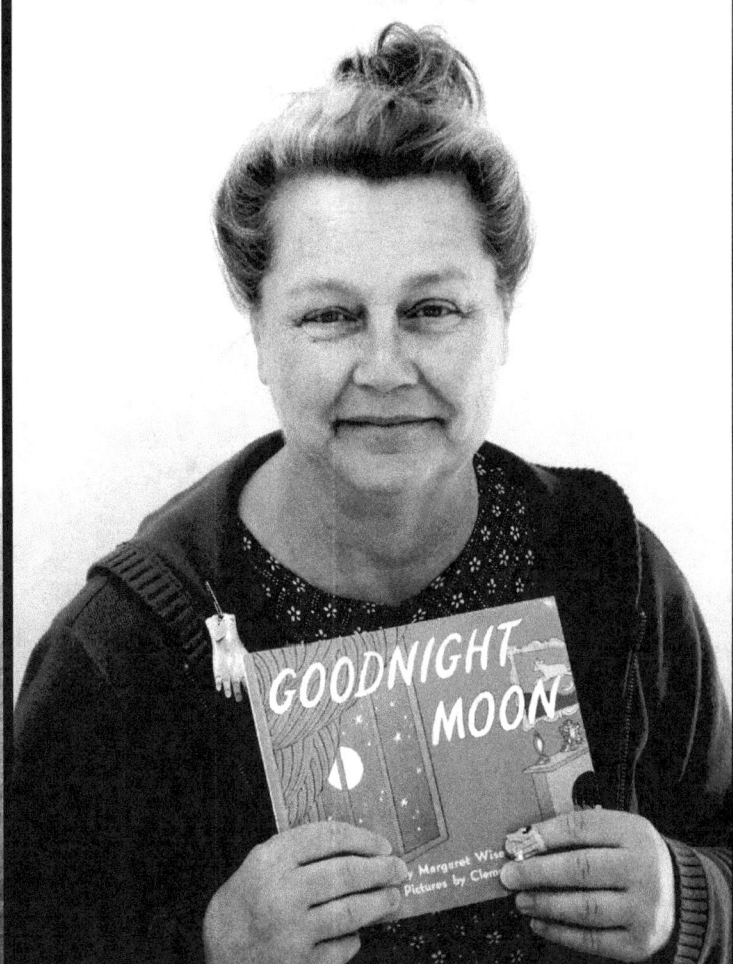
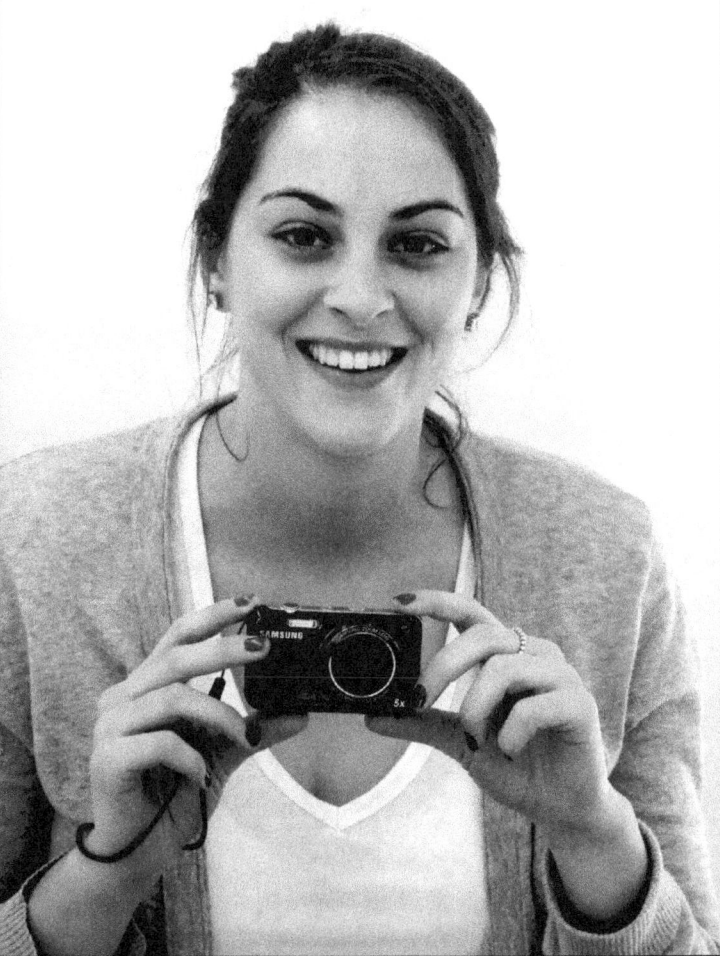
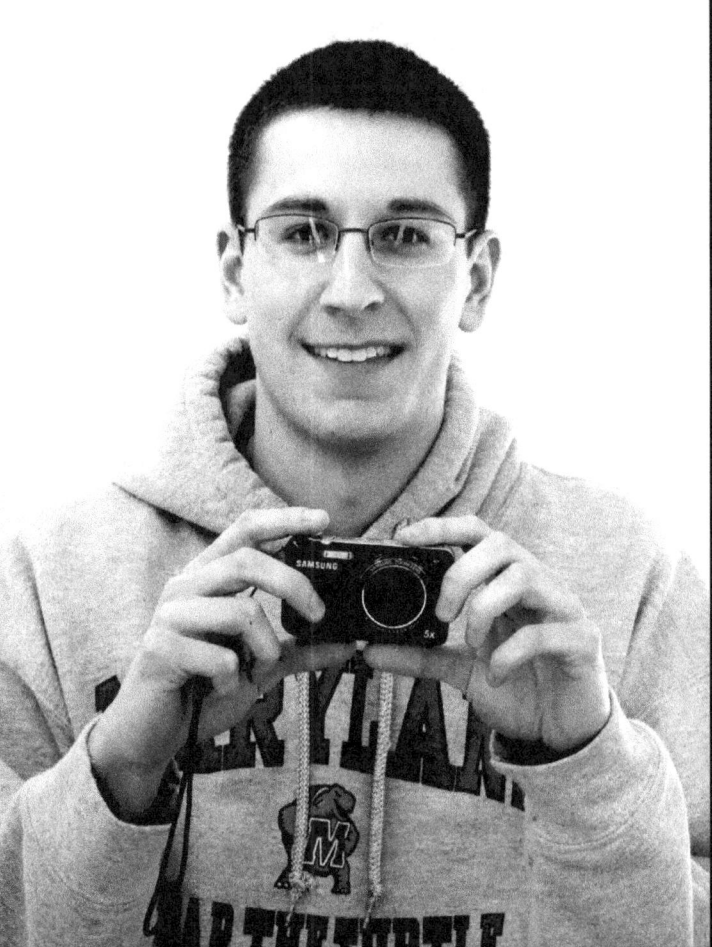

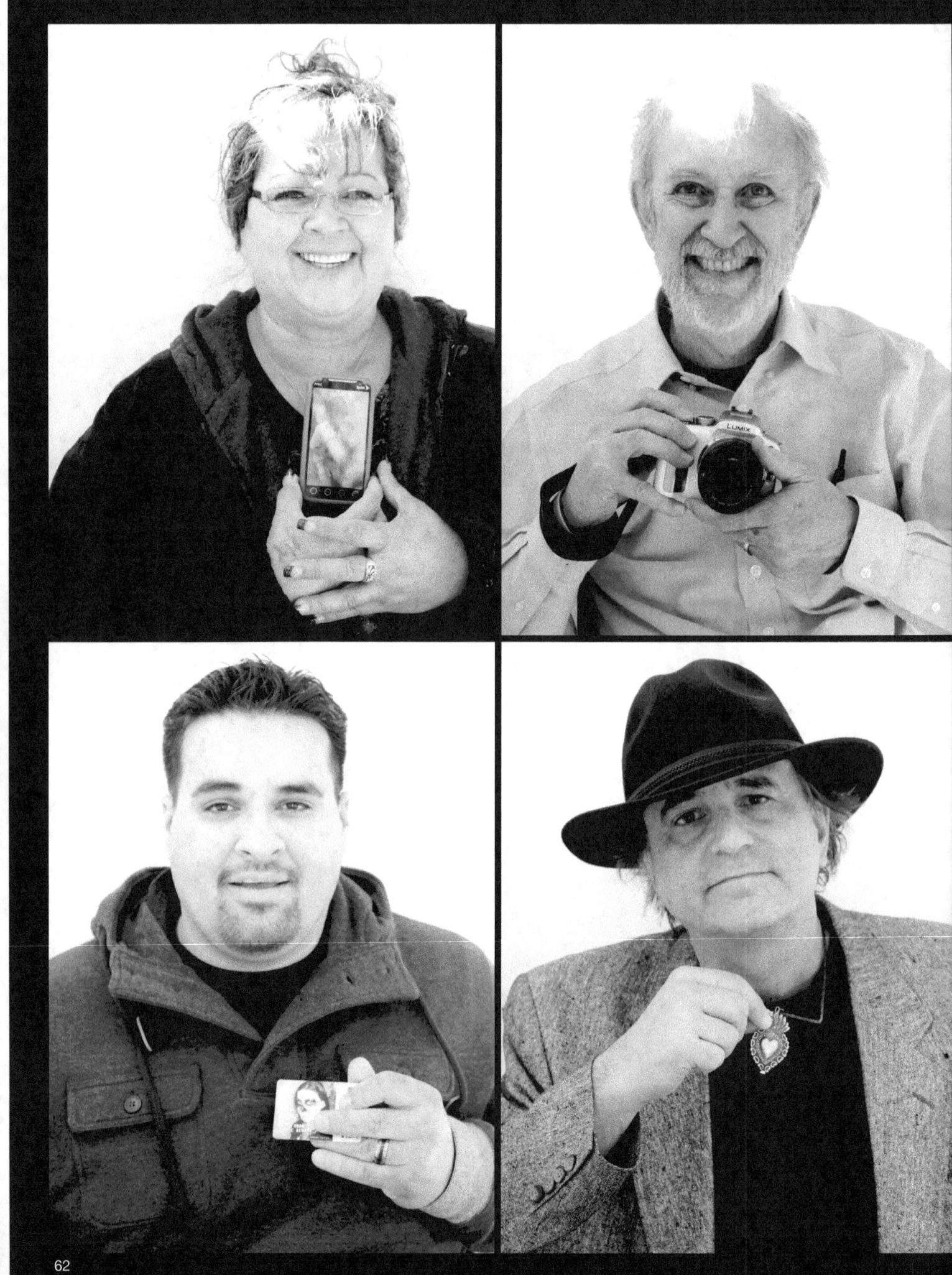

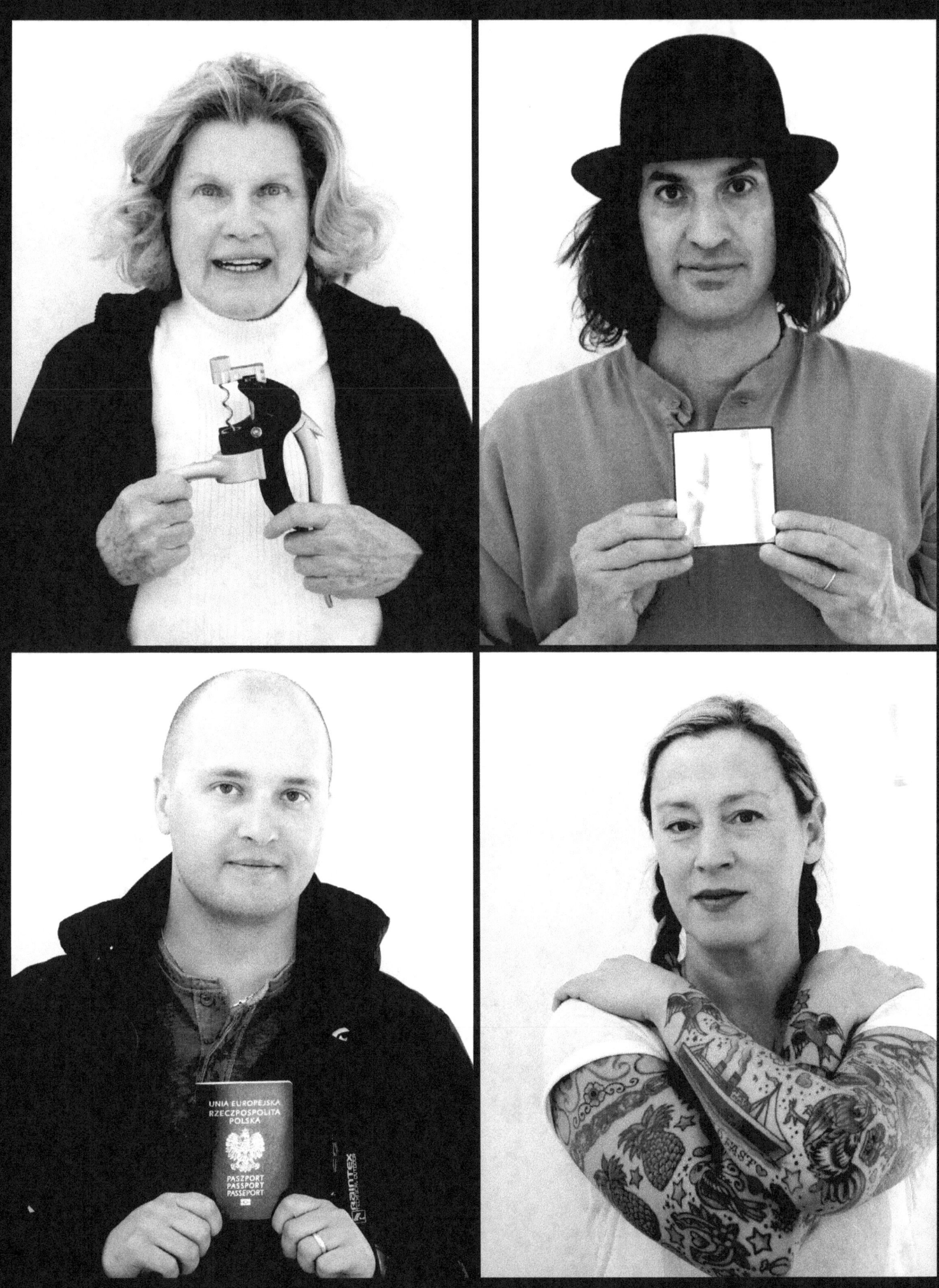

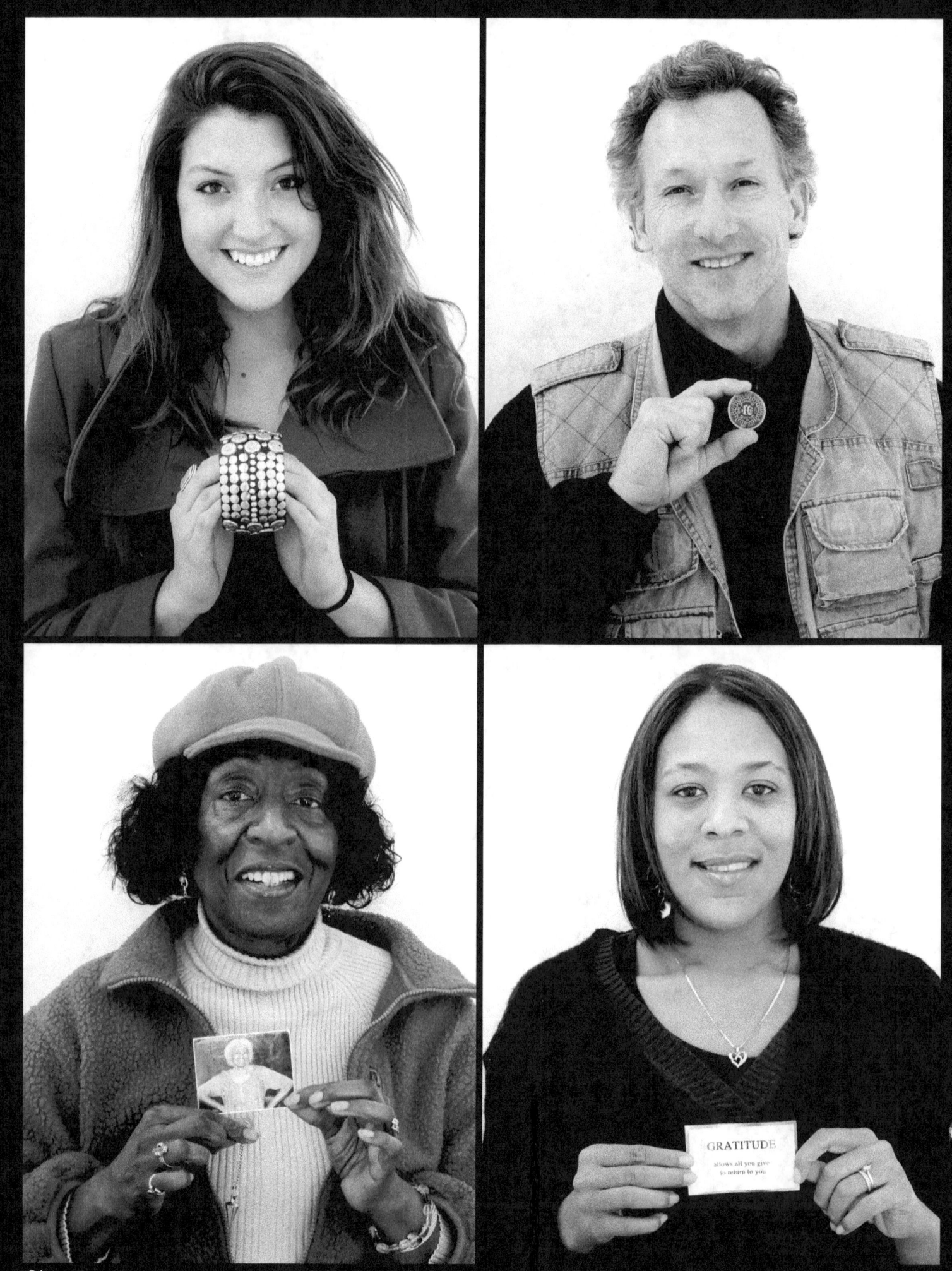

GRATITUDE
allows all you give
to return to you

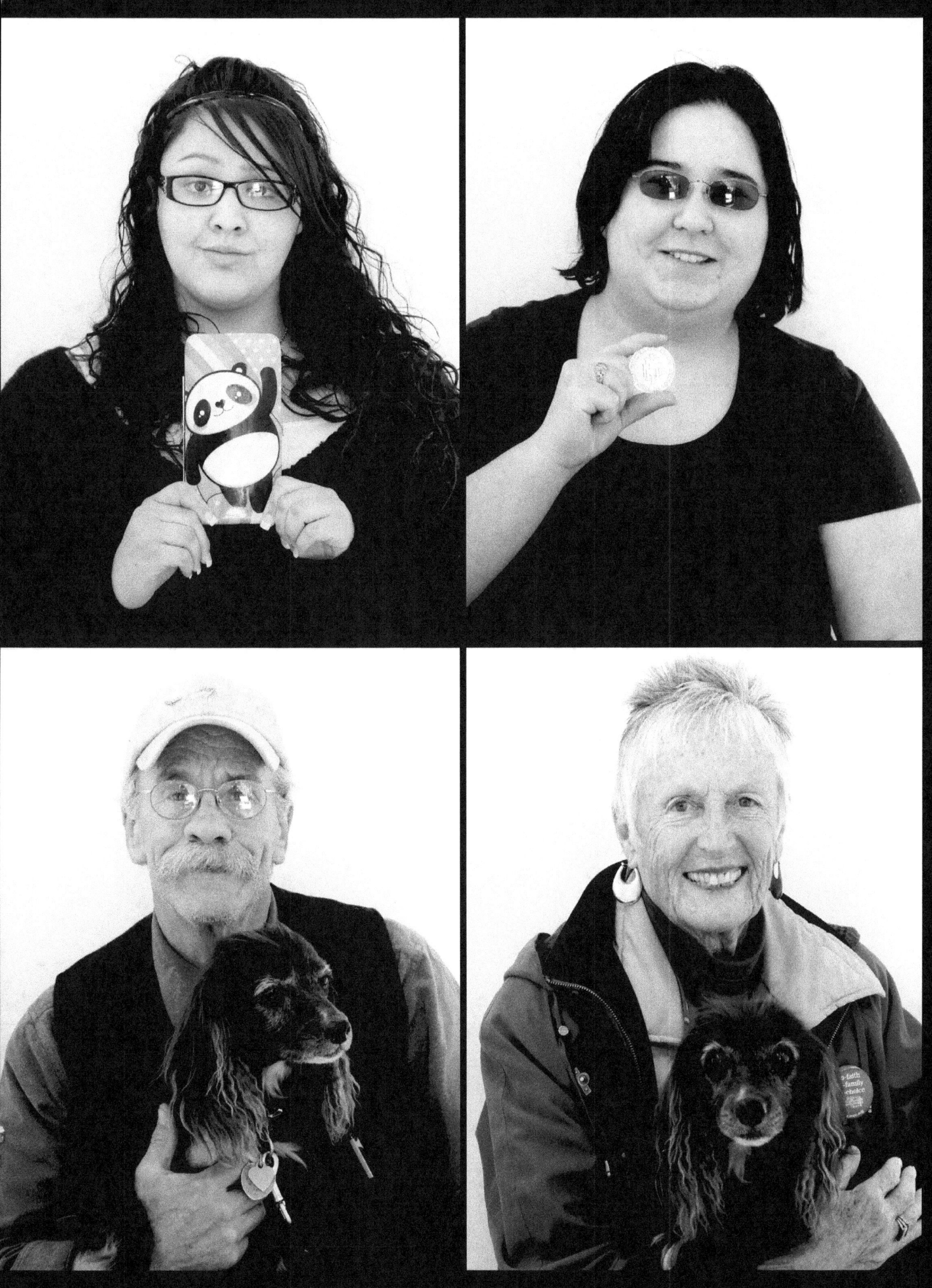

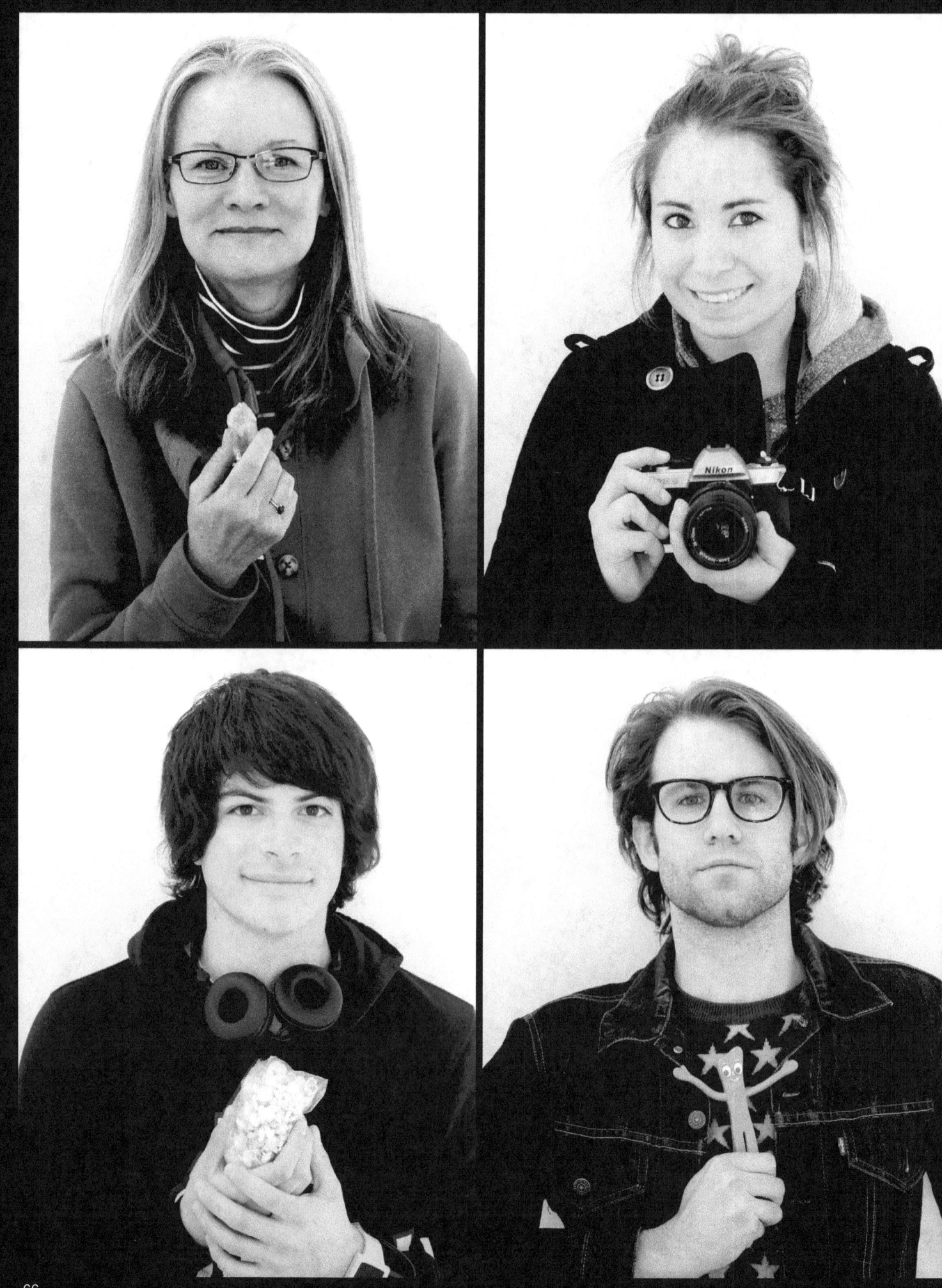

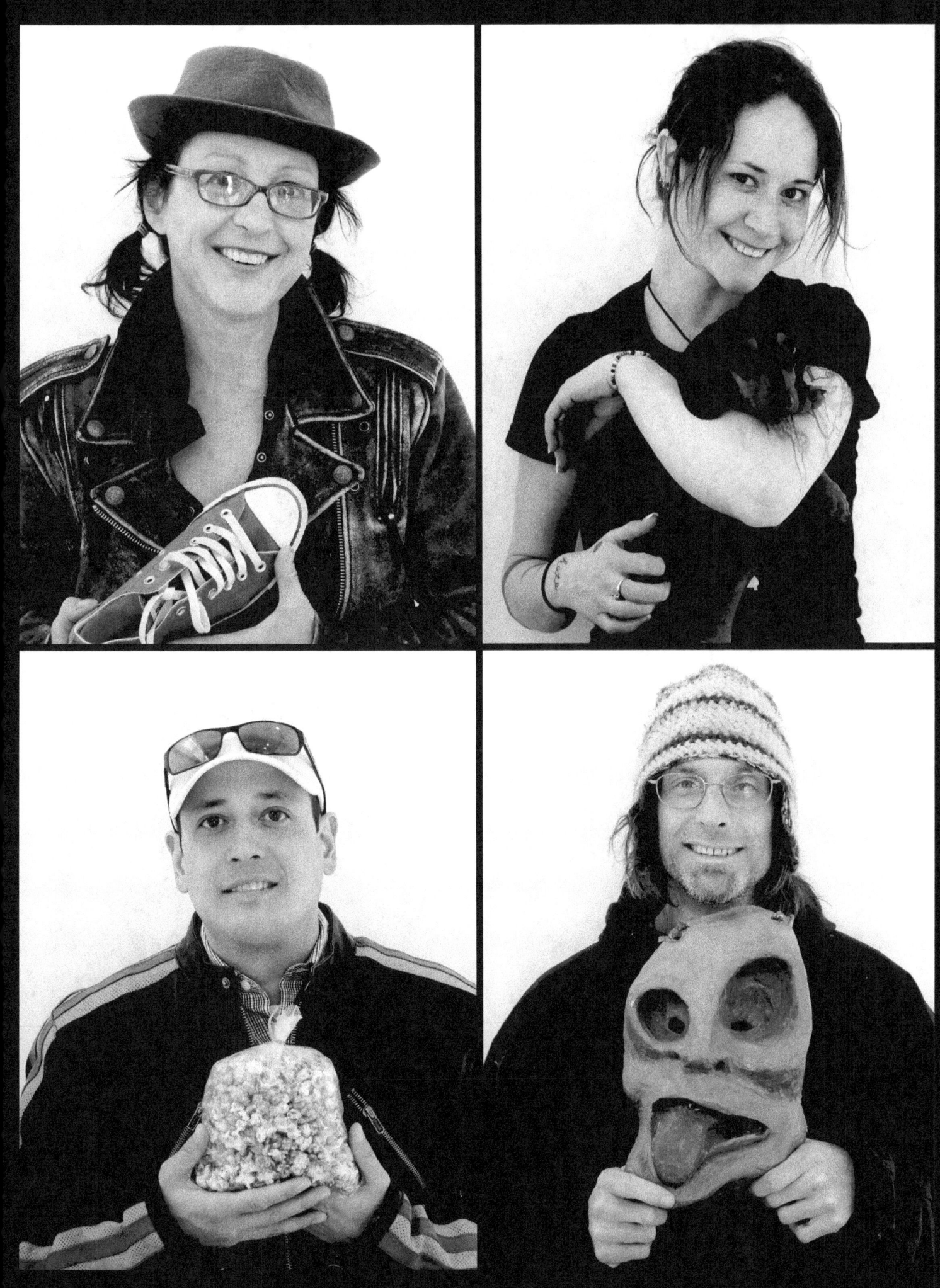

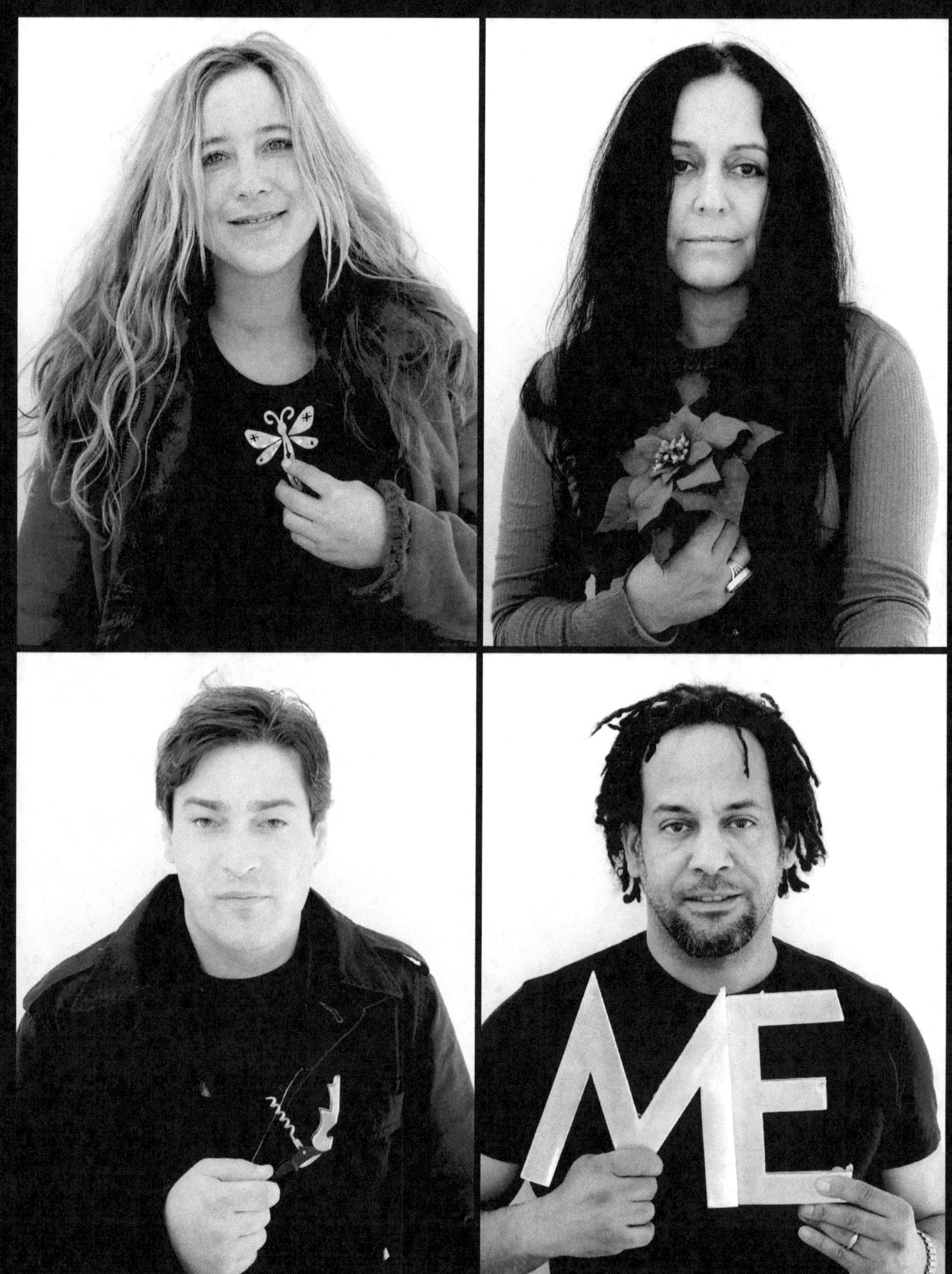

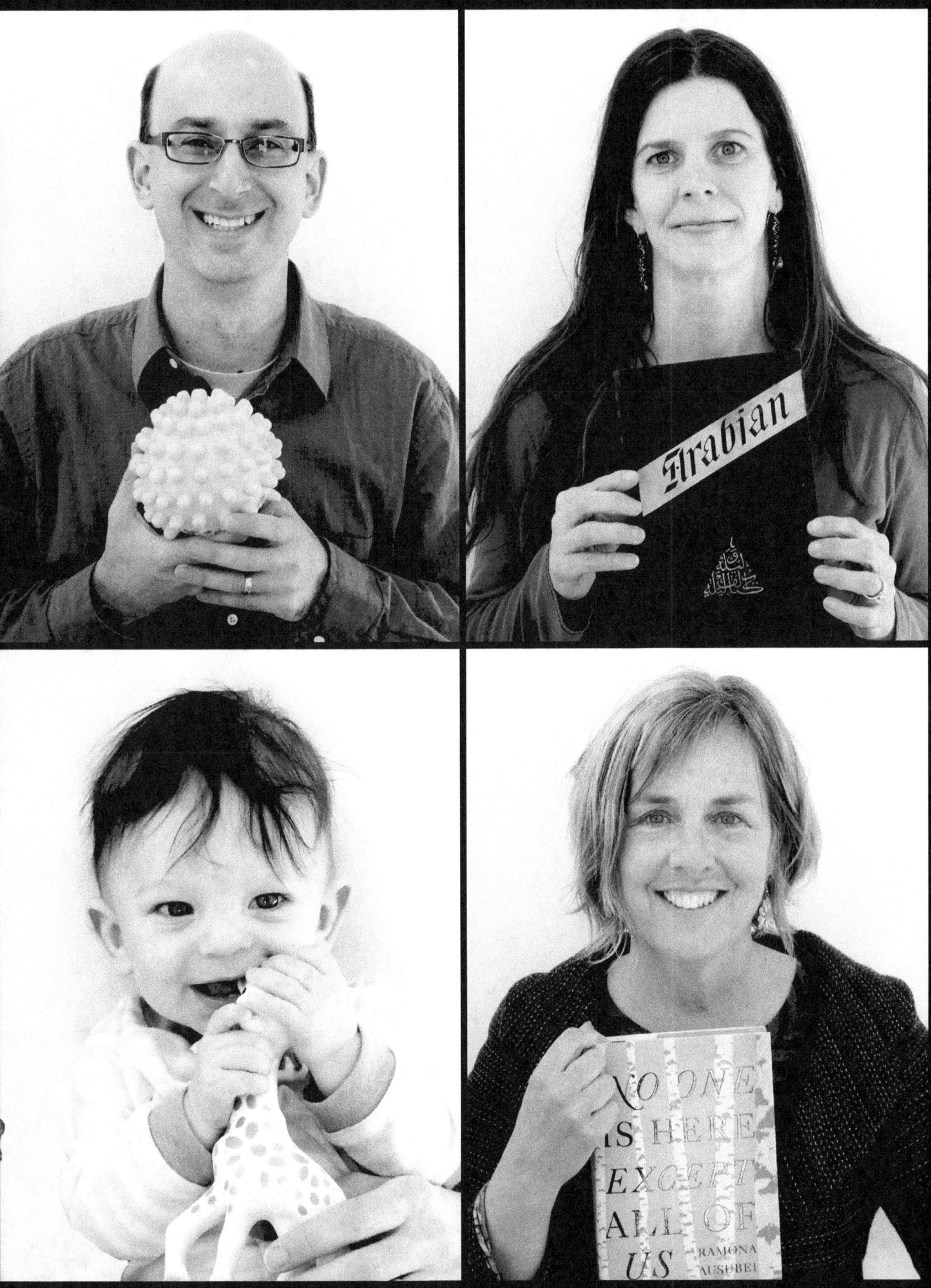

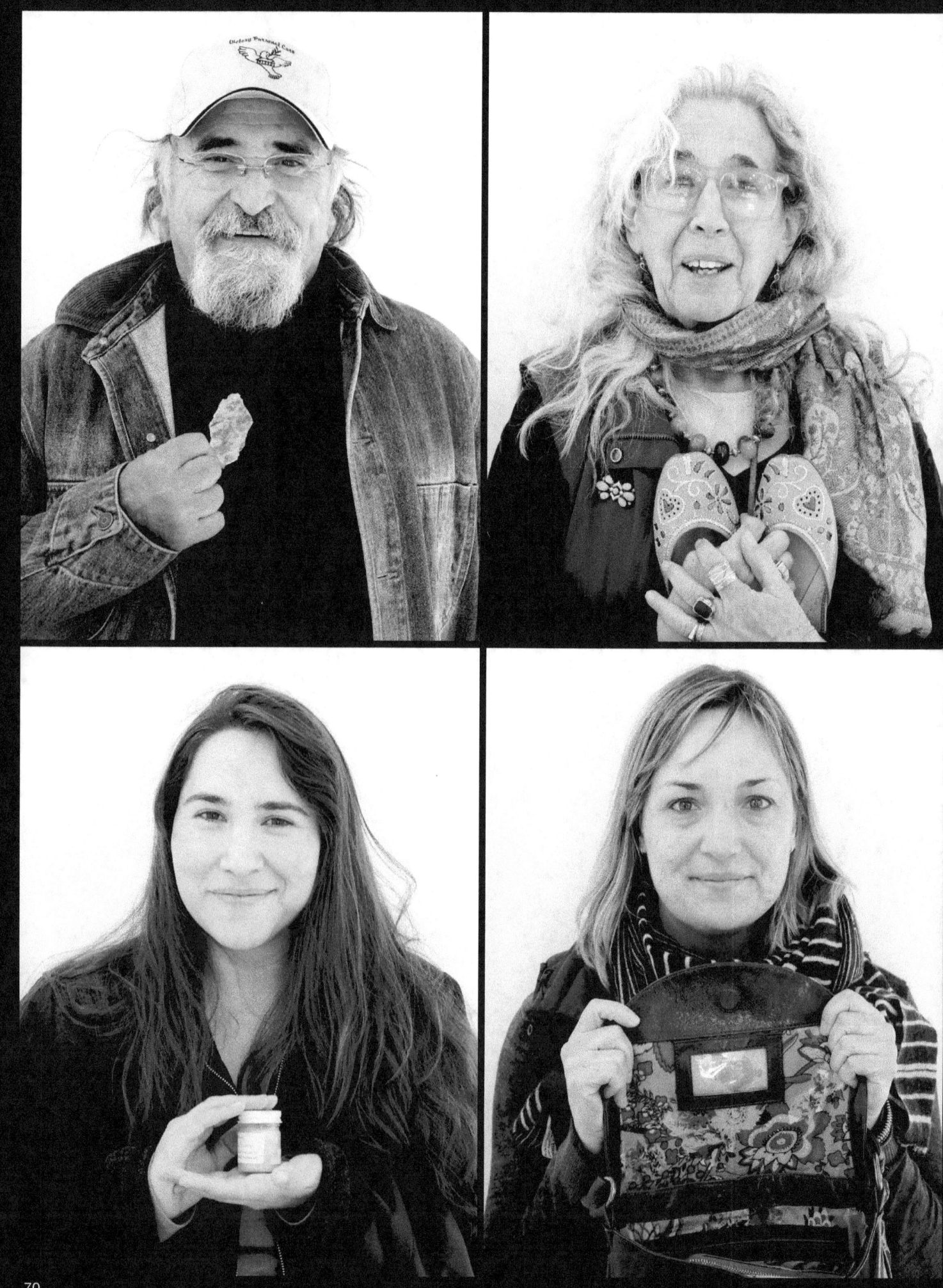

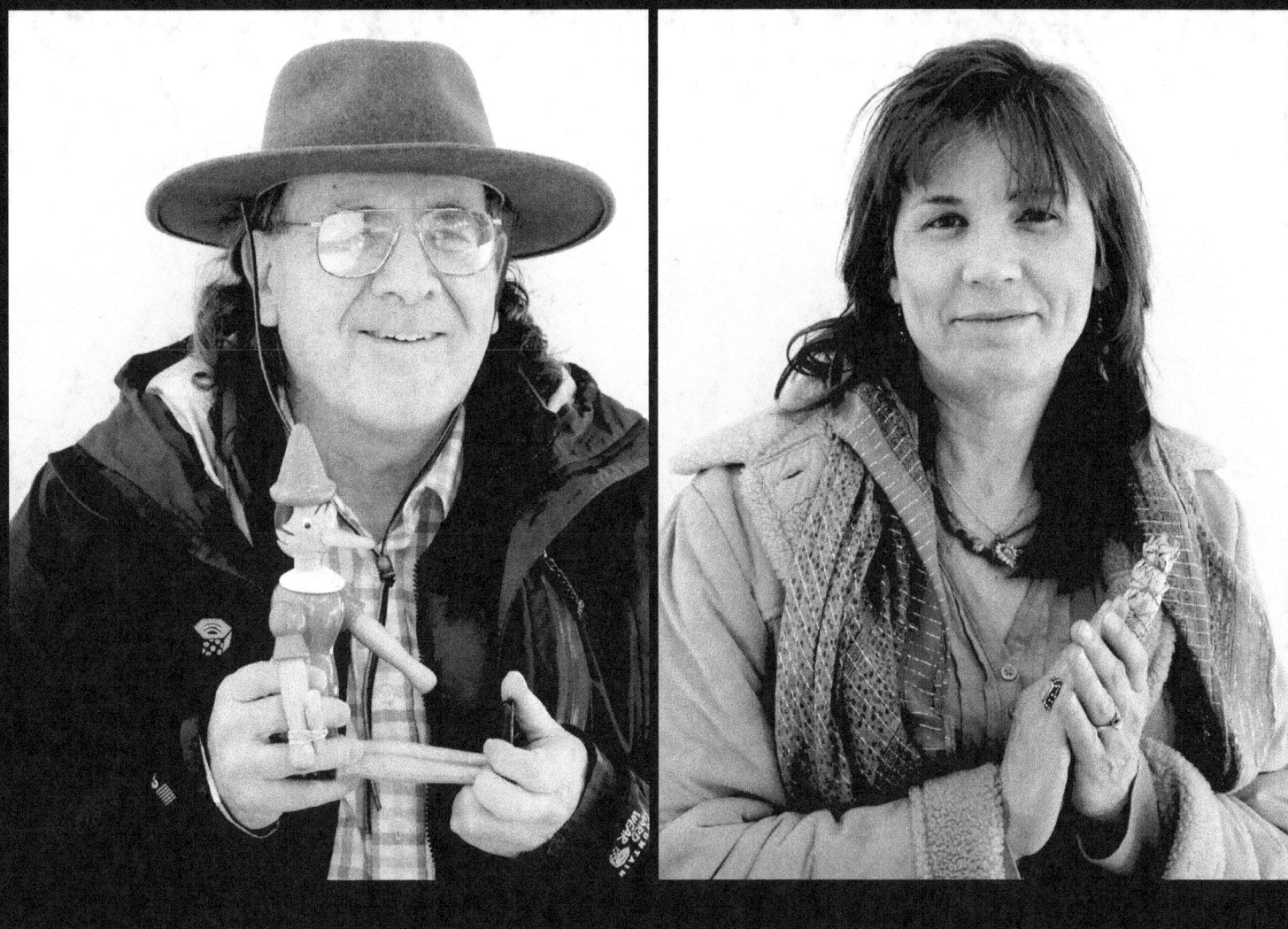

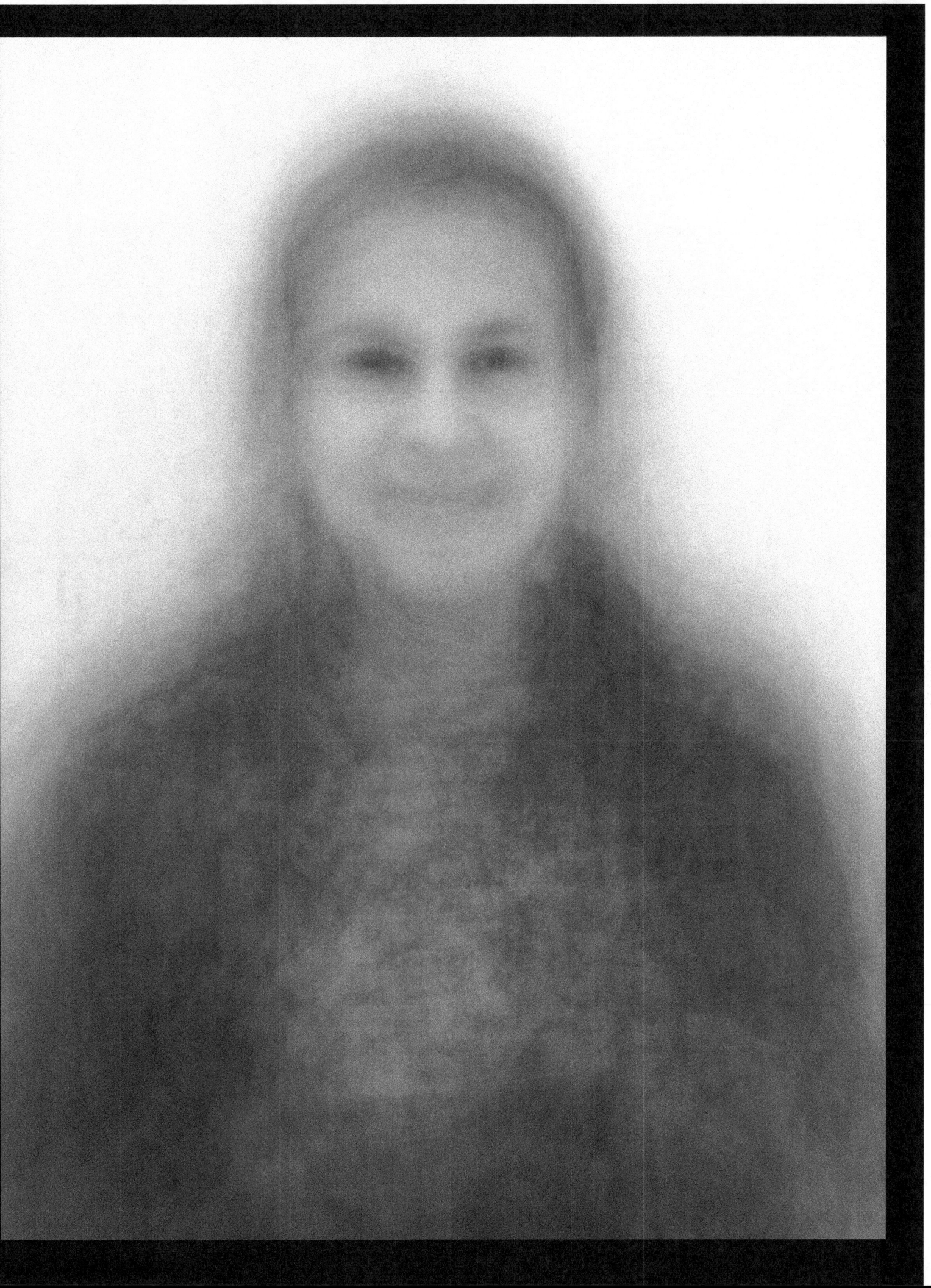

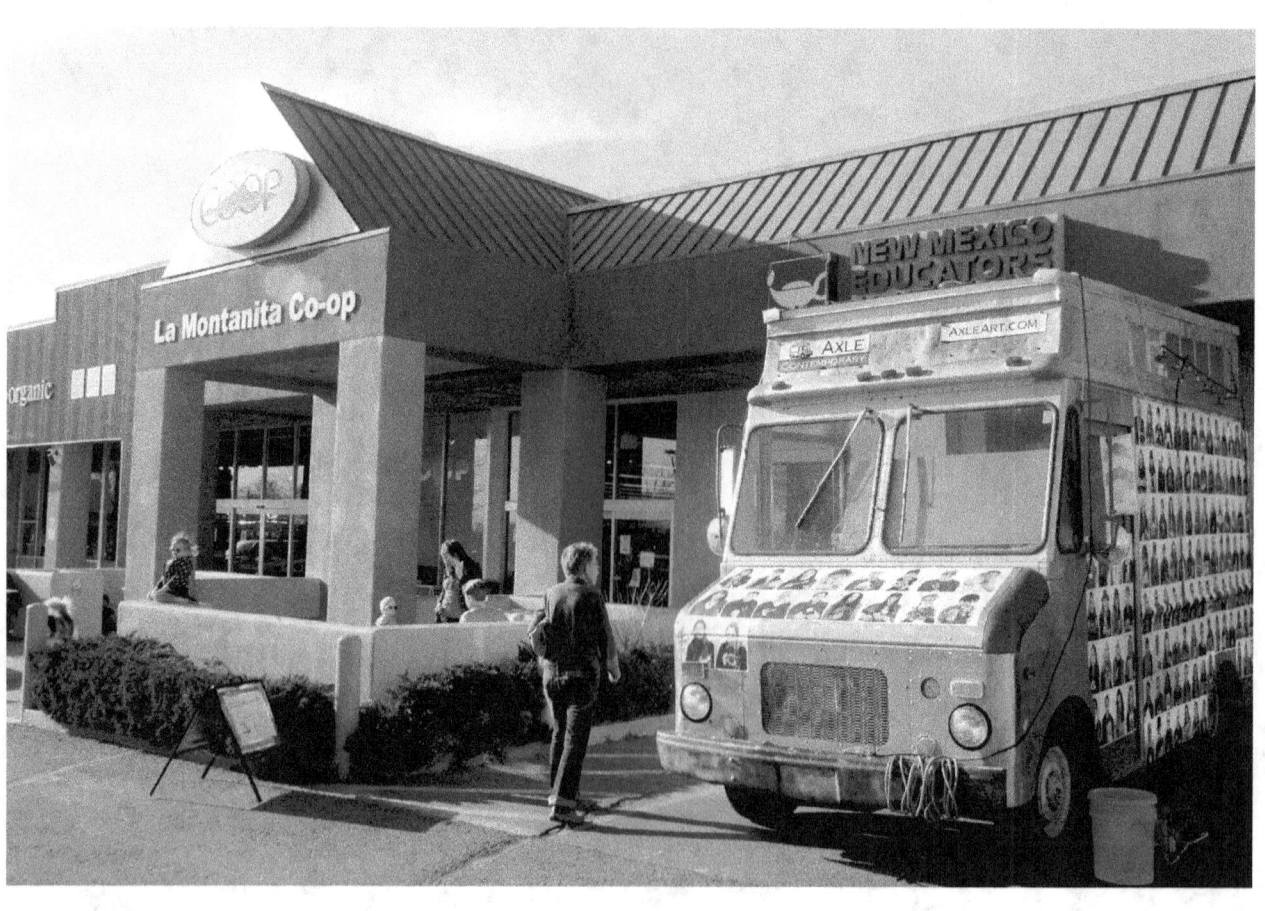

La Montañita Co-op Market

913 West Alameda

Monday

March 5

12pm-6pm

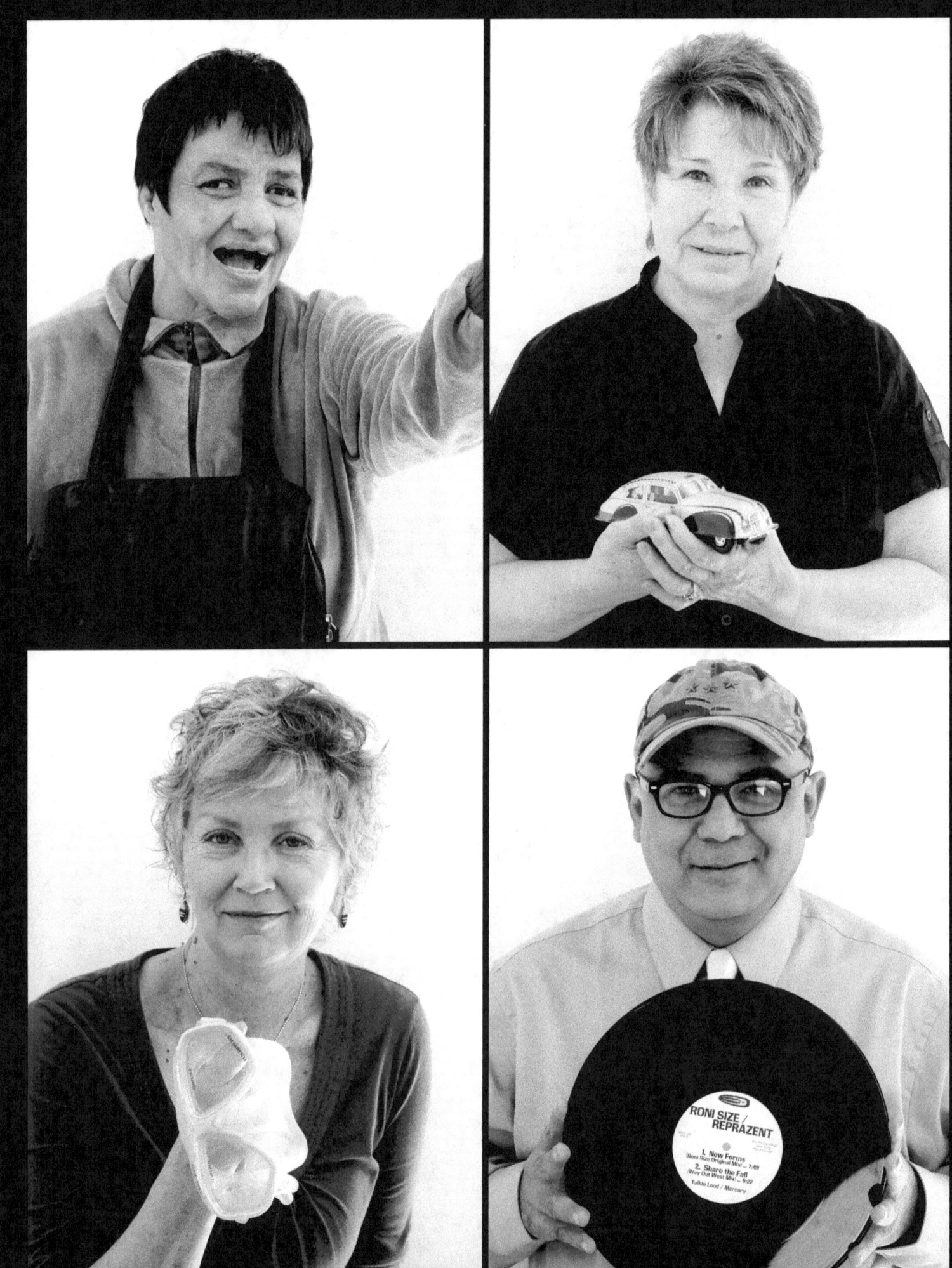

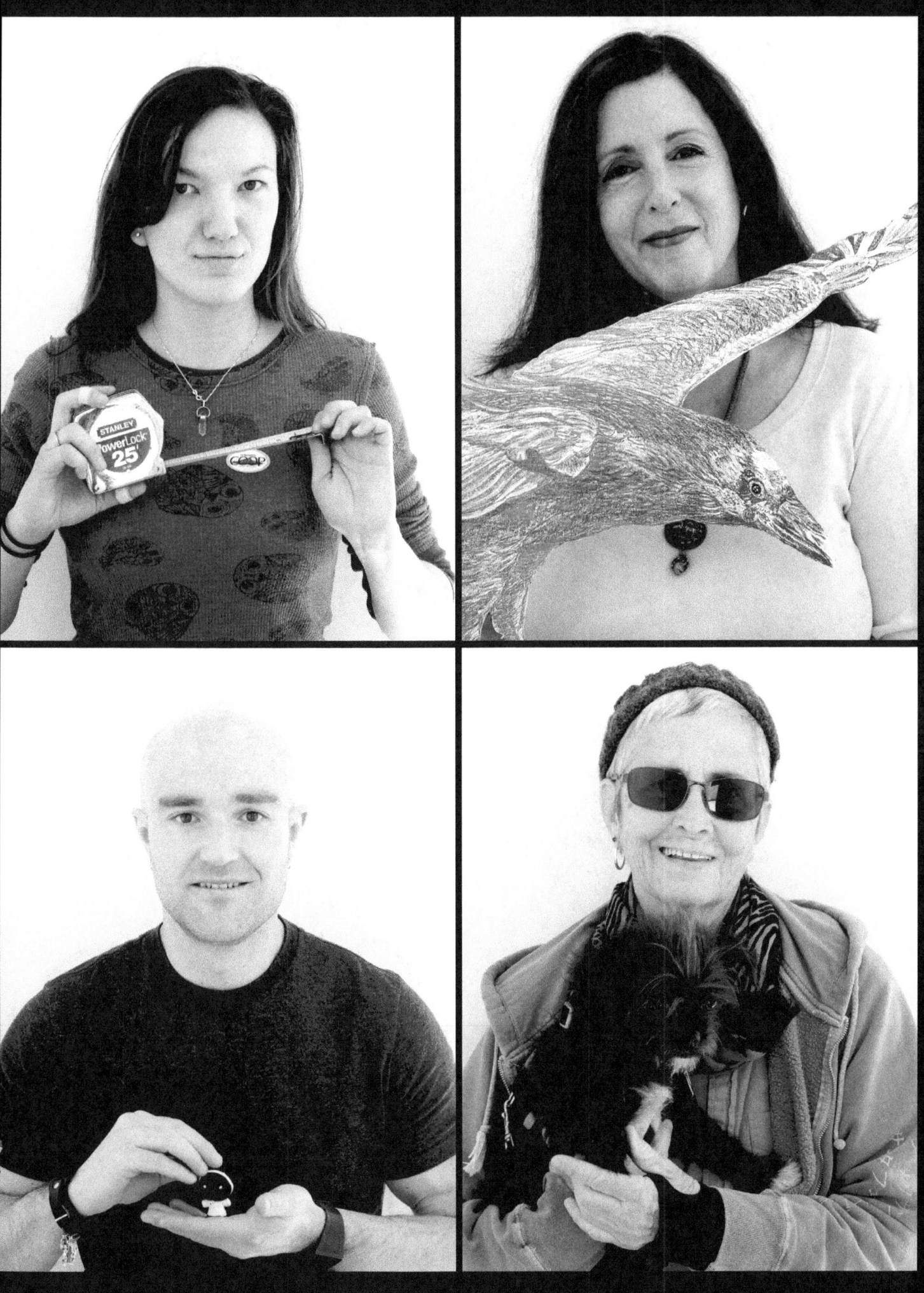

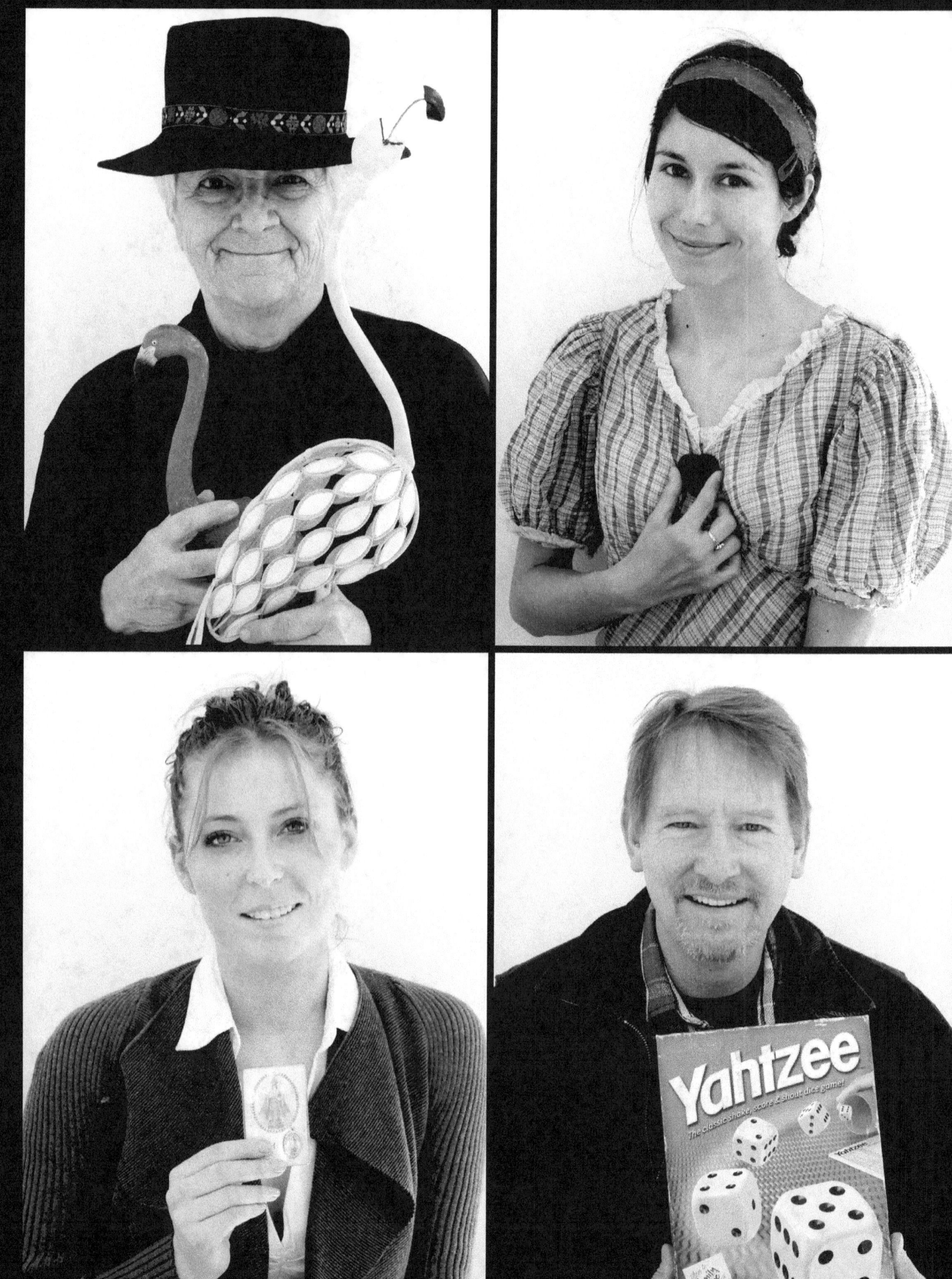

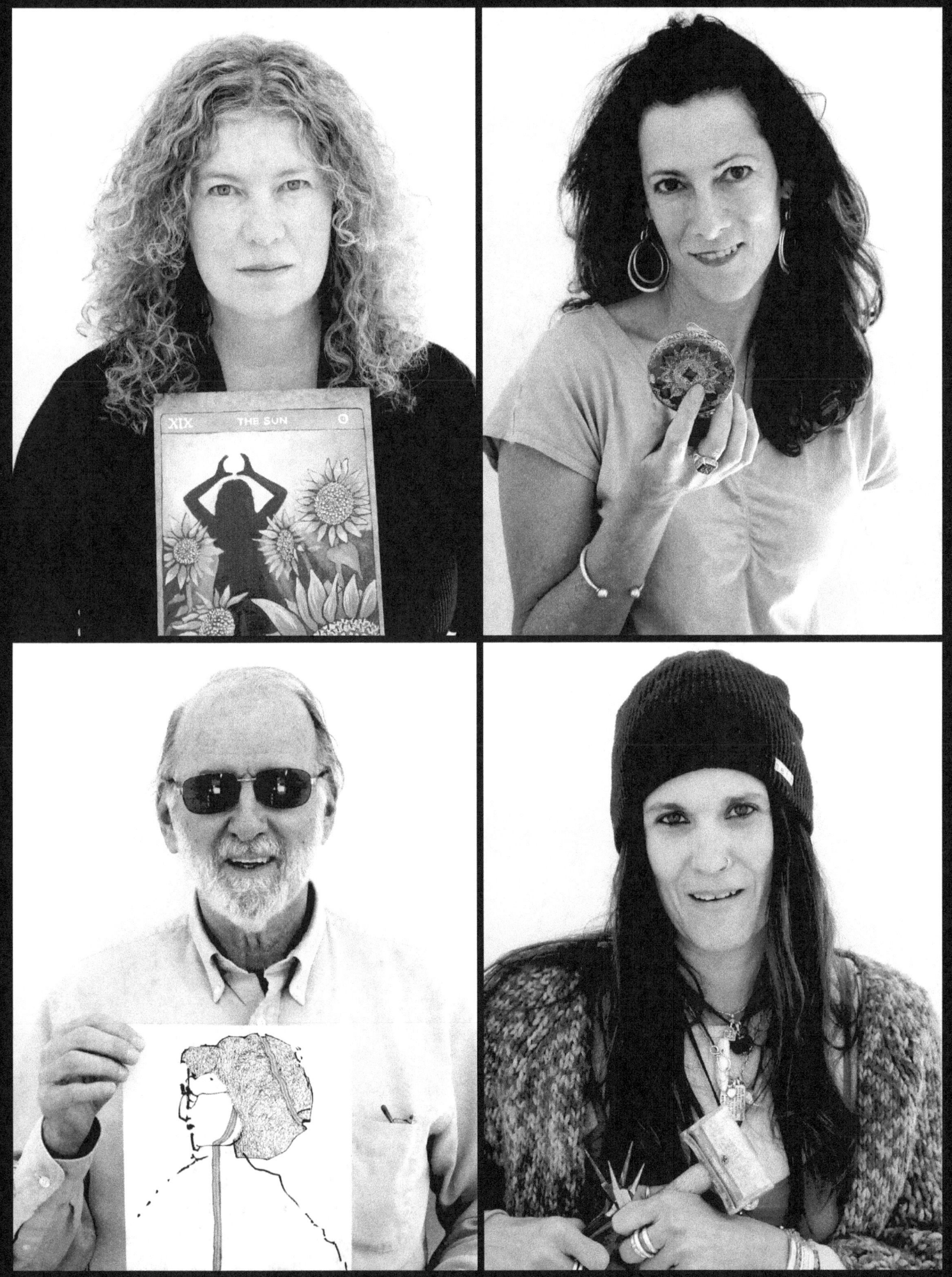

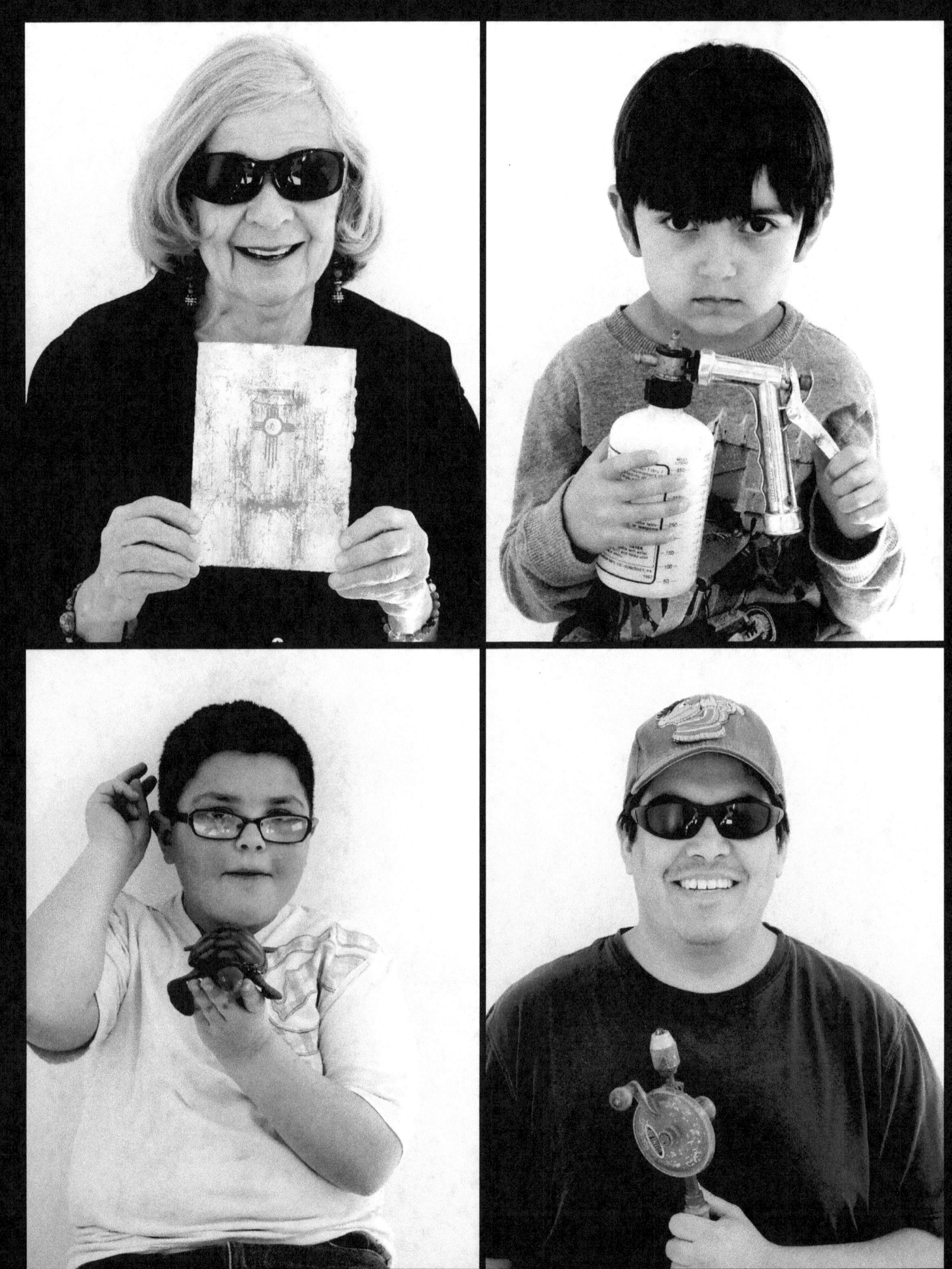

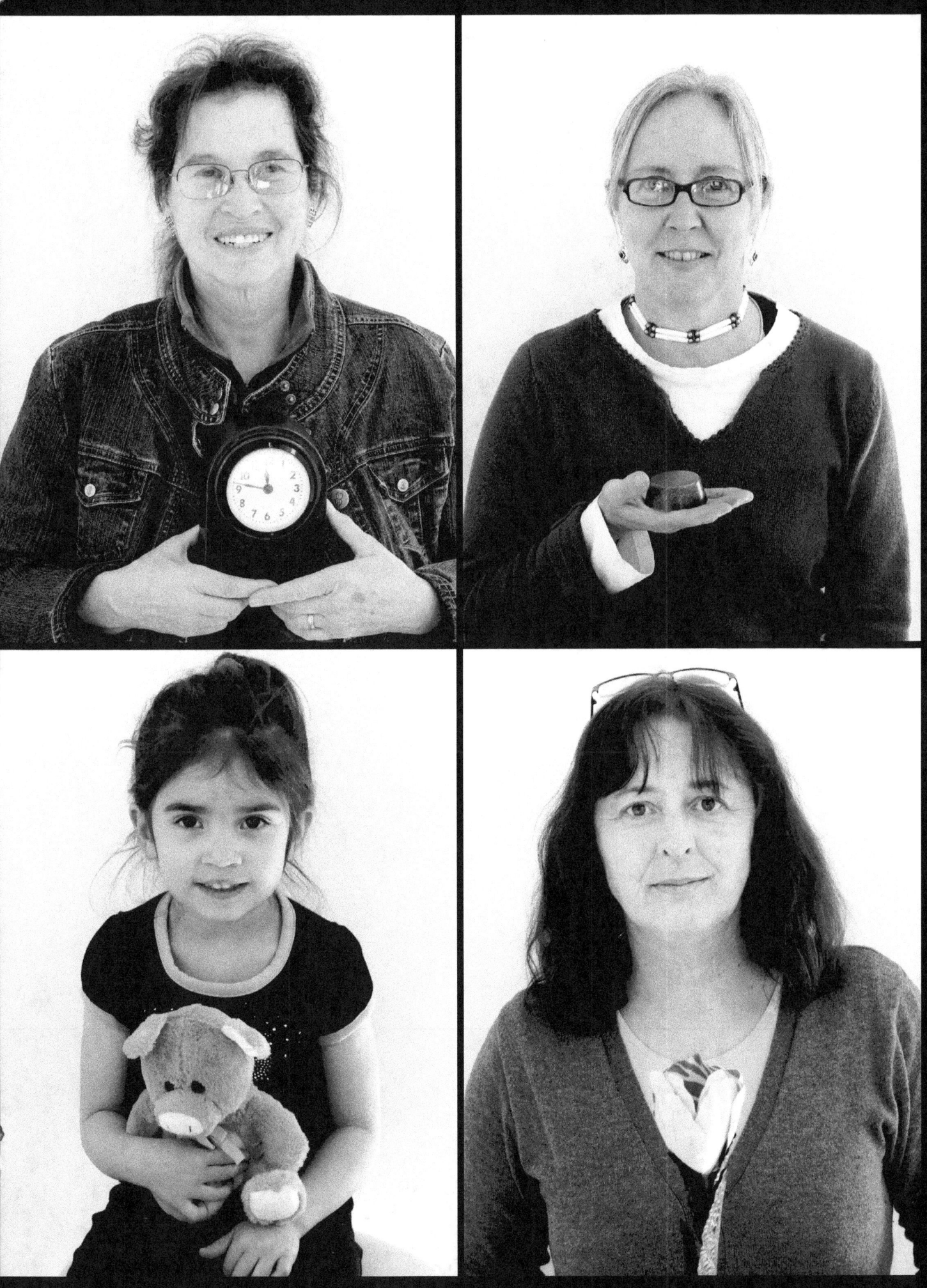

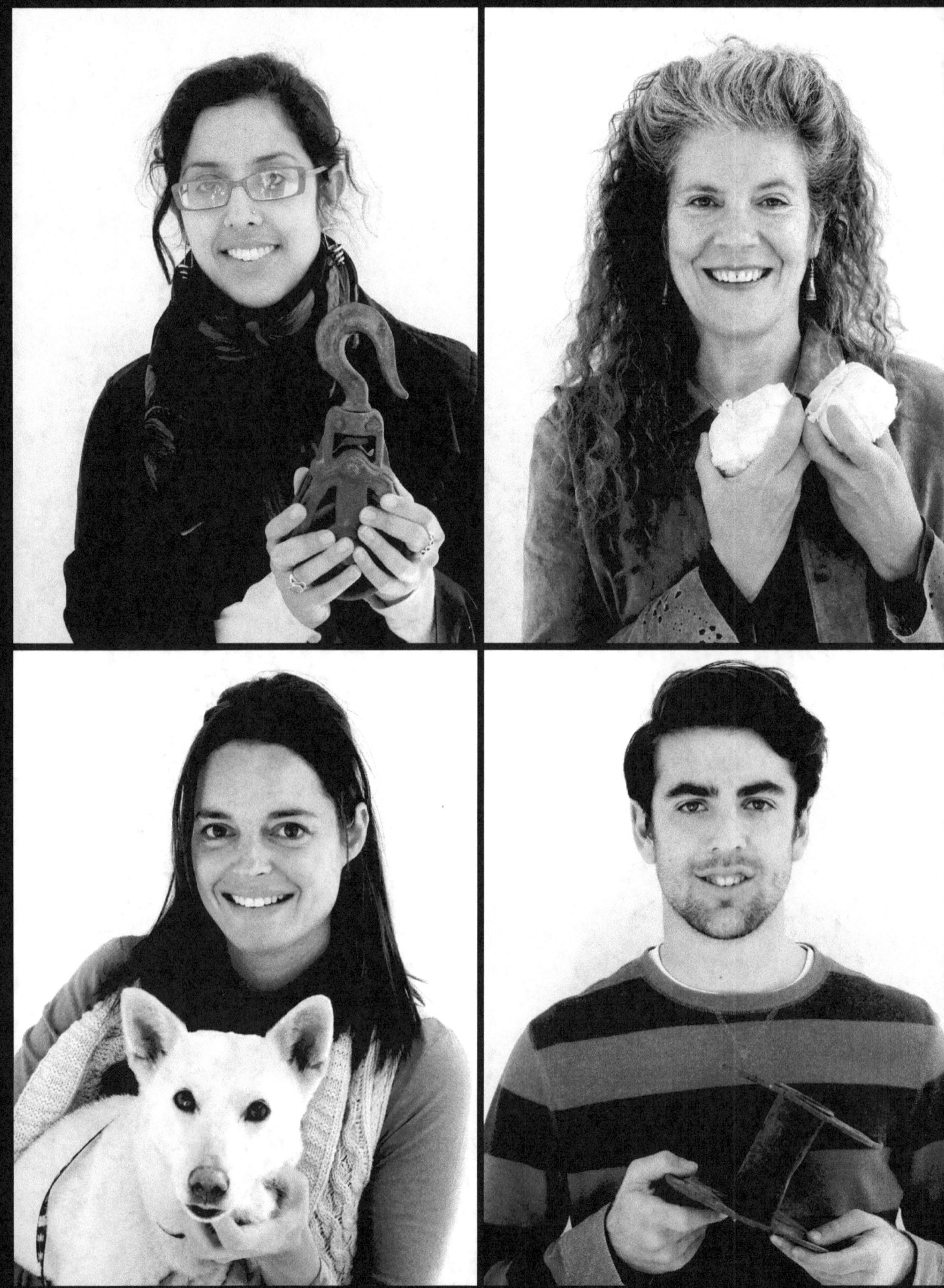

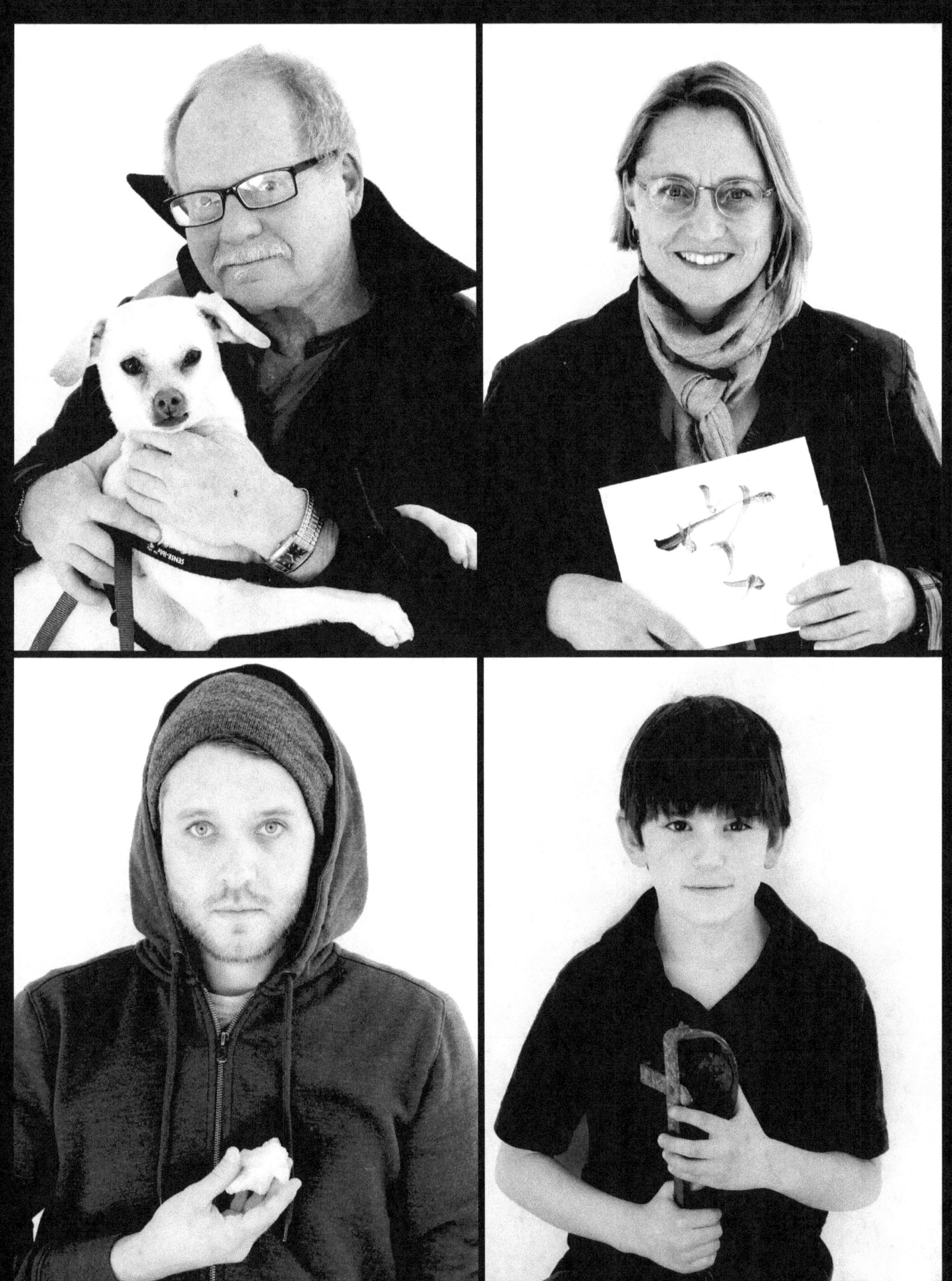

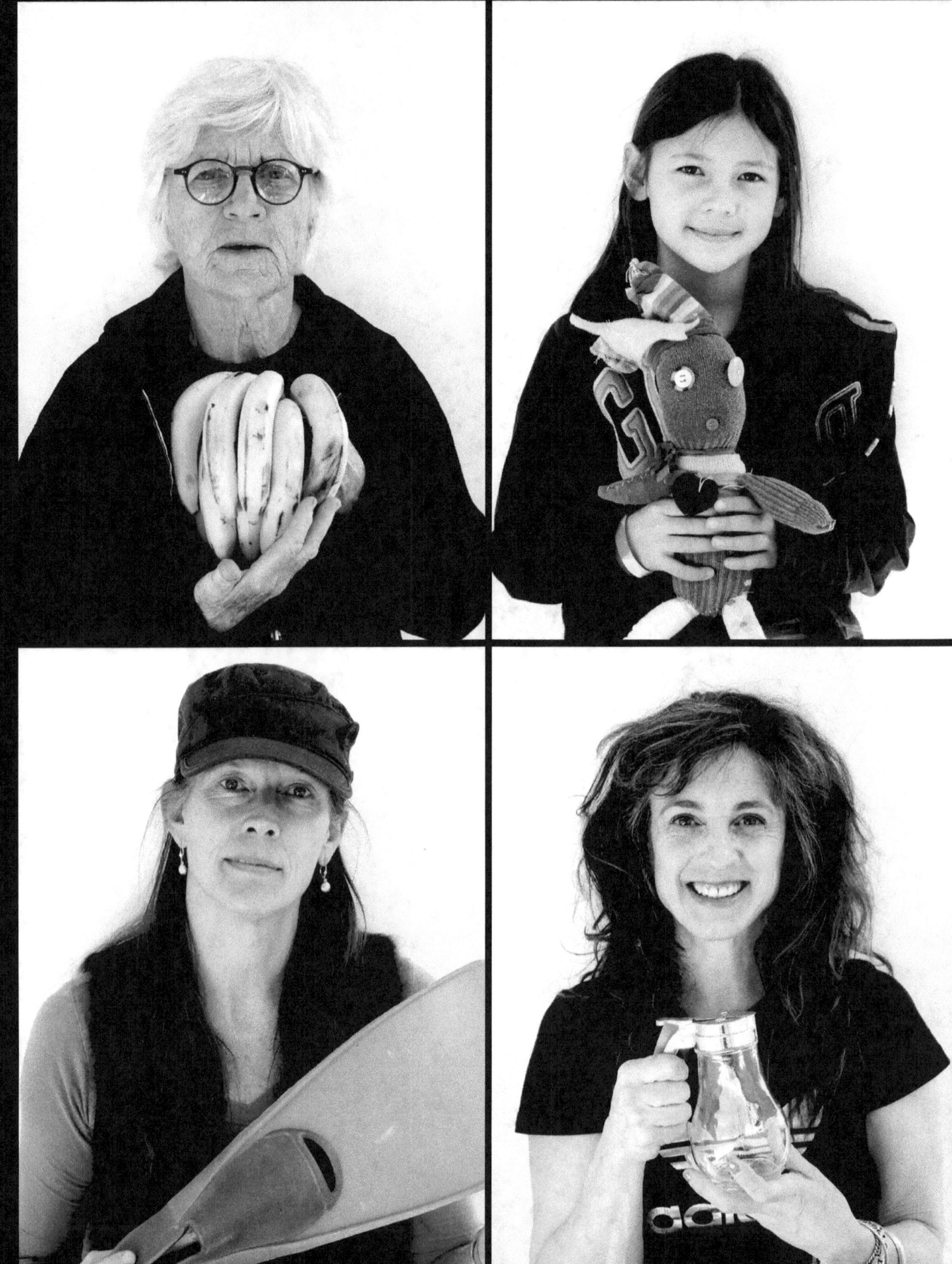

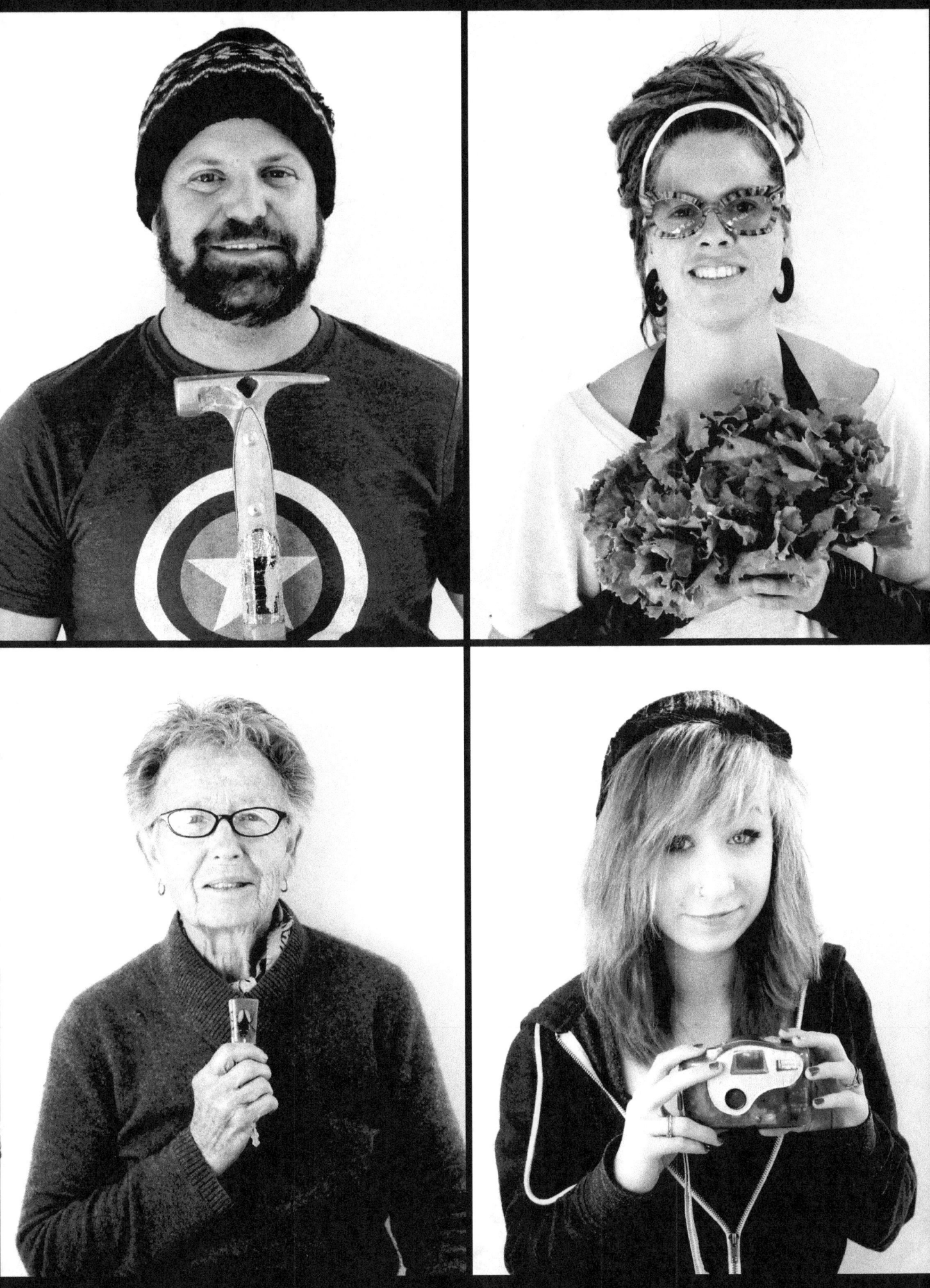

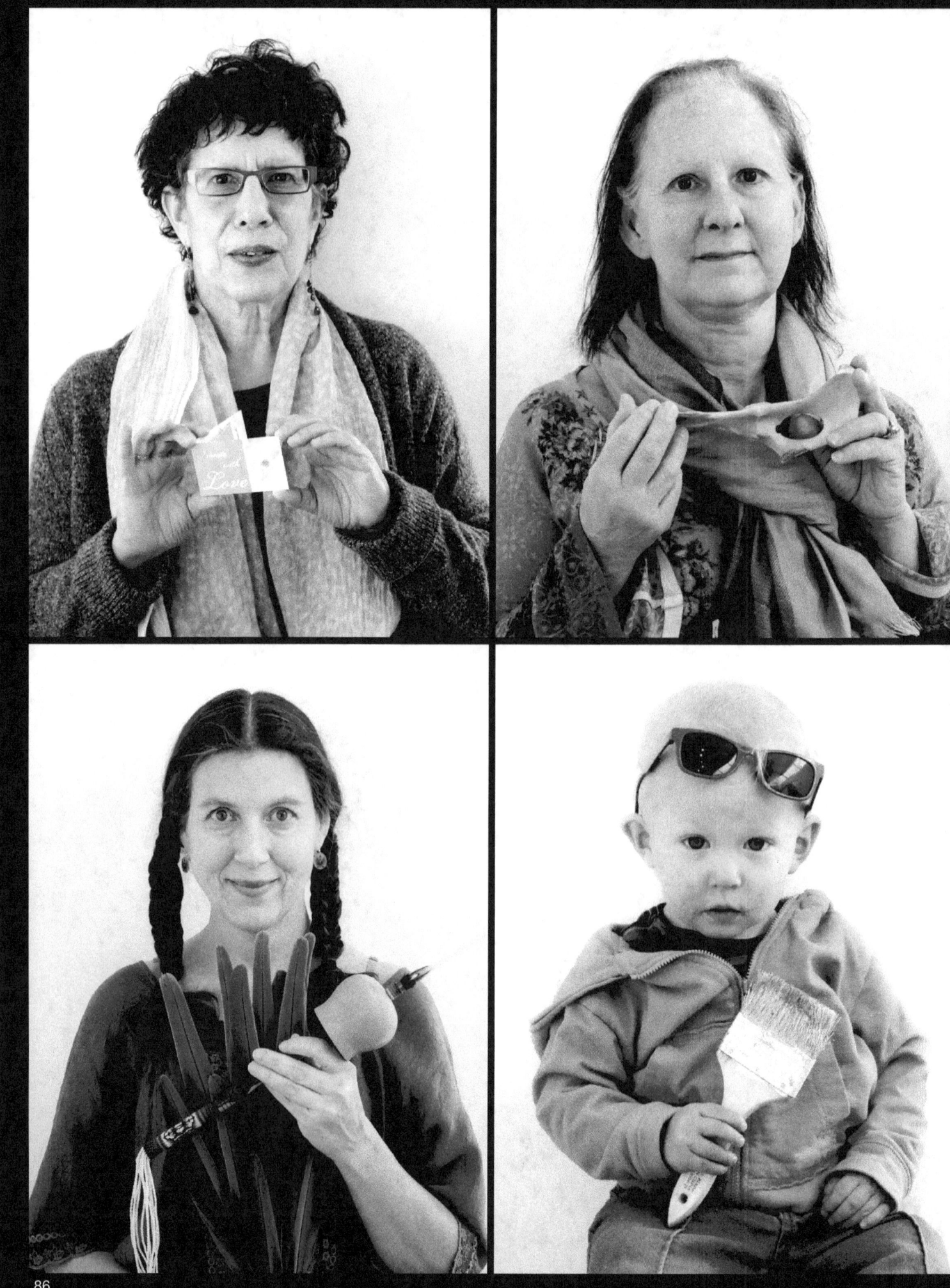

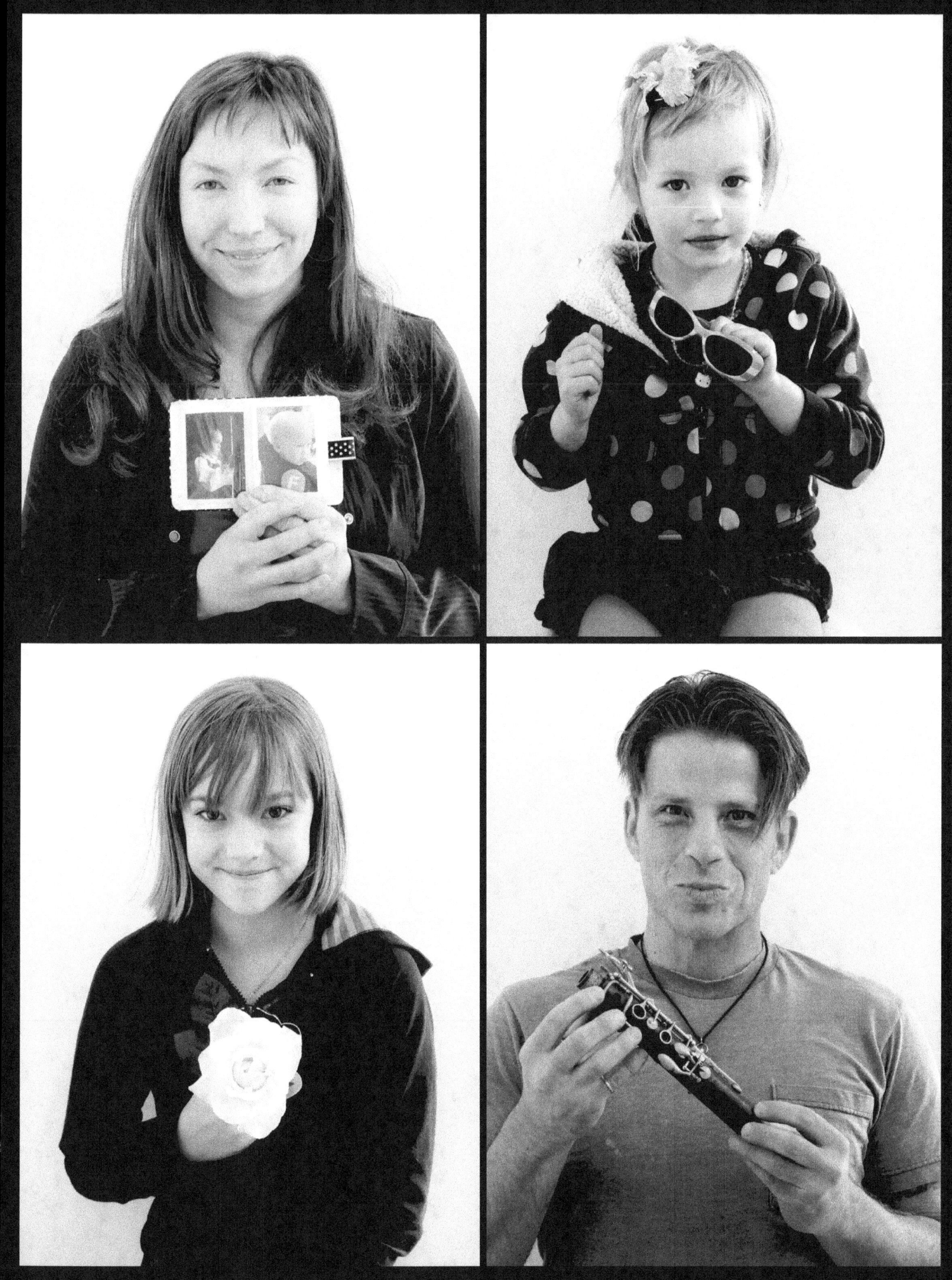

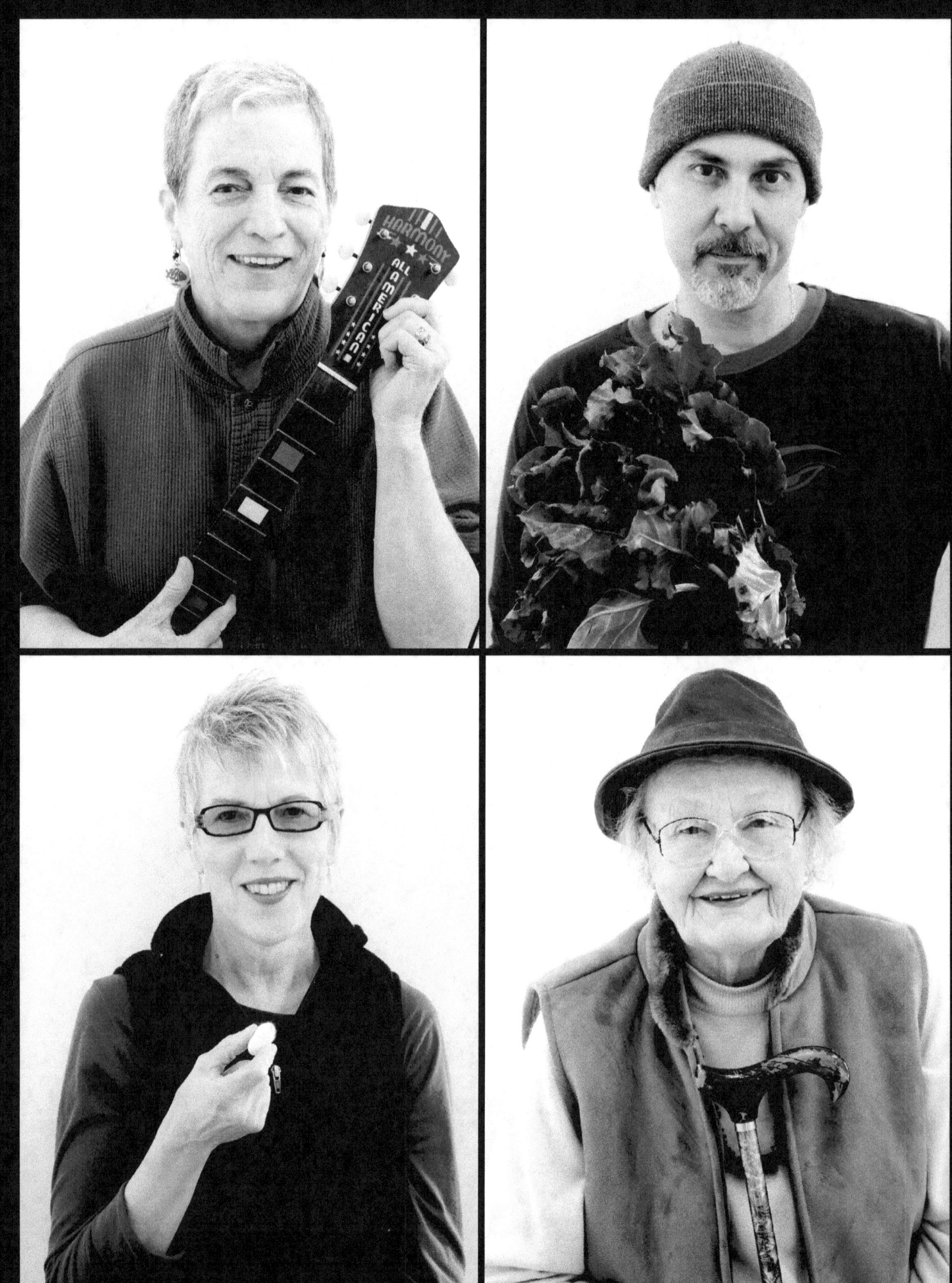

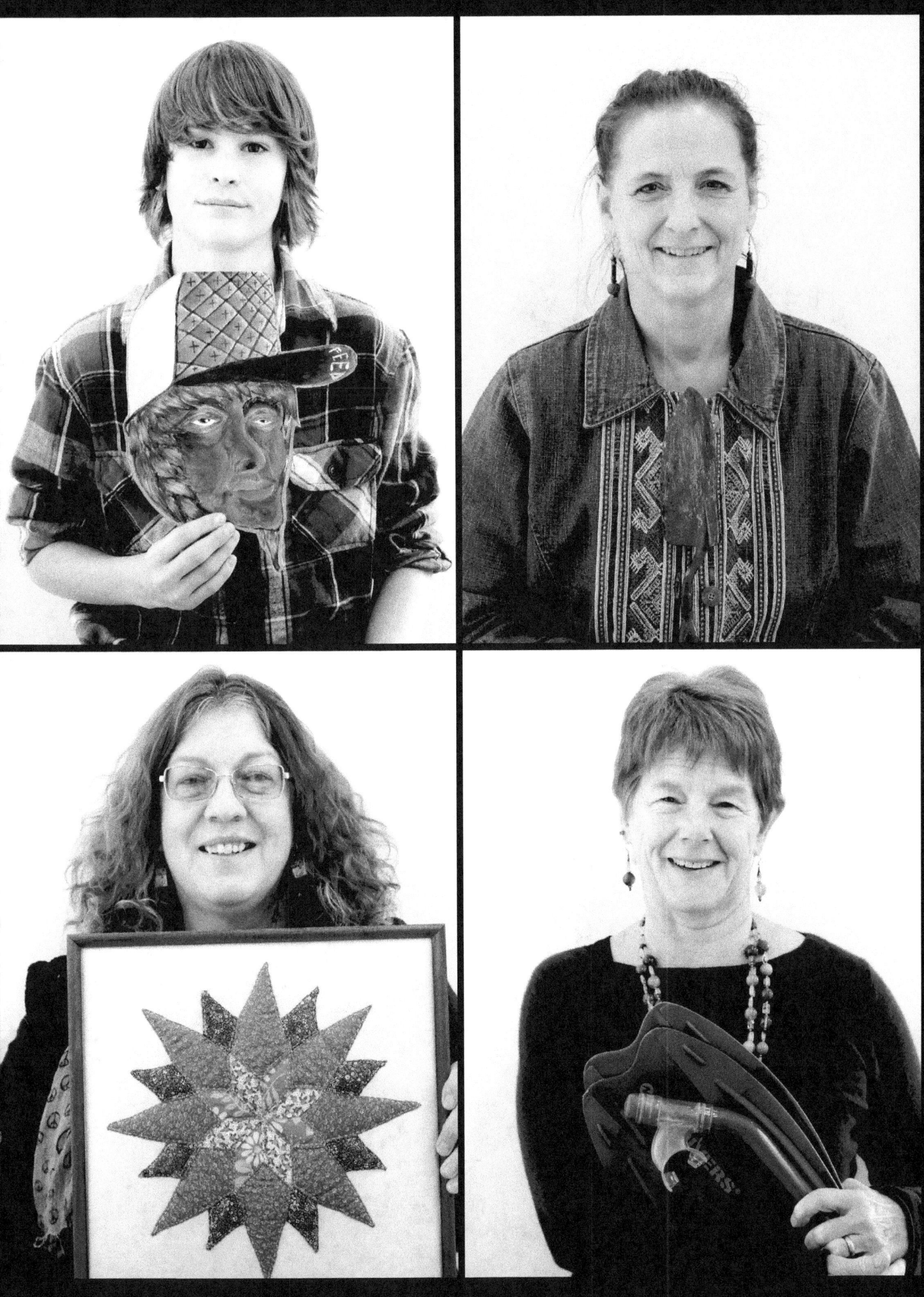

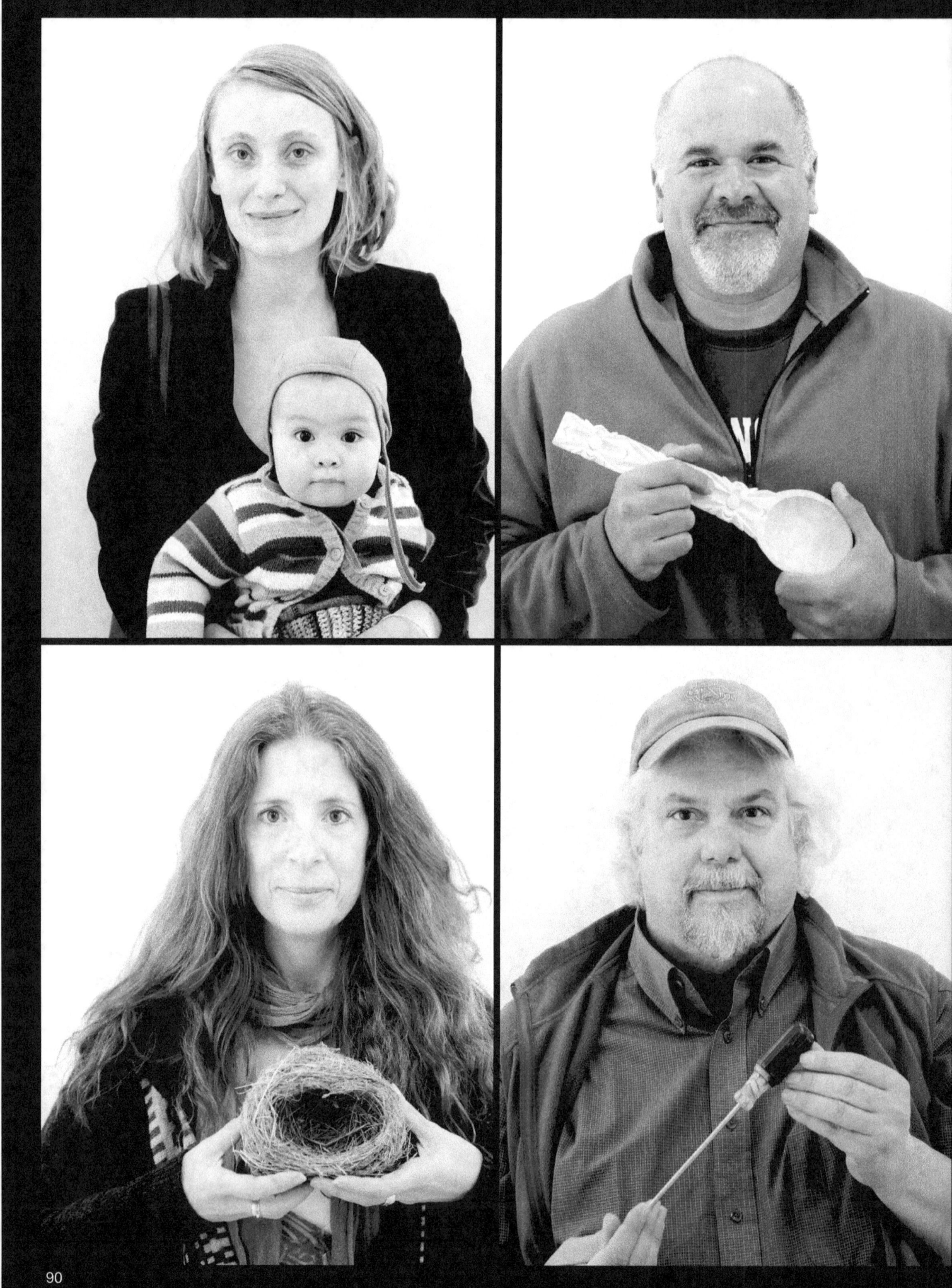

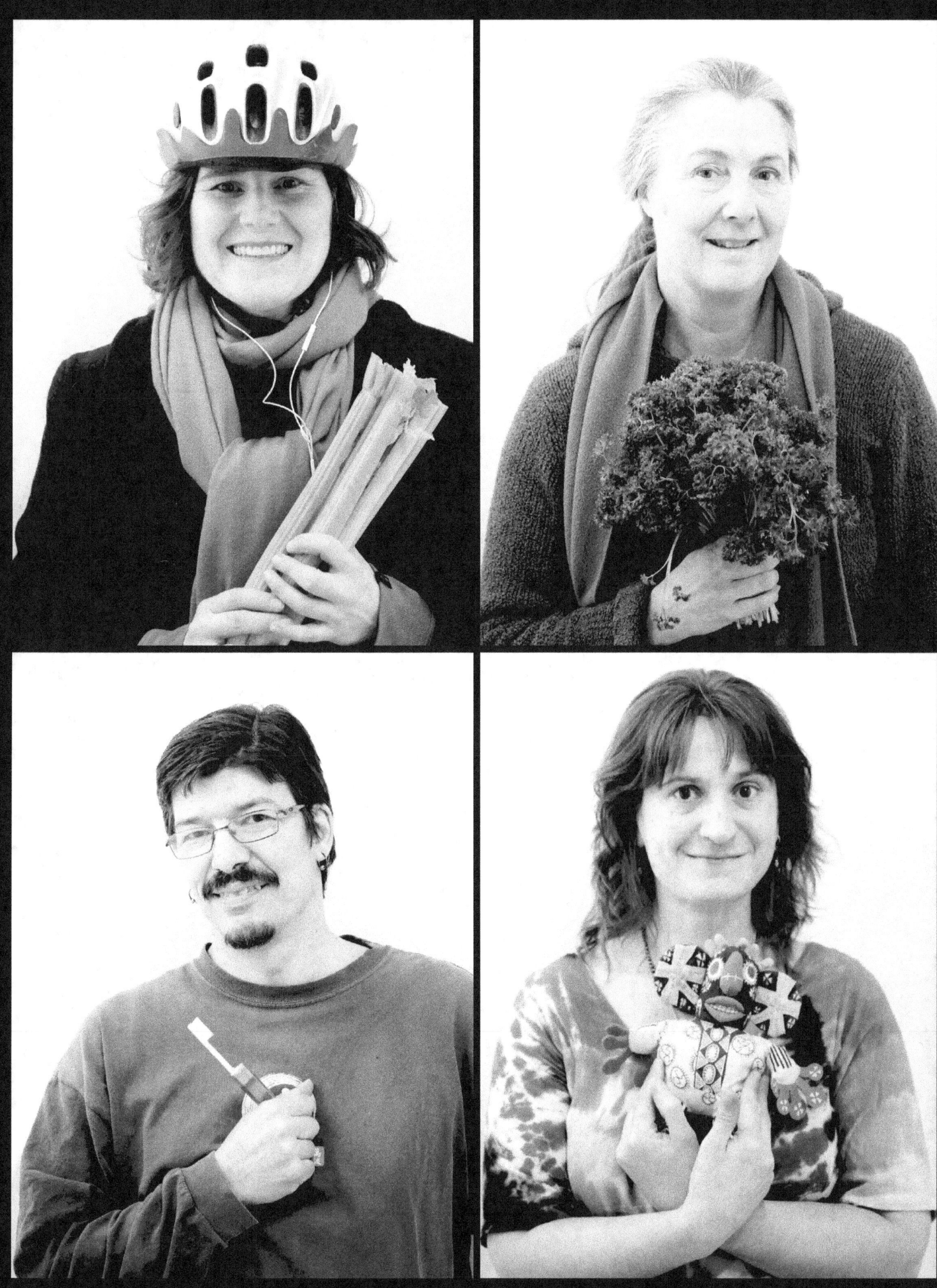

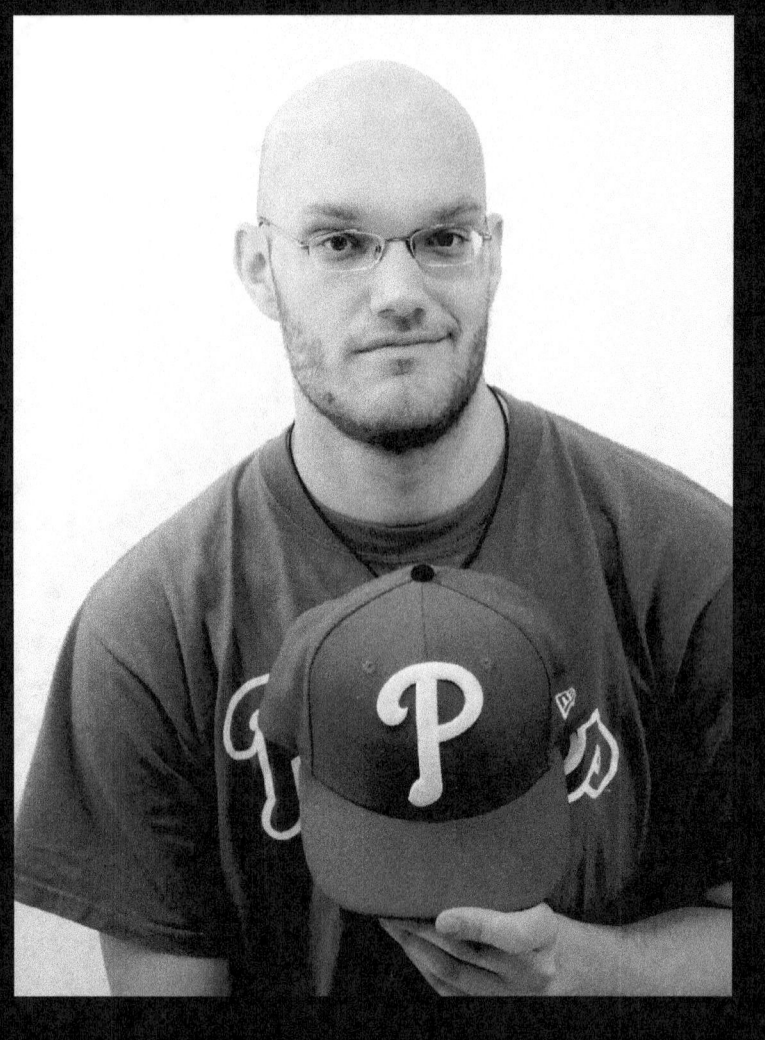

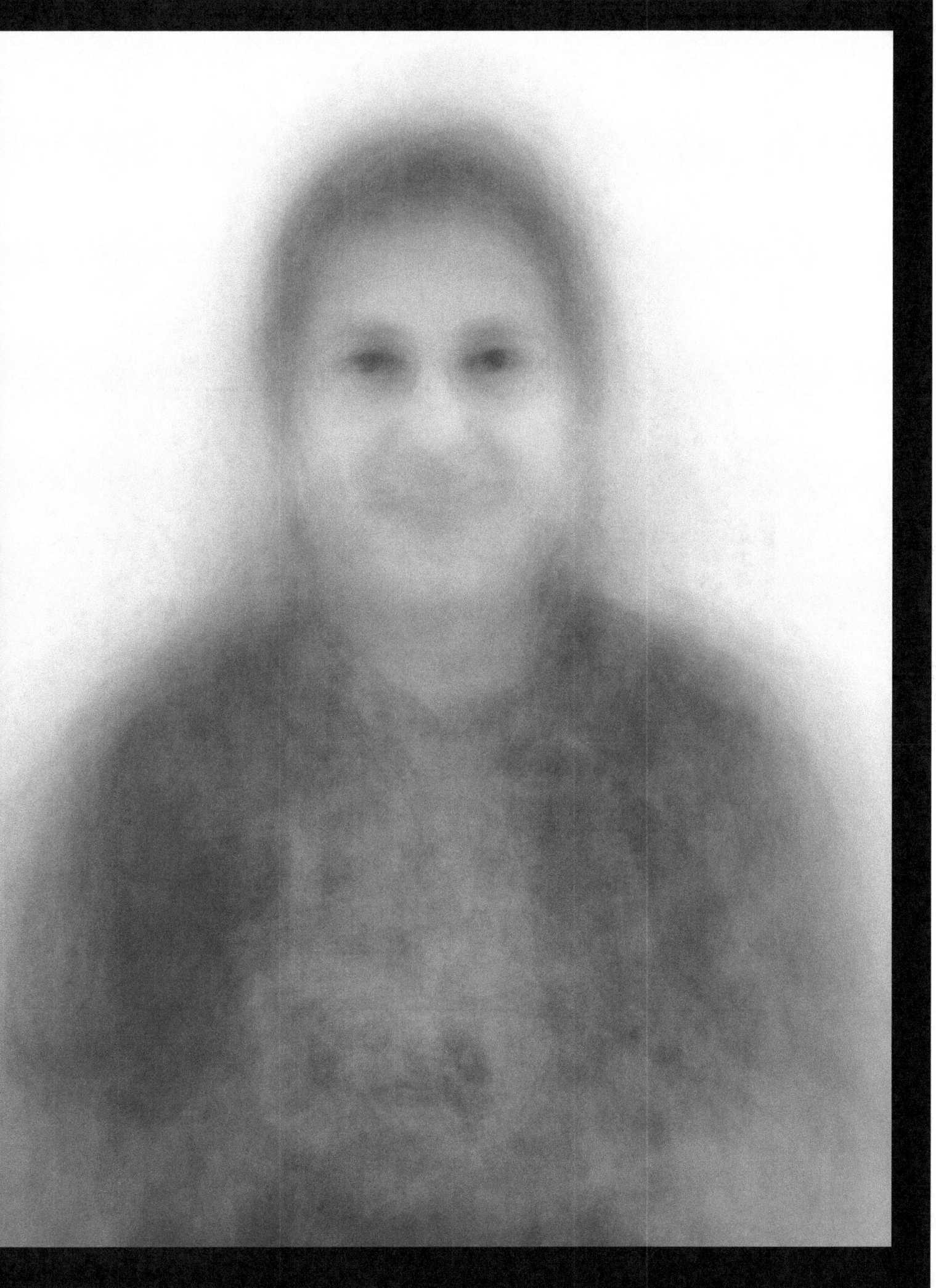

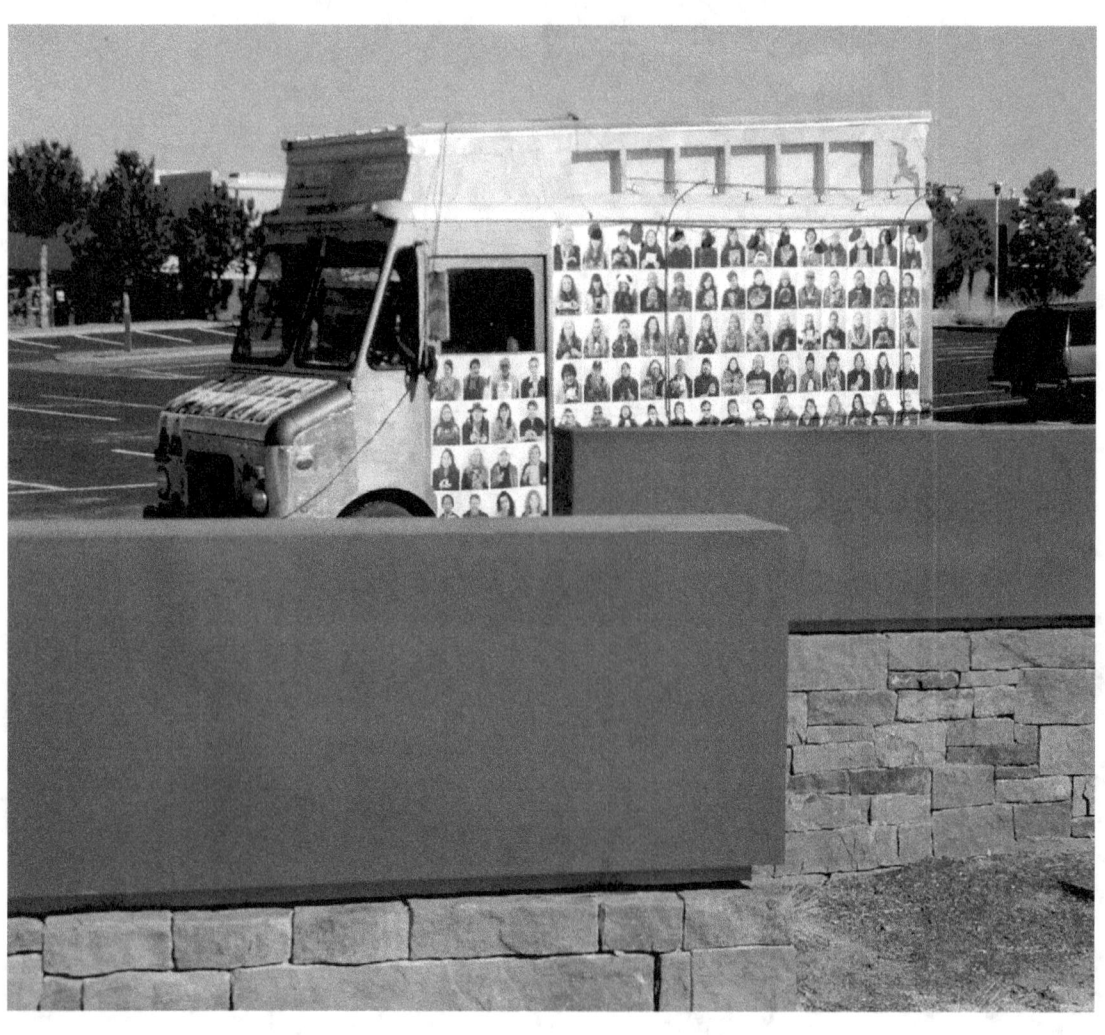

Santa Fe University of Art & Design

1600 St. Michael's Drive

Tuesday

March 6

11am-1pm

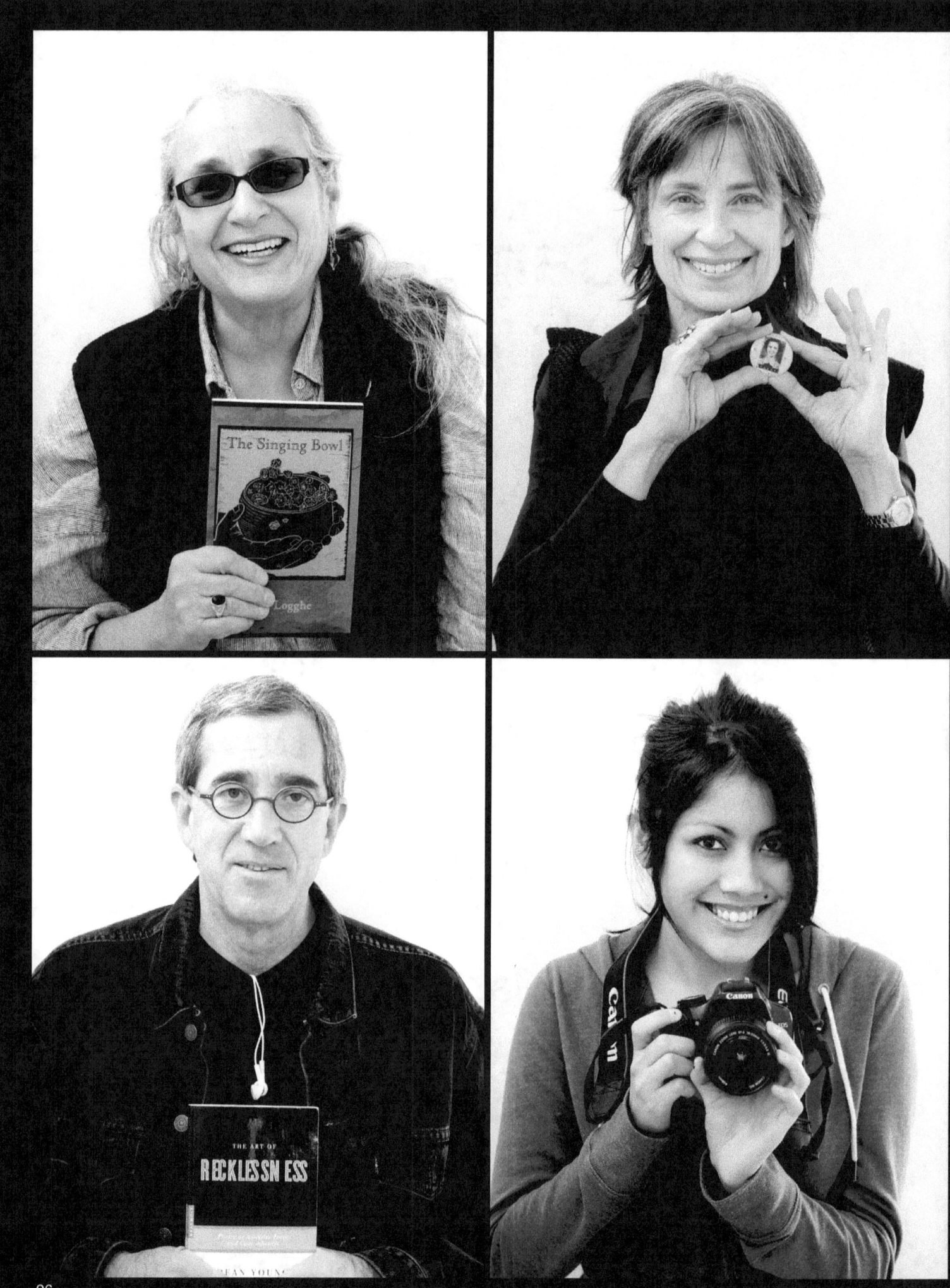

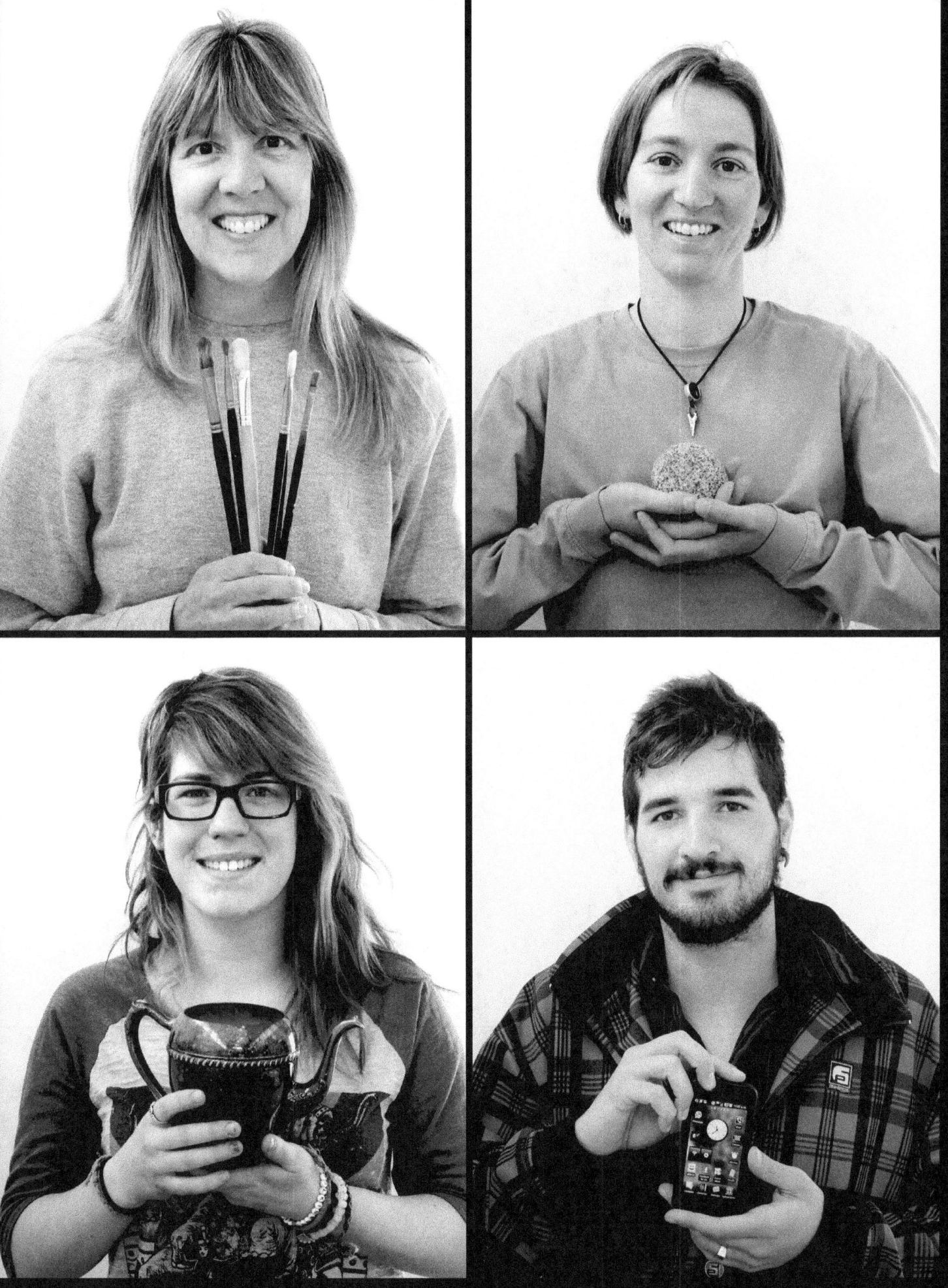

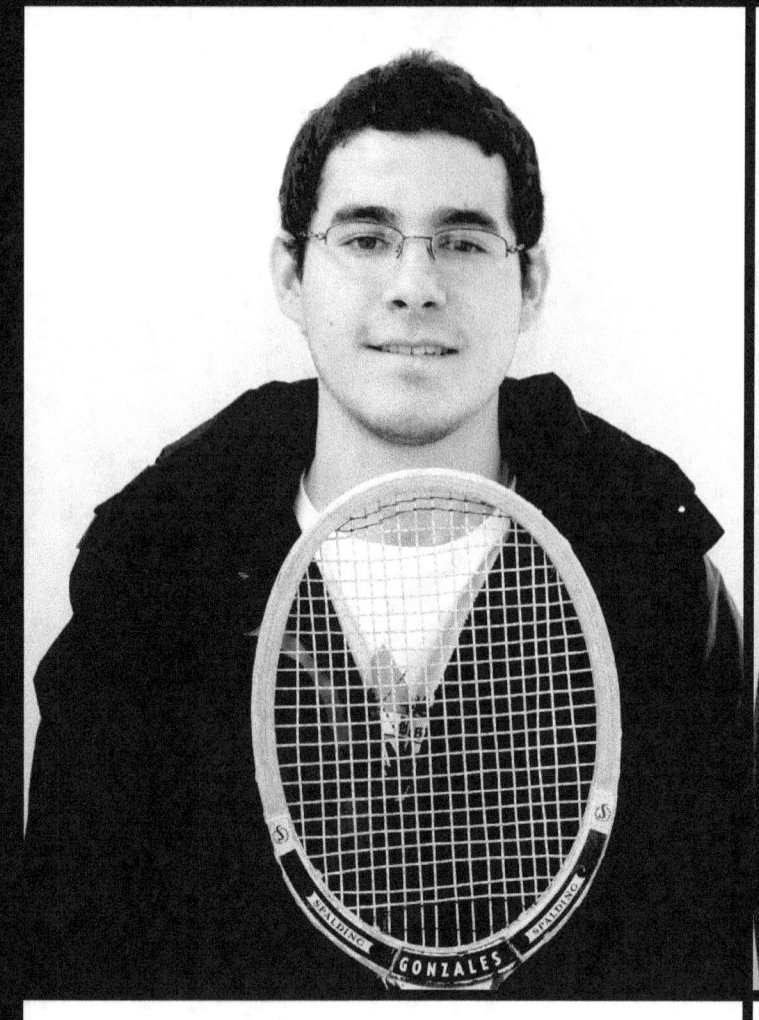
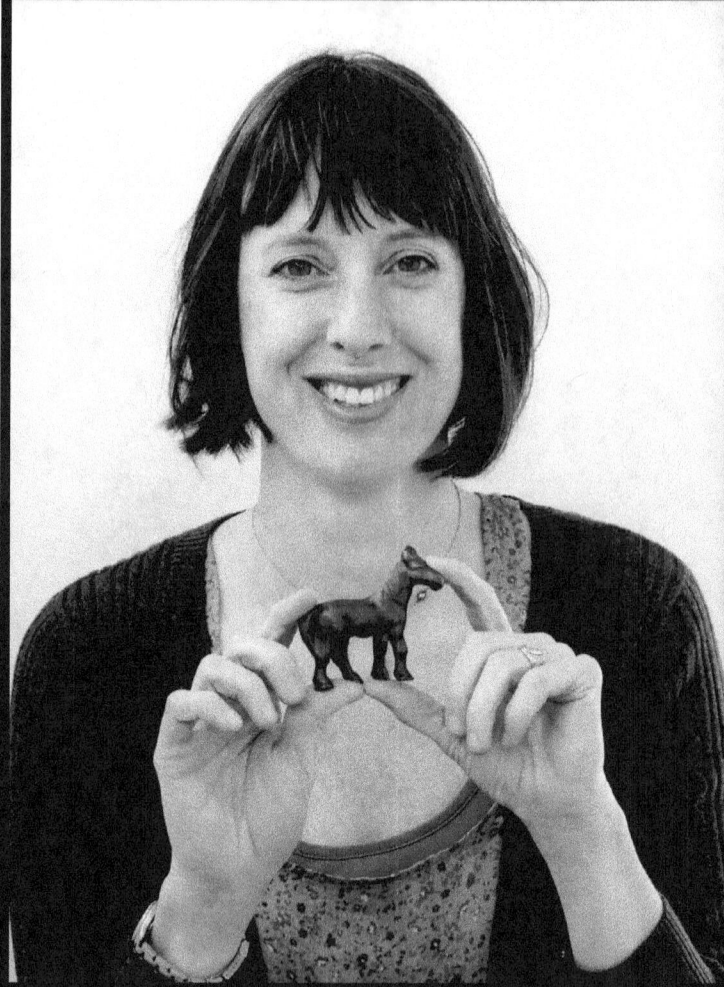
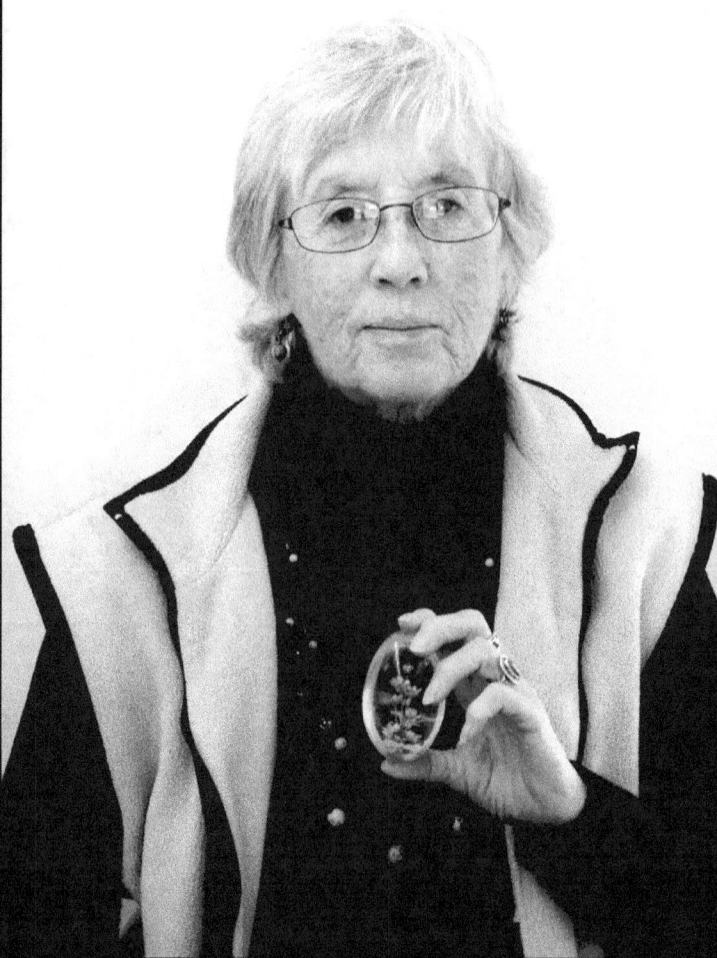
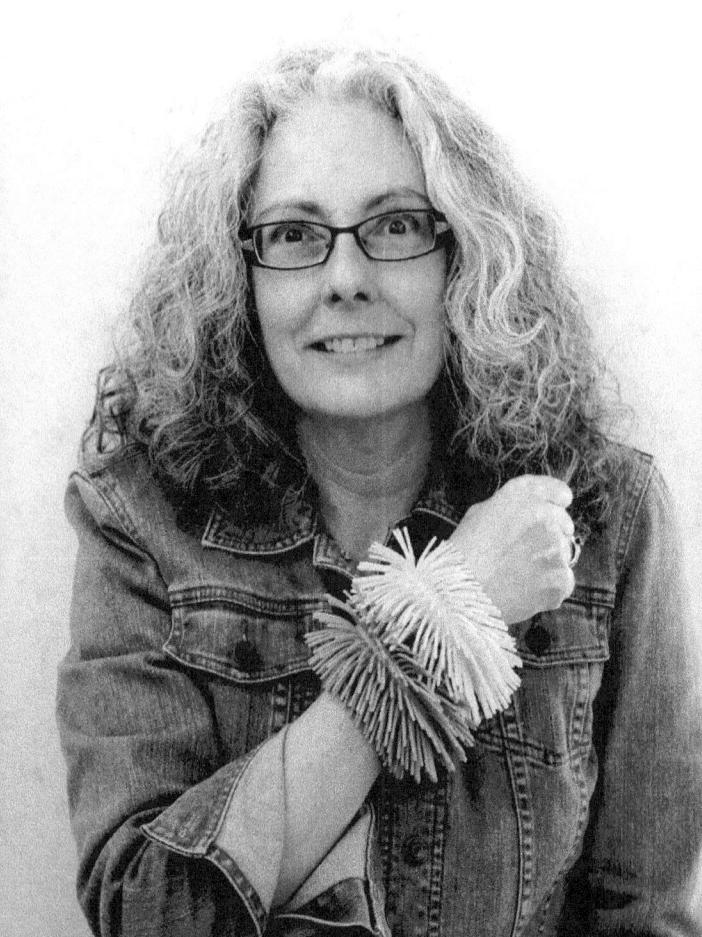

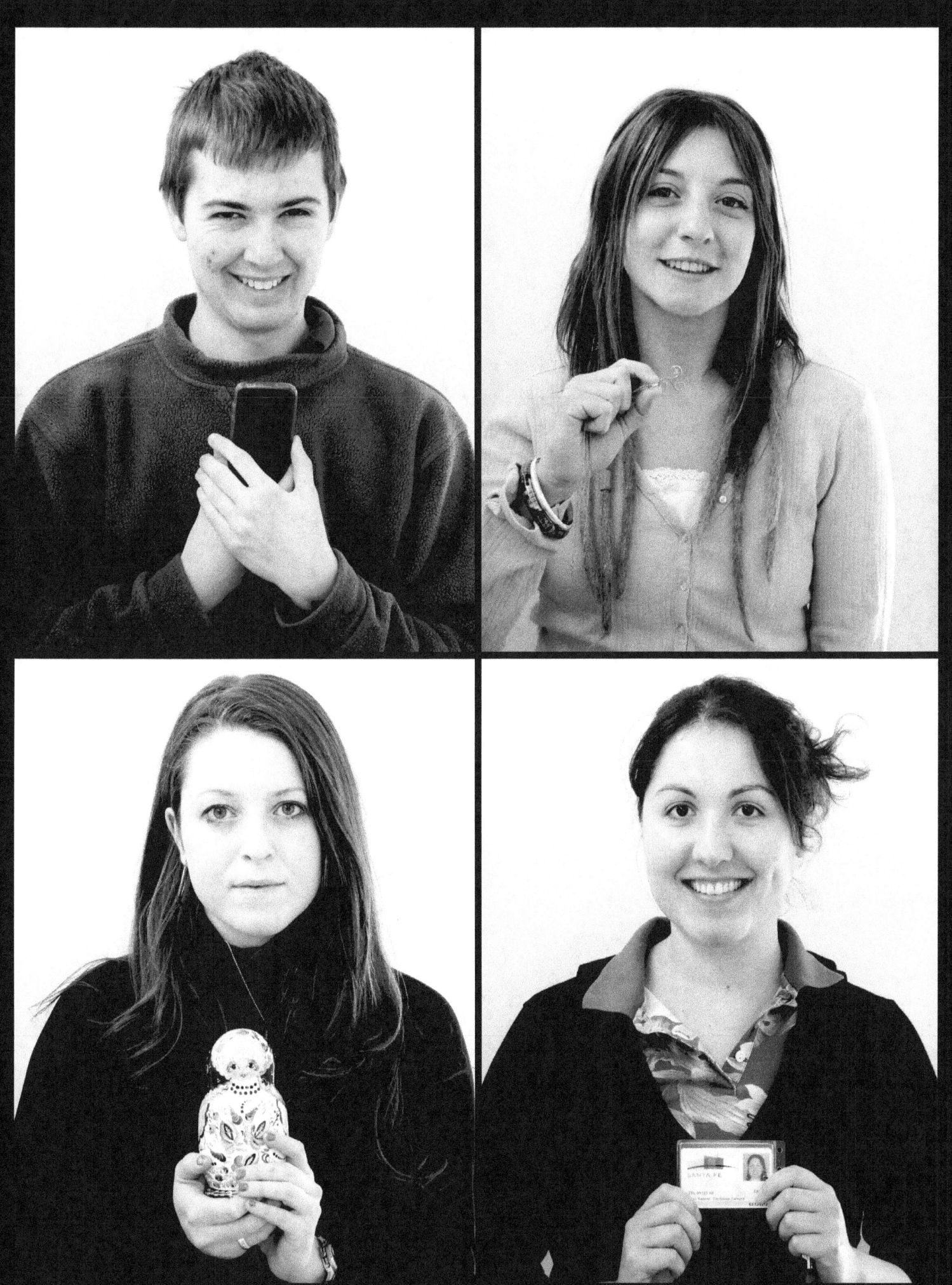

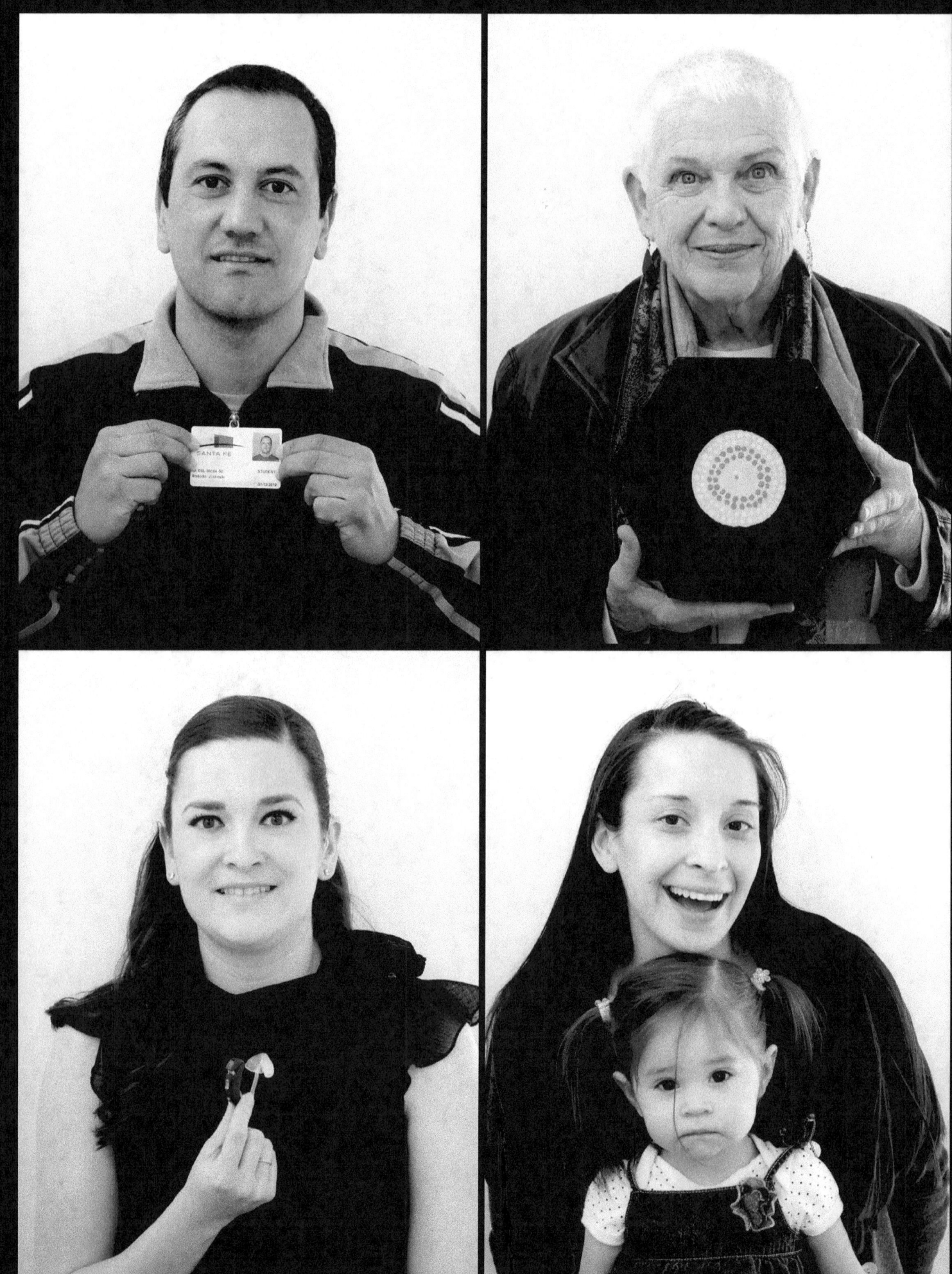

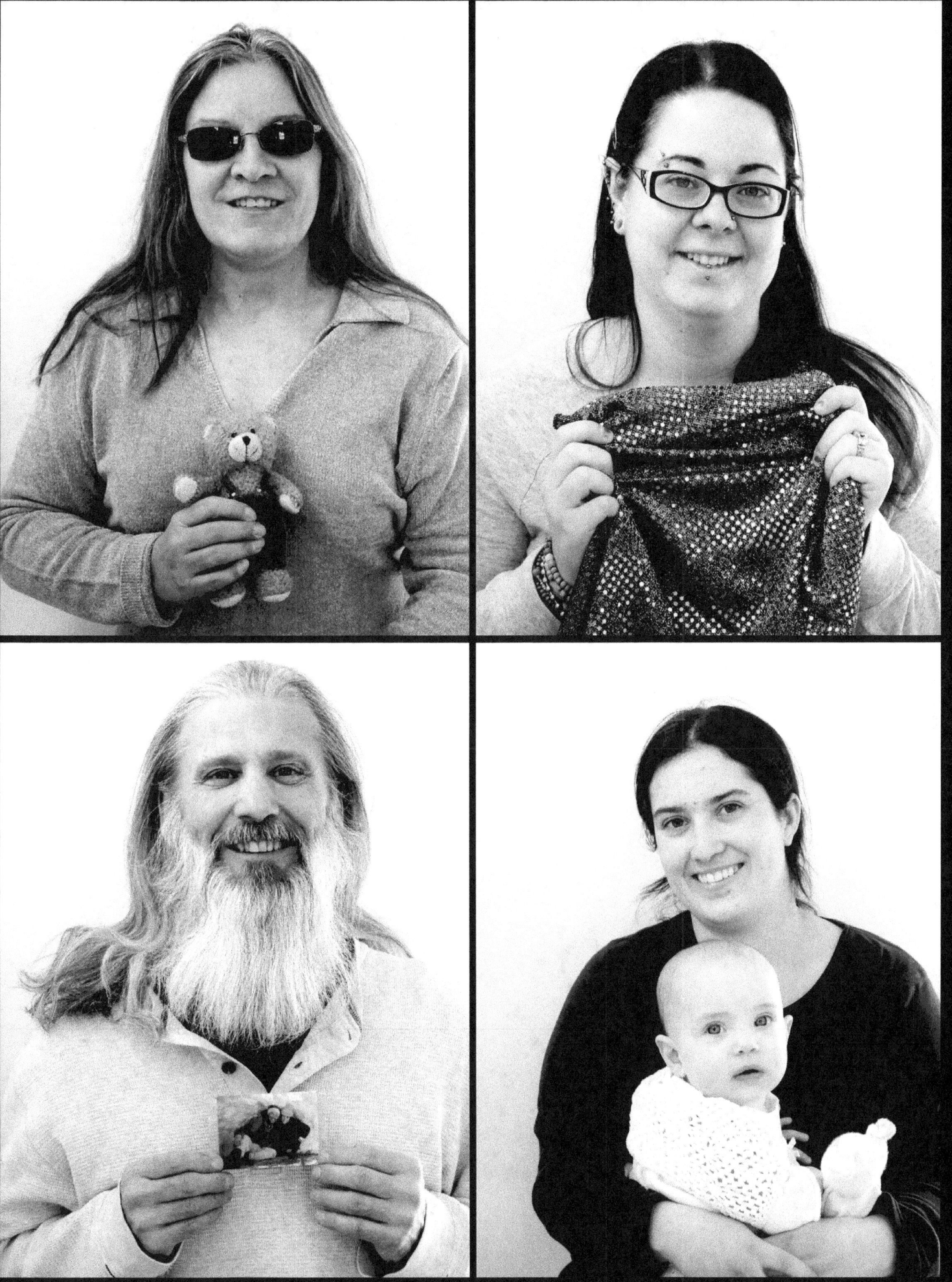

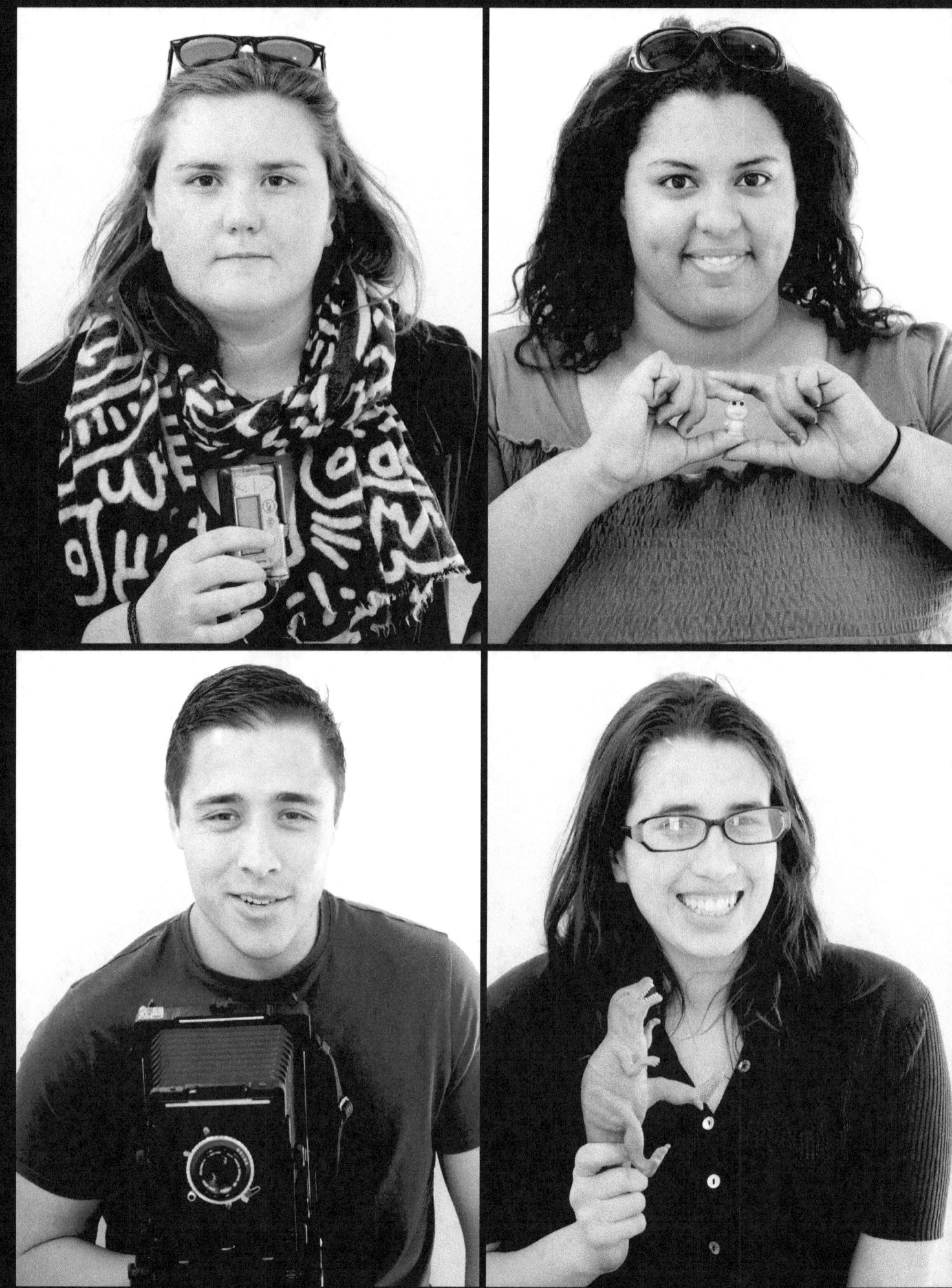

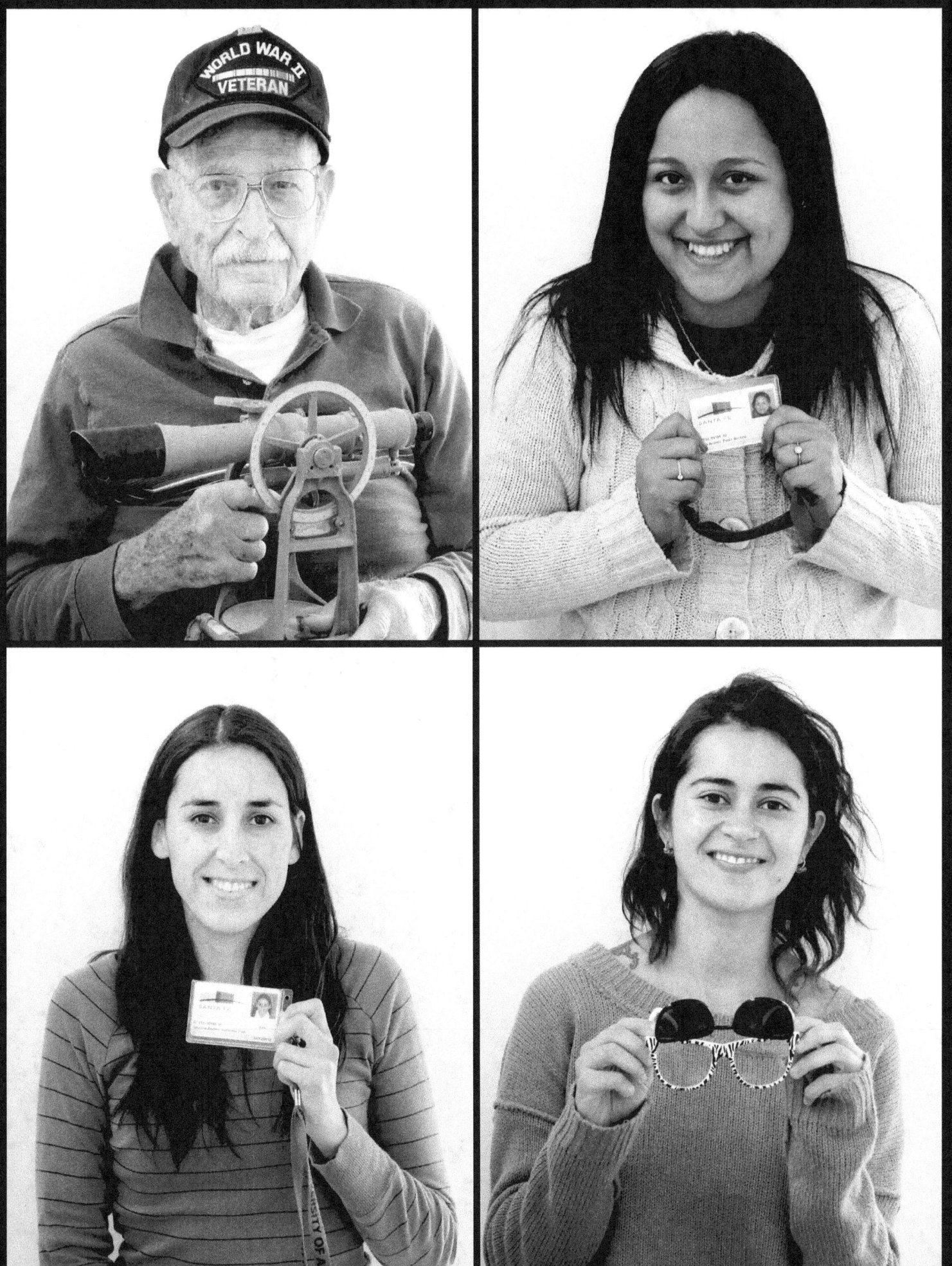

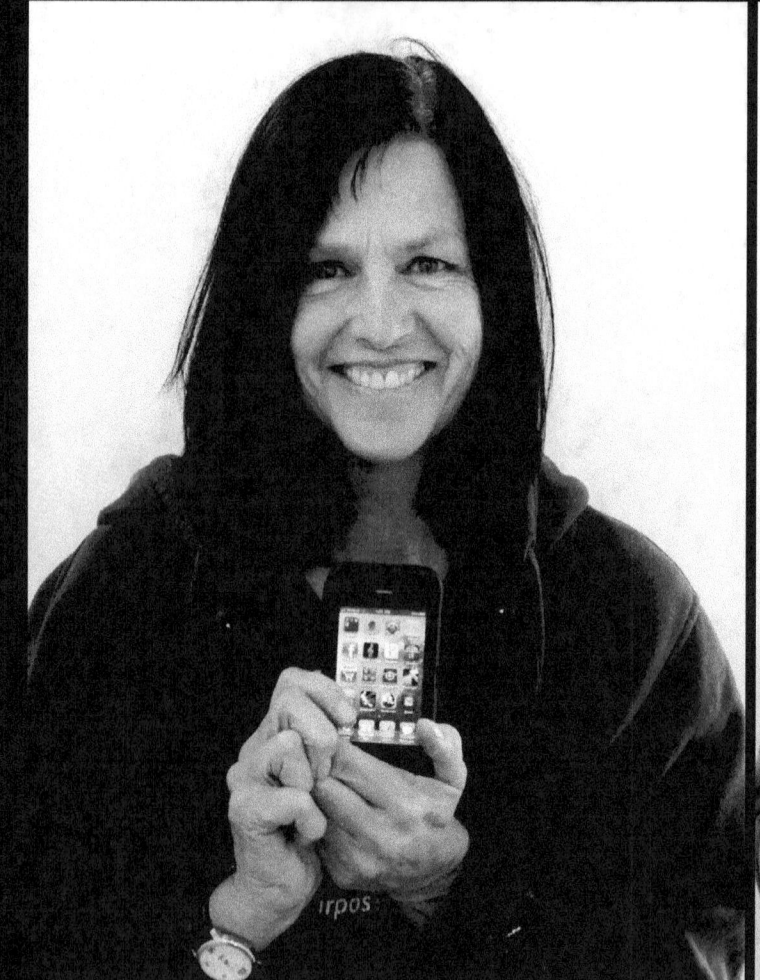
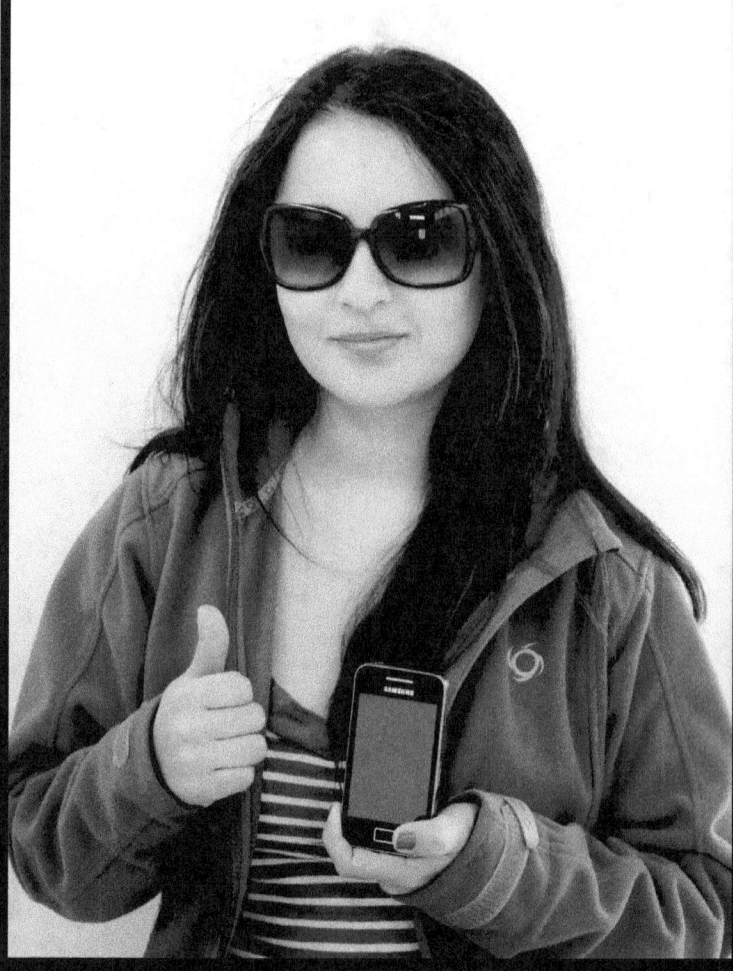
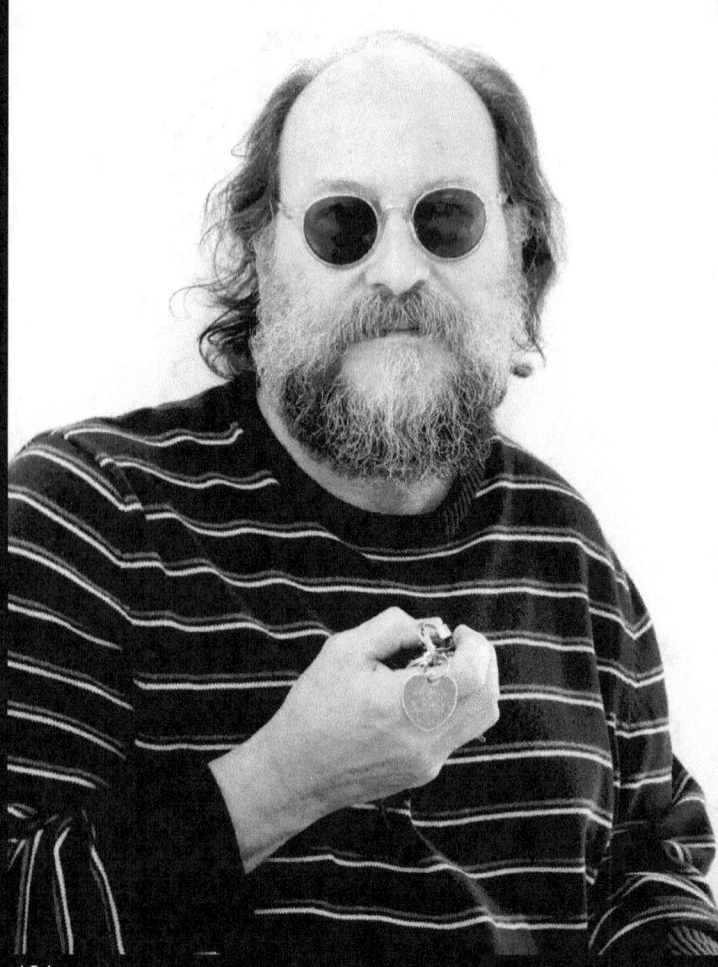

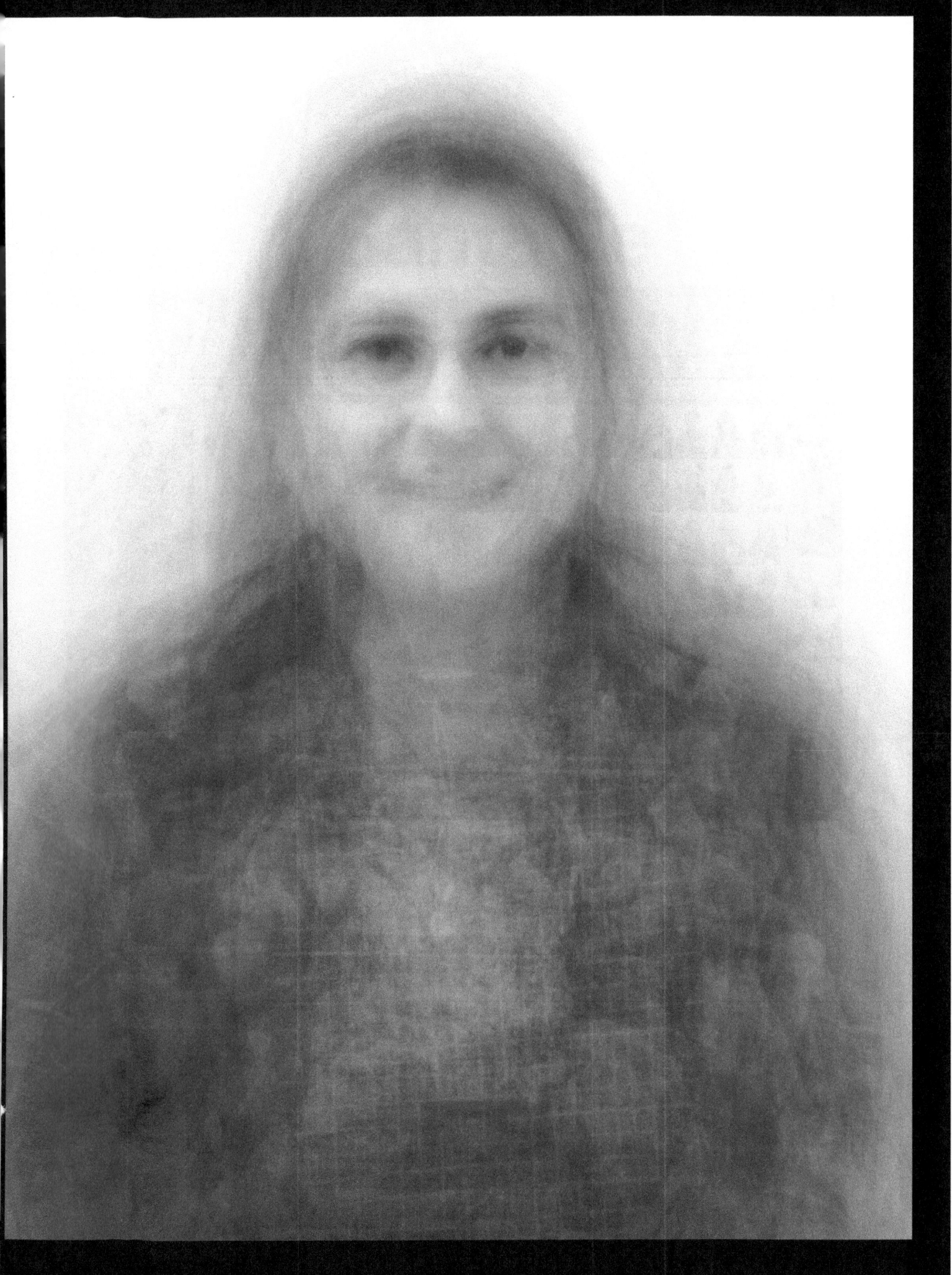

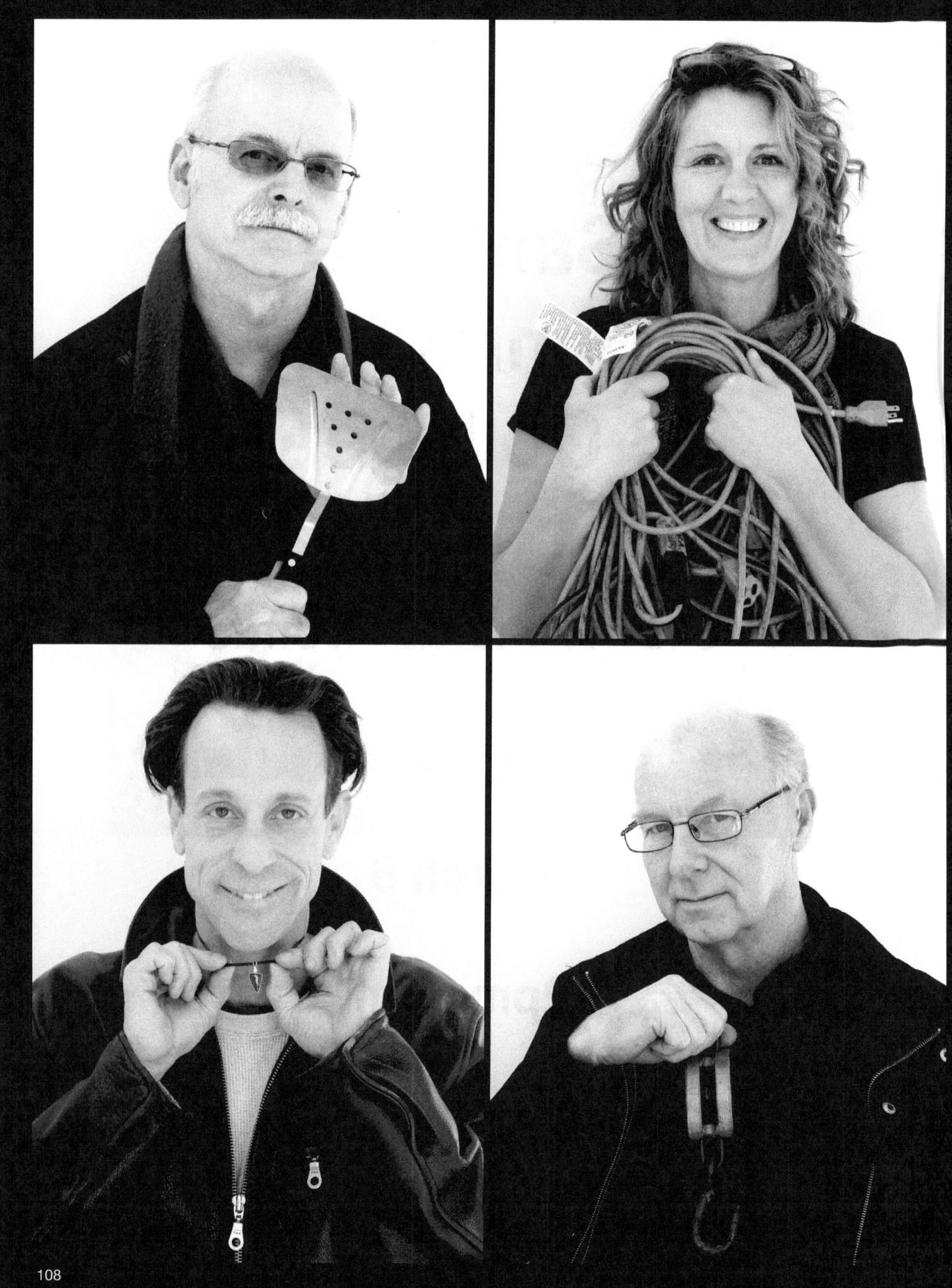

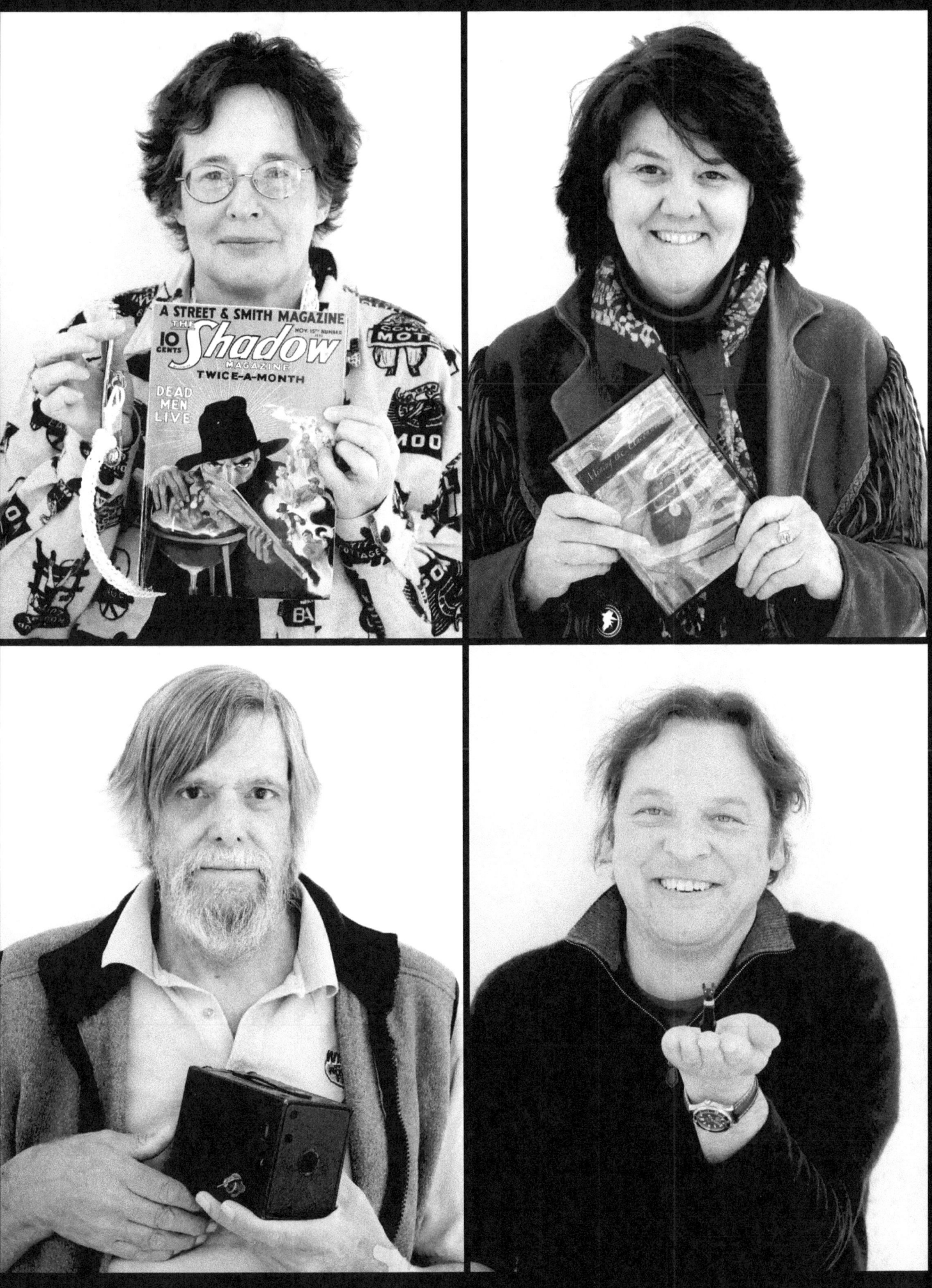

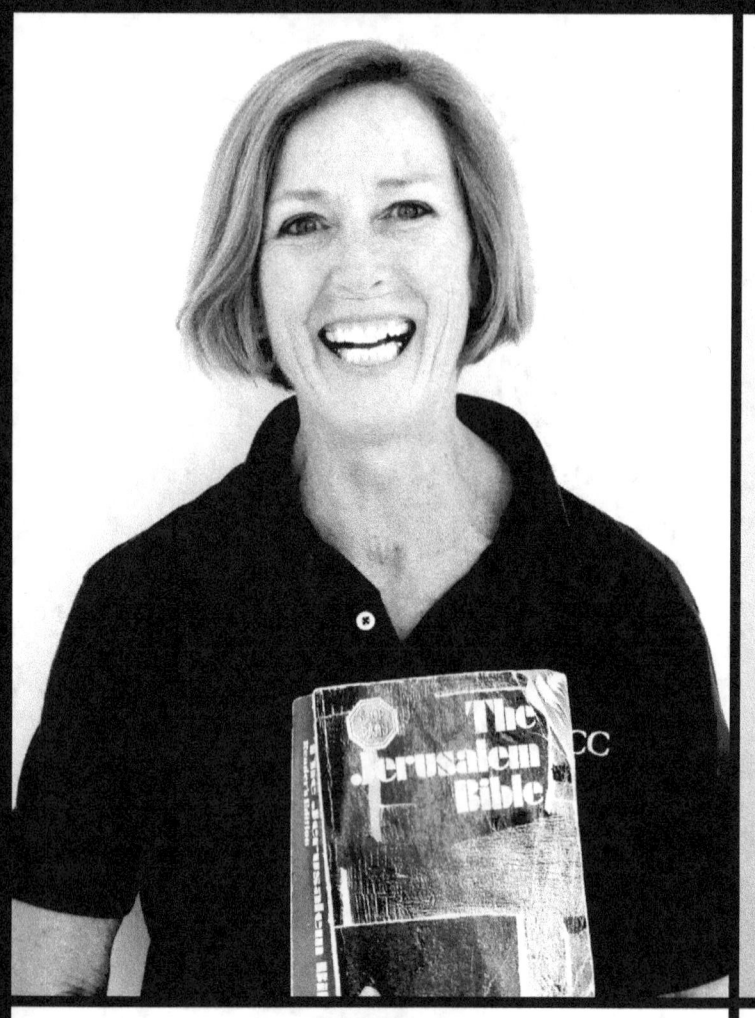
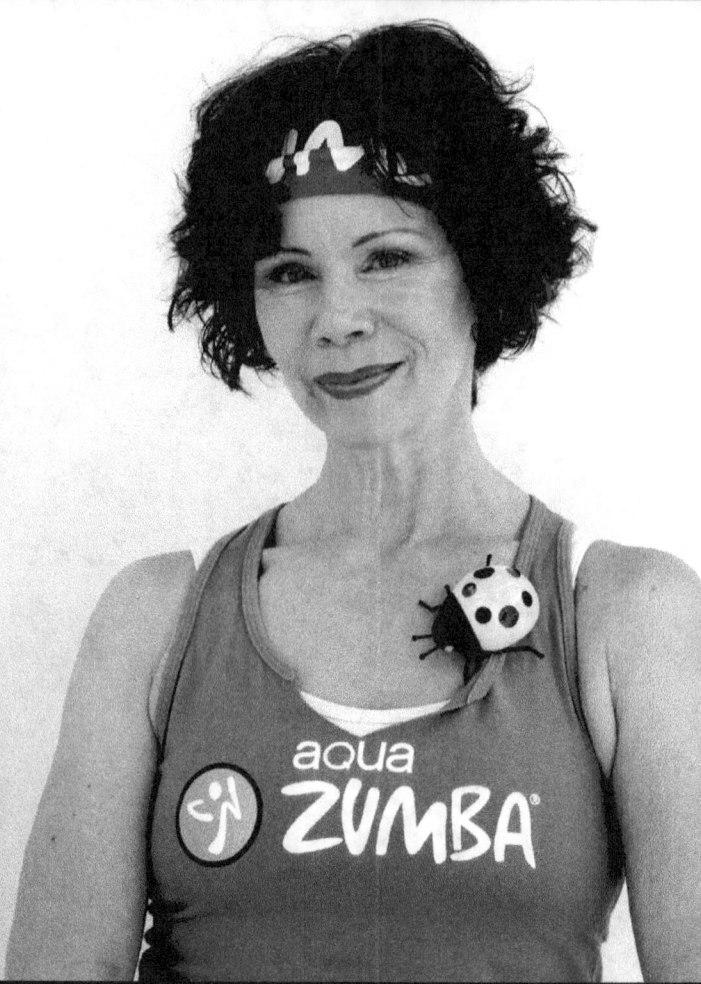
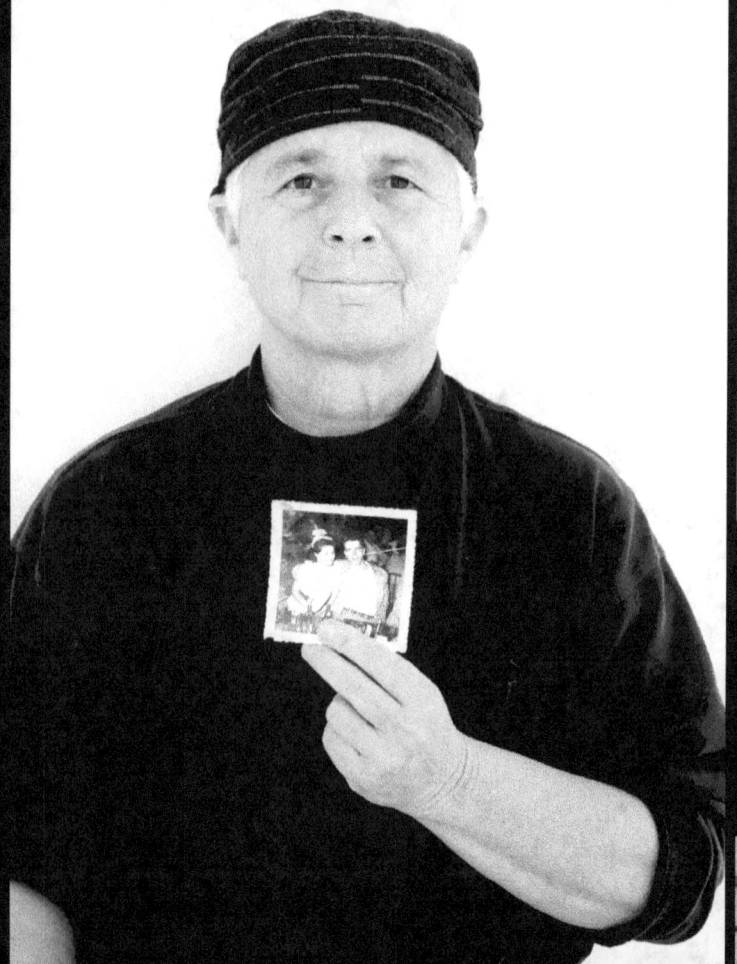
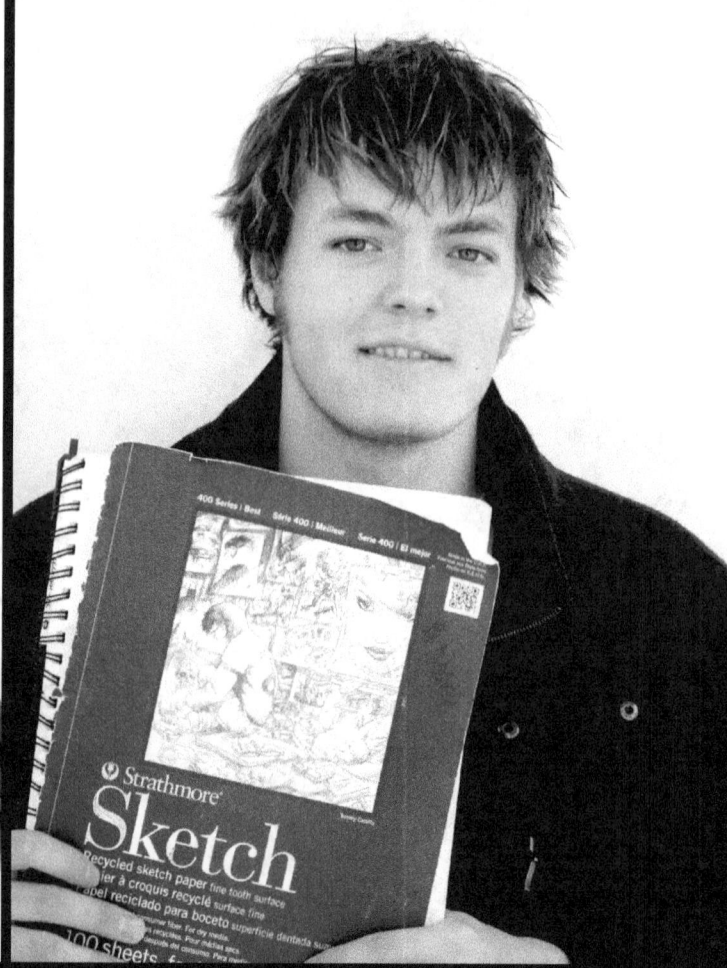

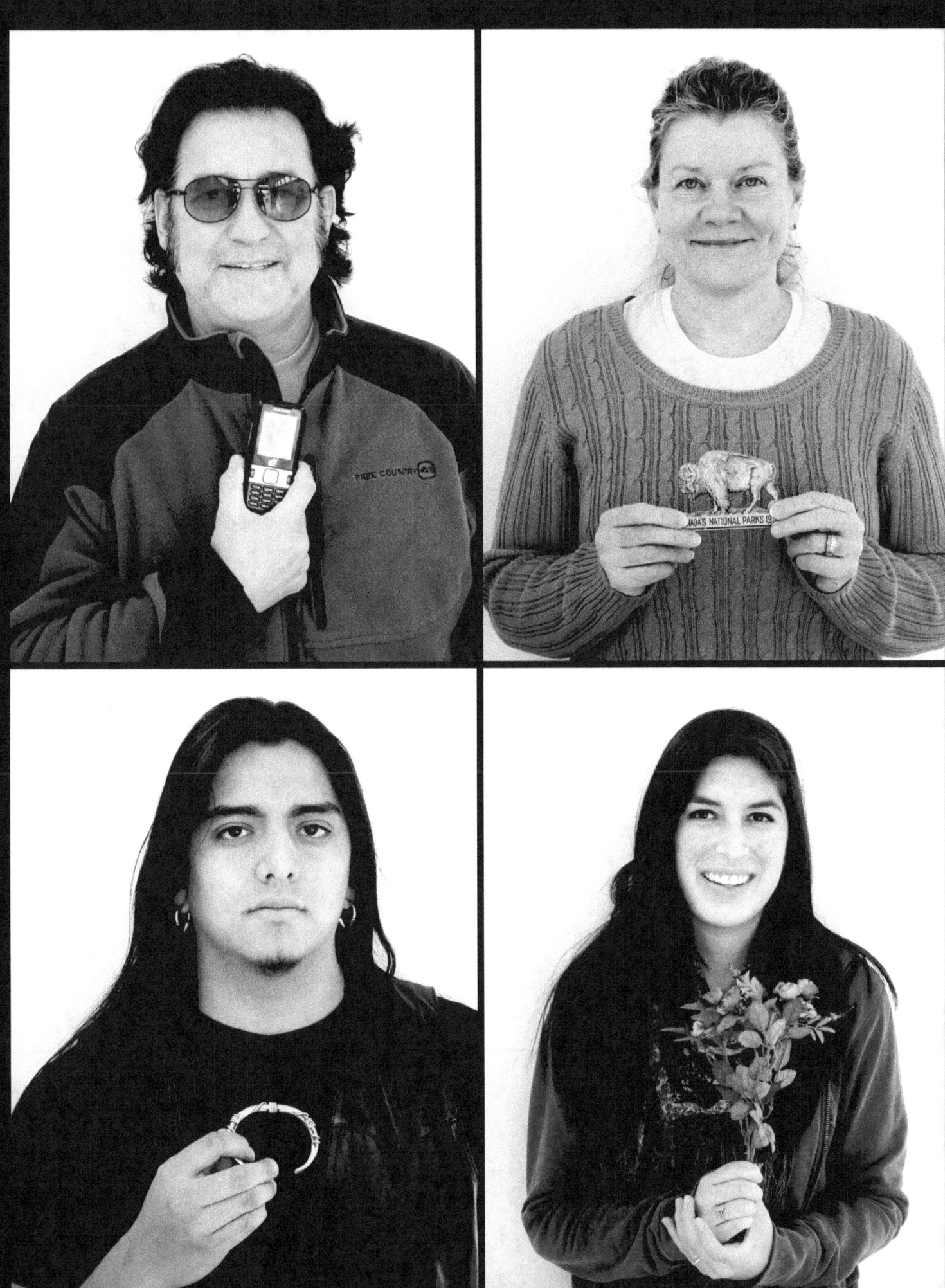

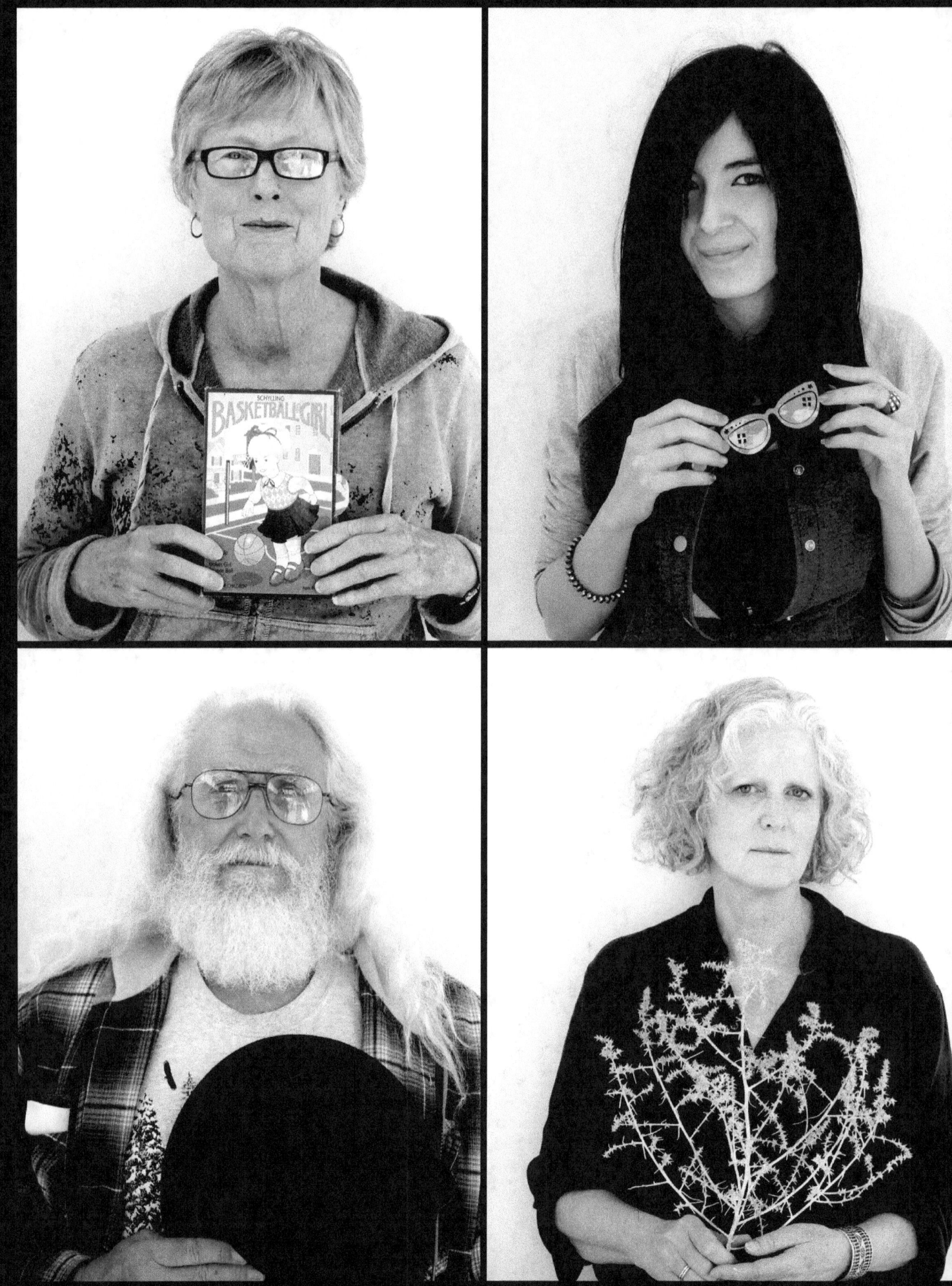

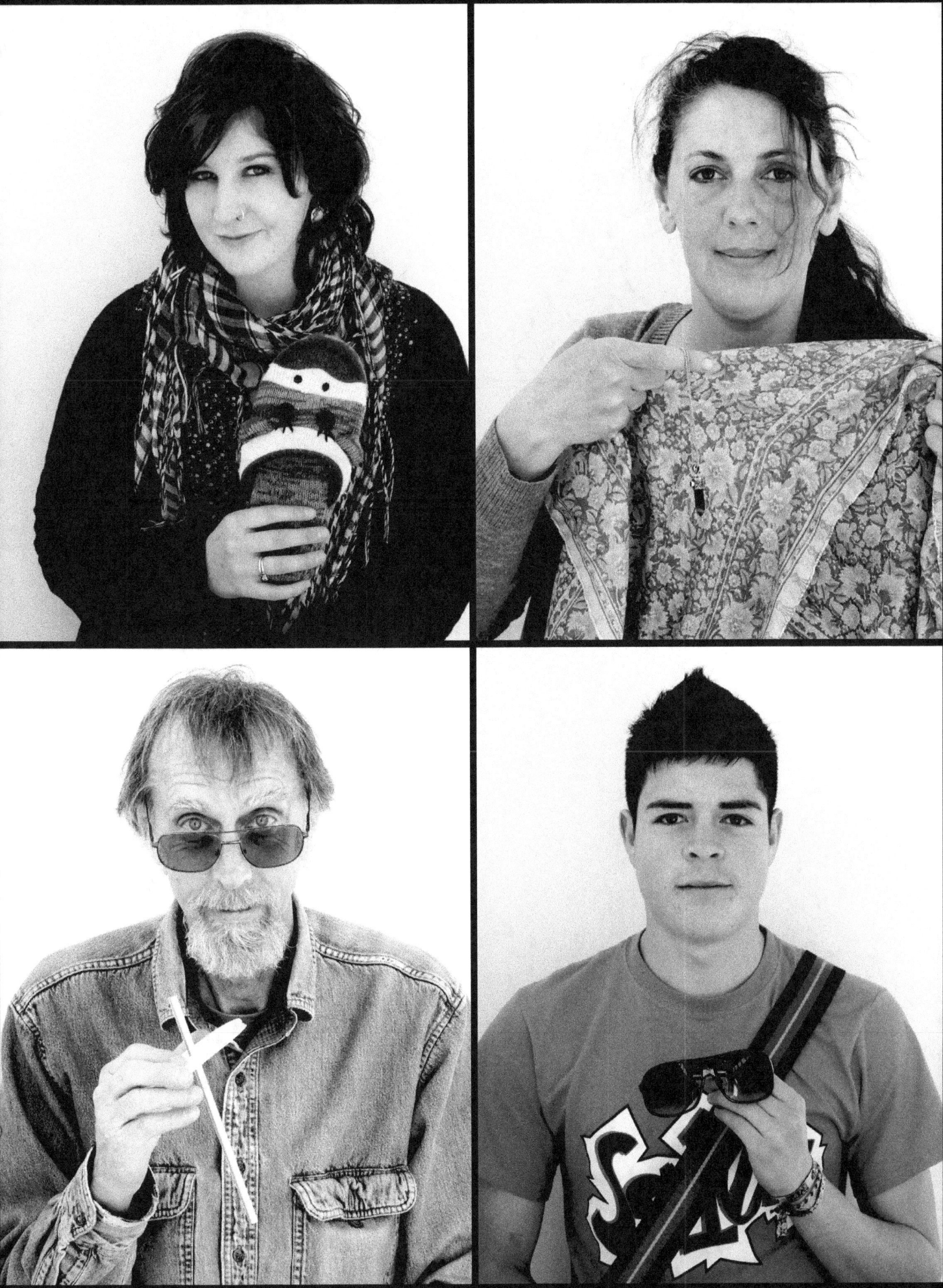

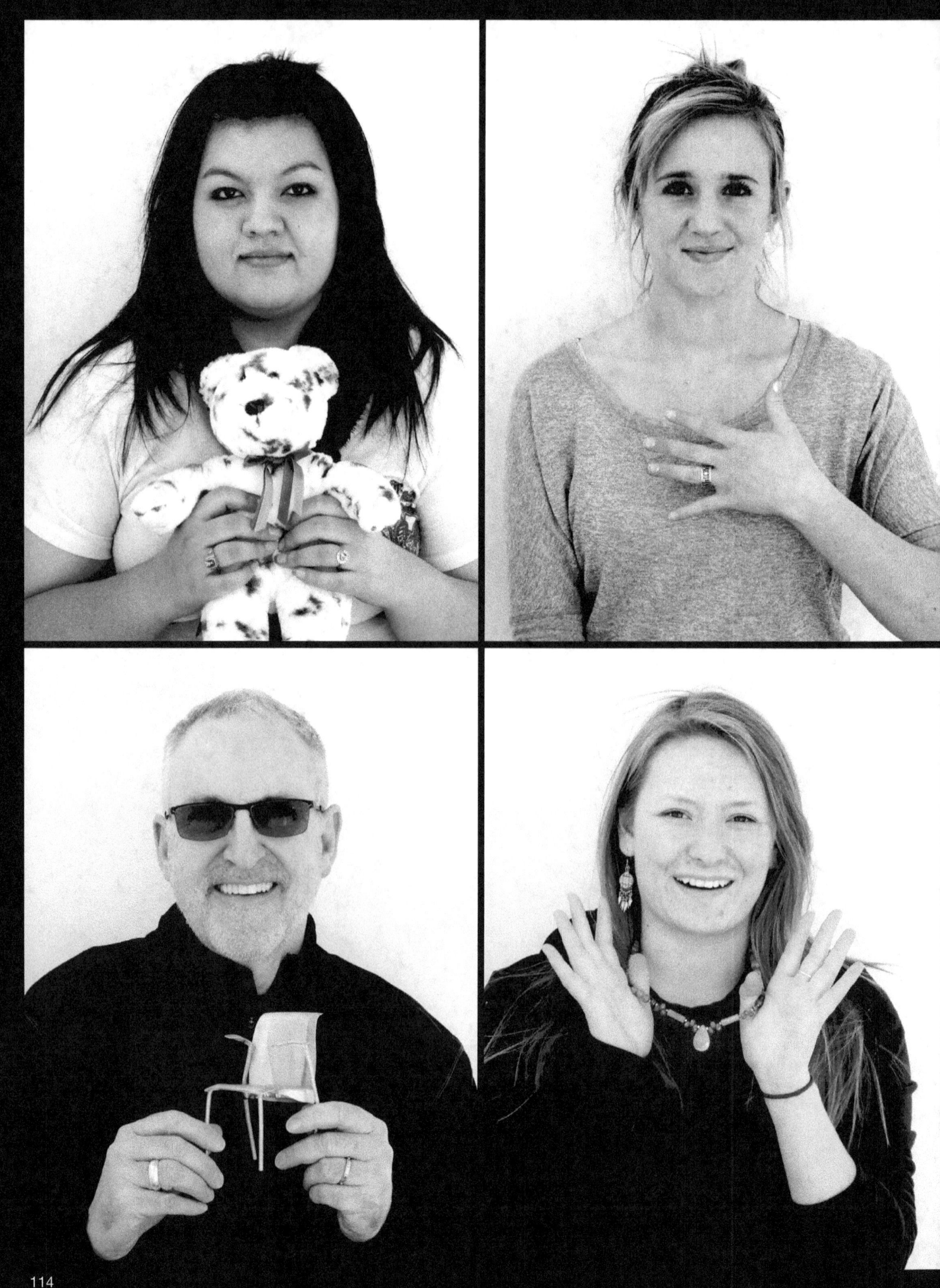

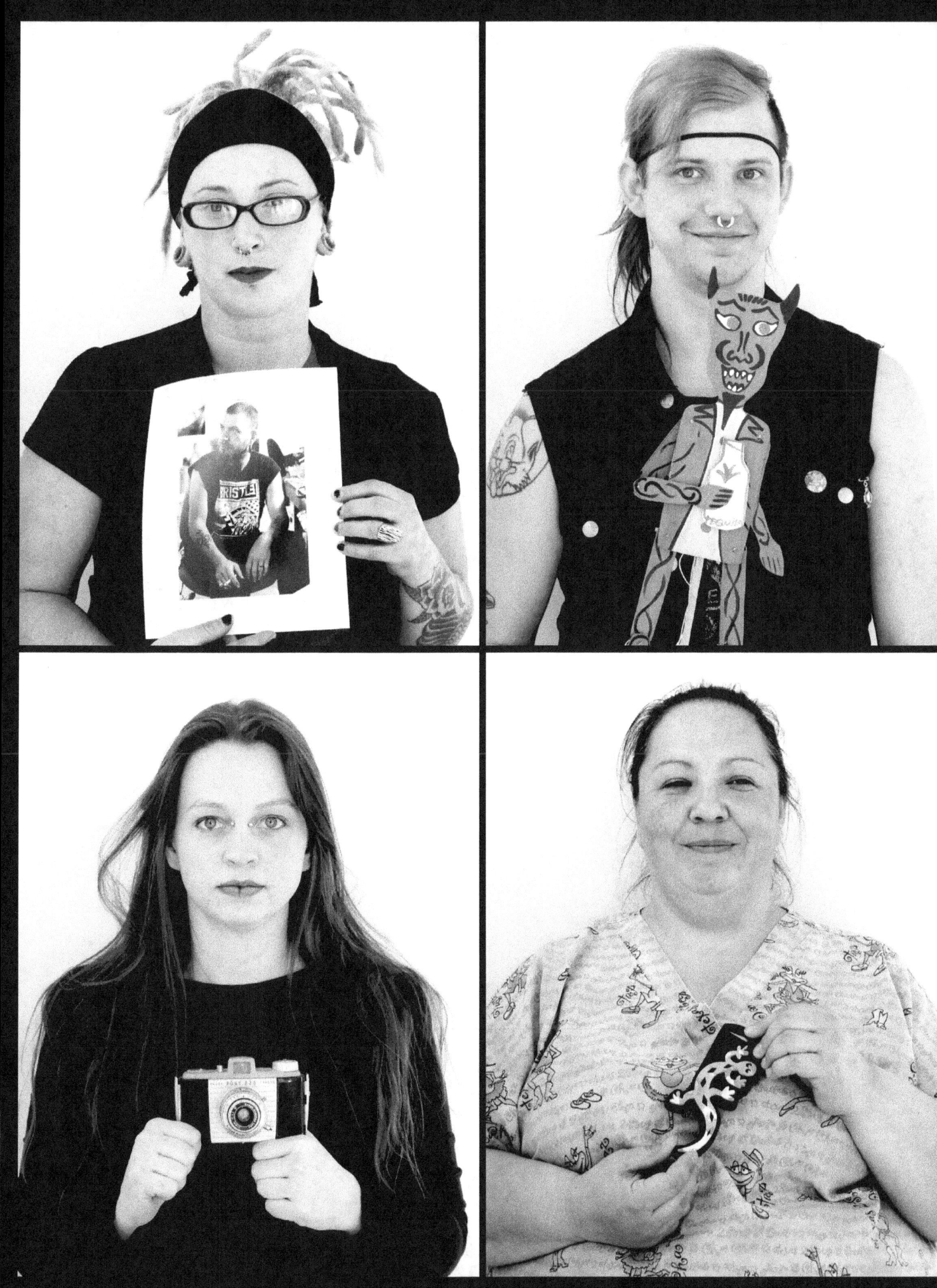

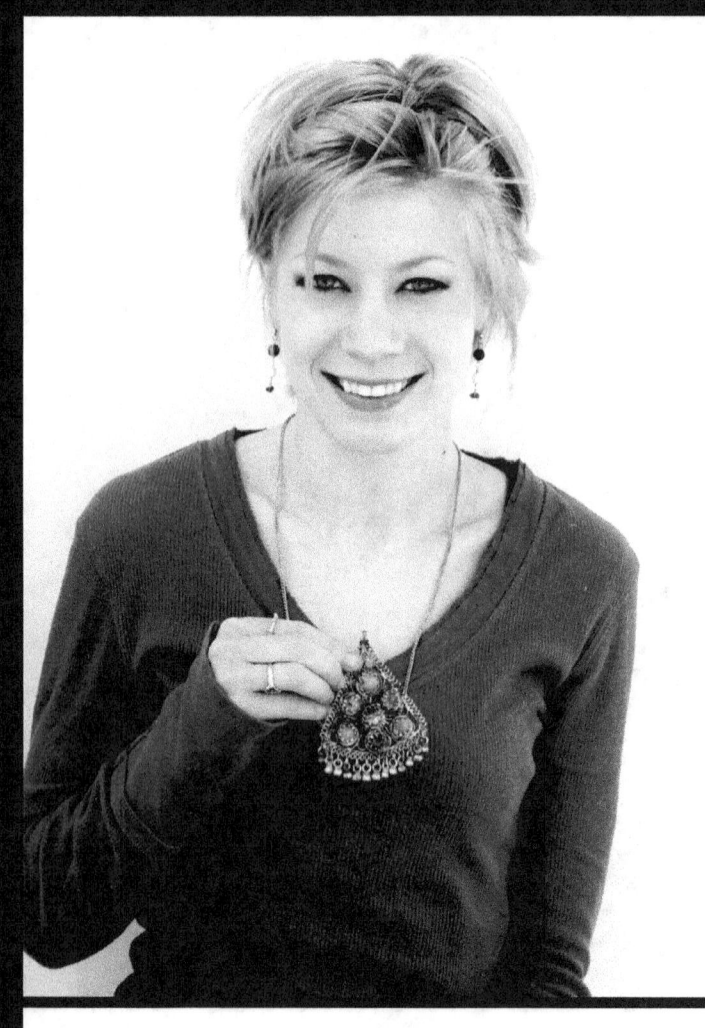
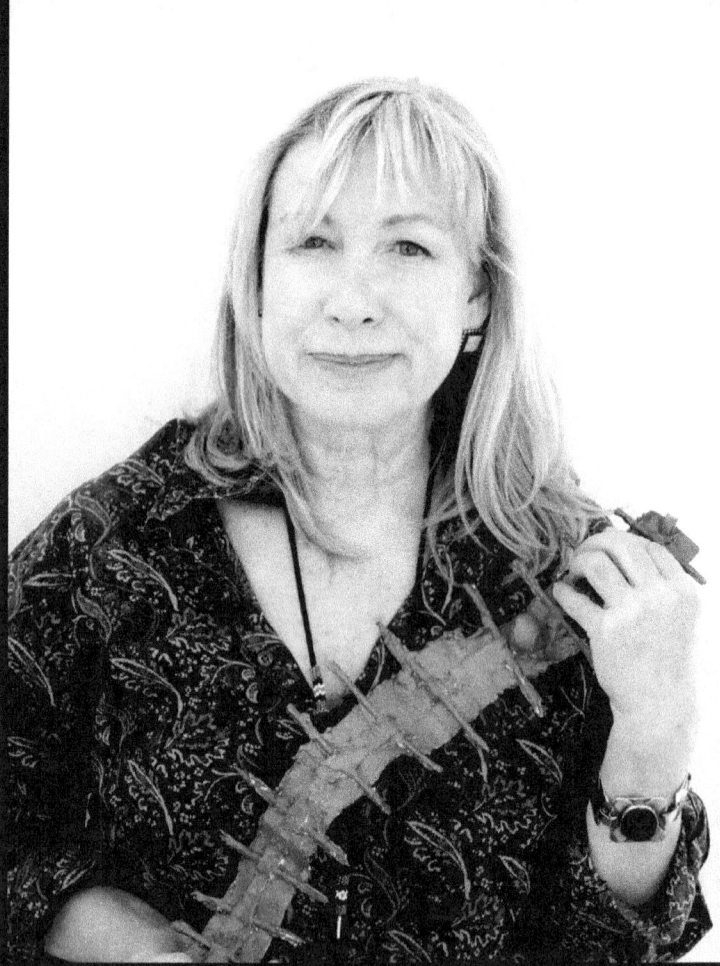
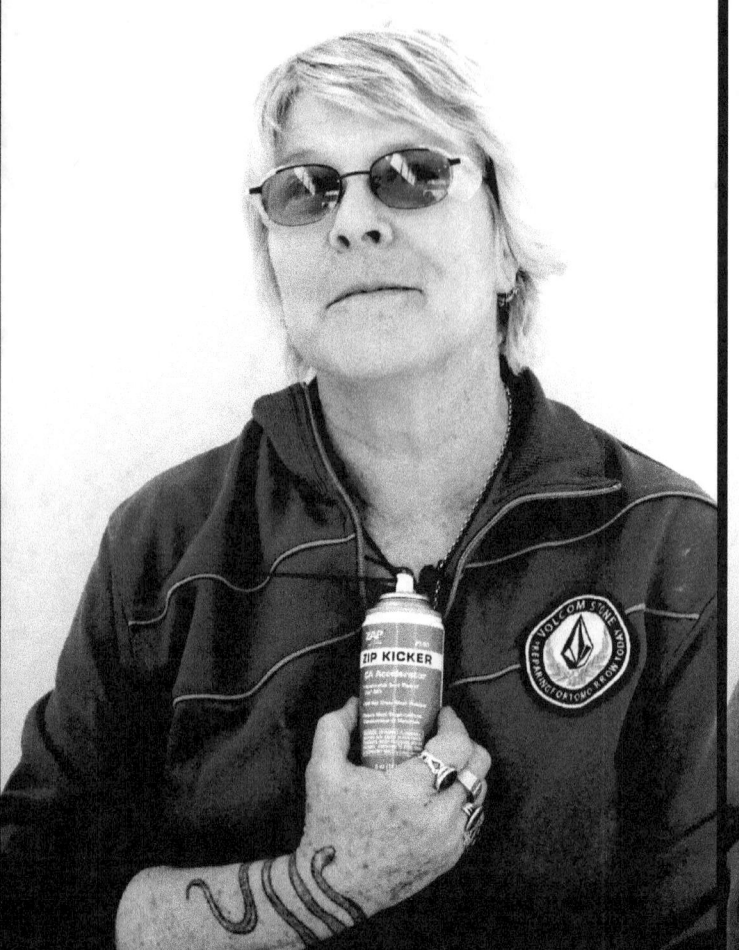
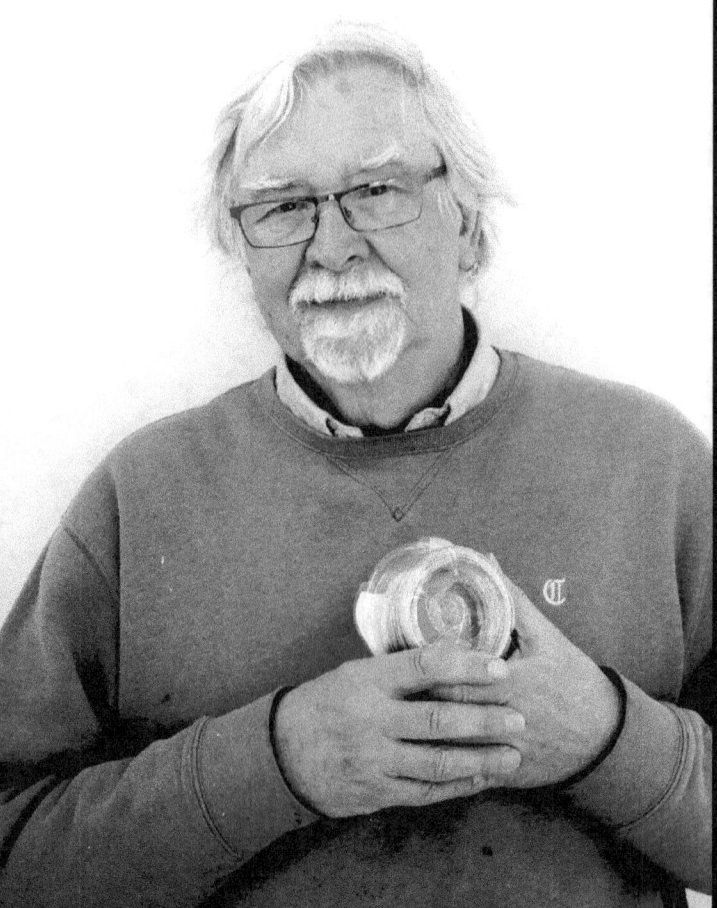

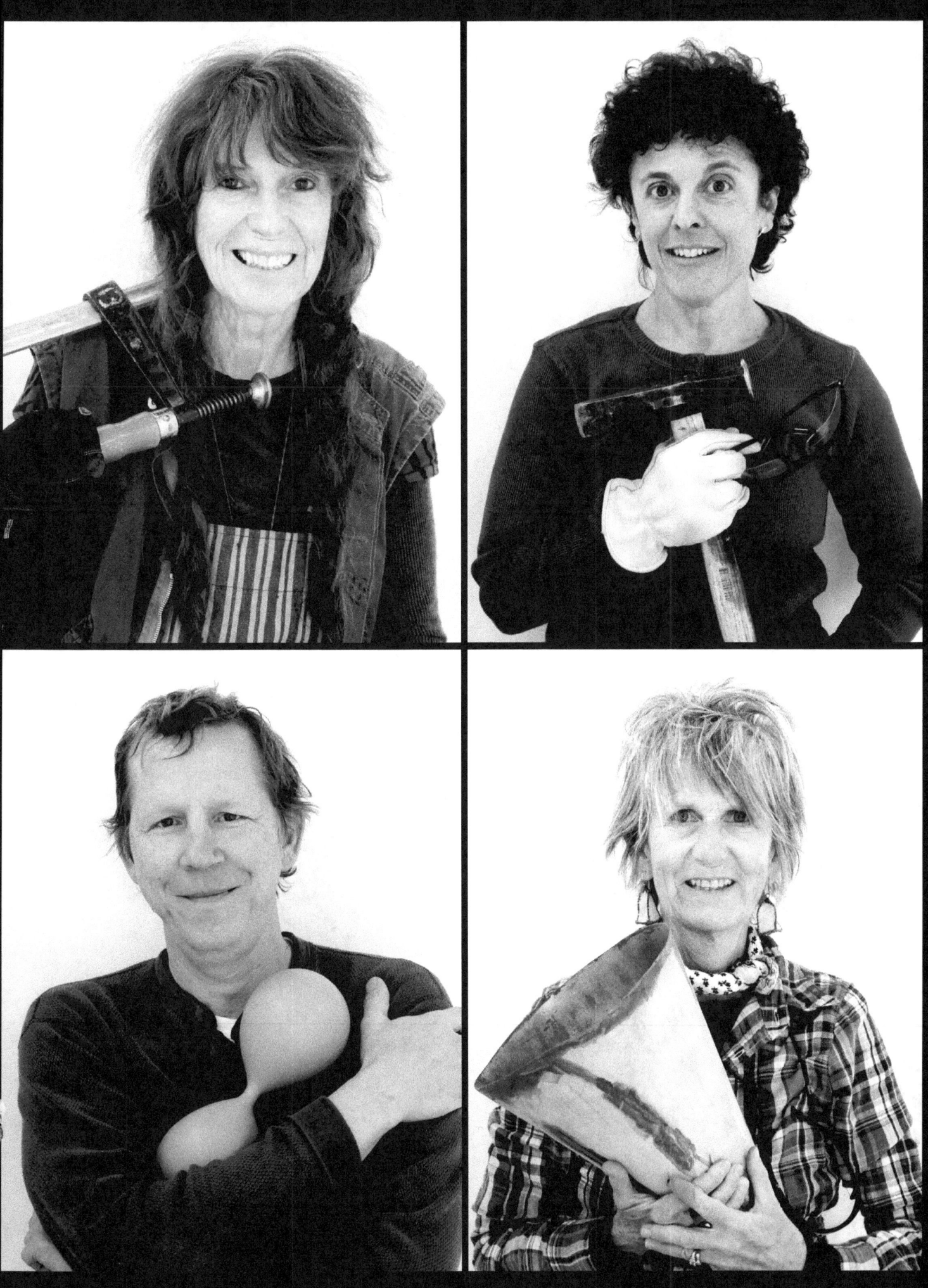

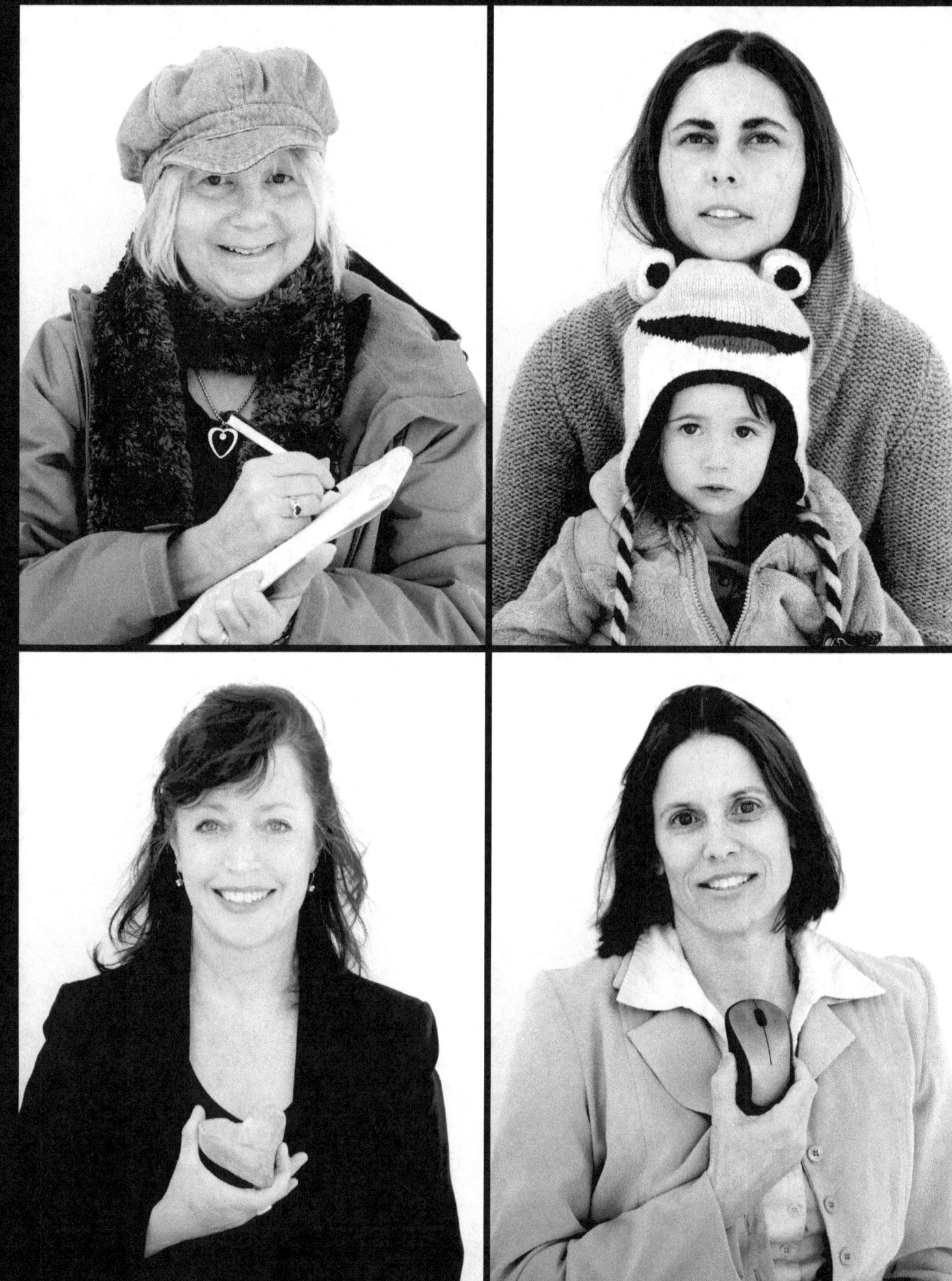

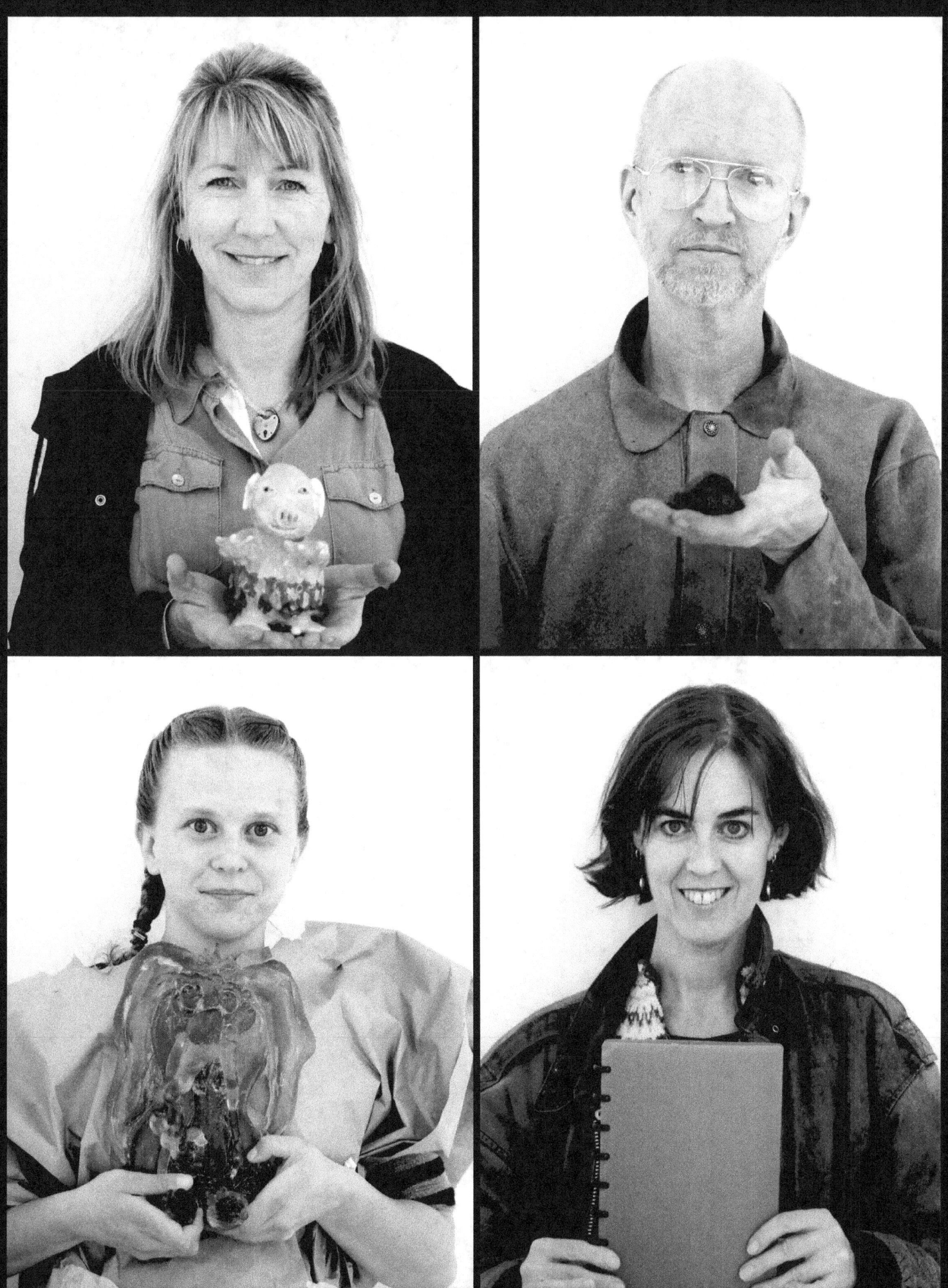

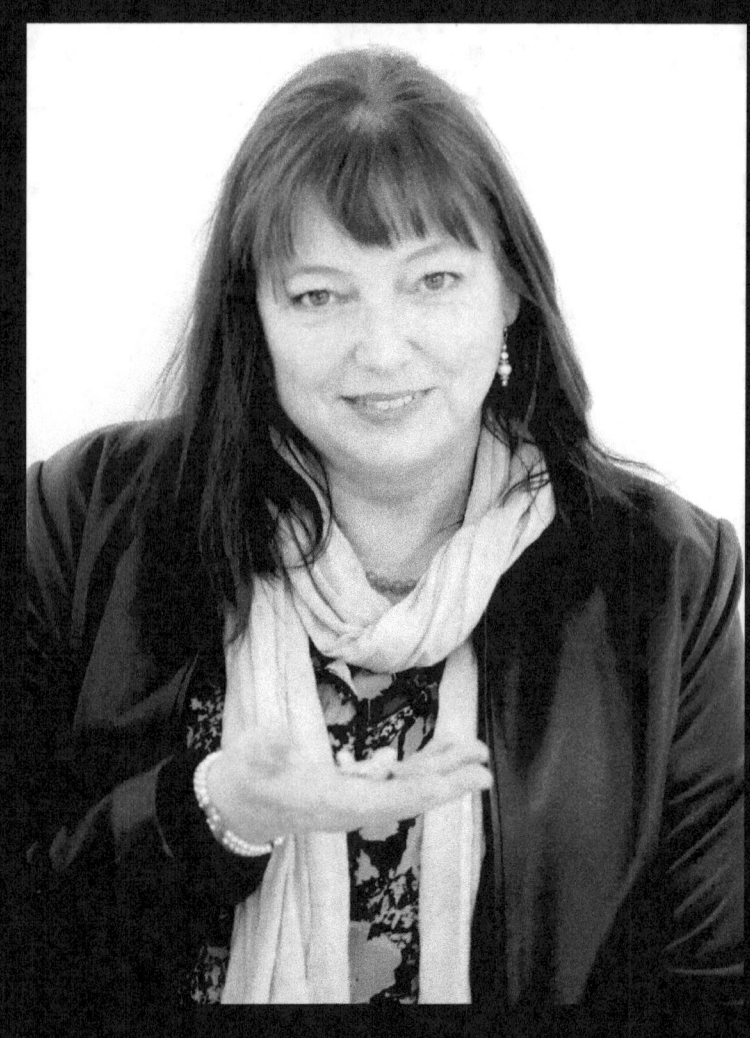

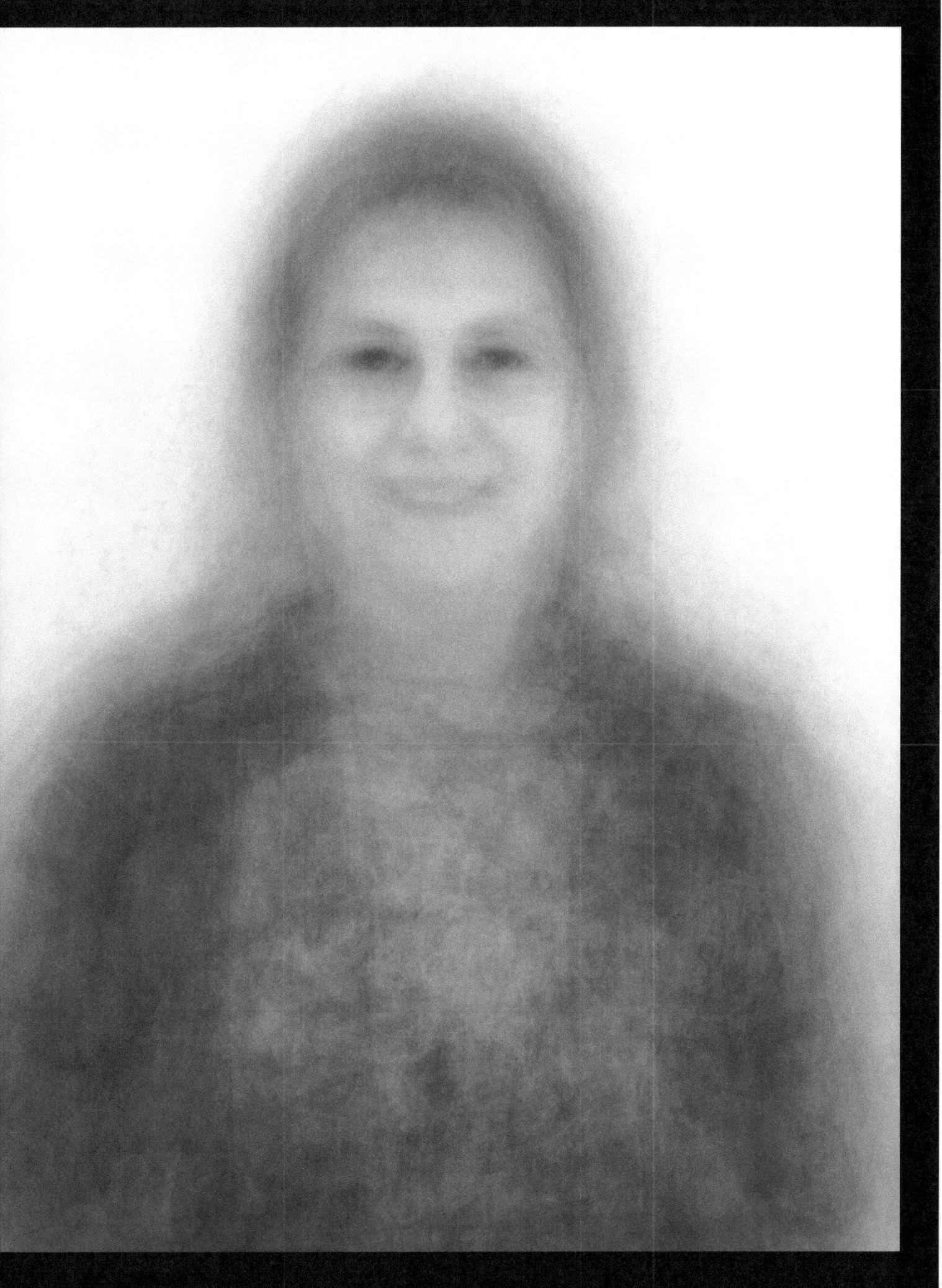

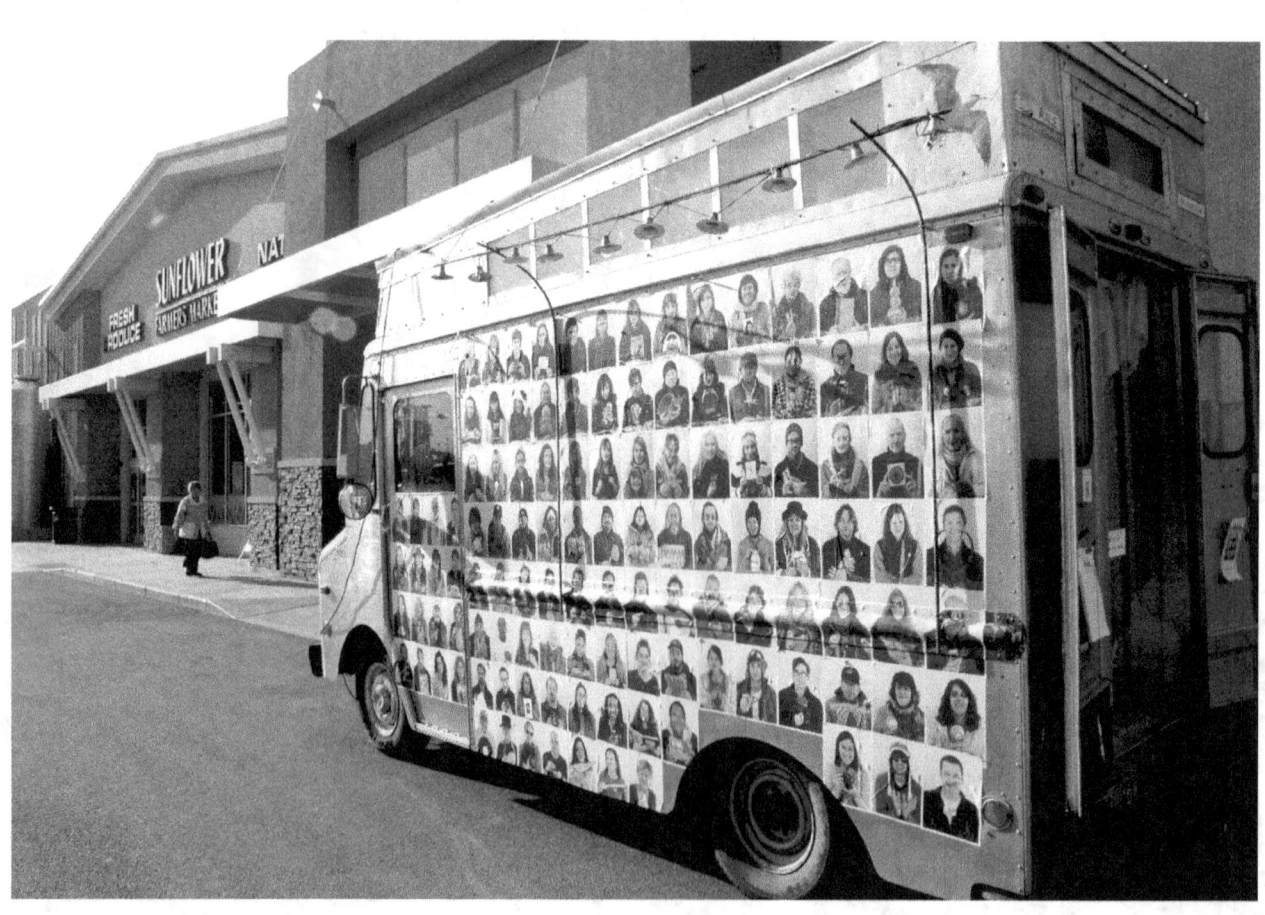

Sunflower Market

3201 Zafarano Drive

Wednesday

March 7

3pm-6pm

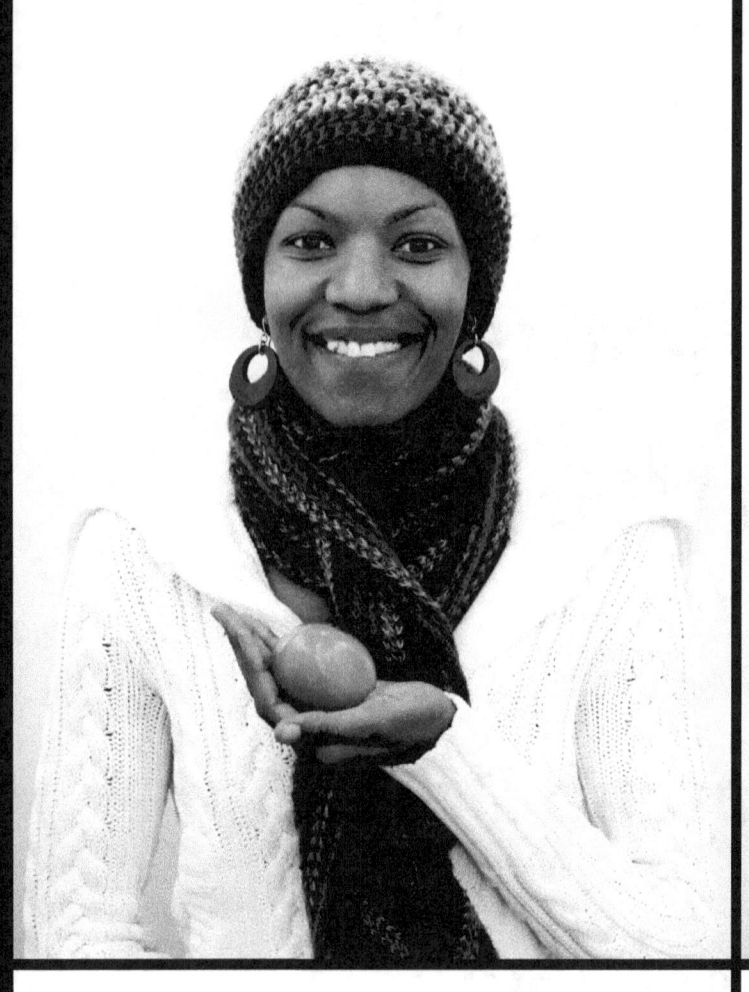
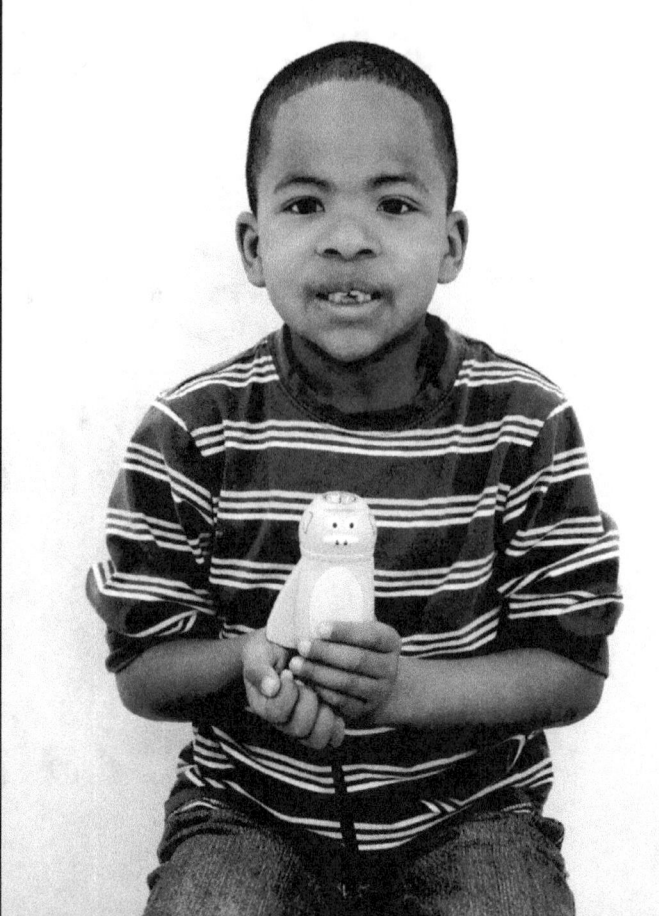
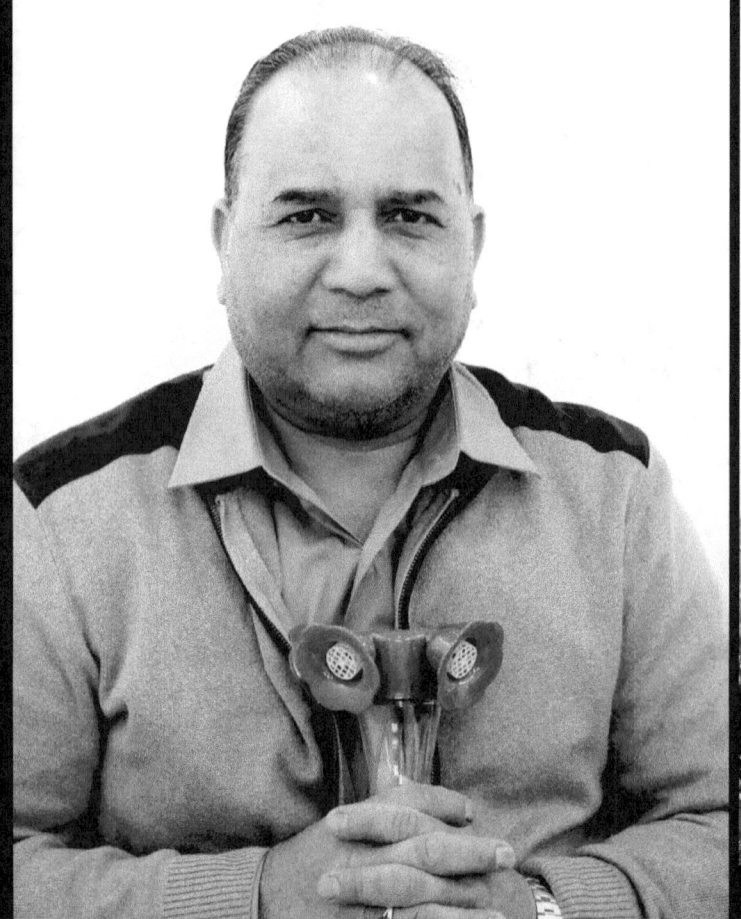
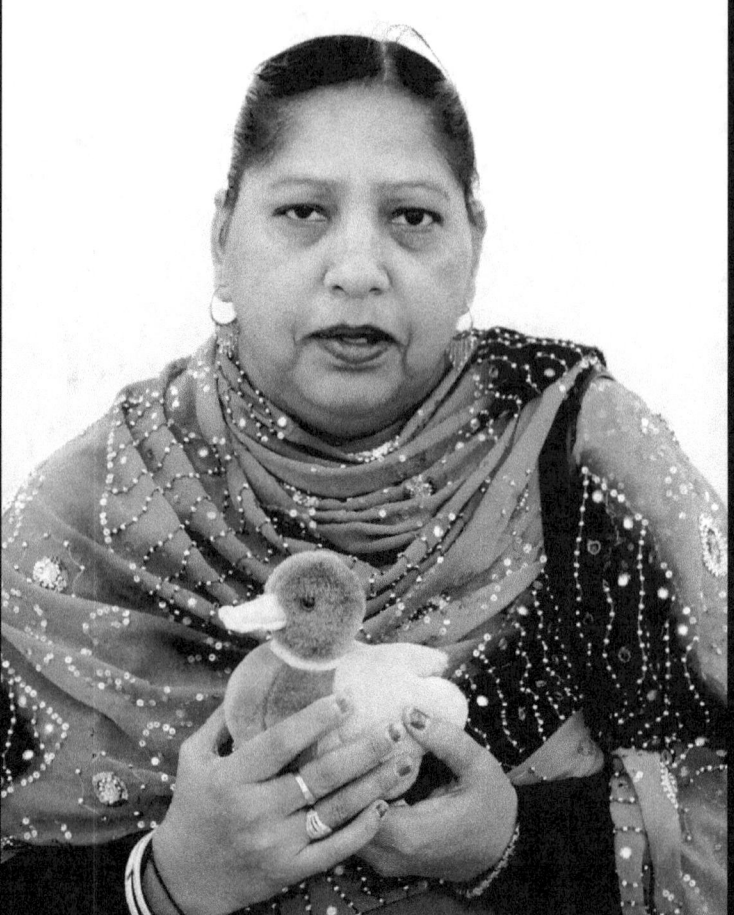

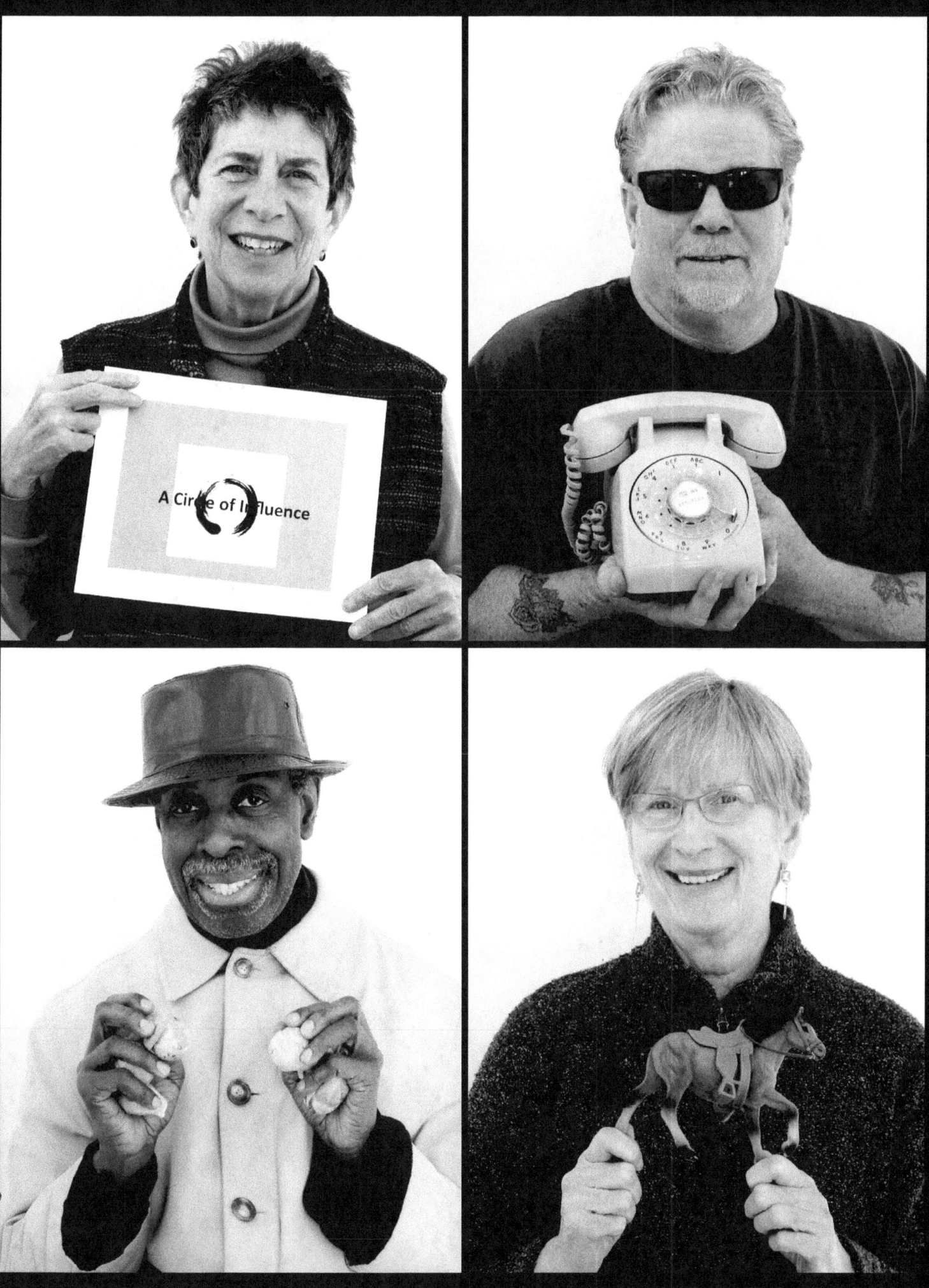

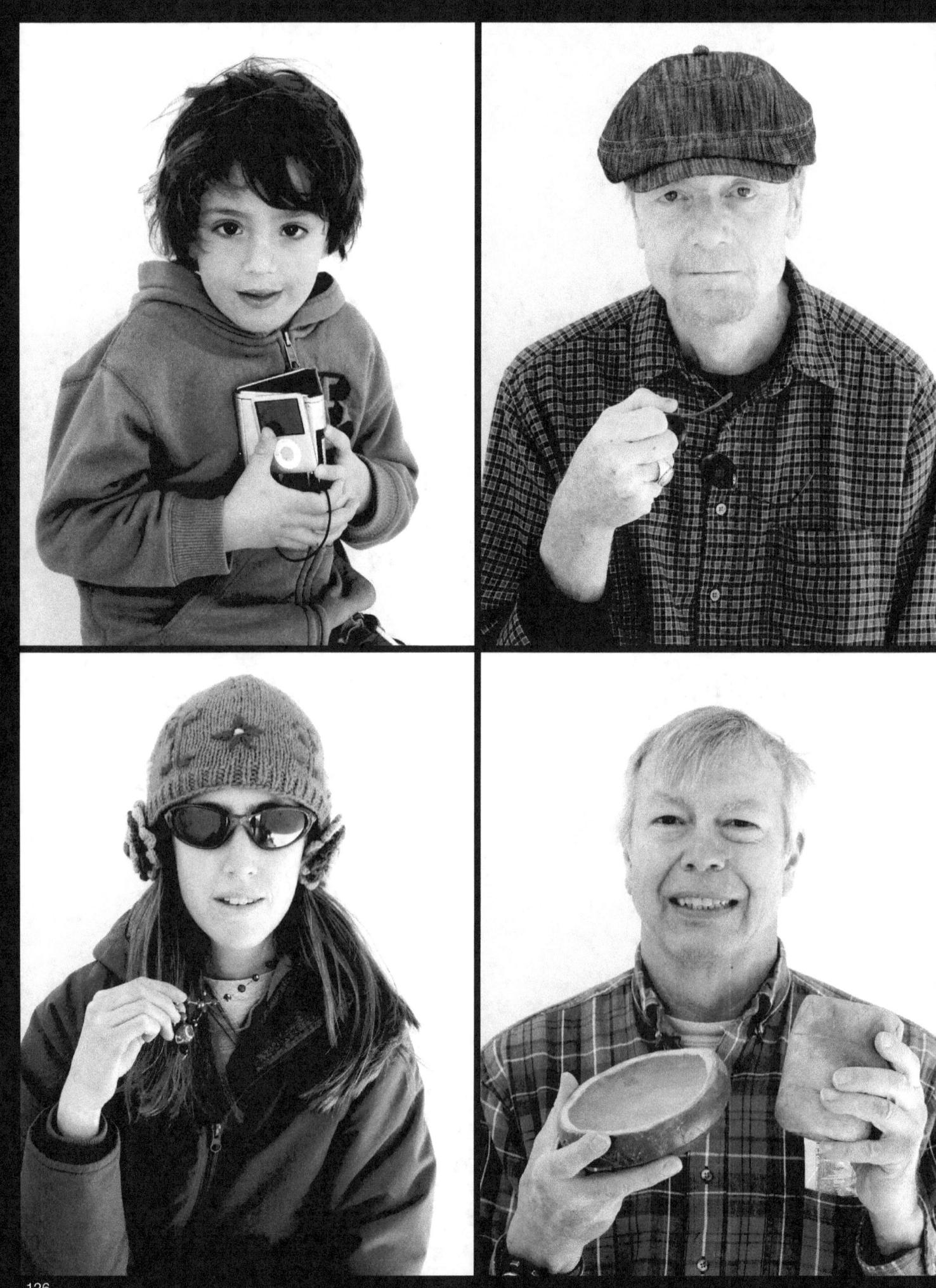

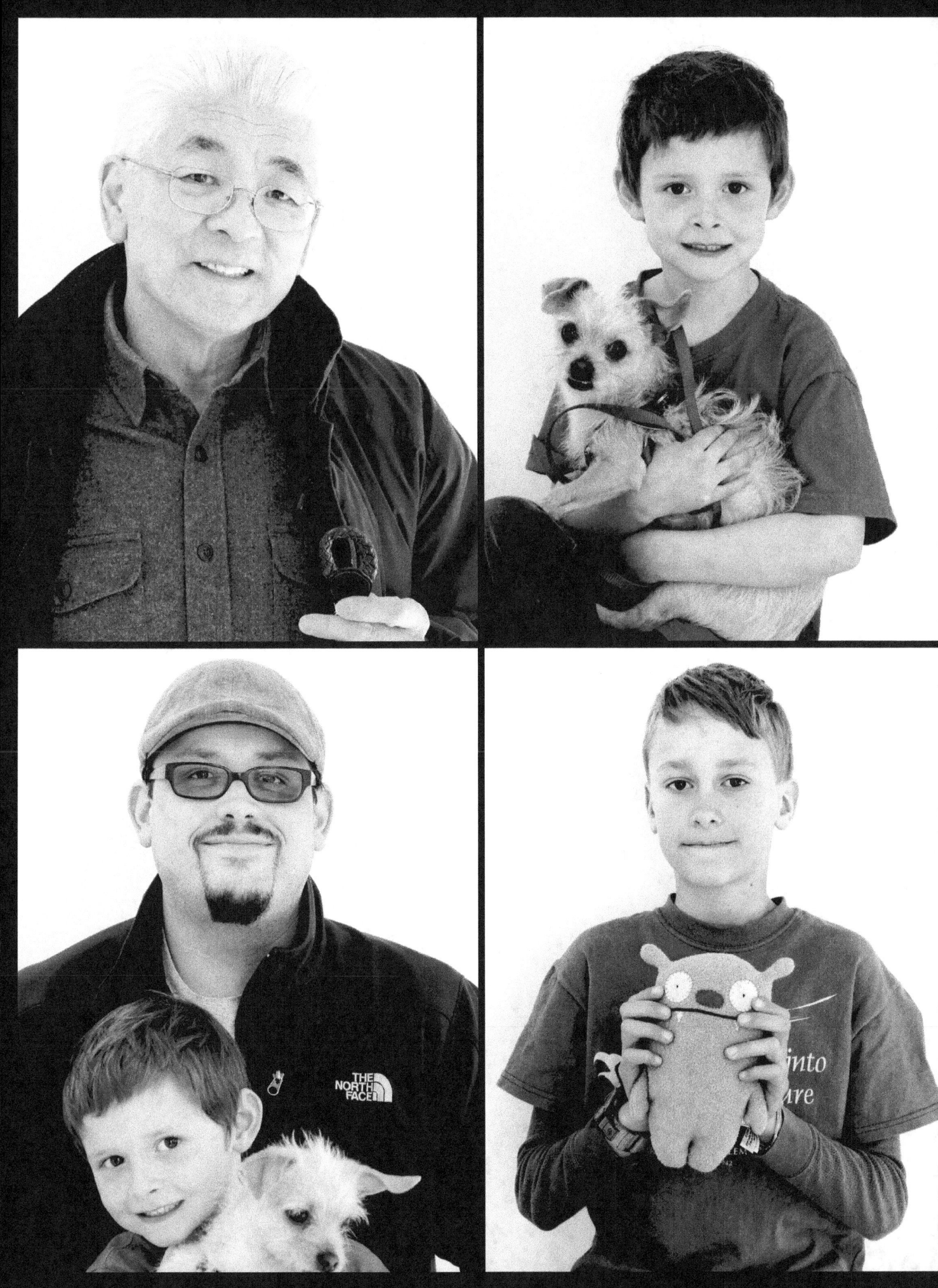

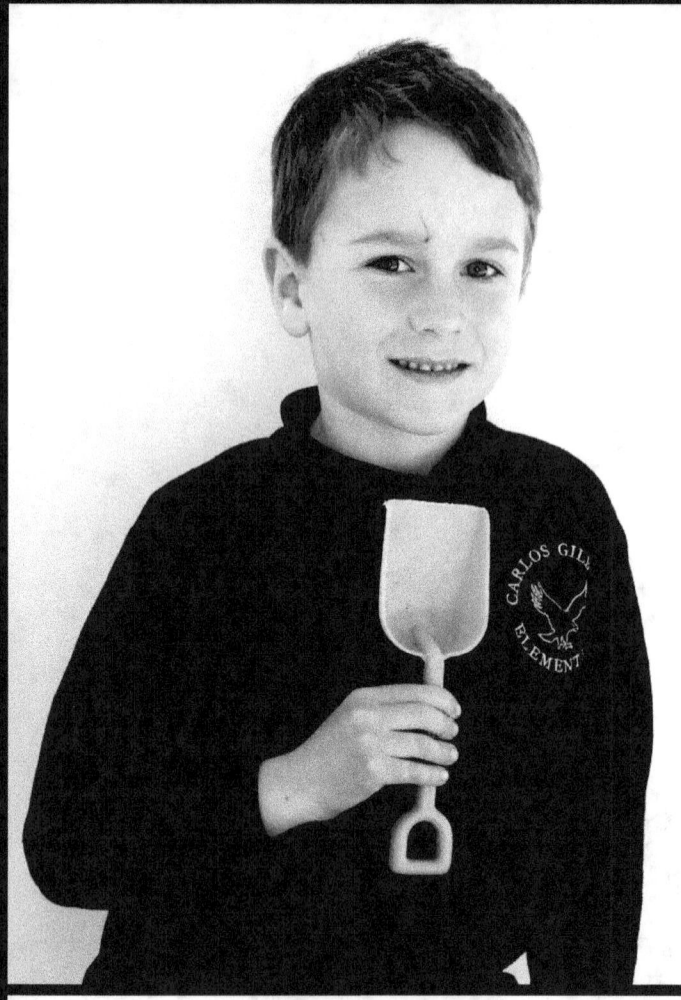
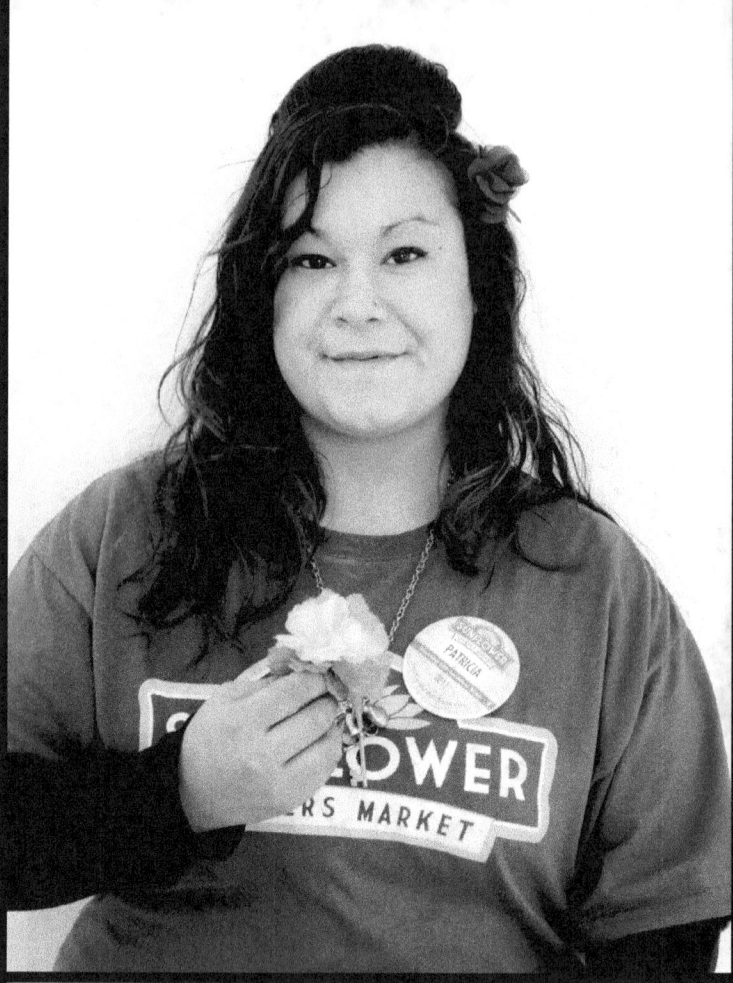
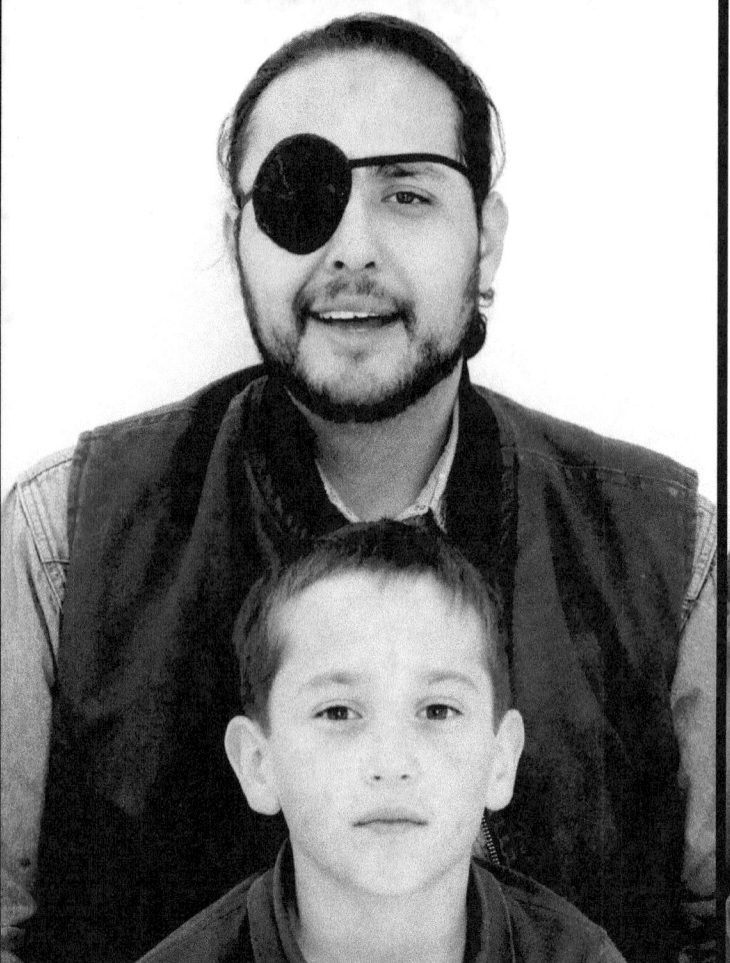
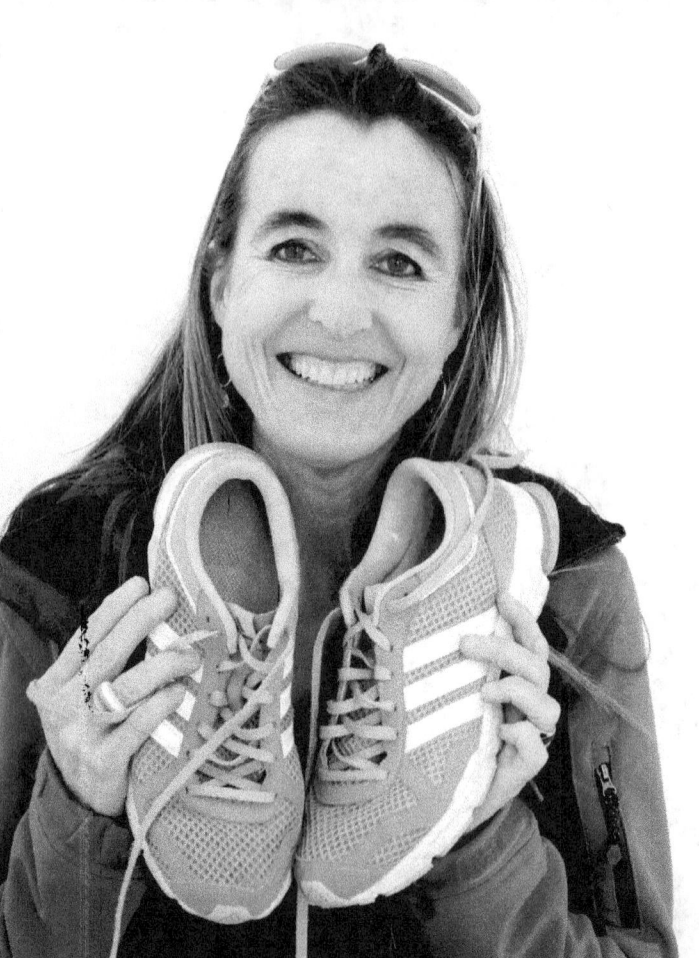

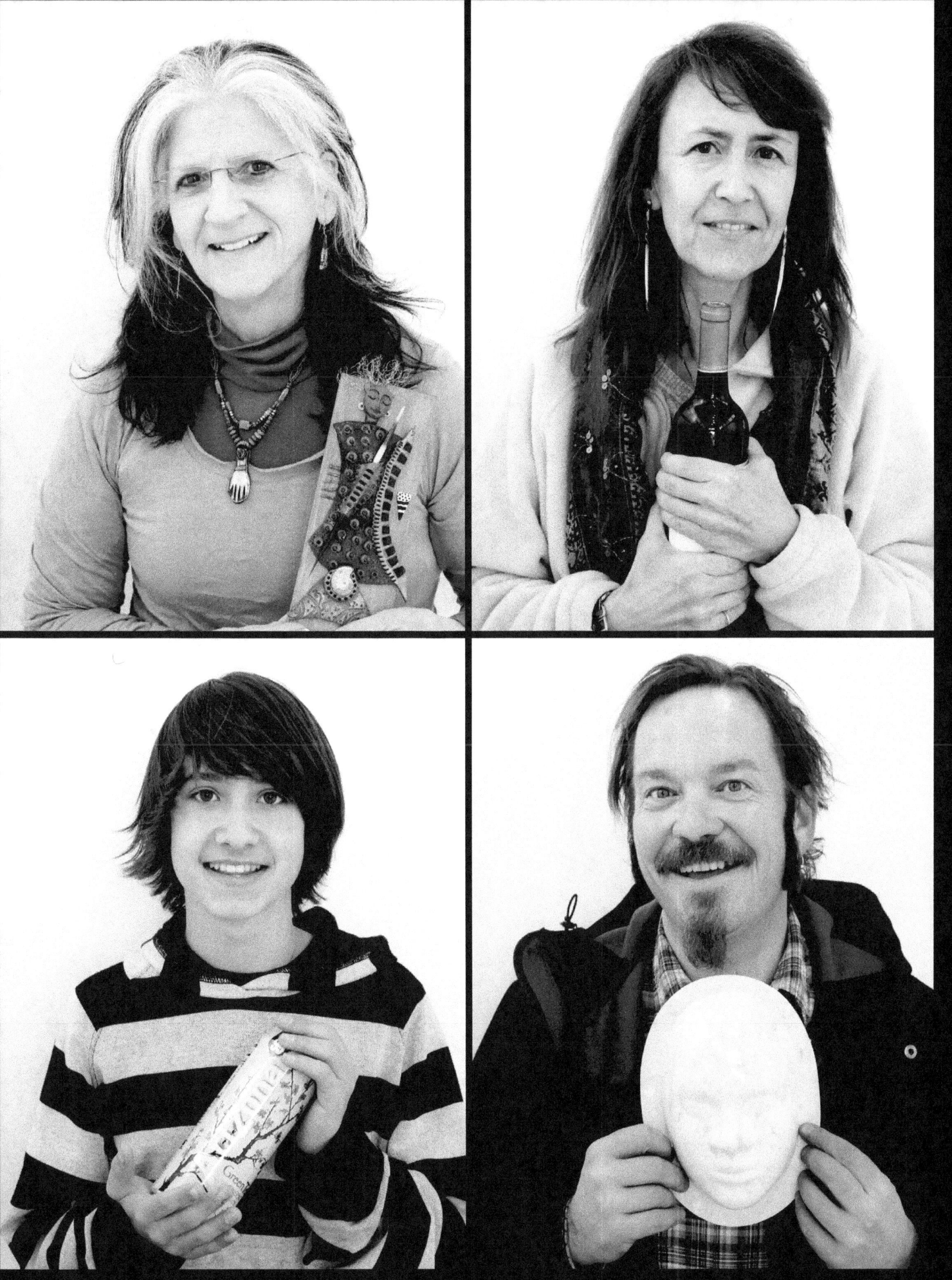

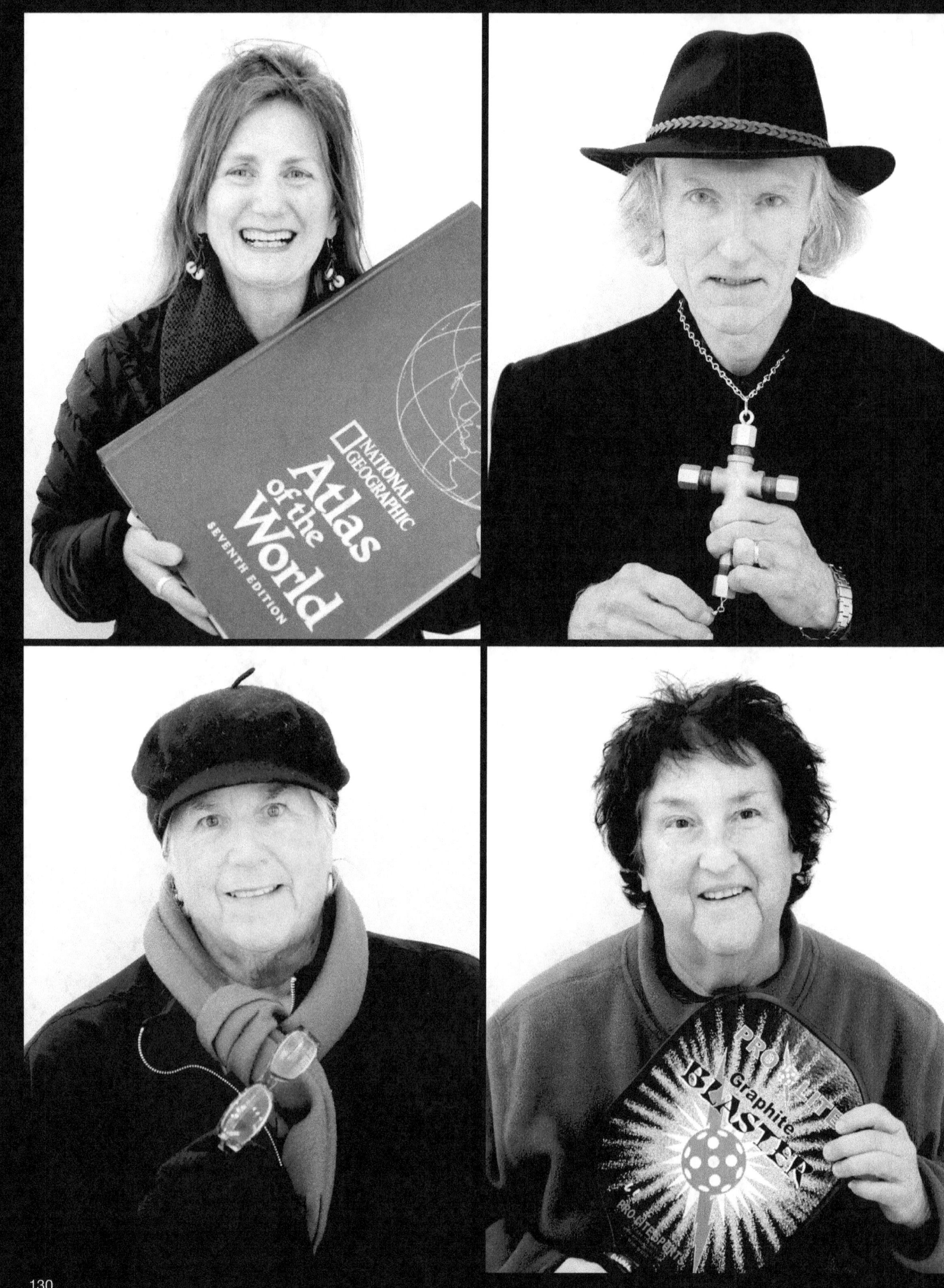

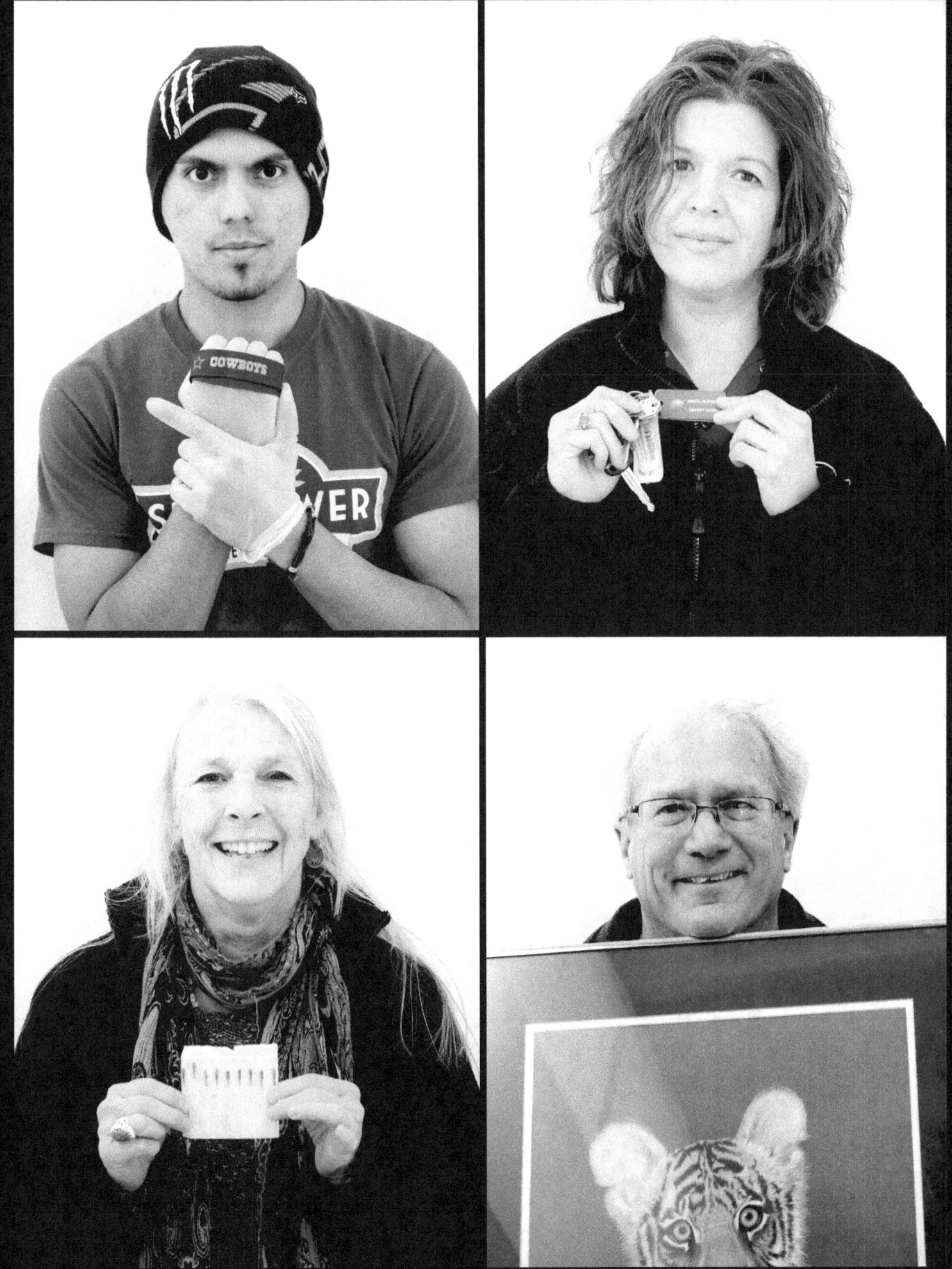

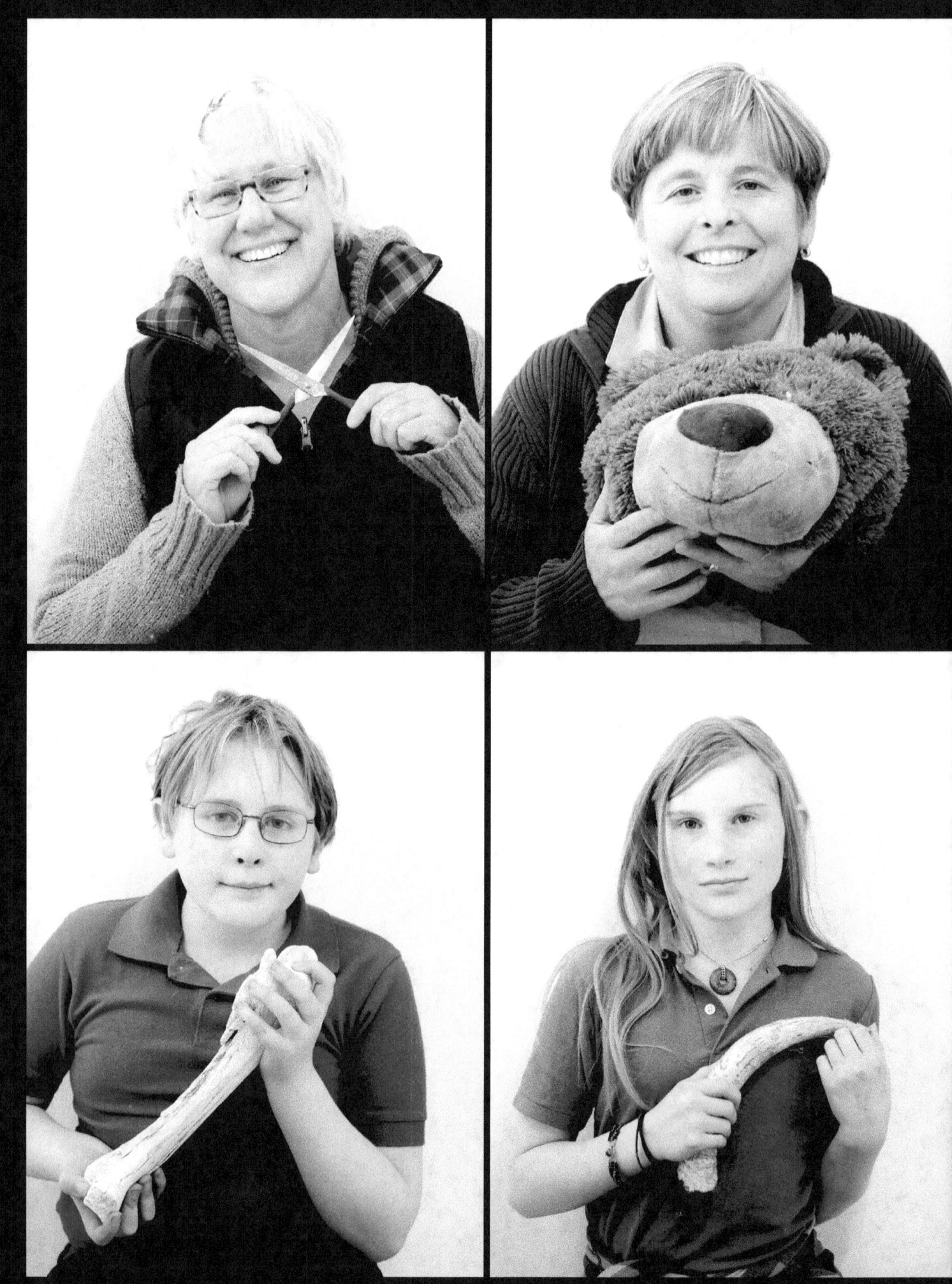

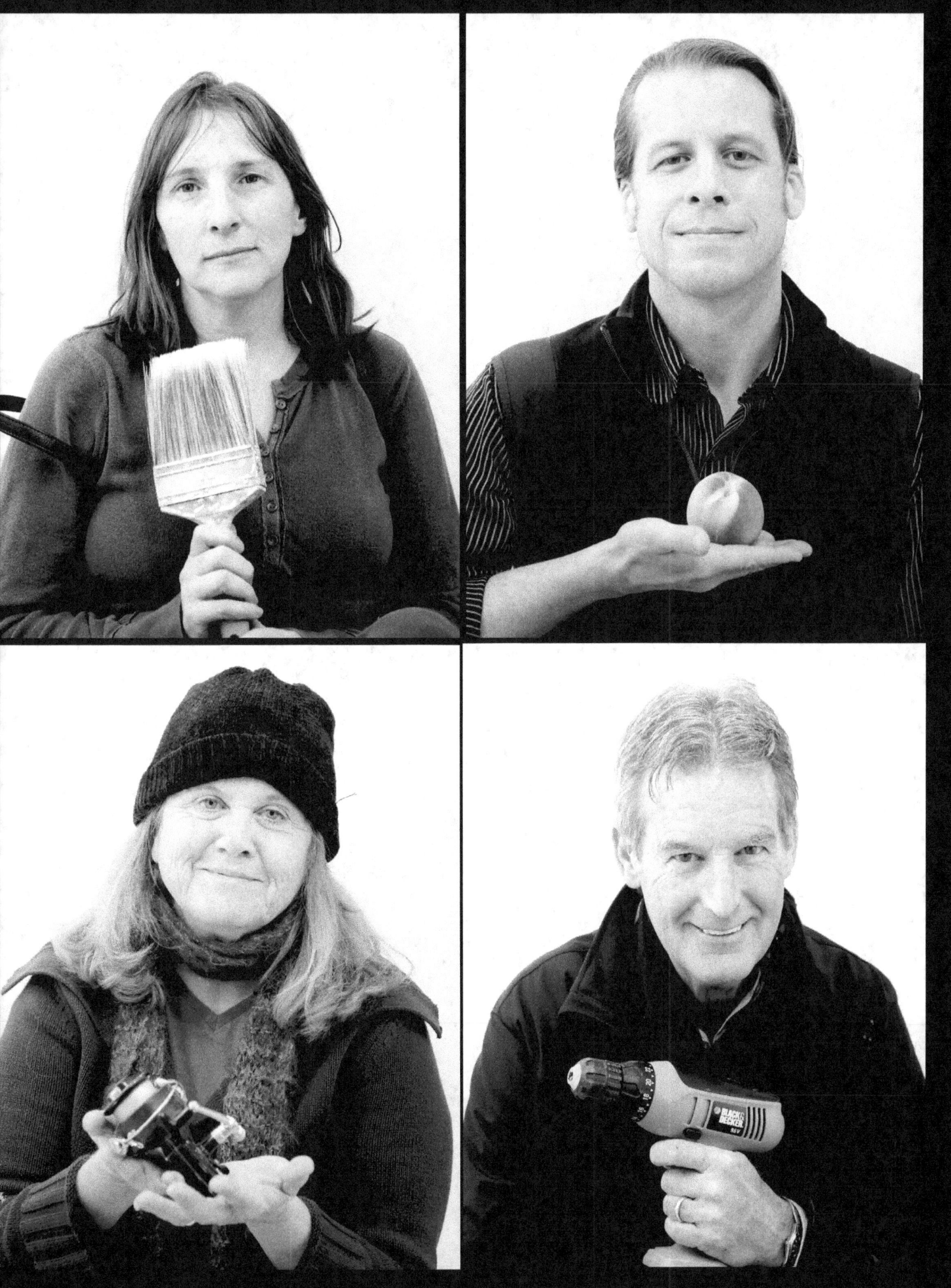

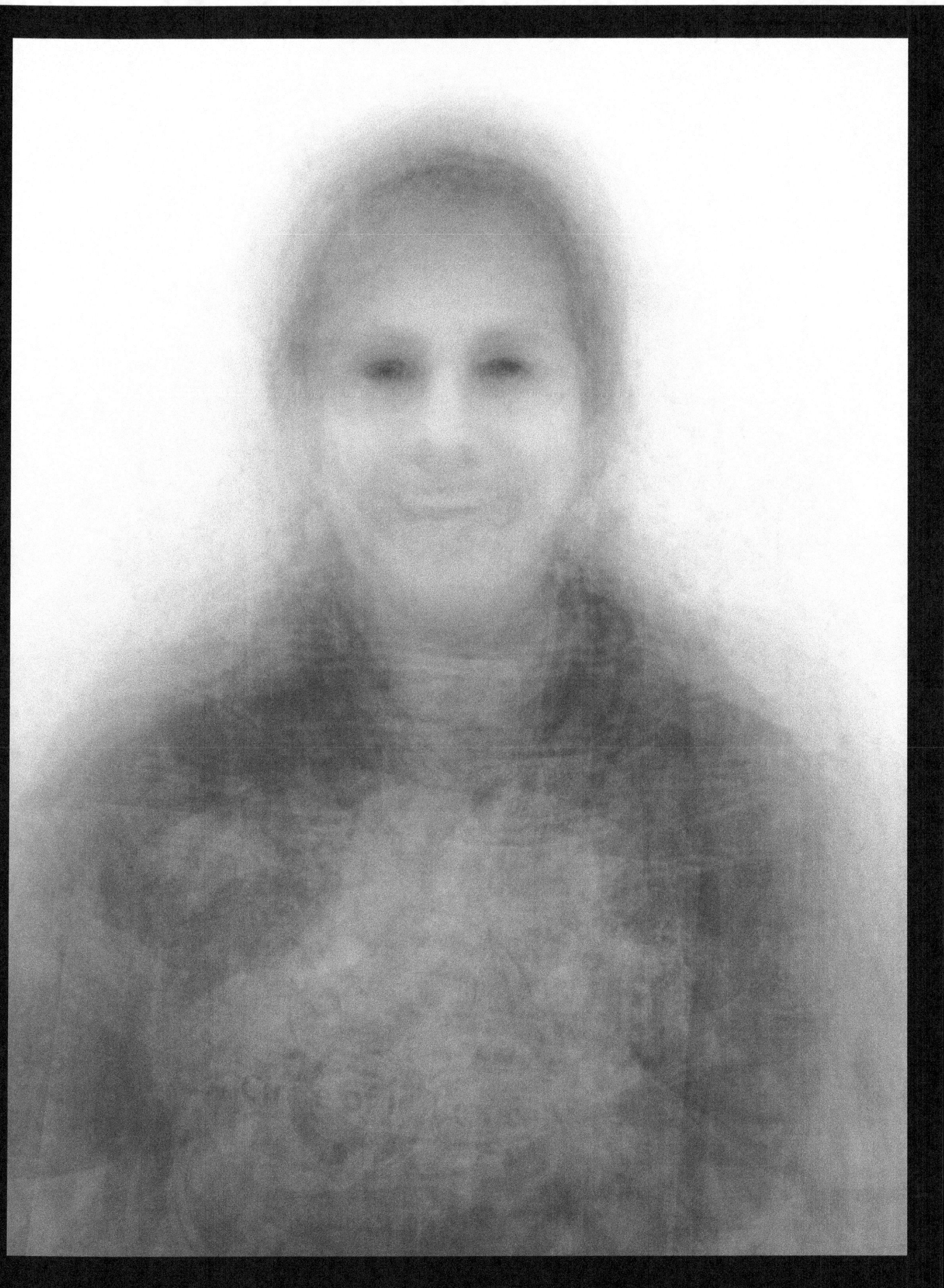

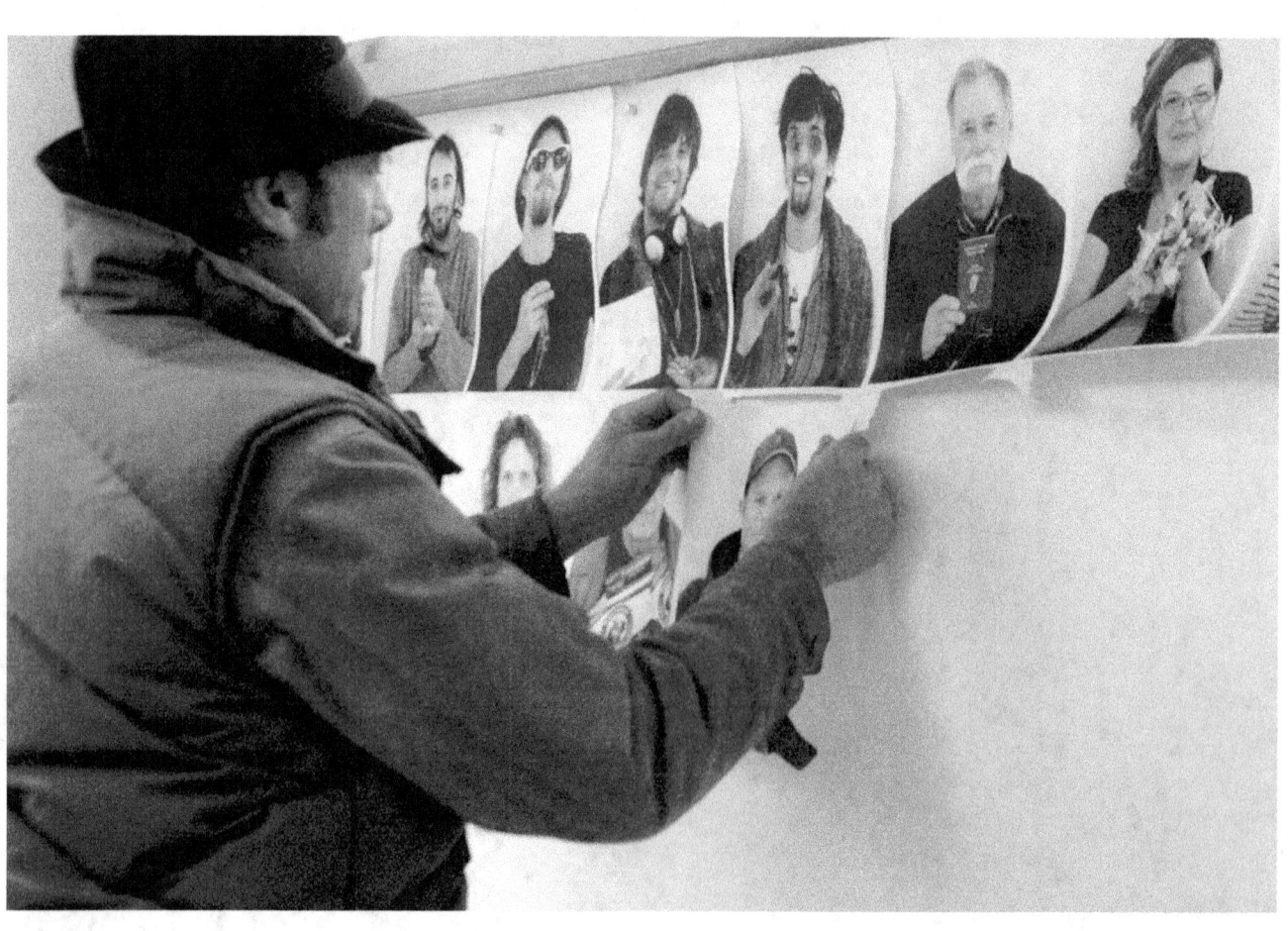

Counter Culture

930 Baca Street

Thursday

March 8

9am-2pm

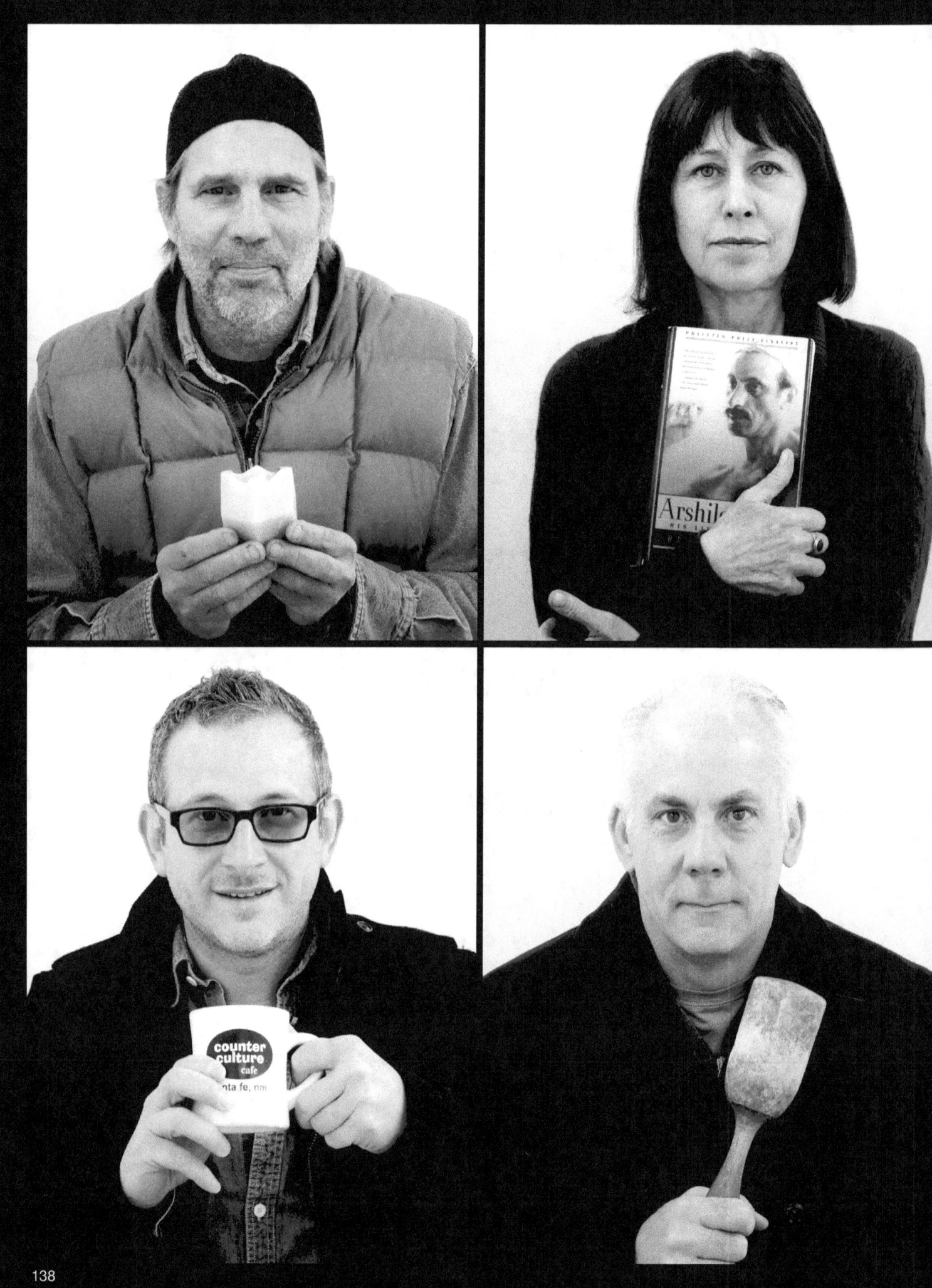

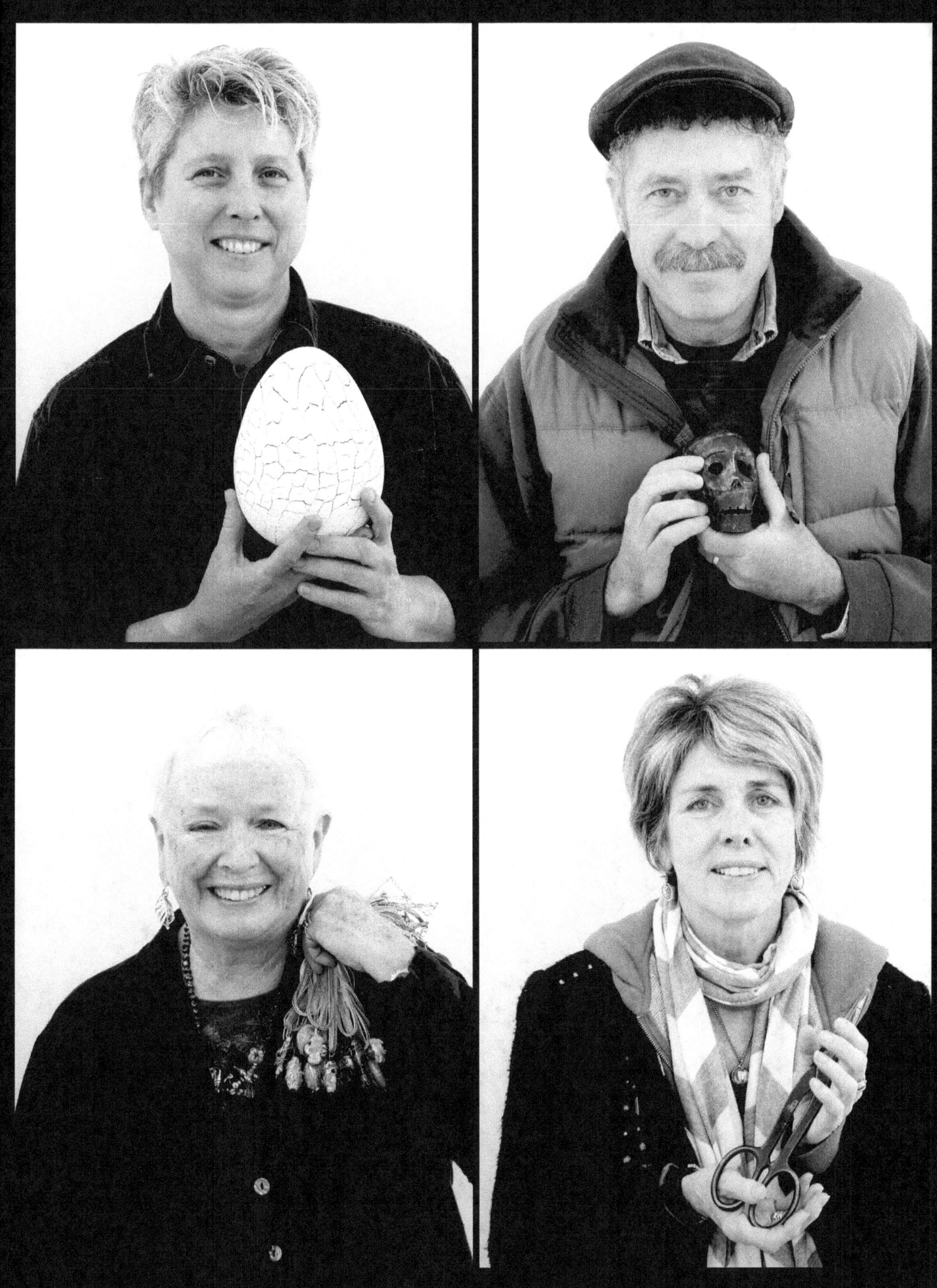

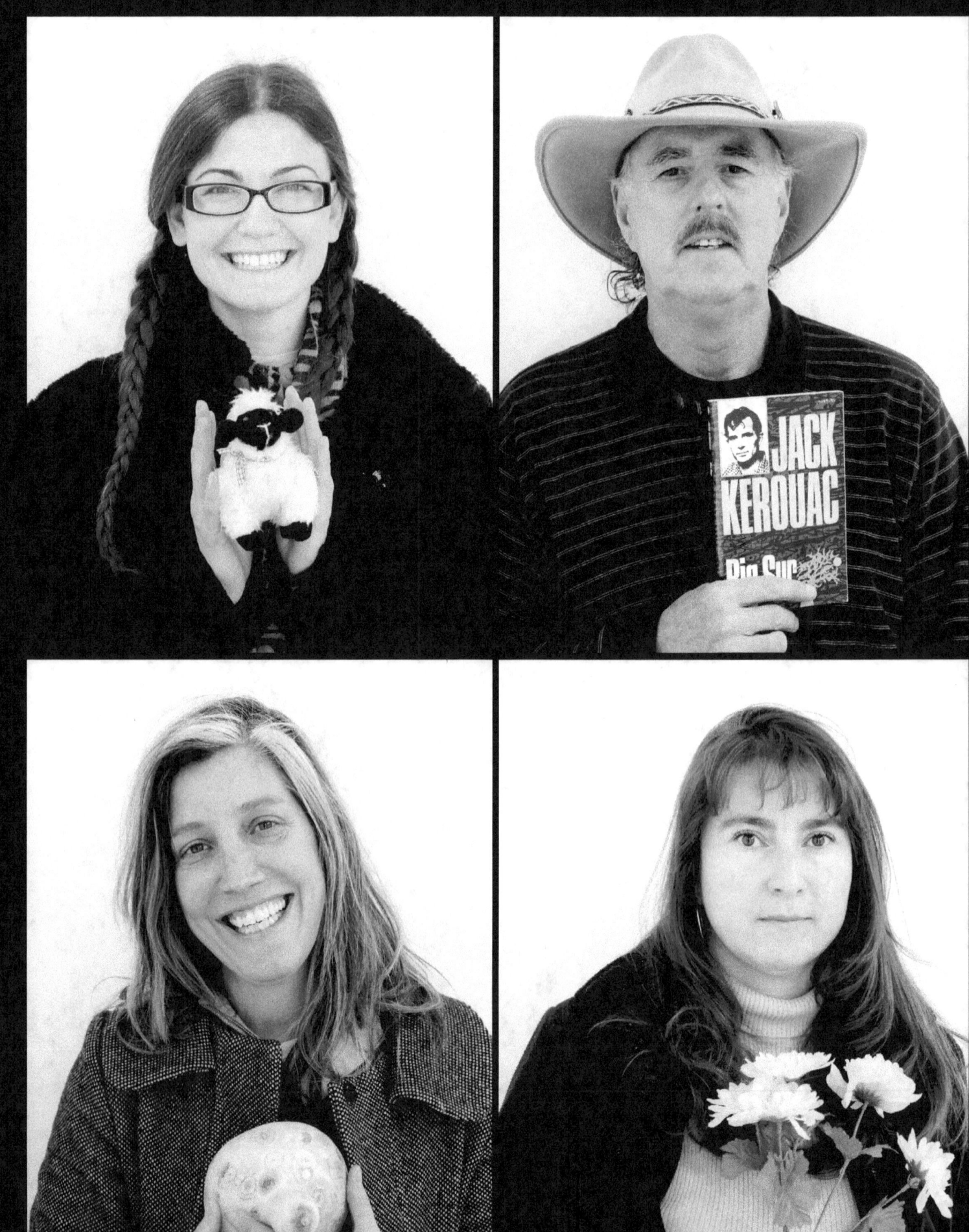

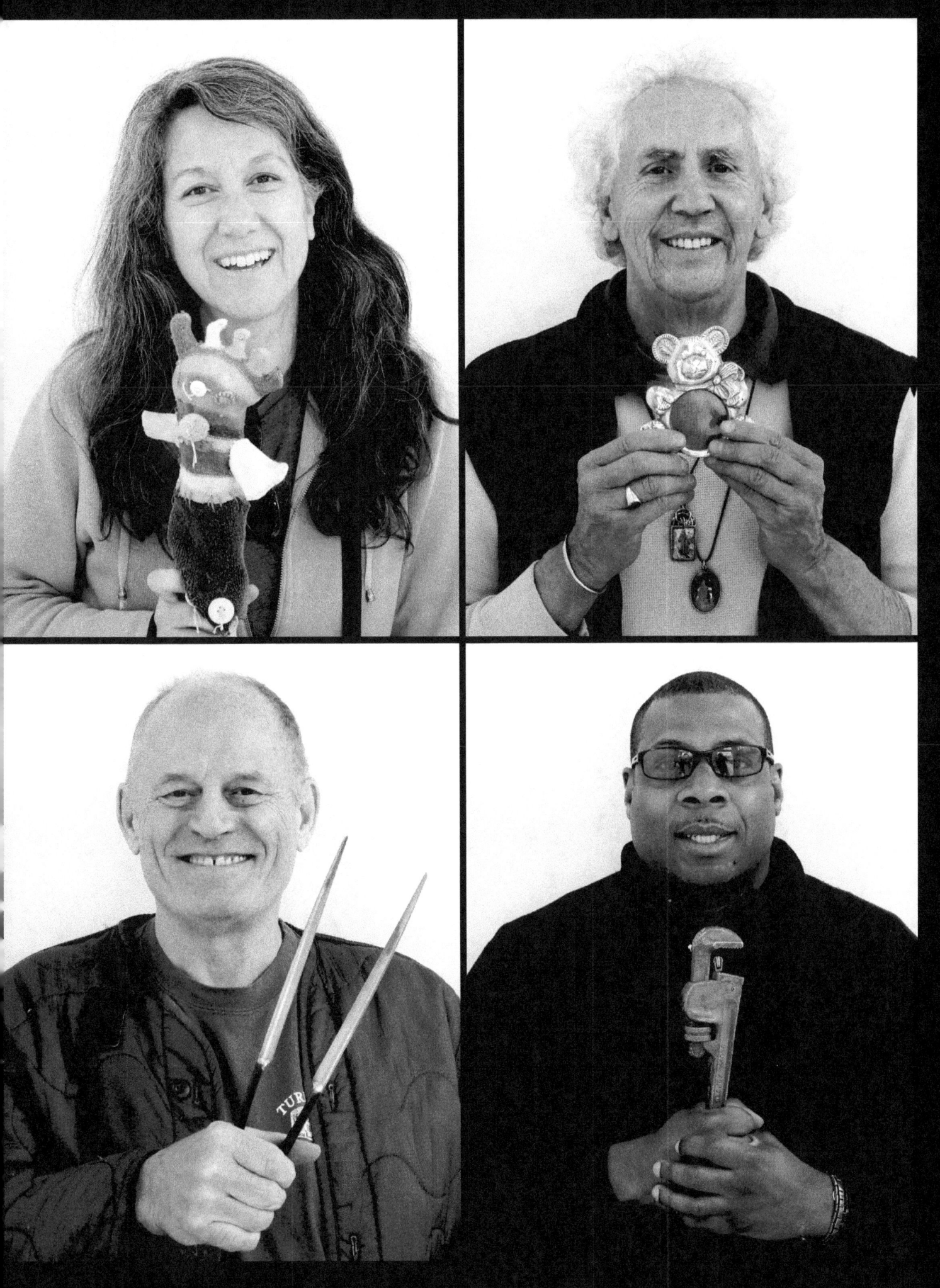

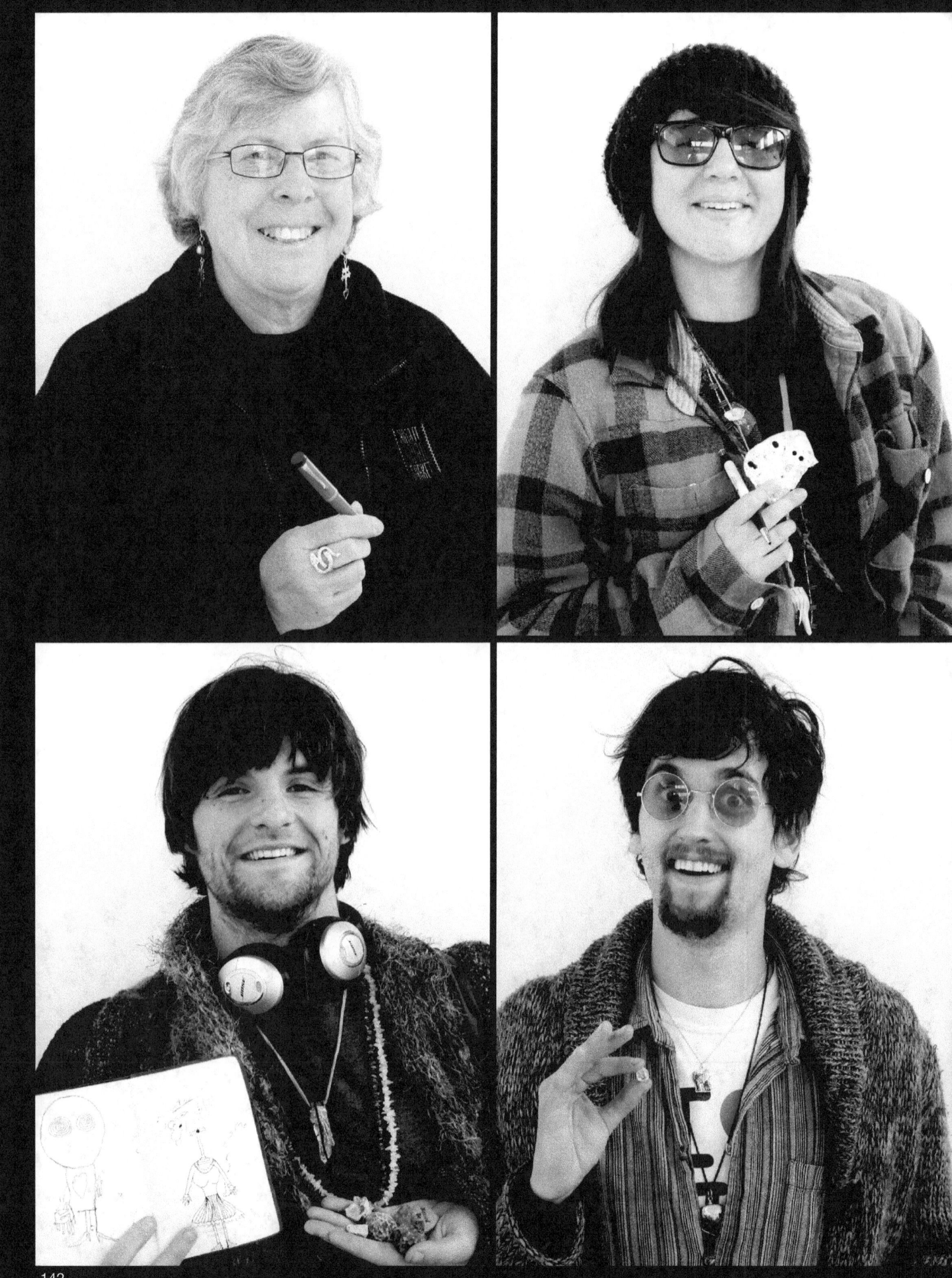

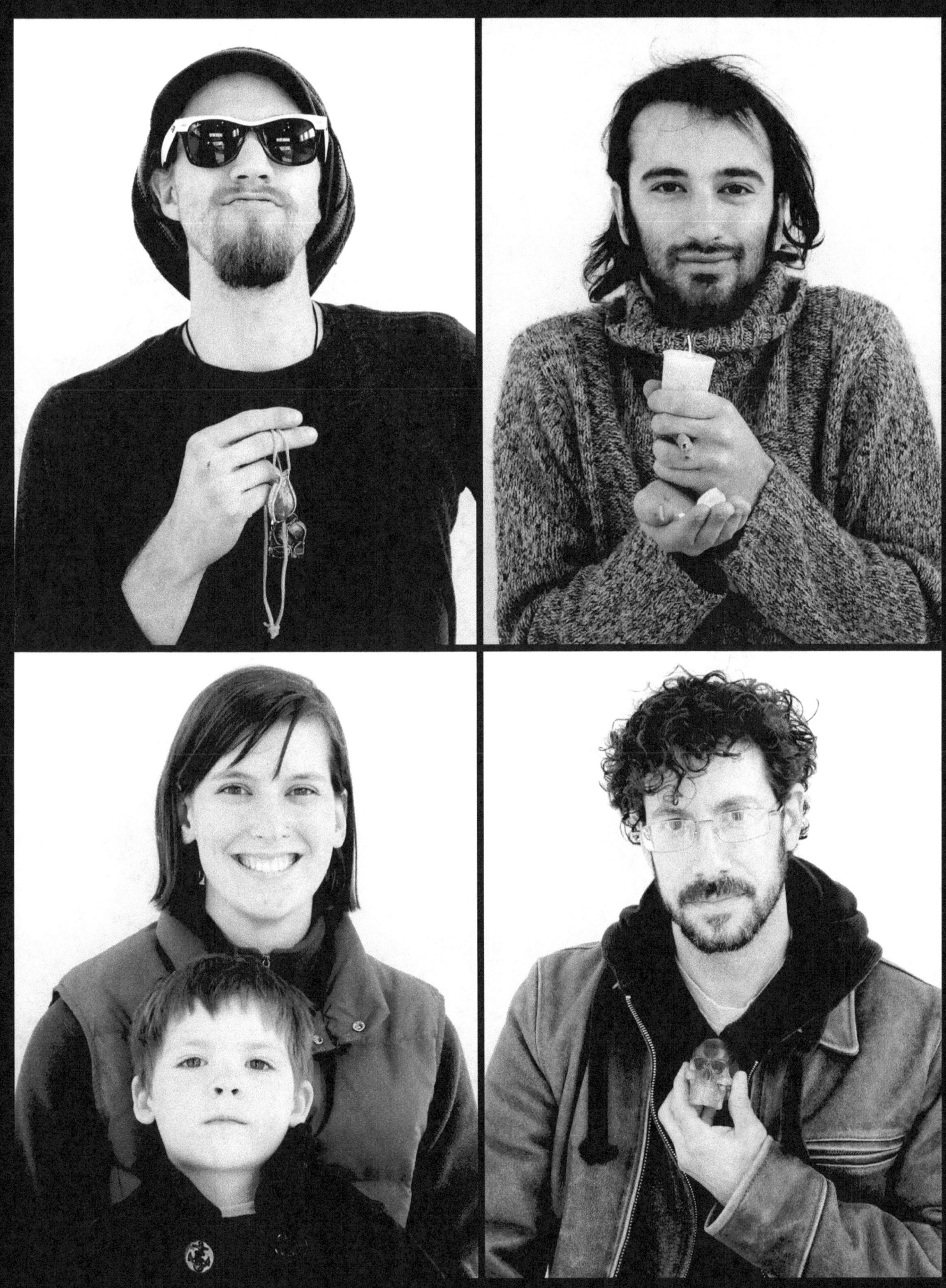

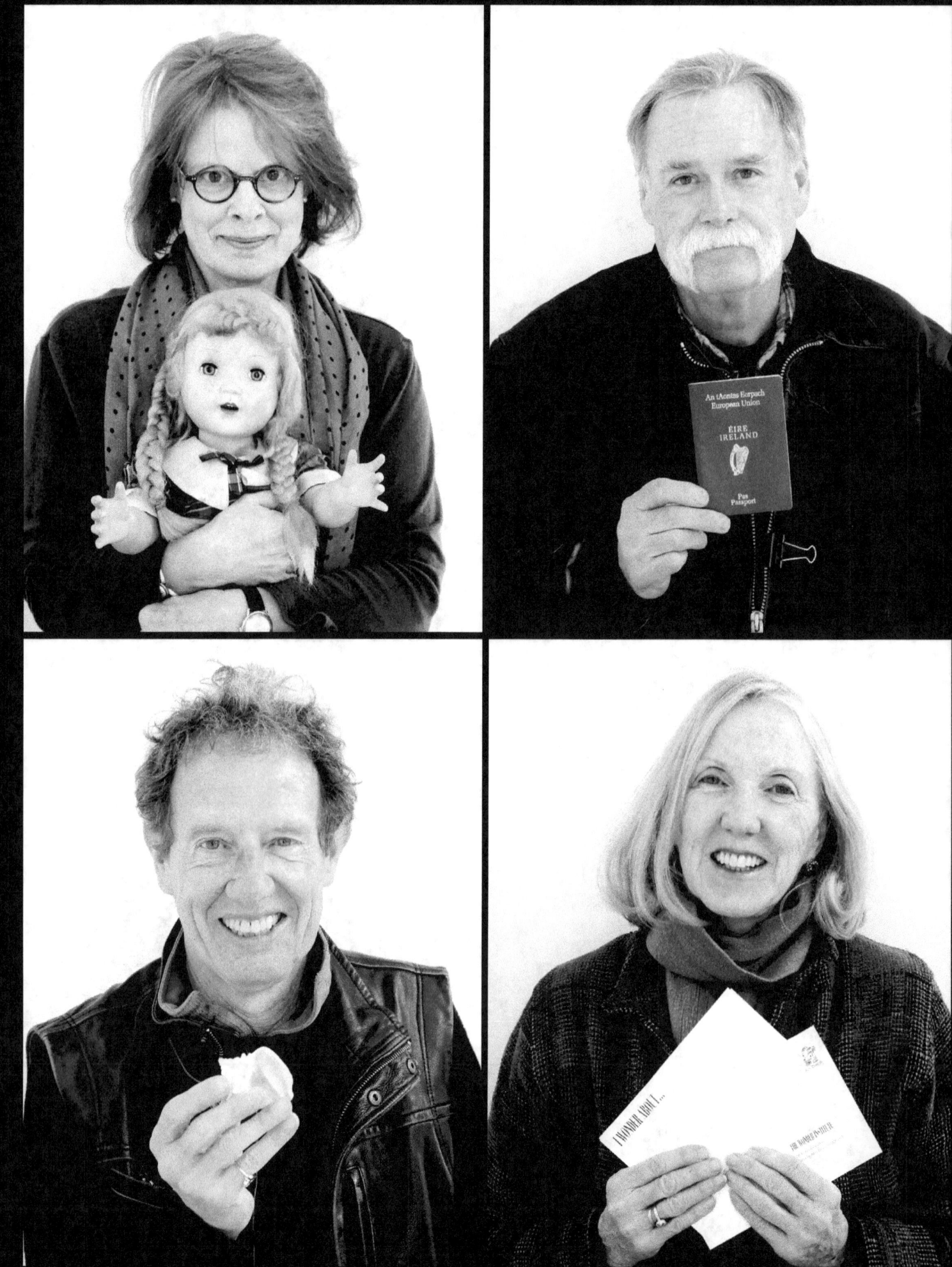

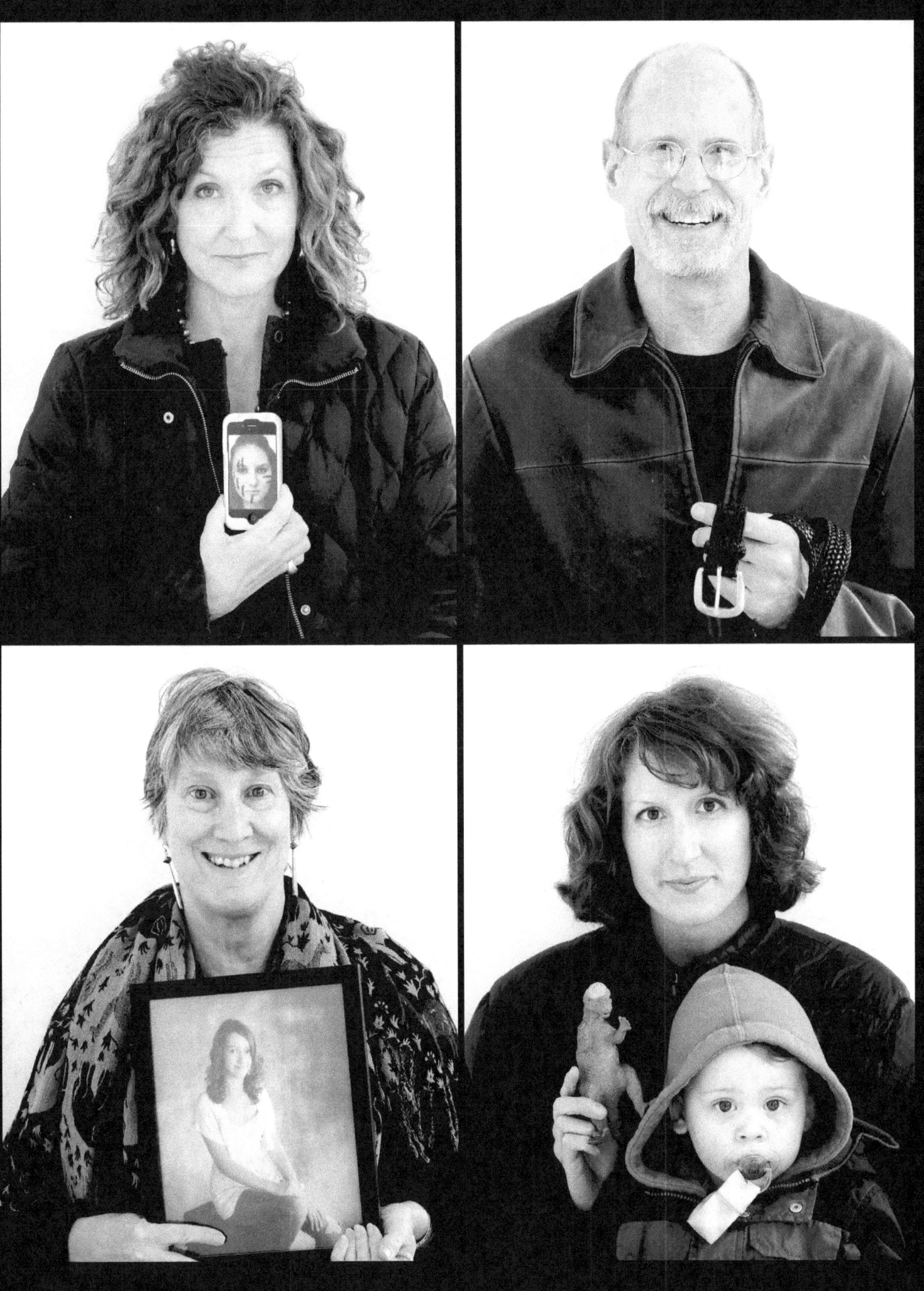

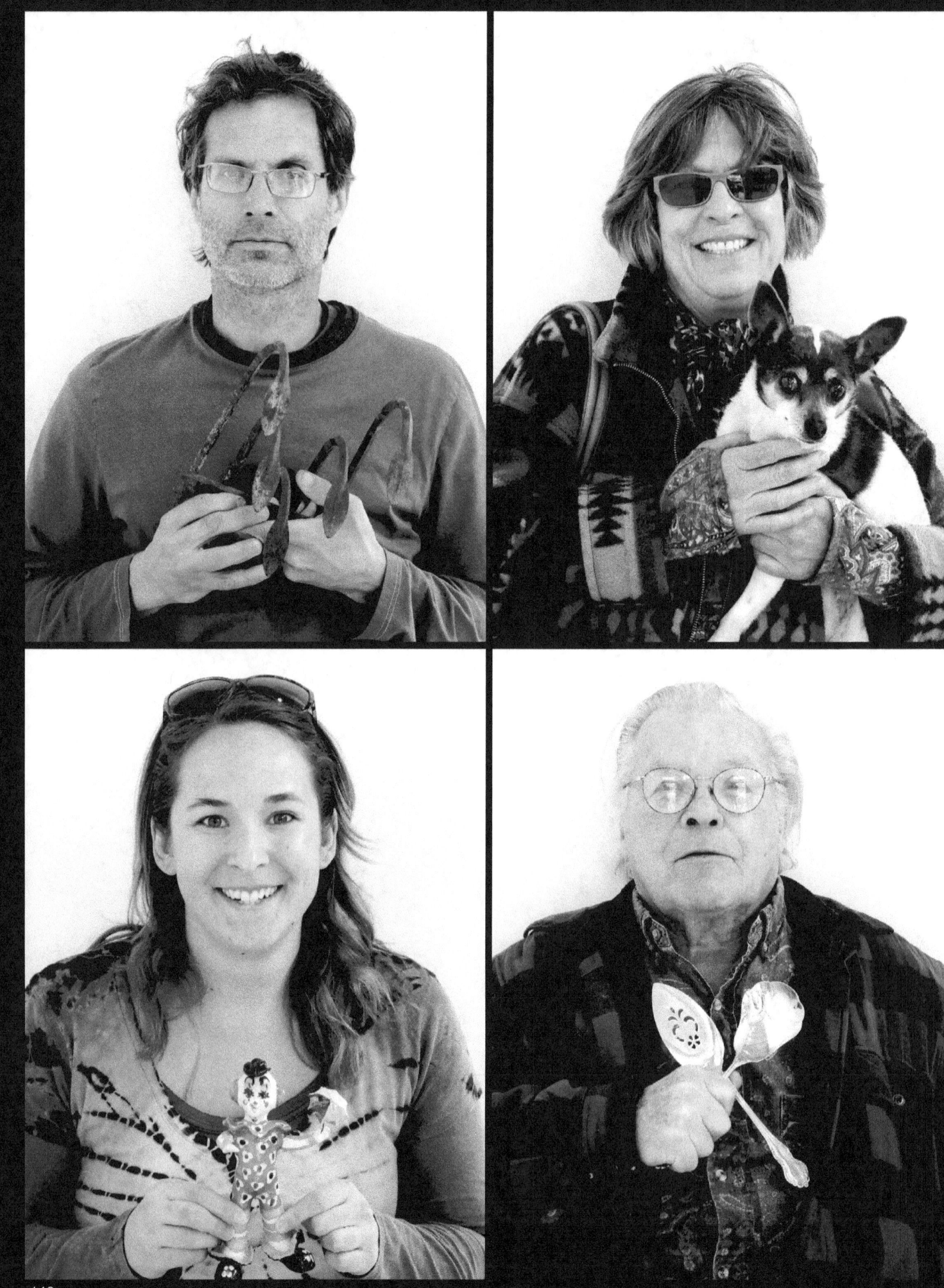

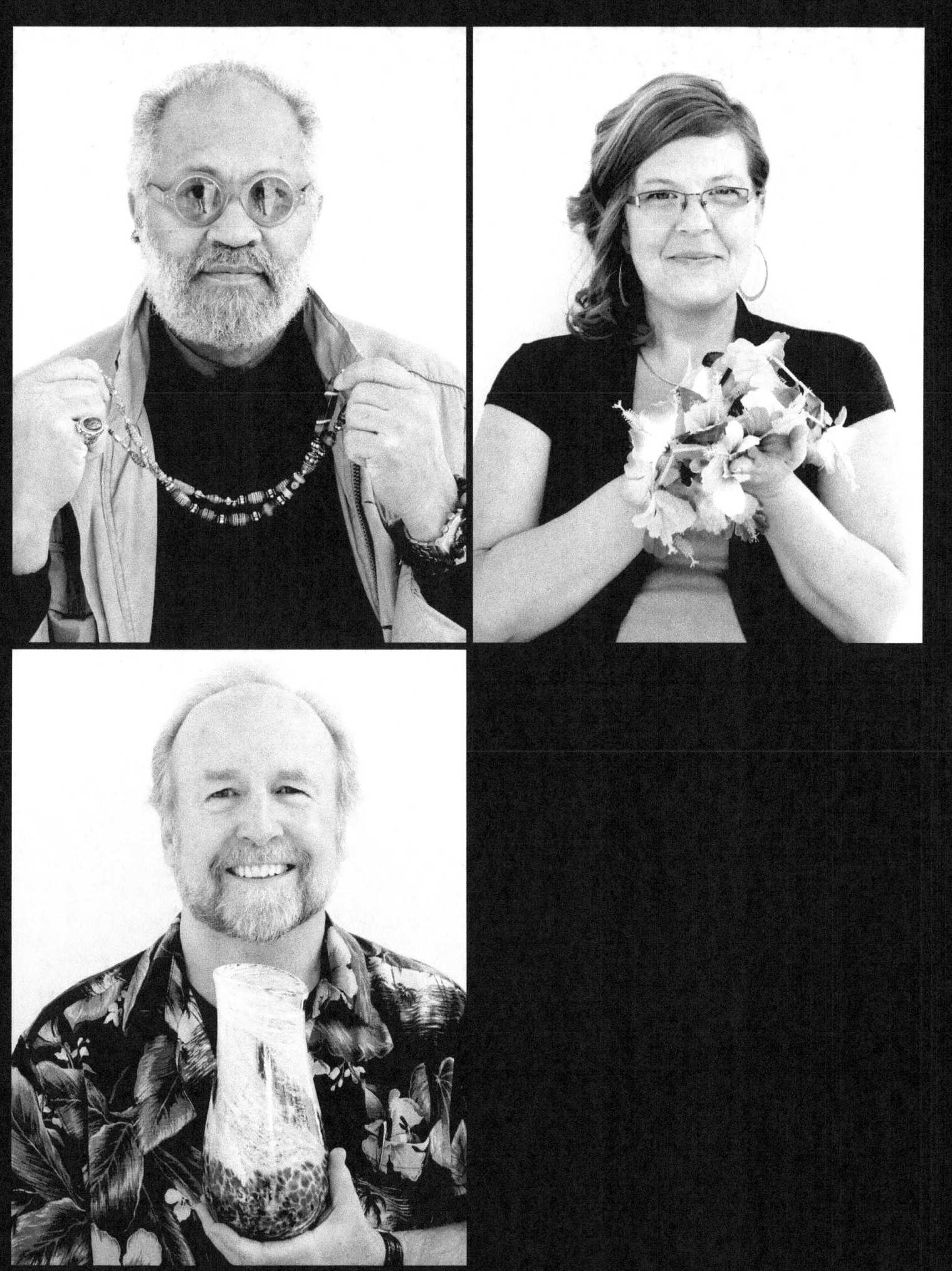

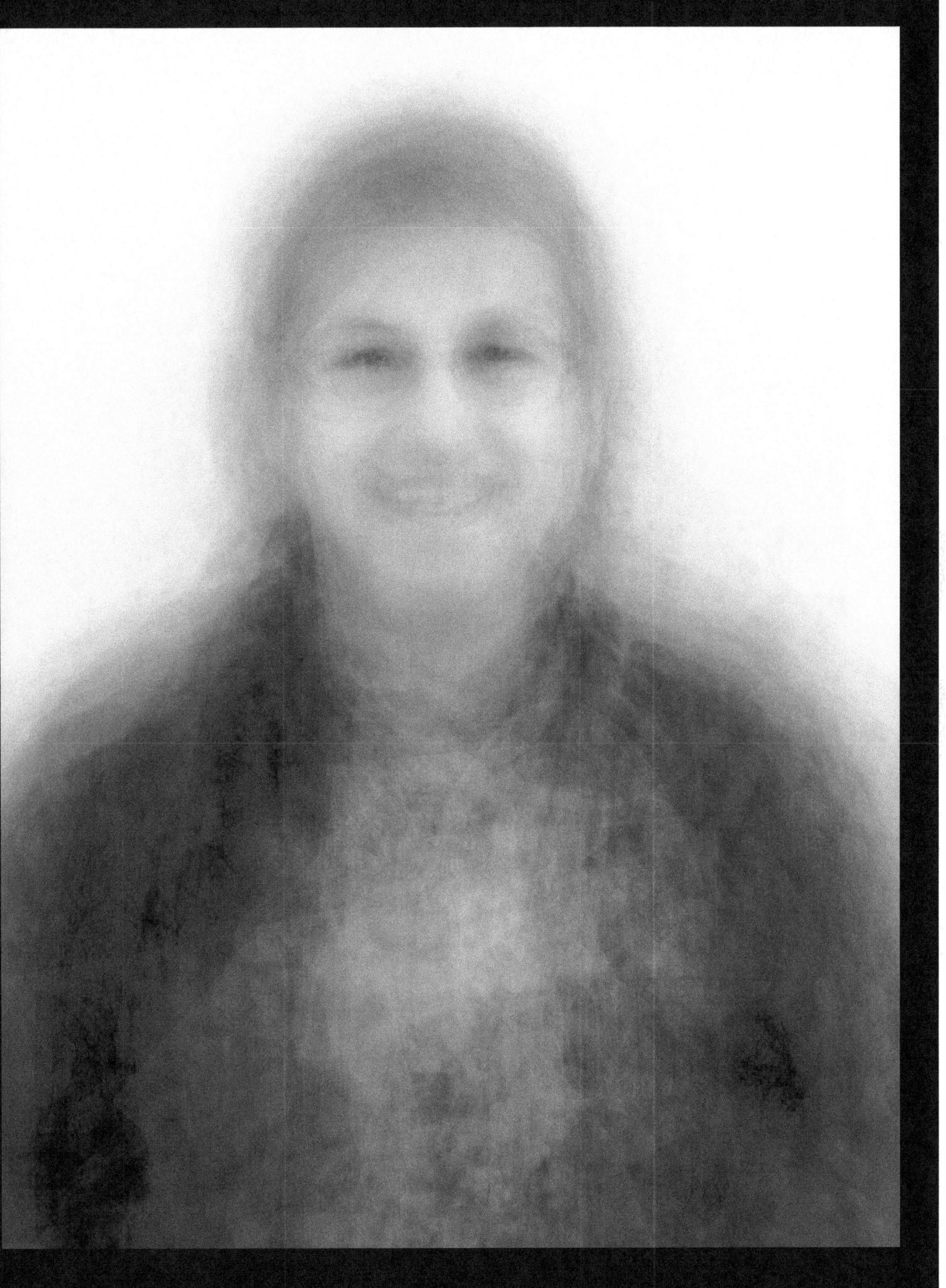

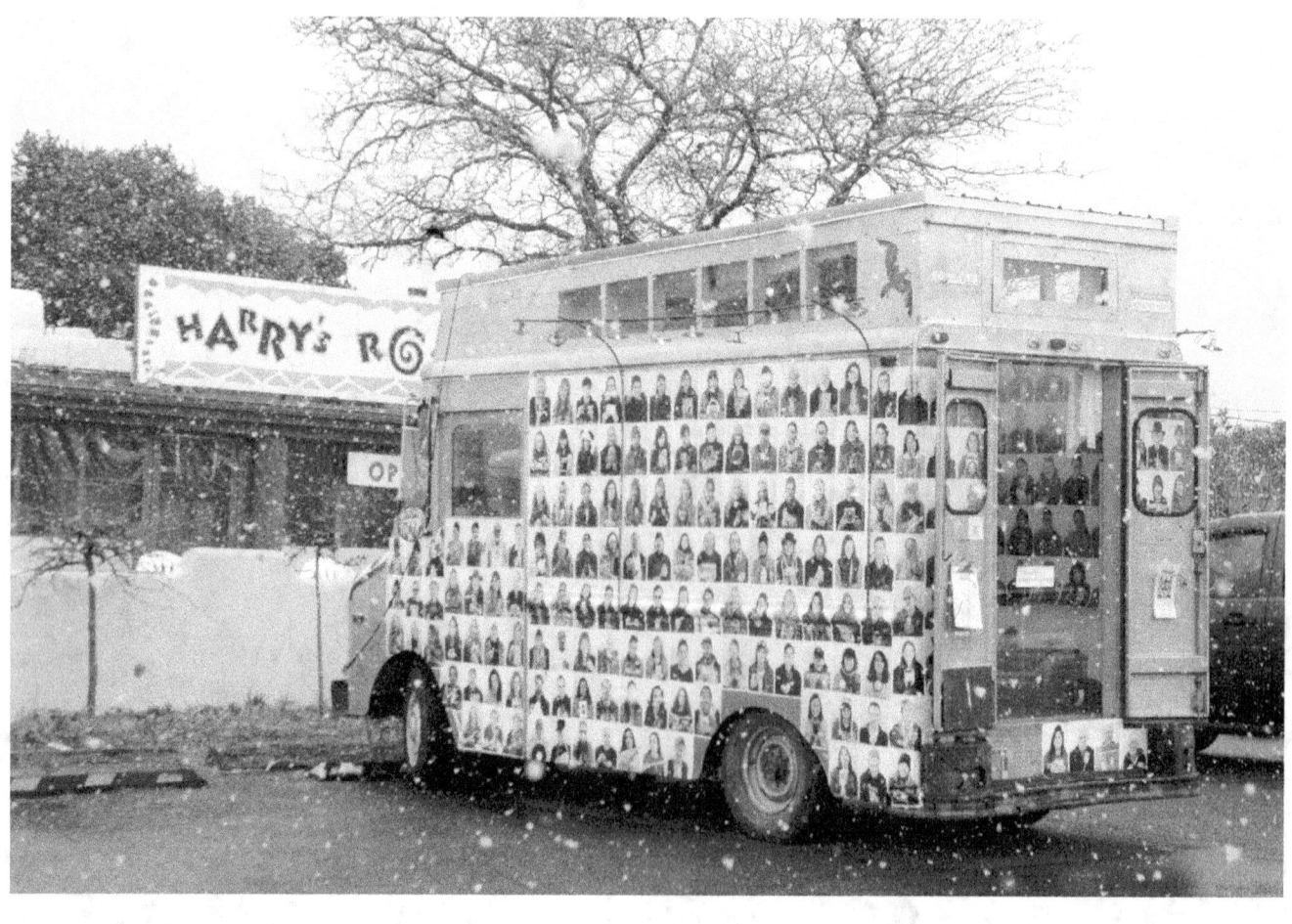

Harry's Roadhouse

96 Old Las Vegas Highway

Friday

March 9

9am-2pm

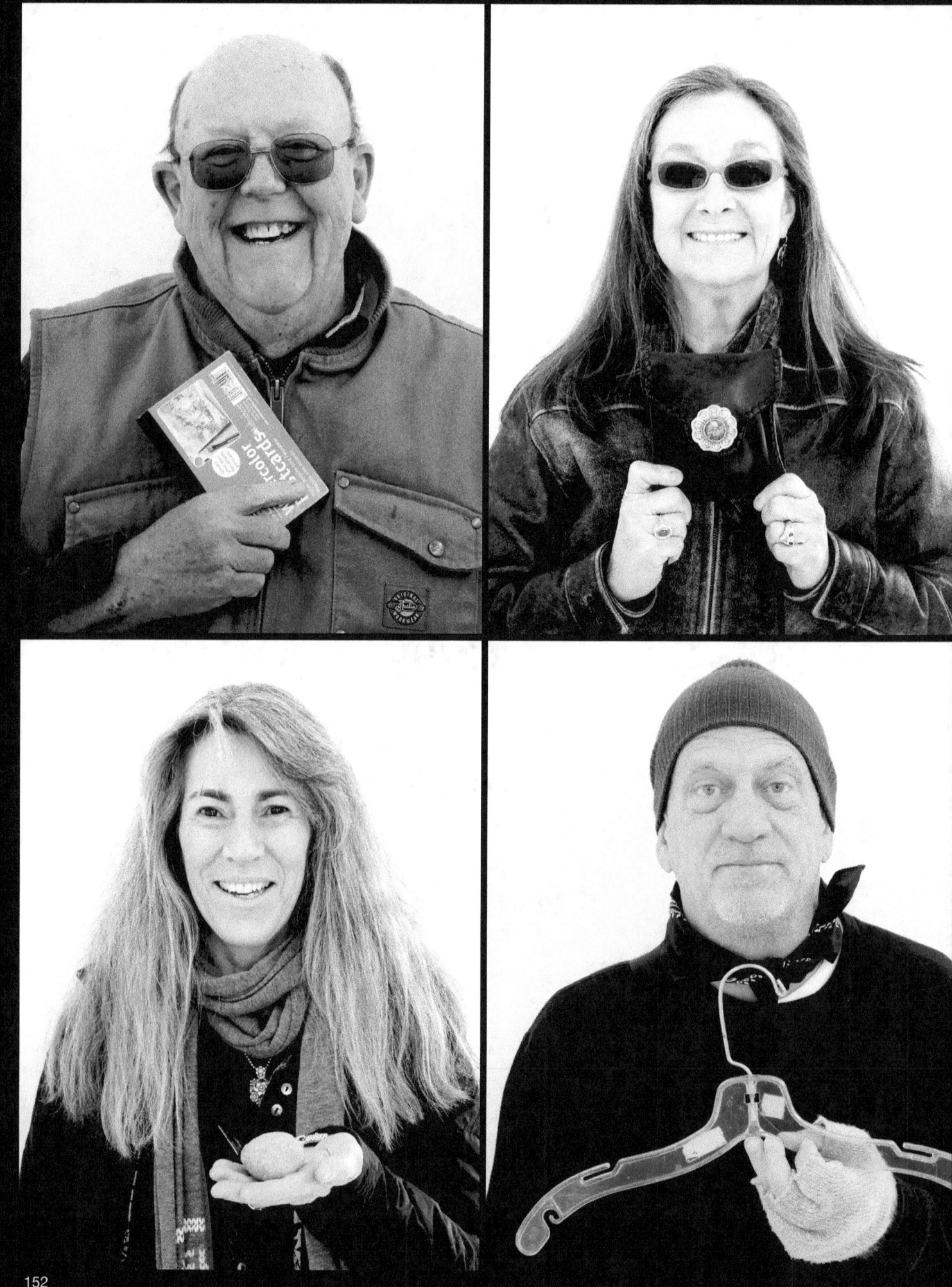

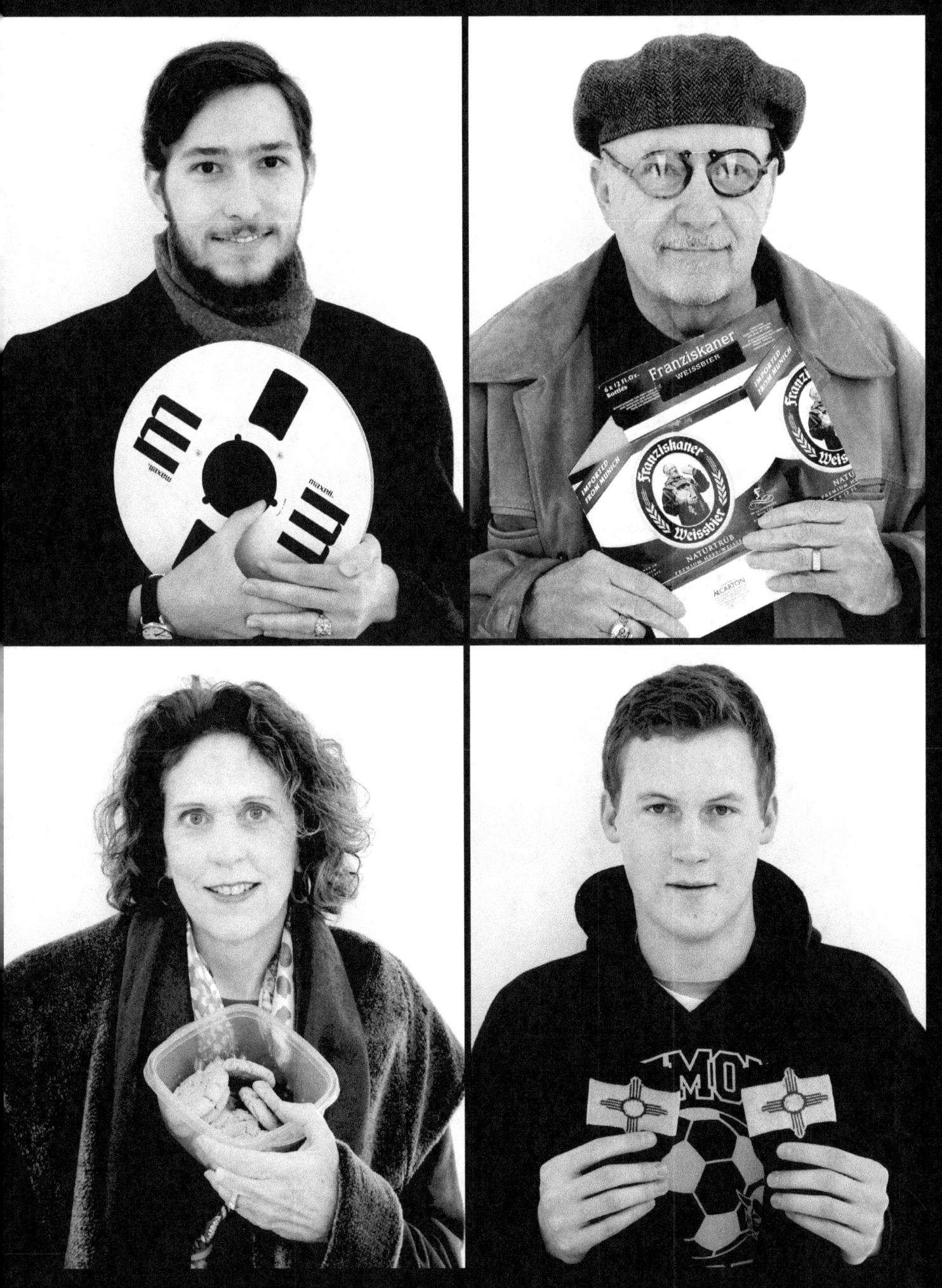

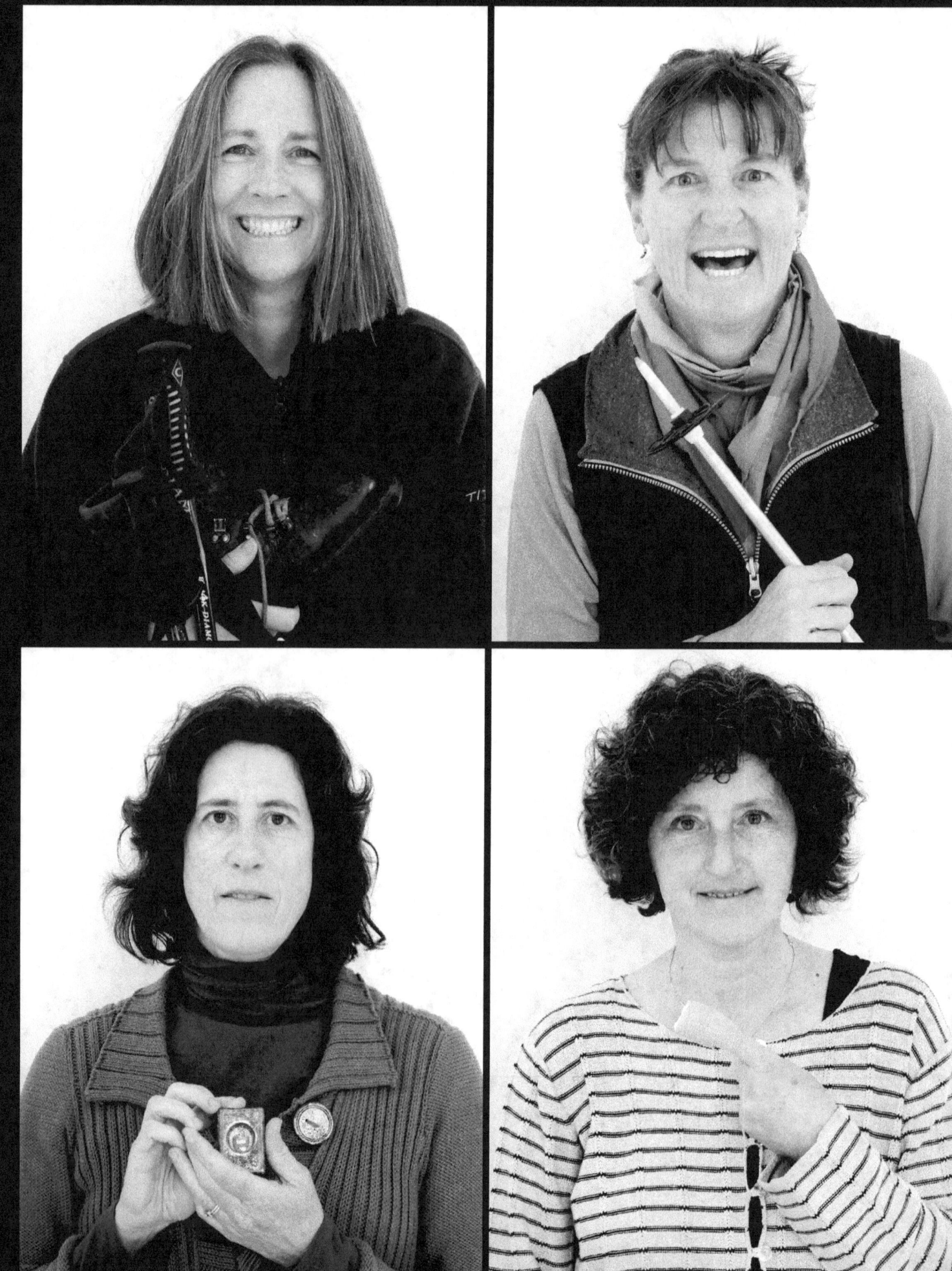

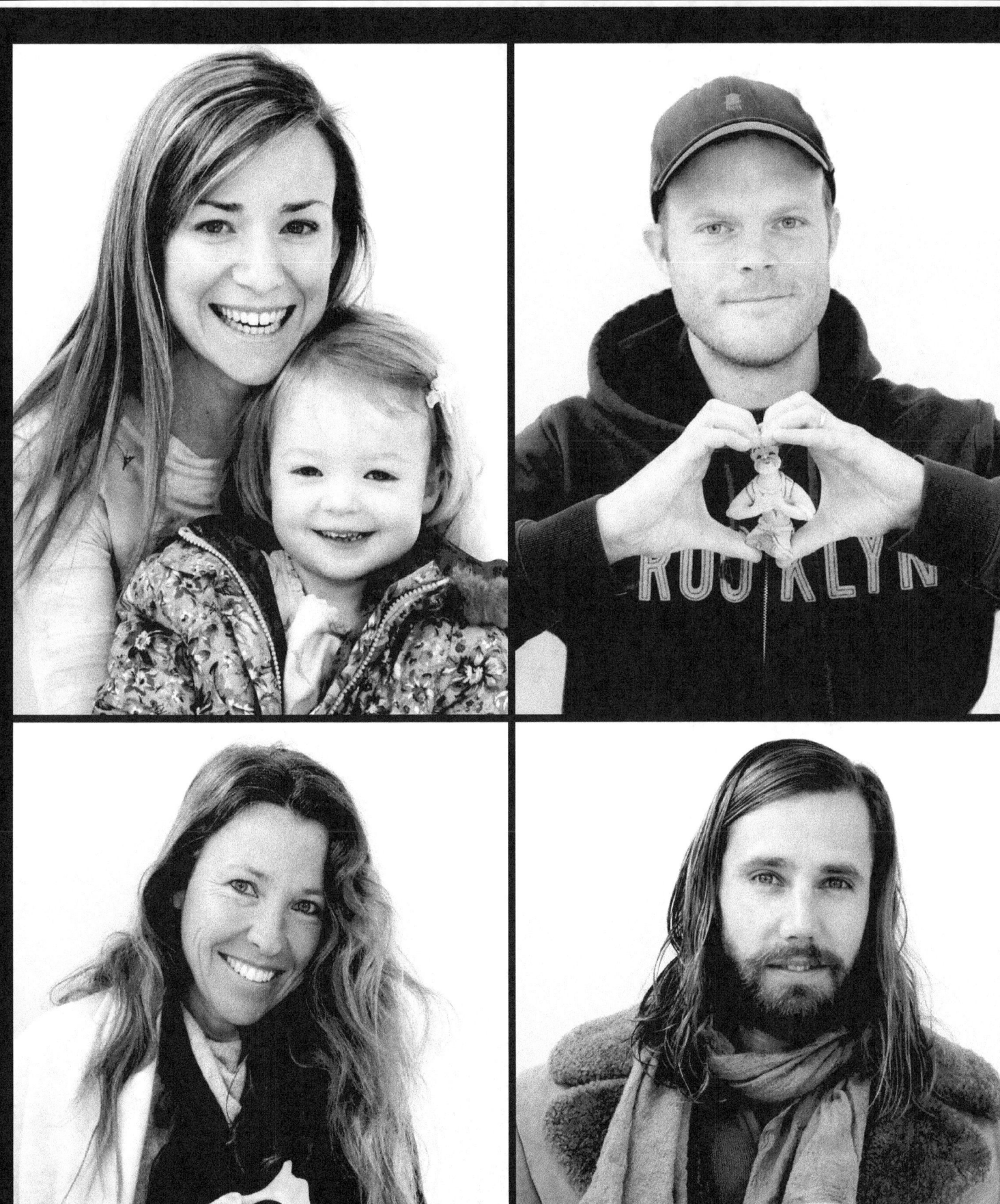

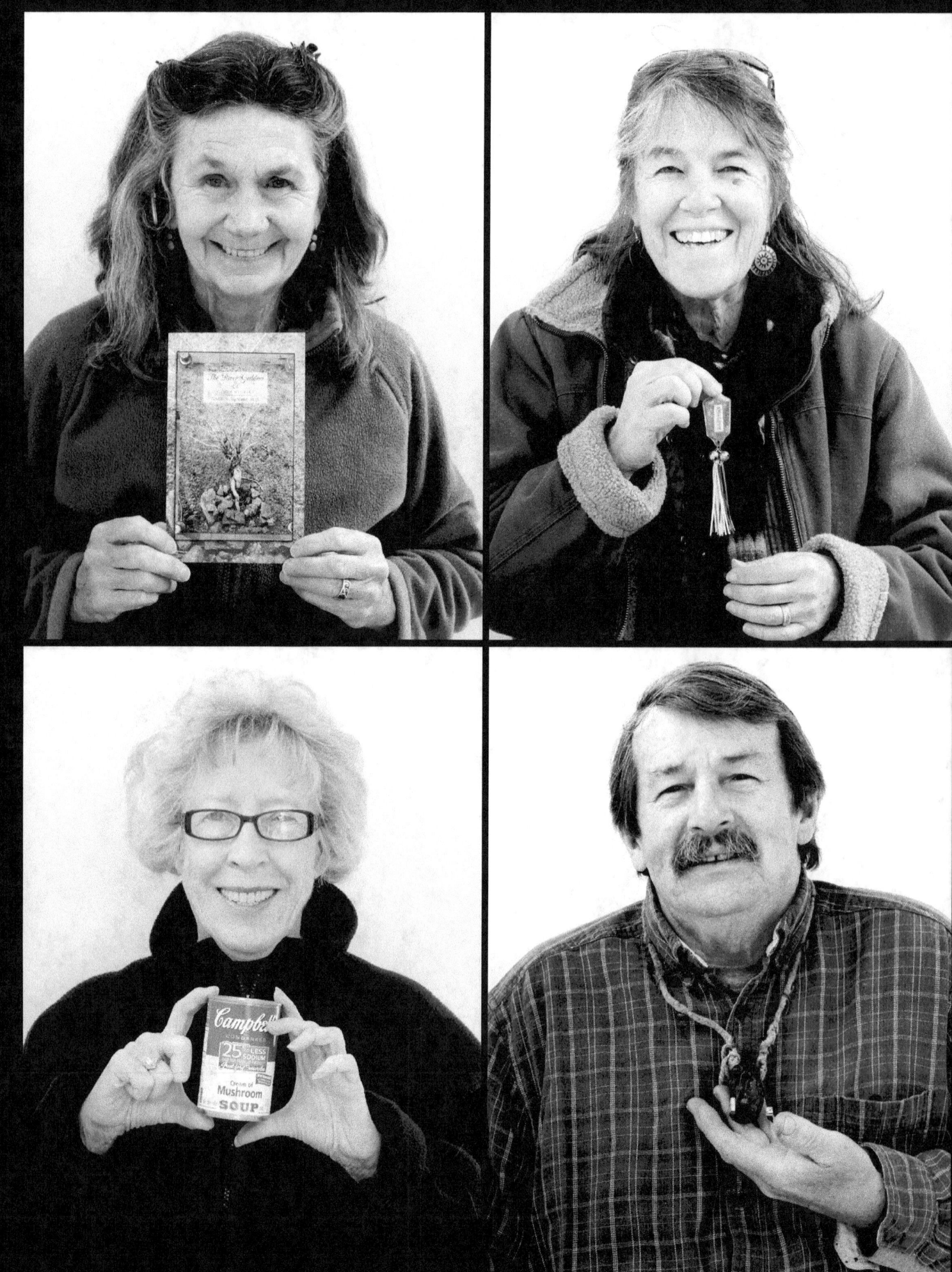

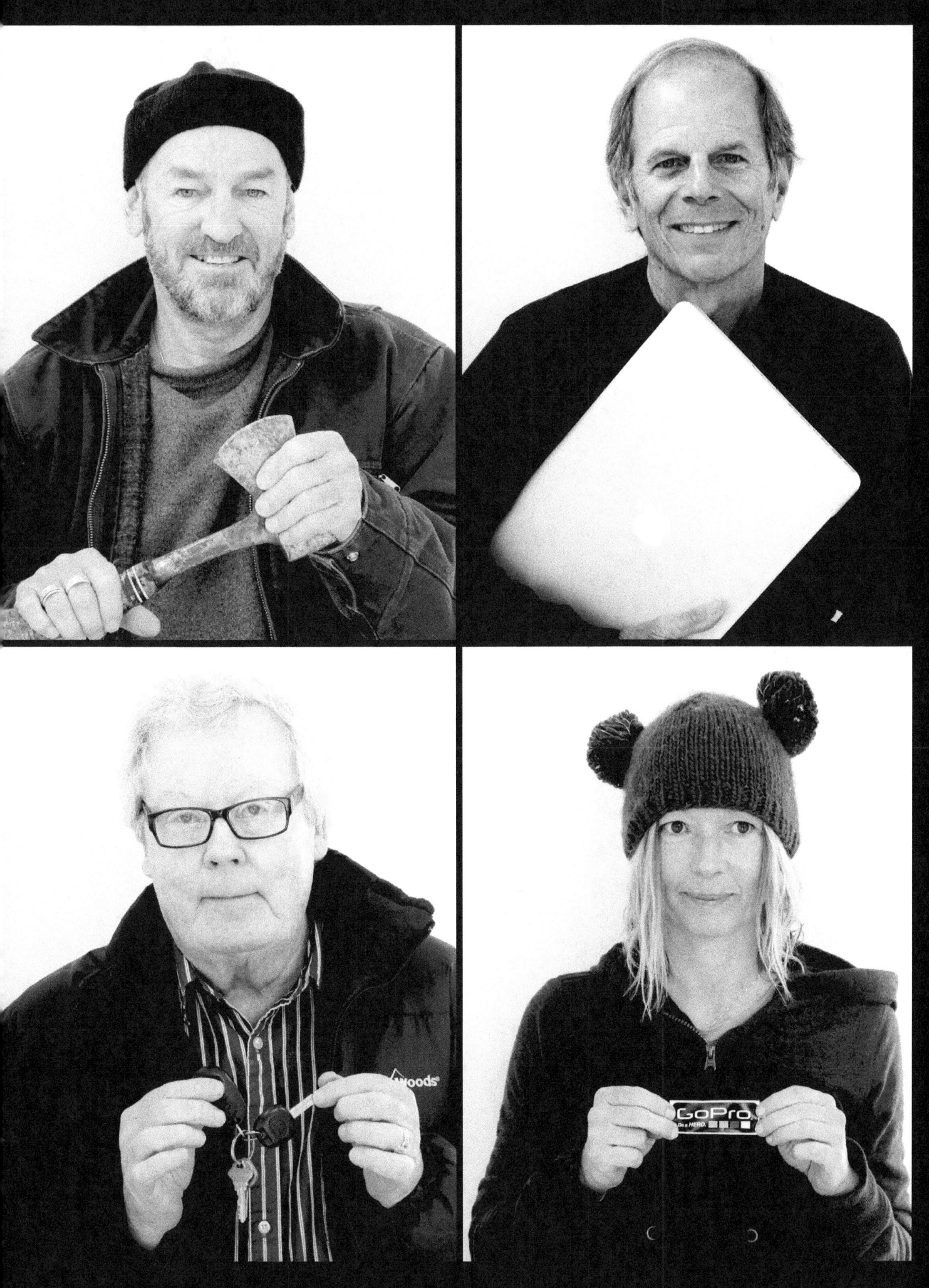

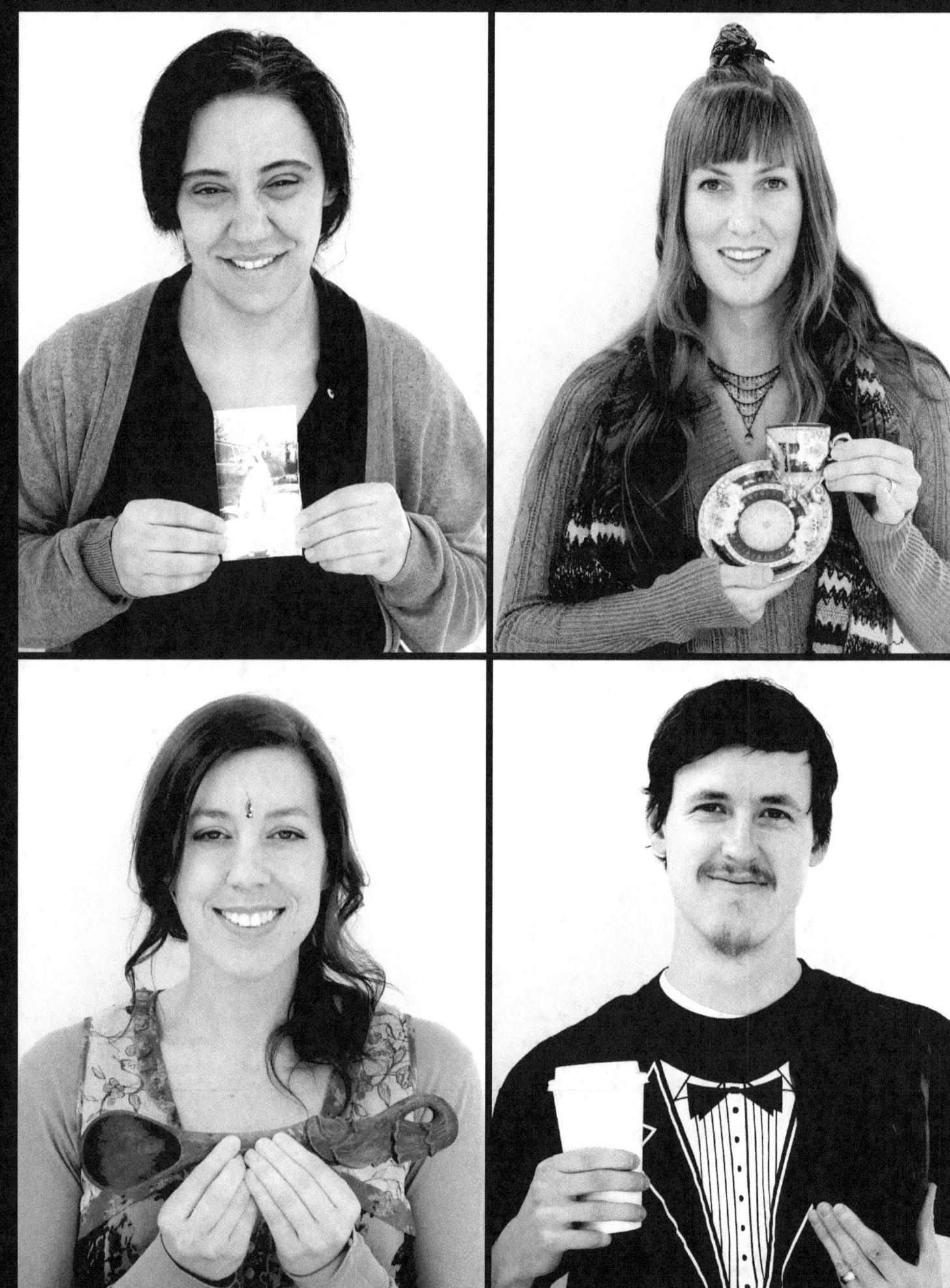

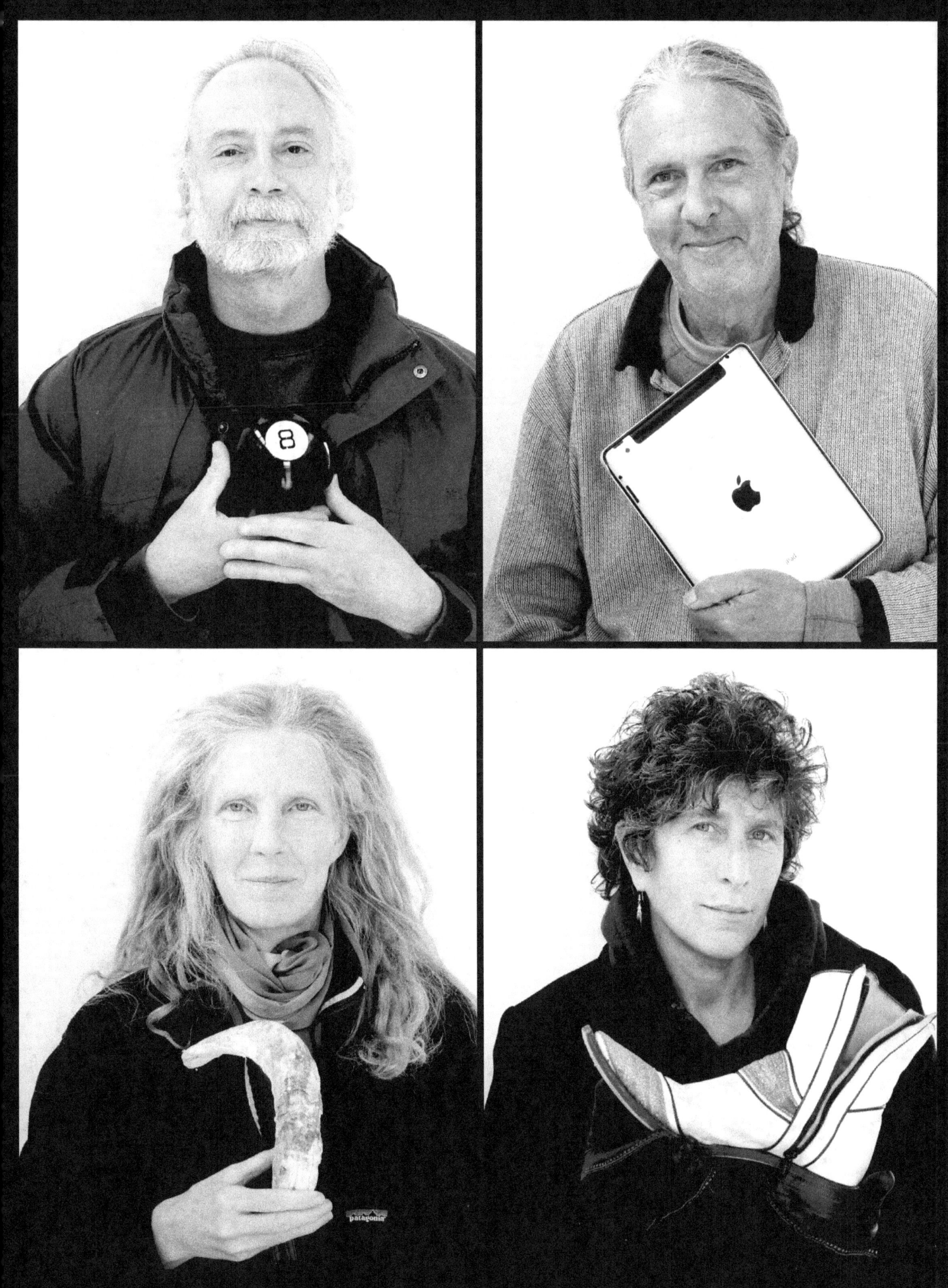

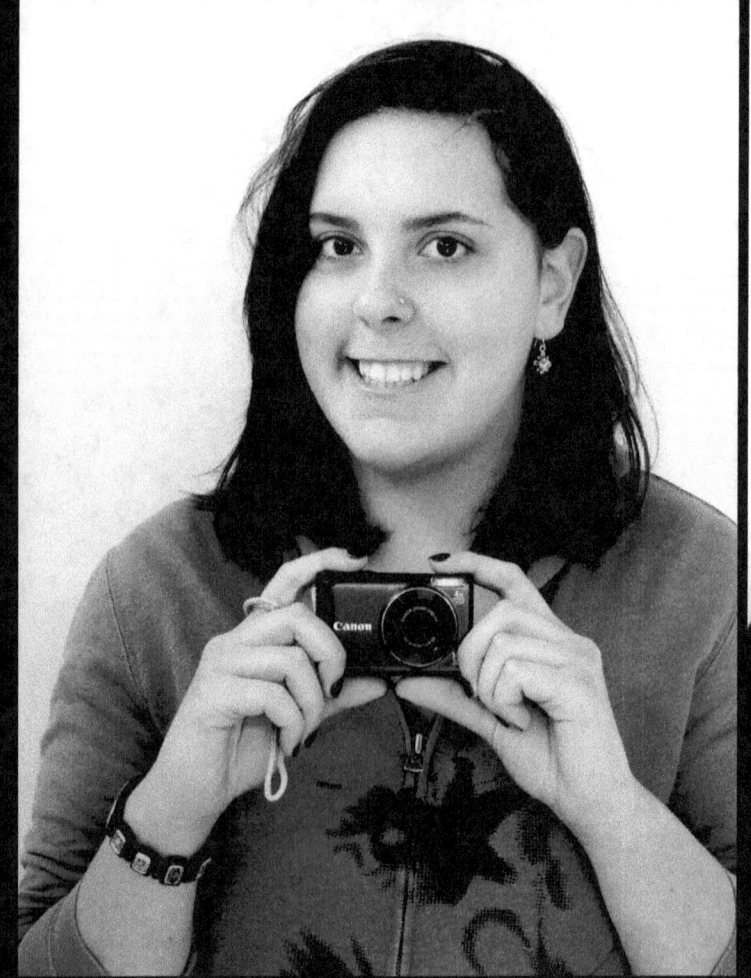

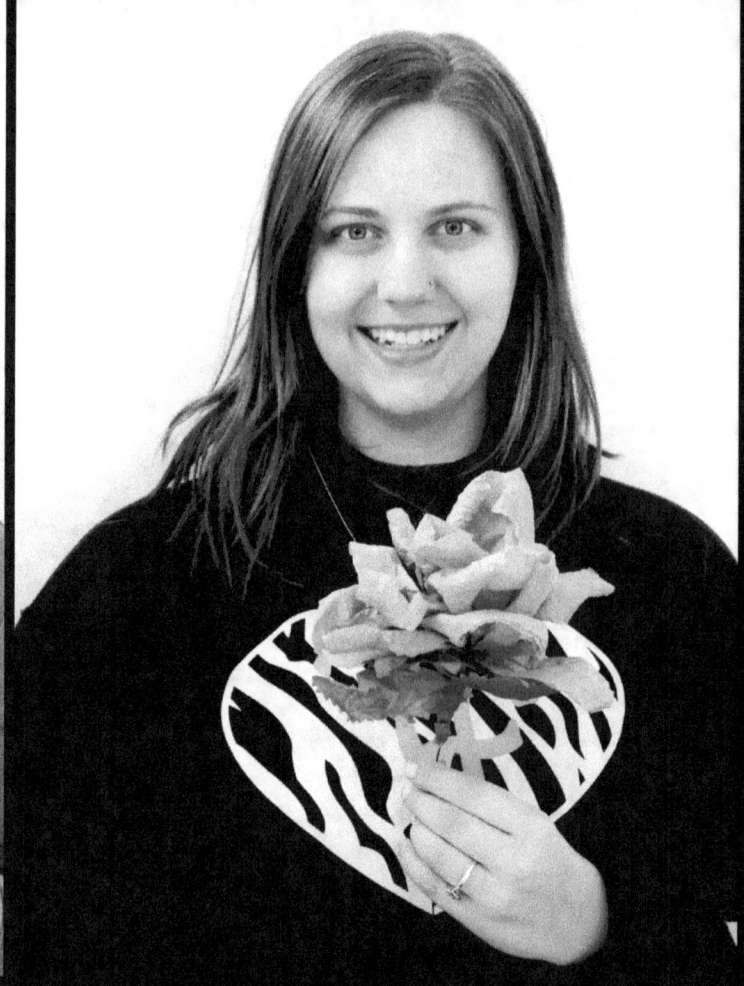

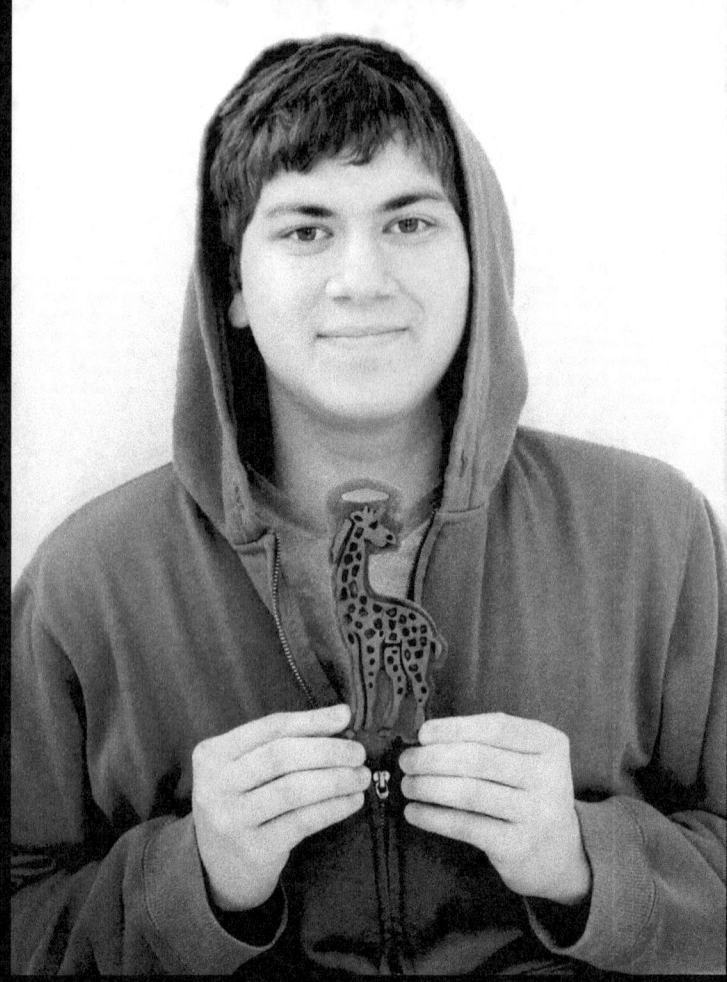

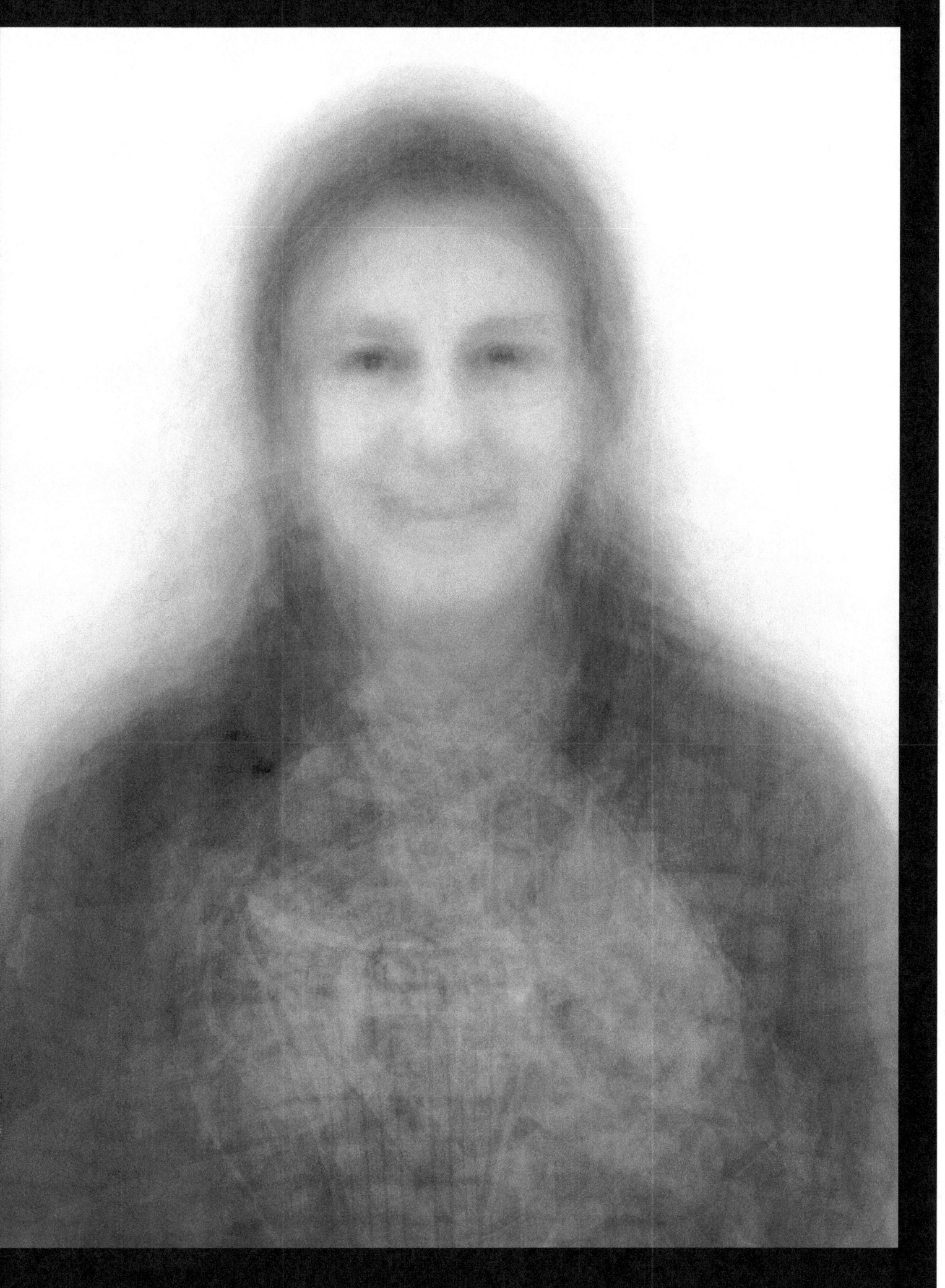

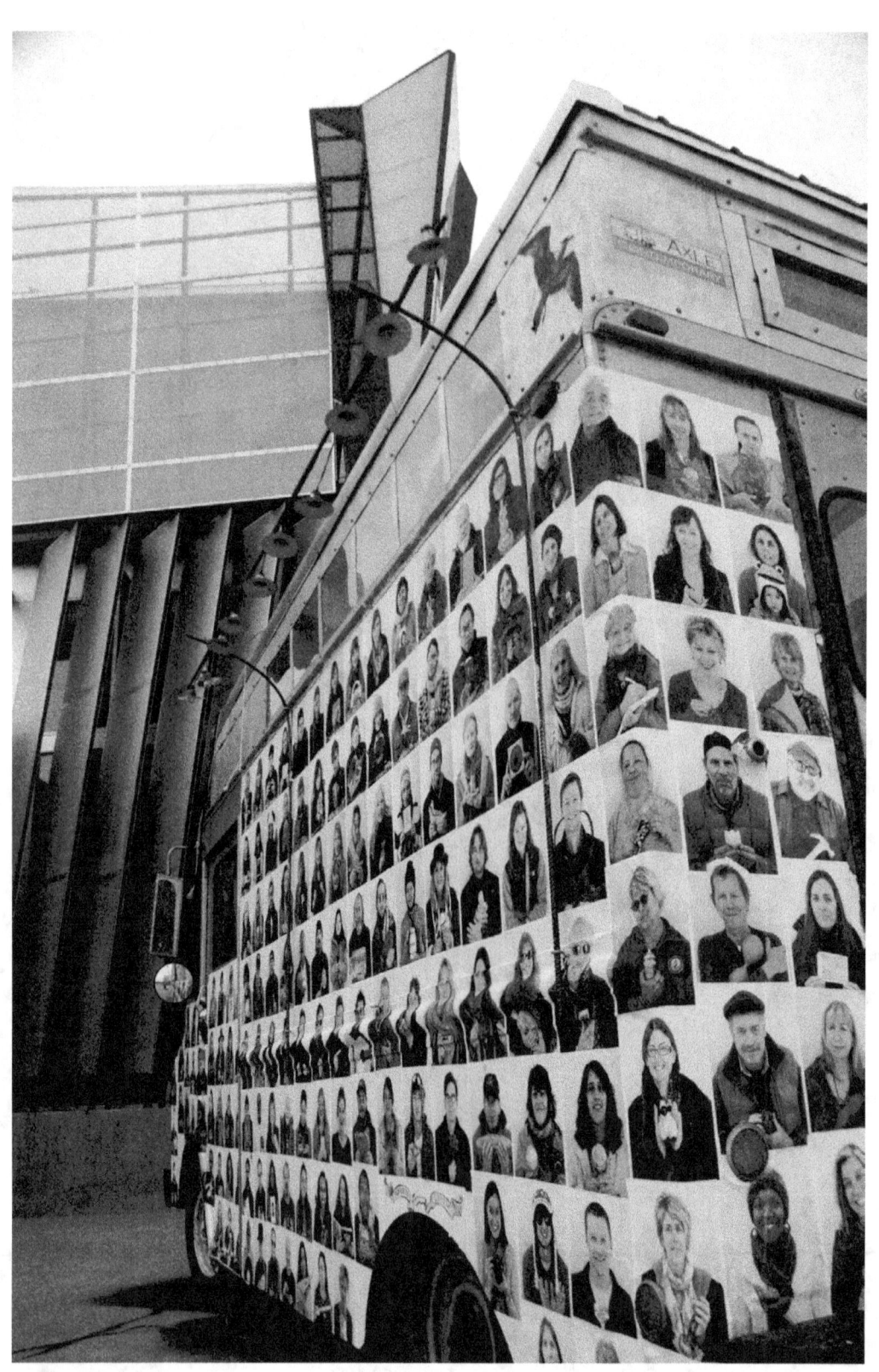

Genoveva Chavez Community Center

3221 Rodeo Road

Saturday

March 10

11am-4pm

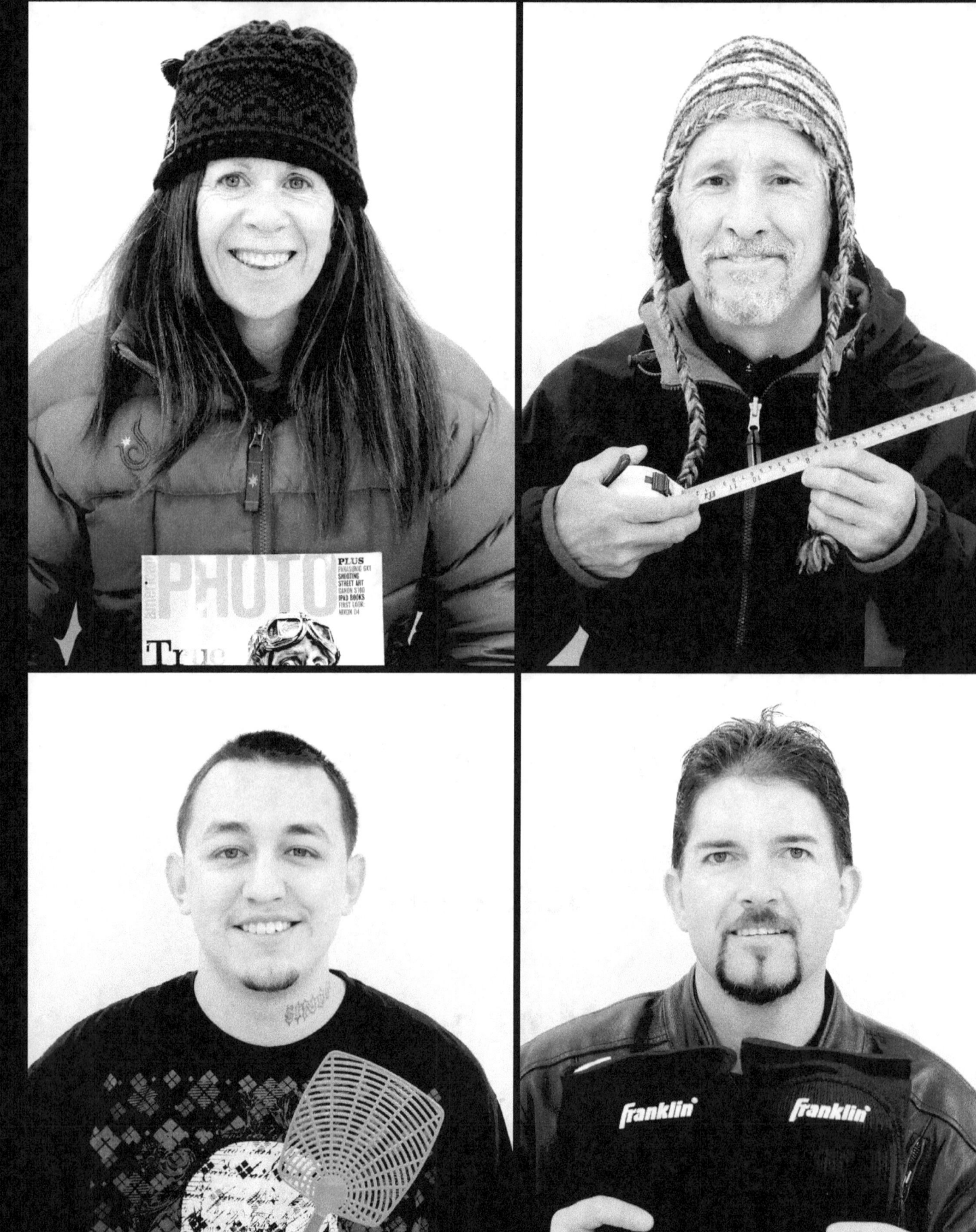

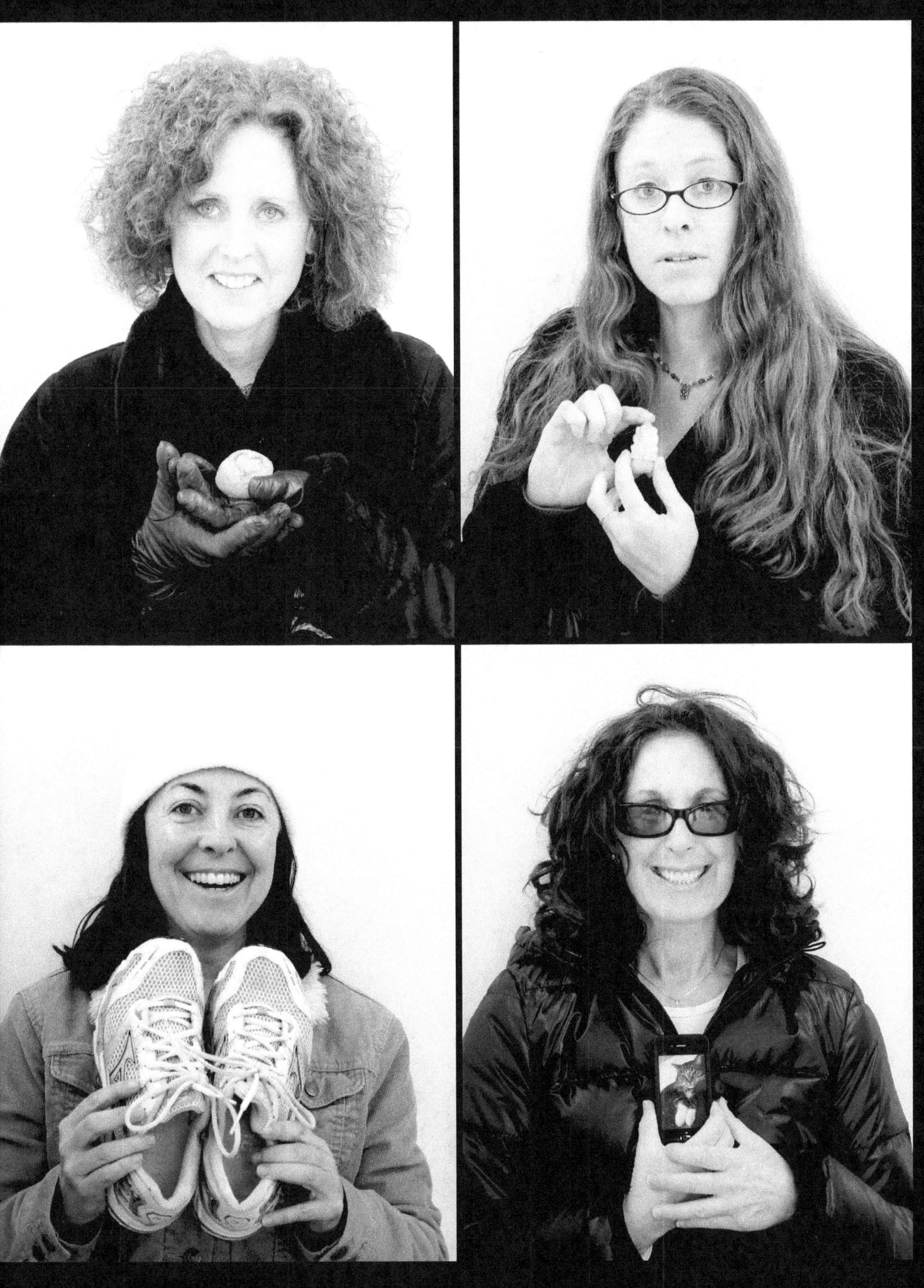

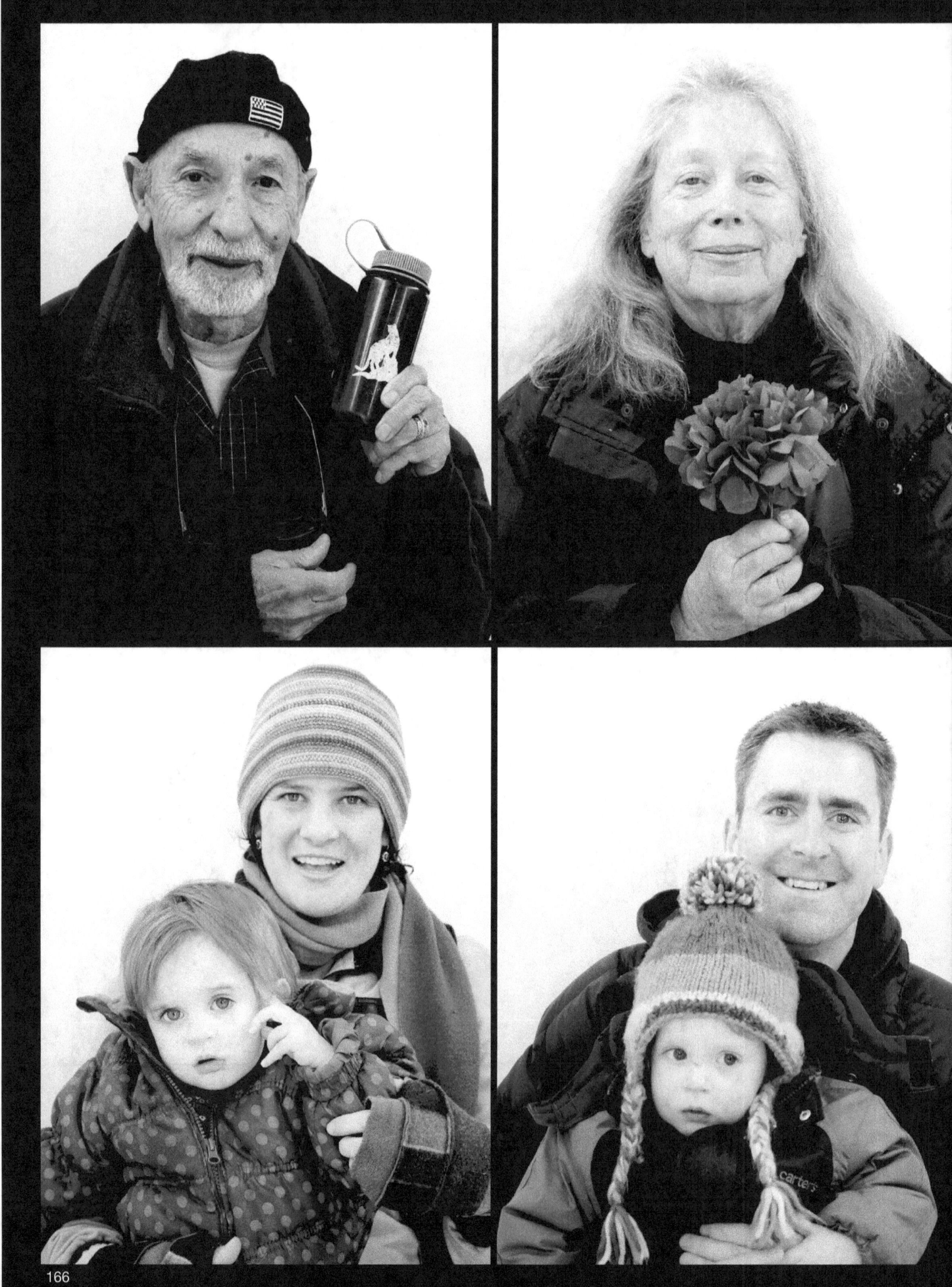

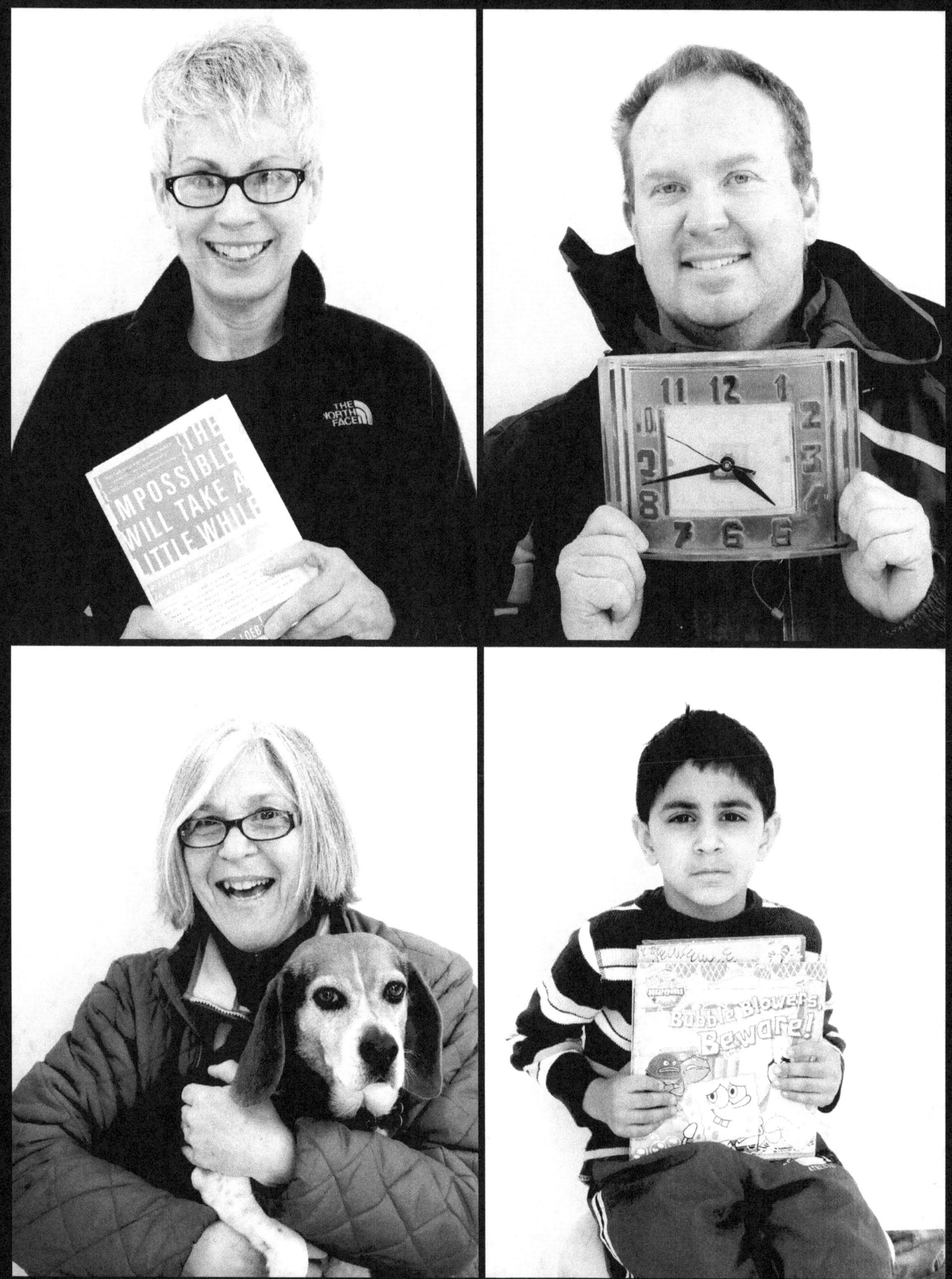

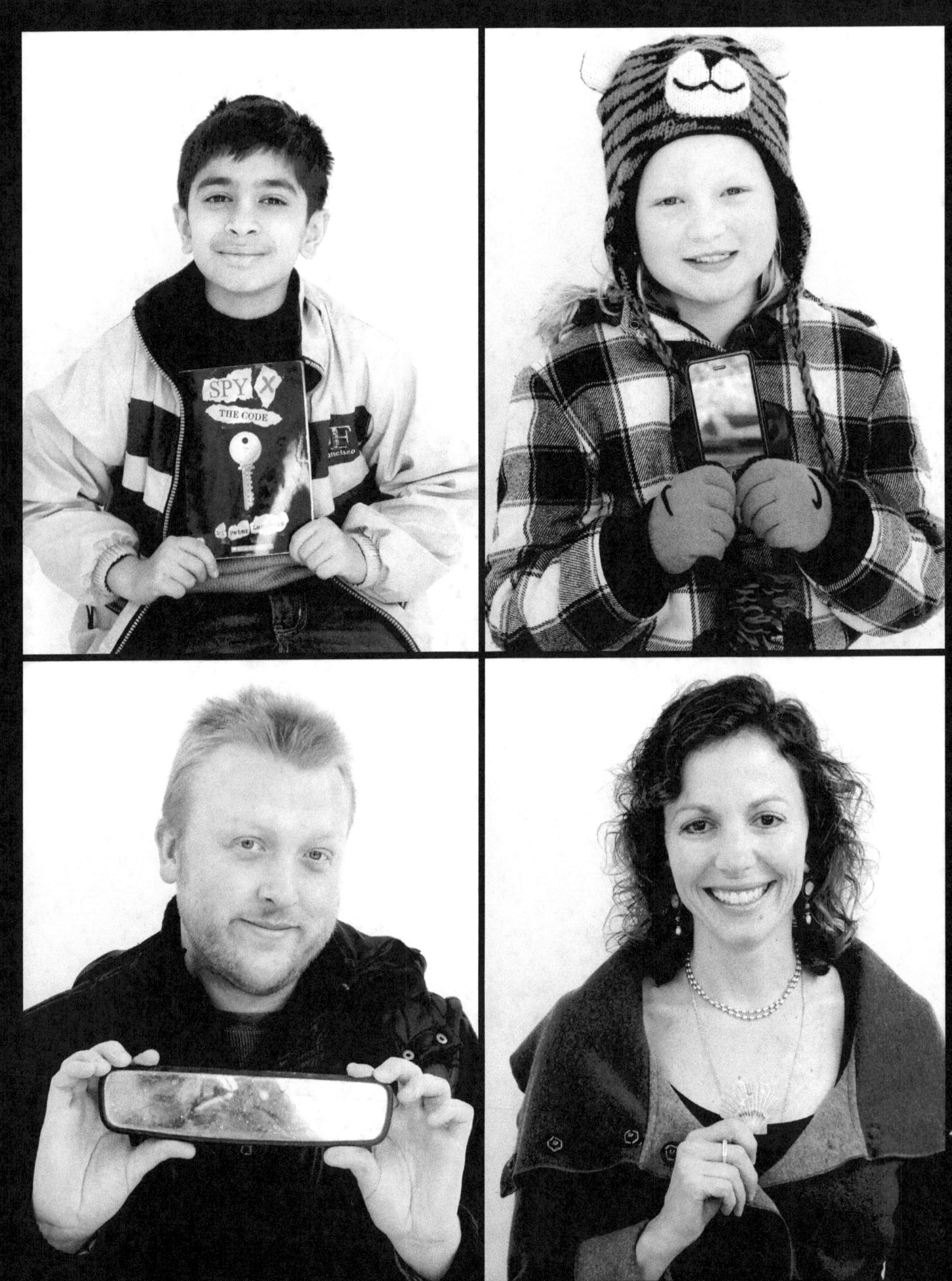

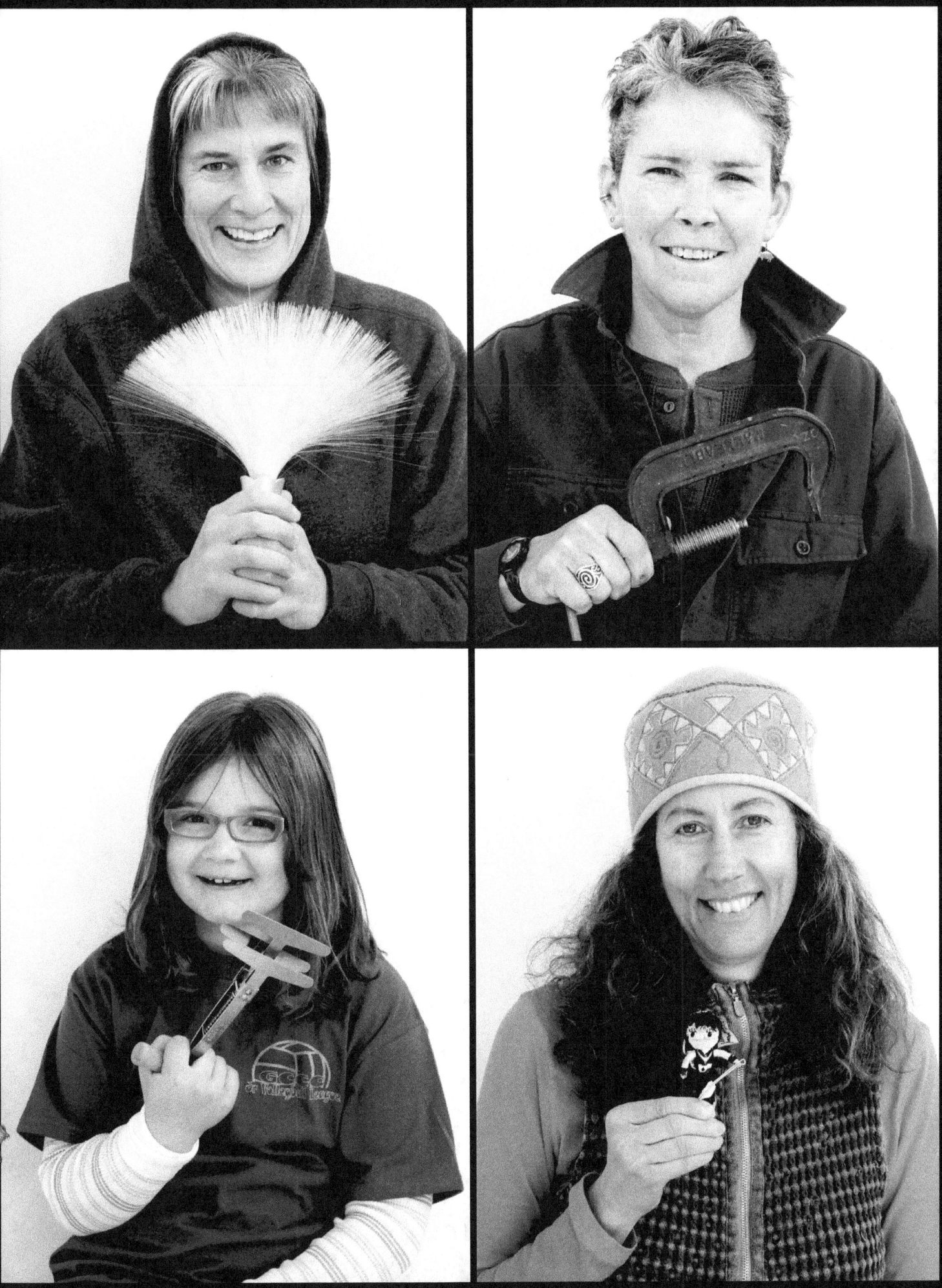

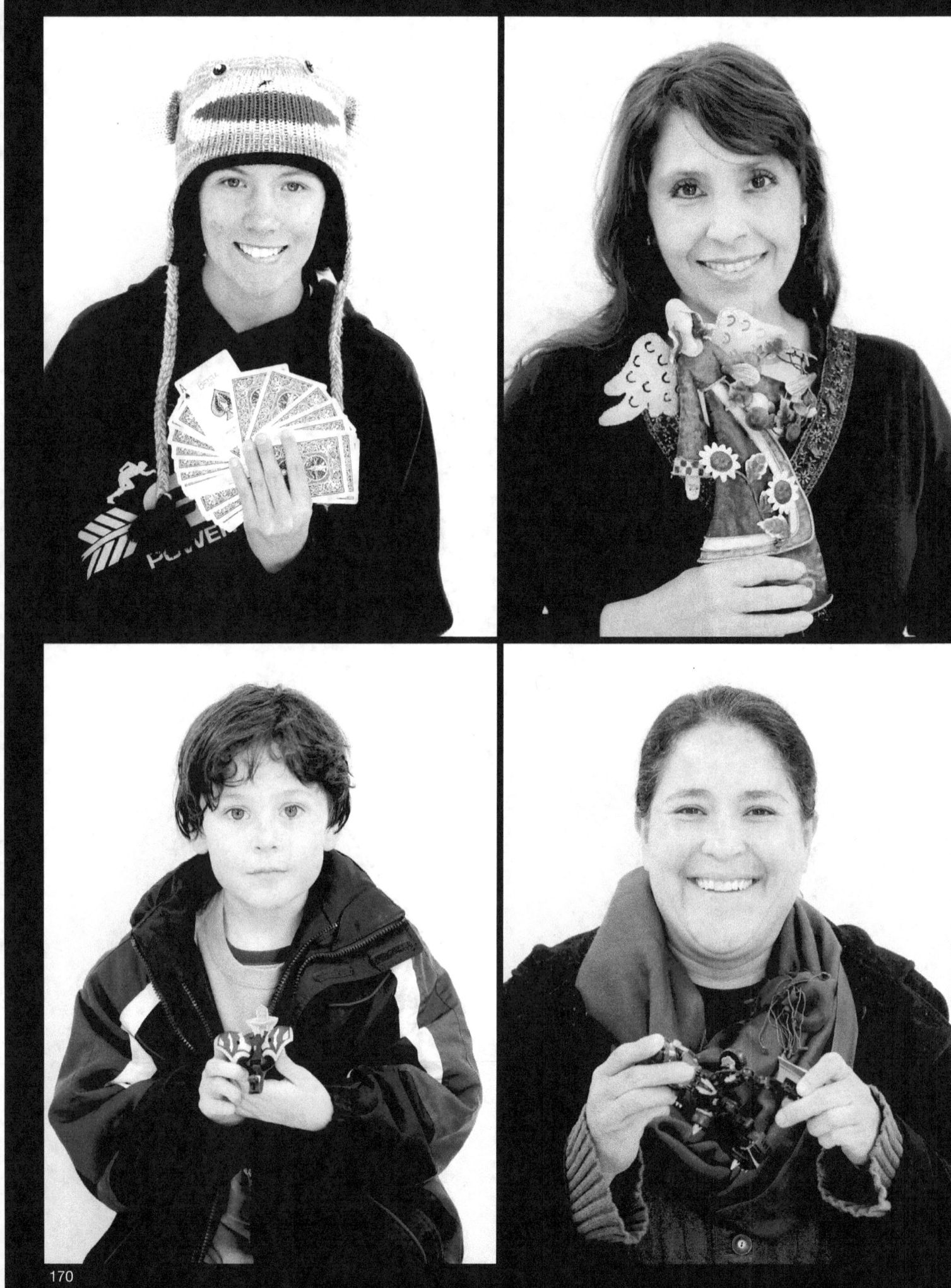

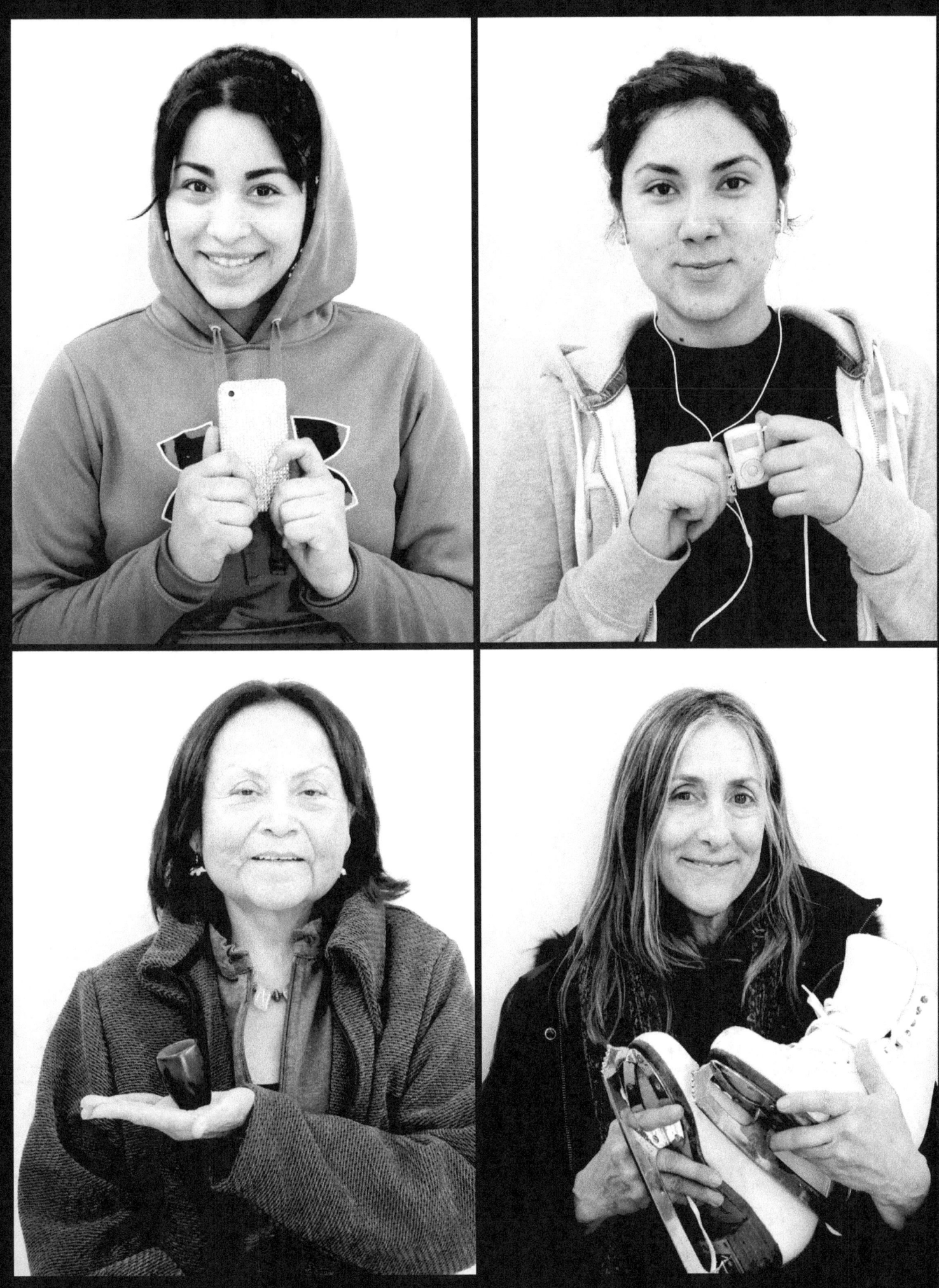

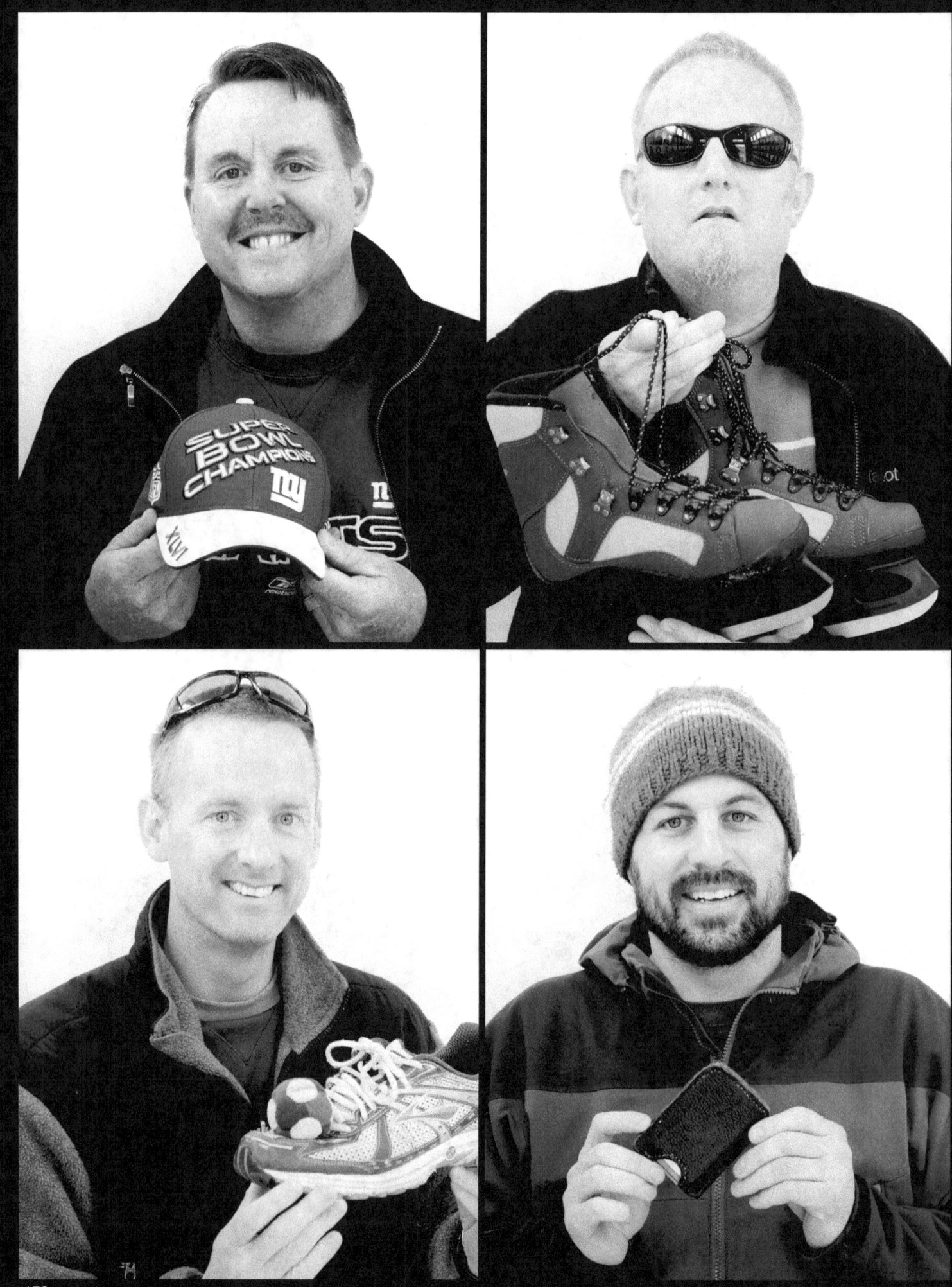

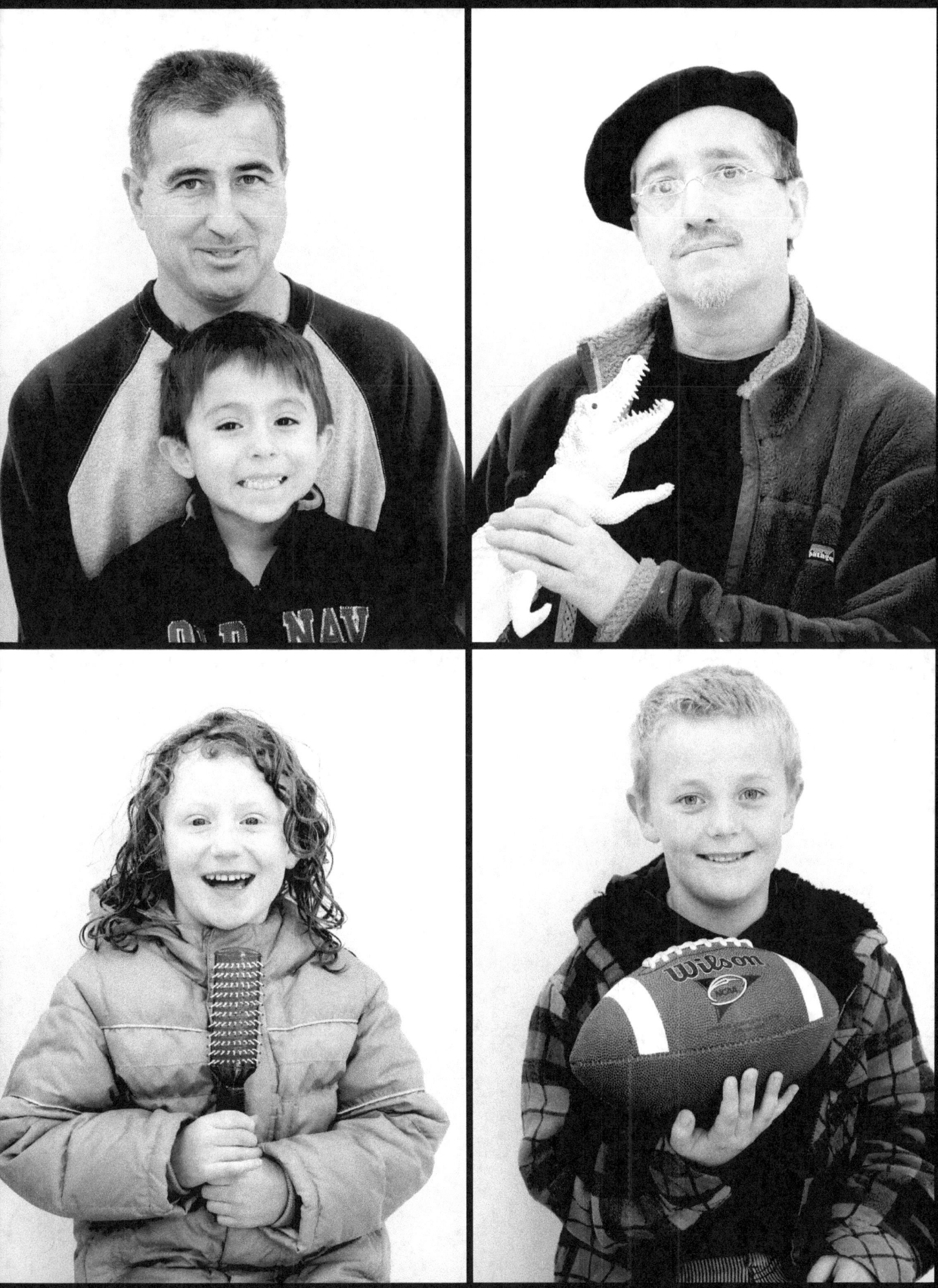

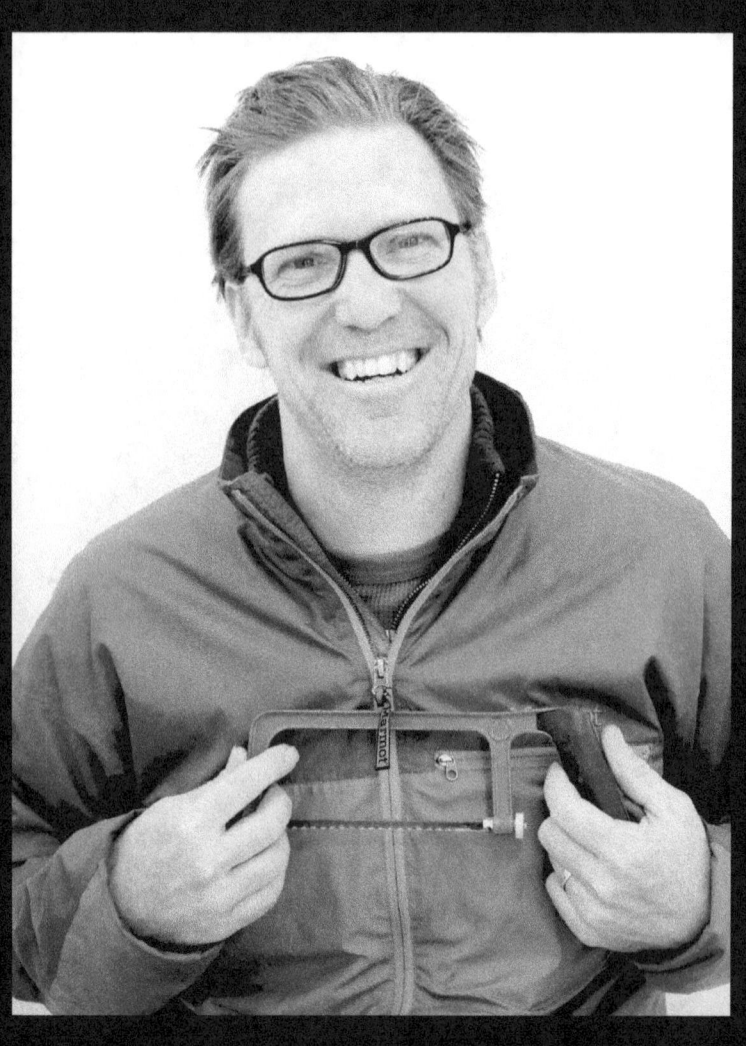

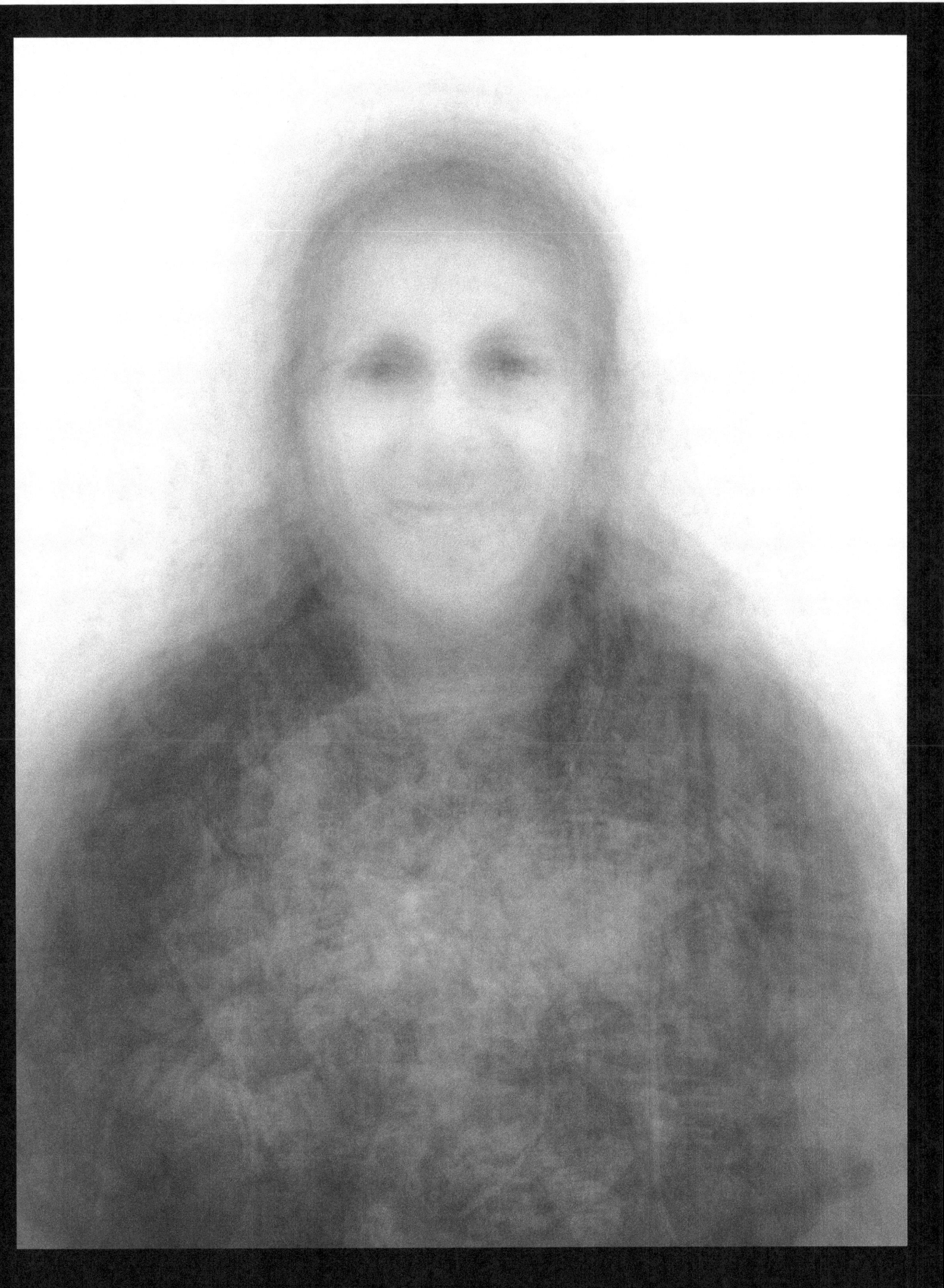

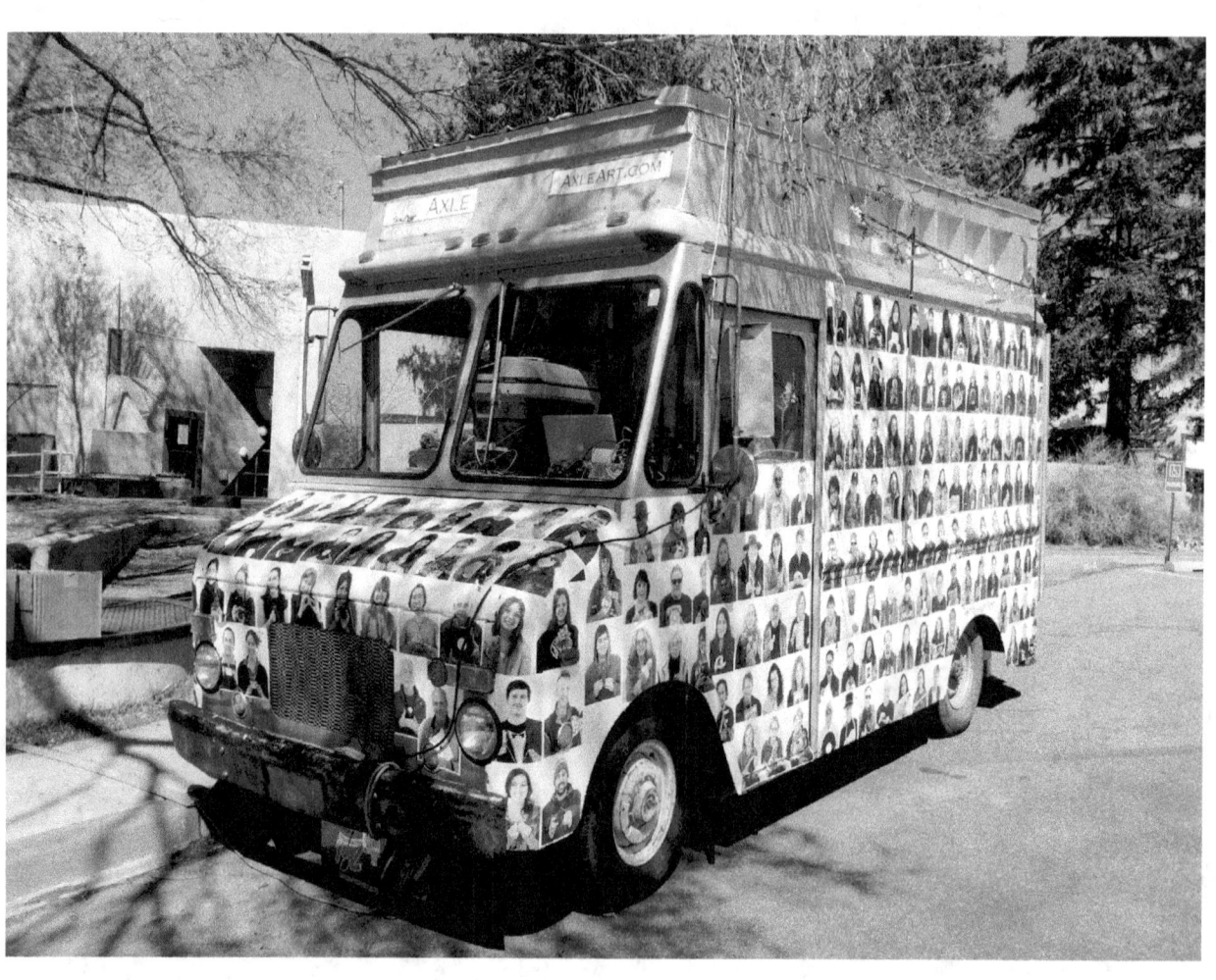

Santa Fe Children's Museum

1050 Old Pecos Trail

Sunday

March 11

12pm-4pm

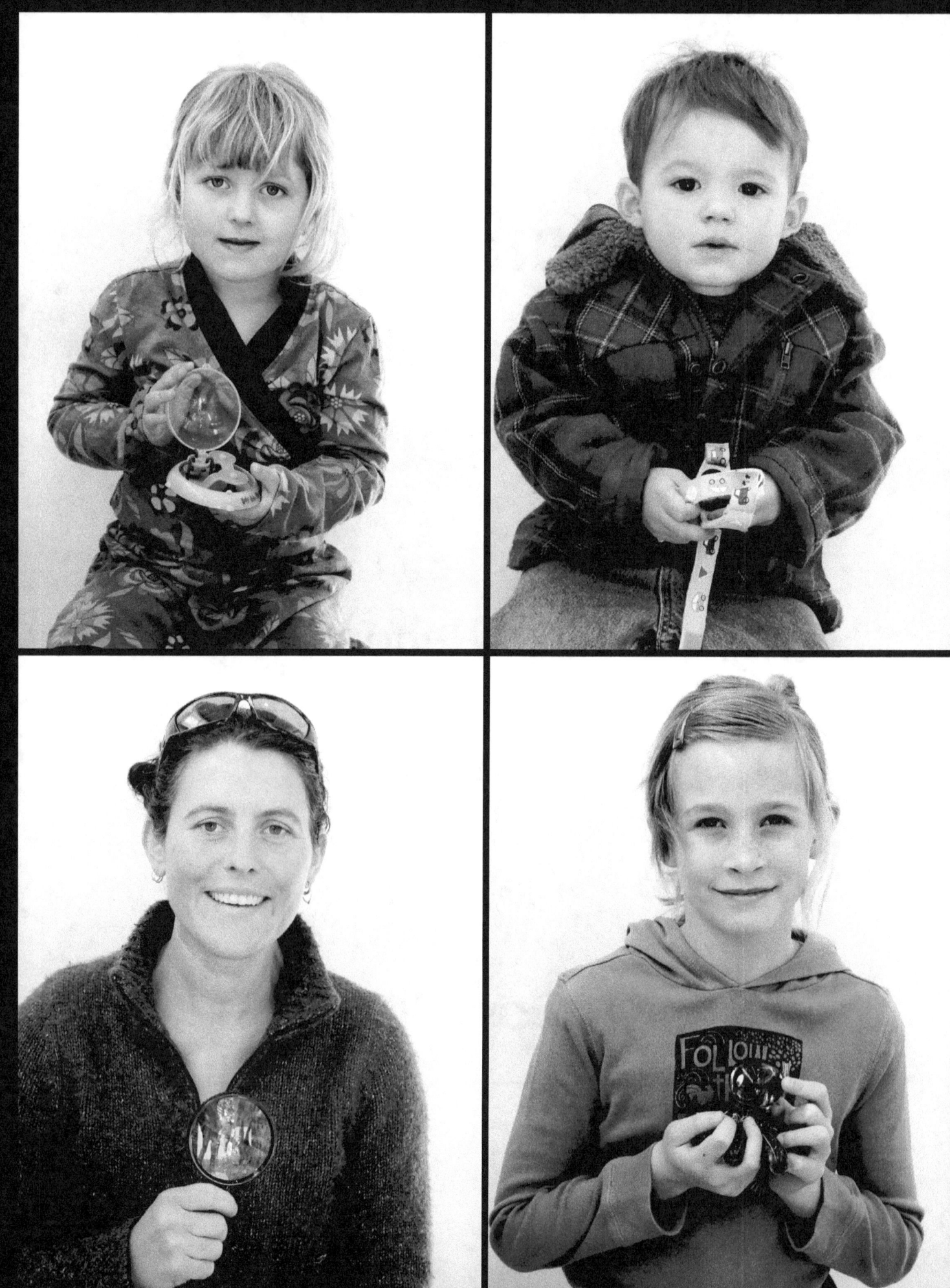

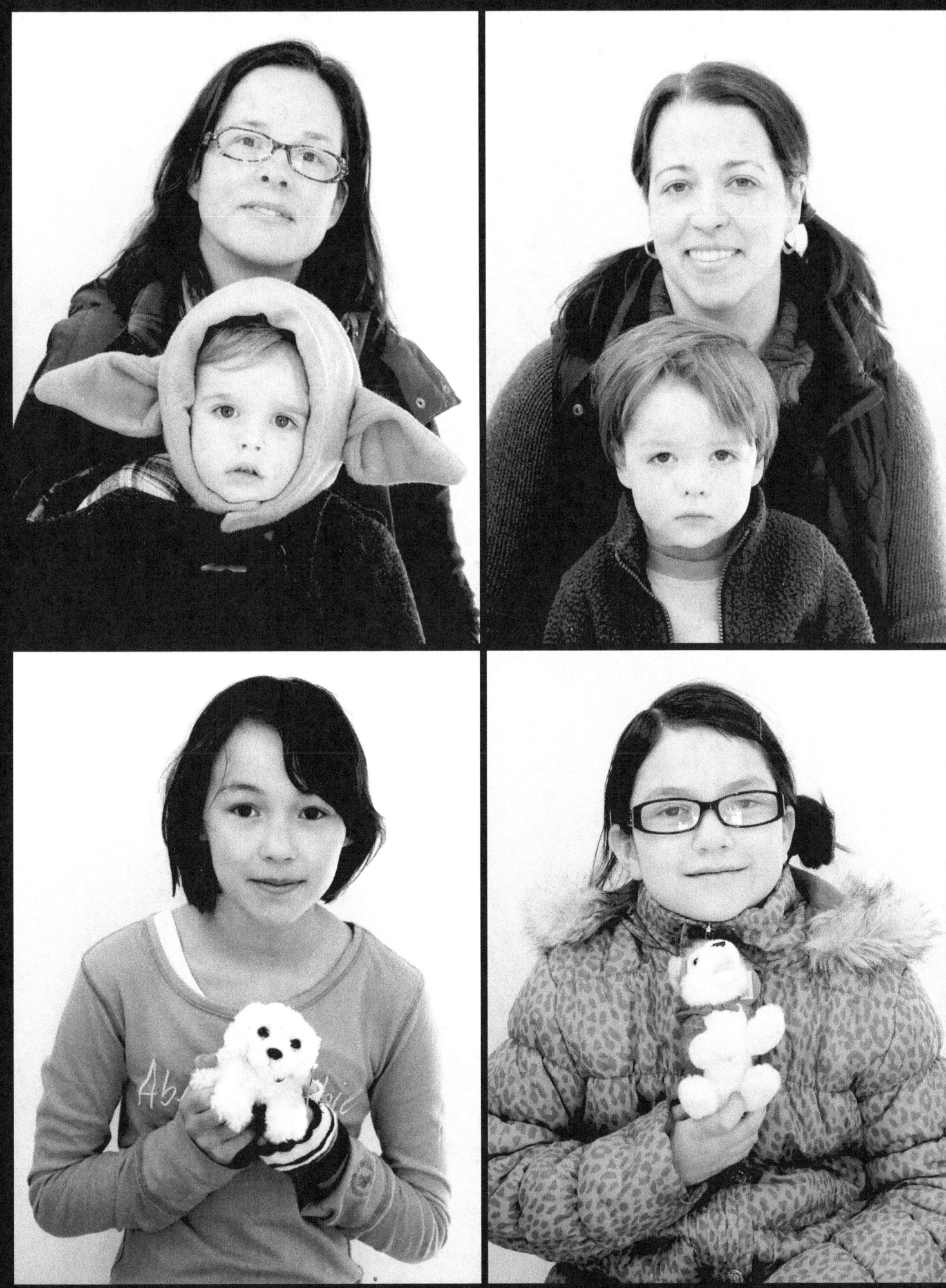

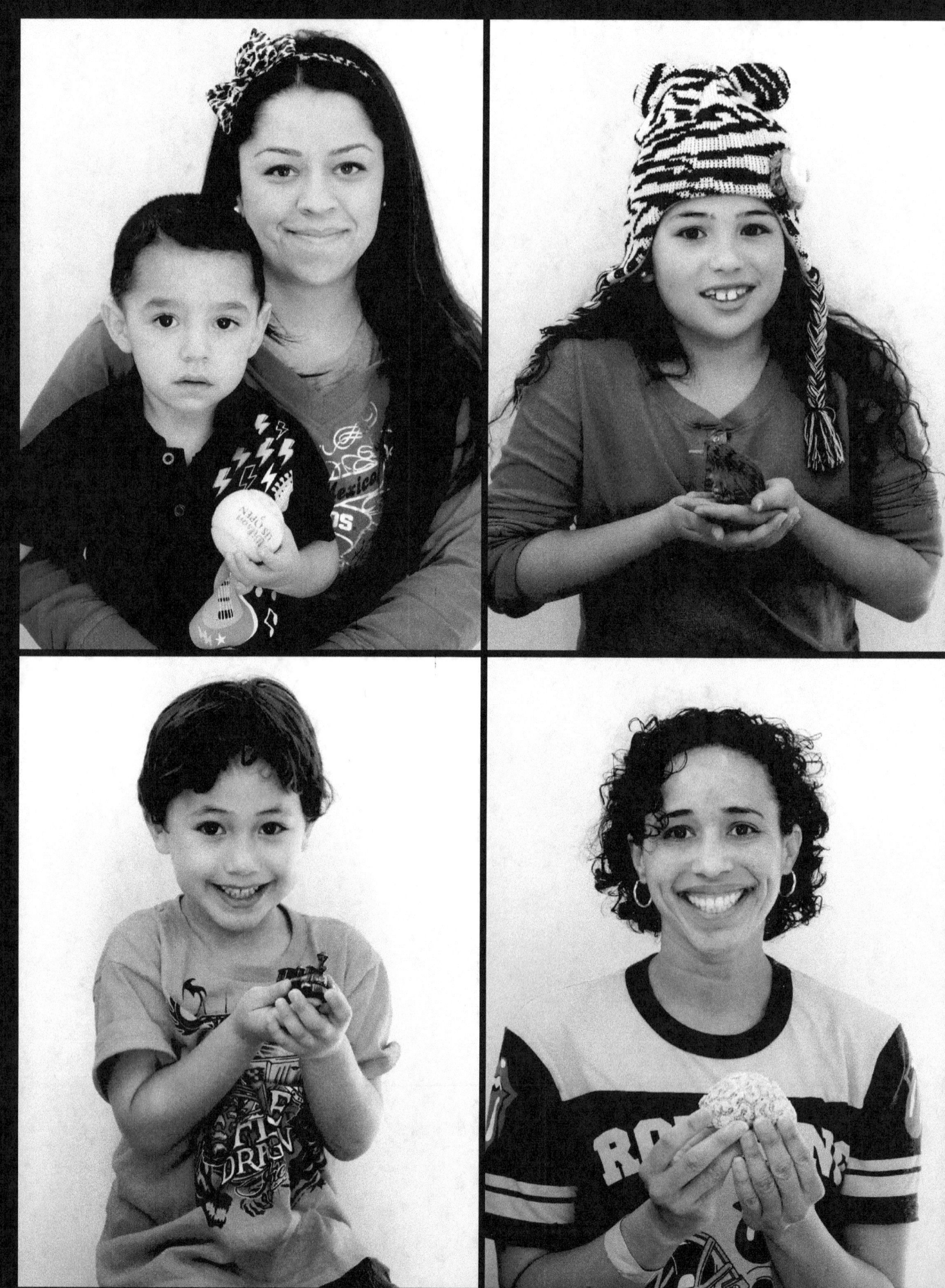

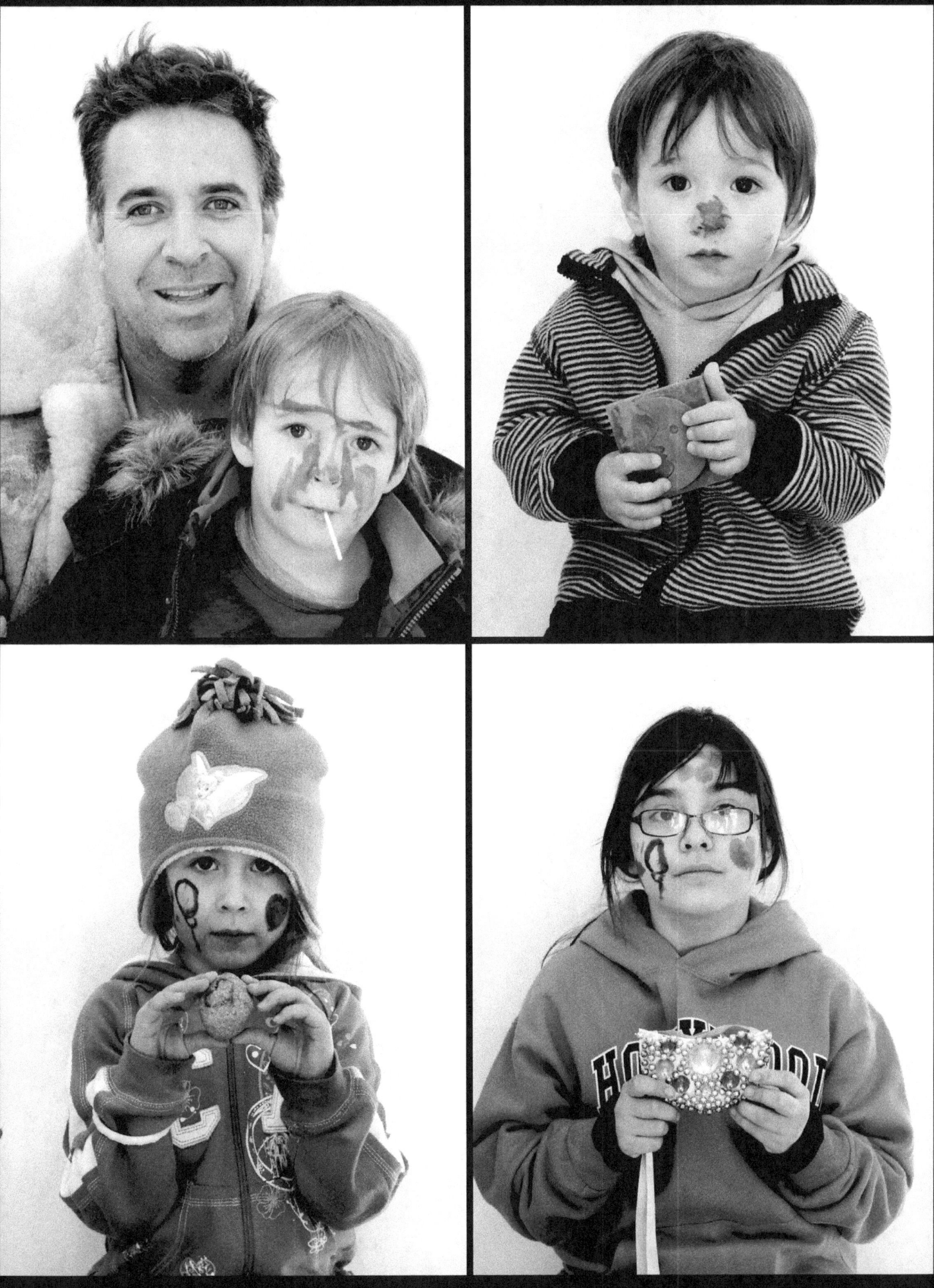

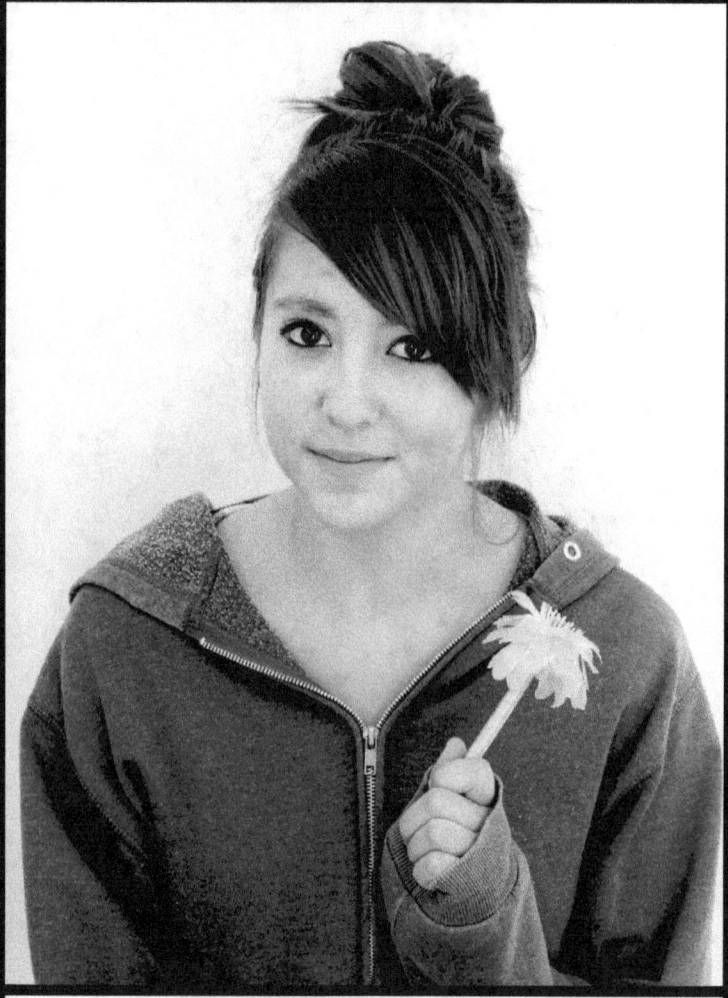
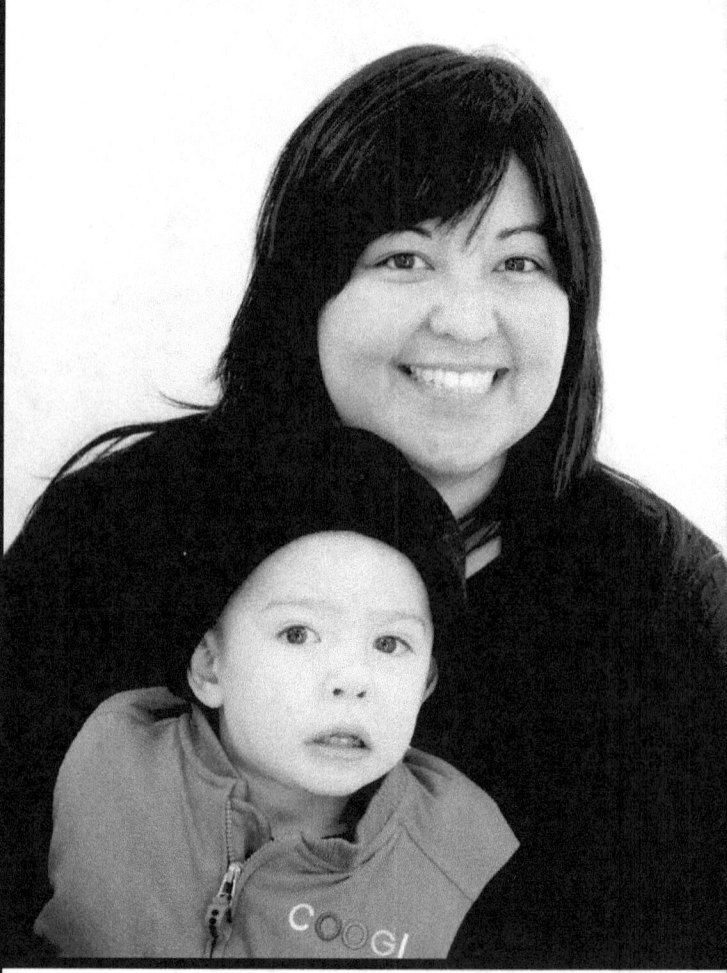
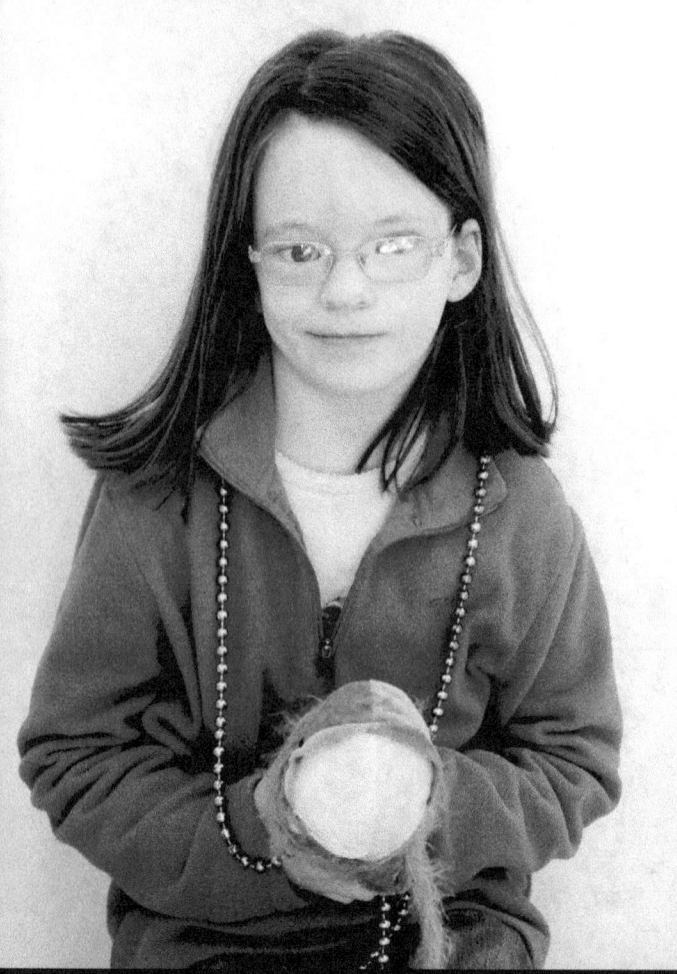
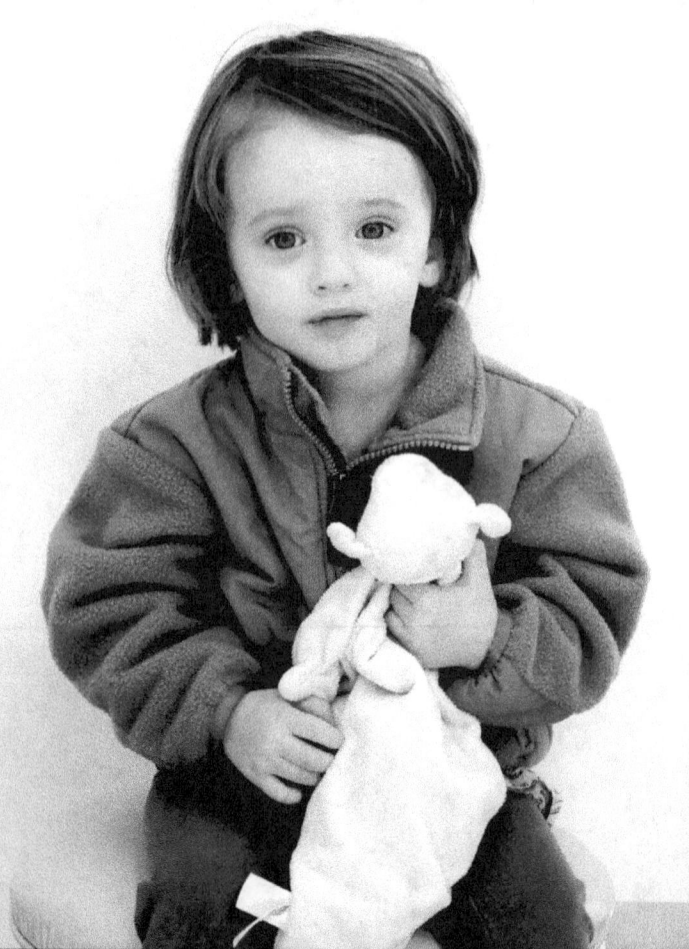

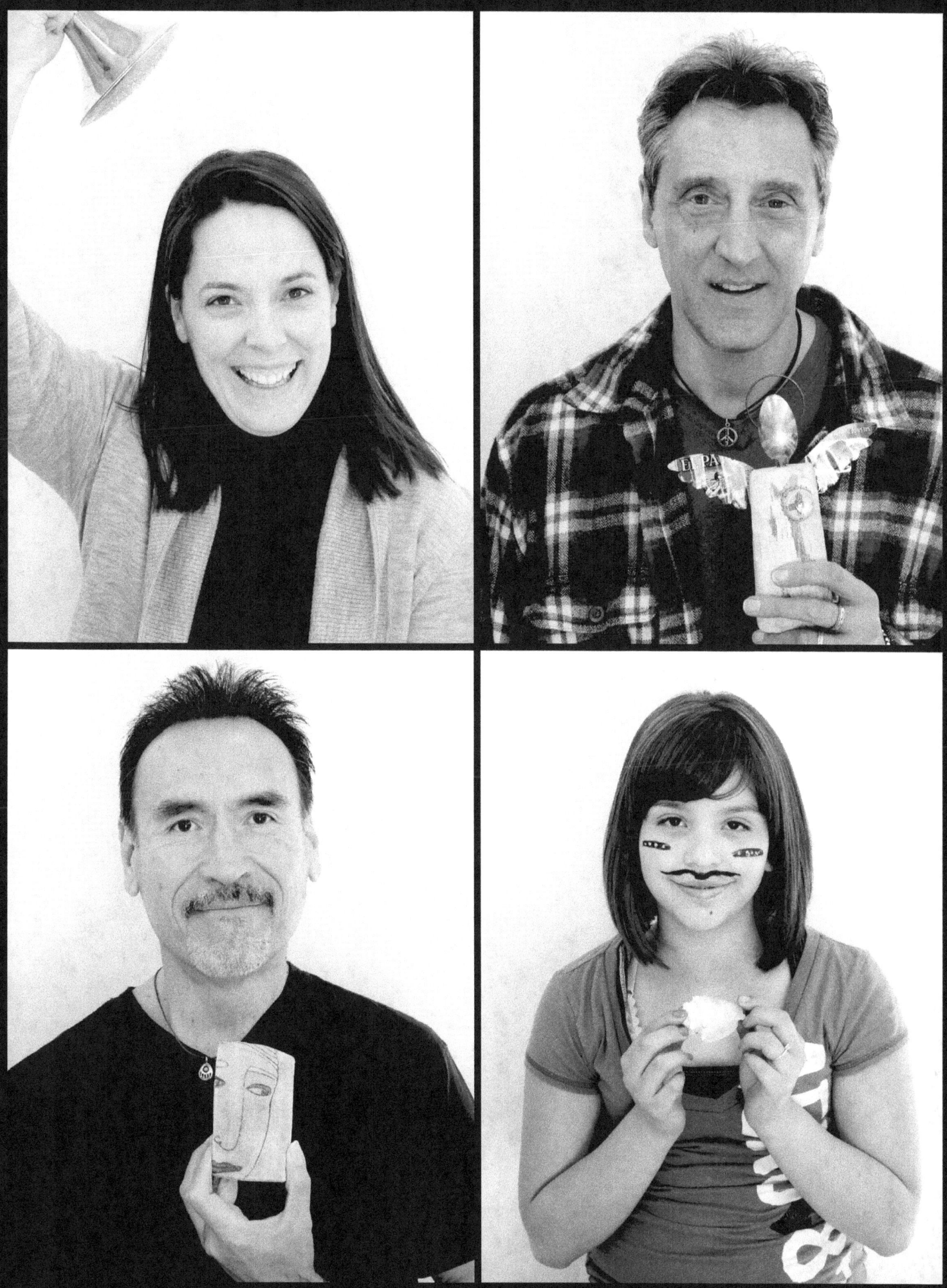

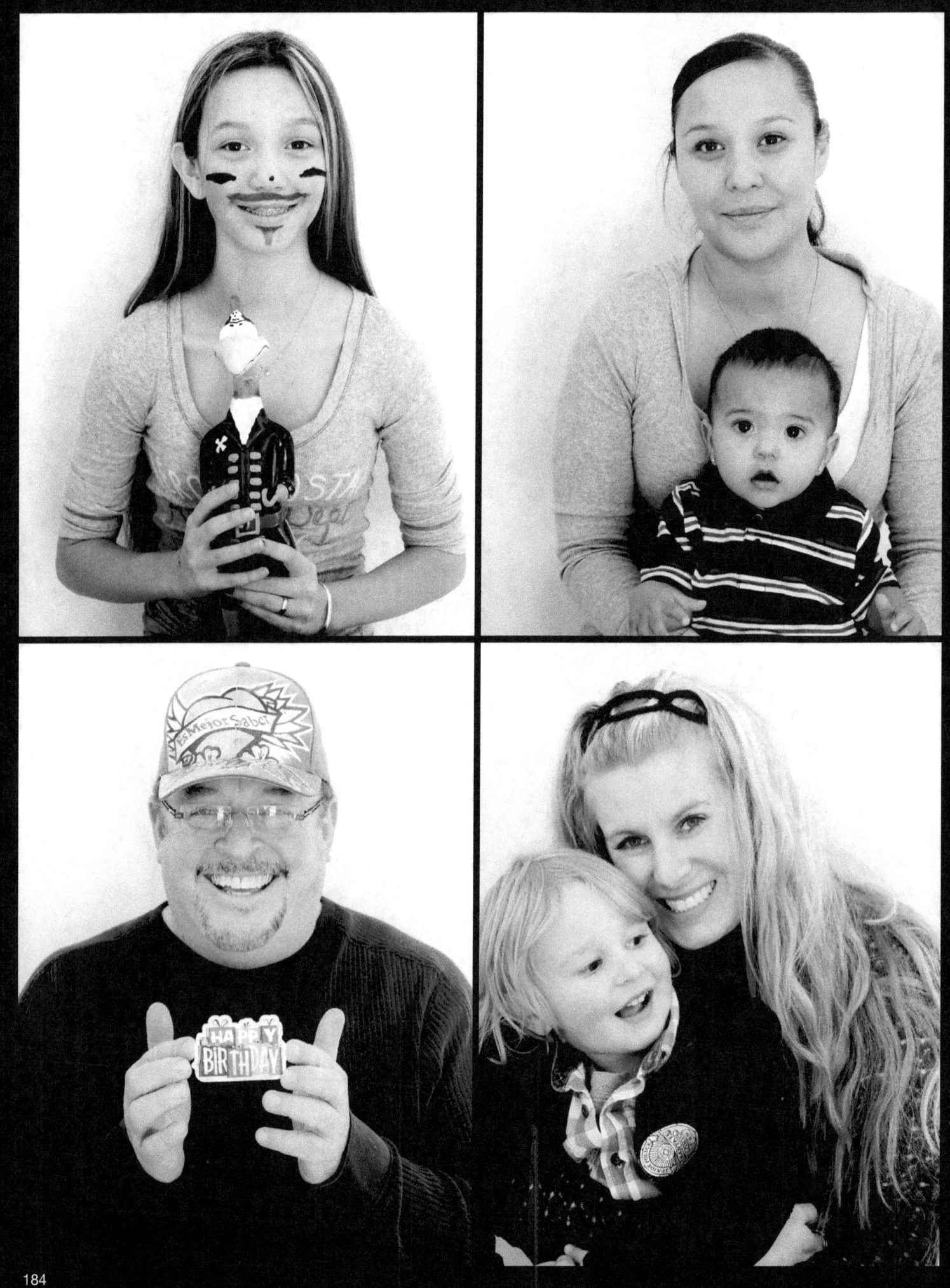

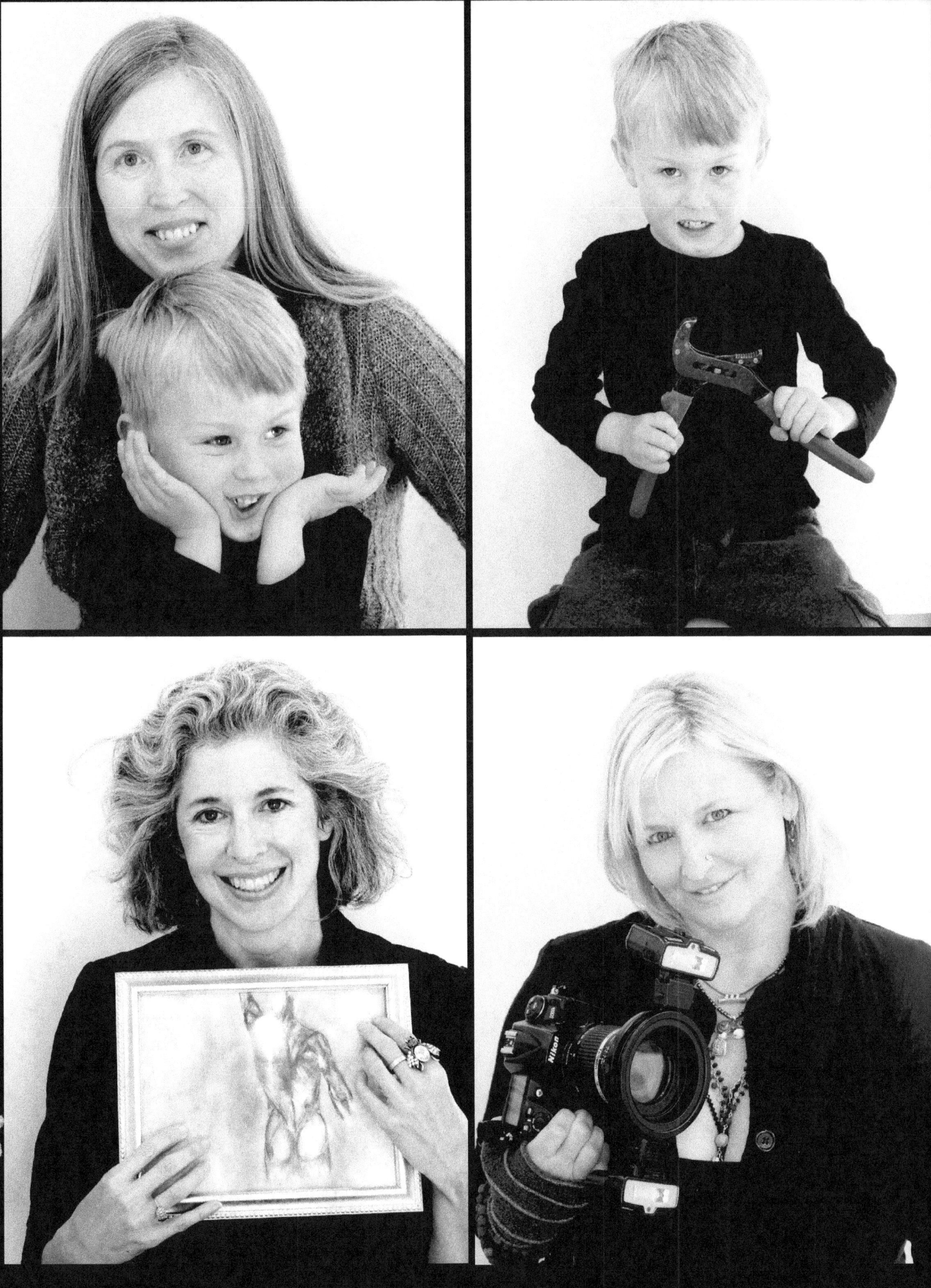

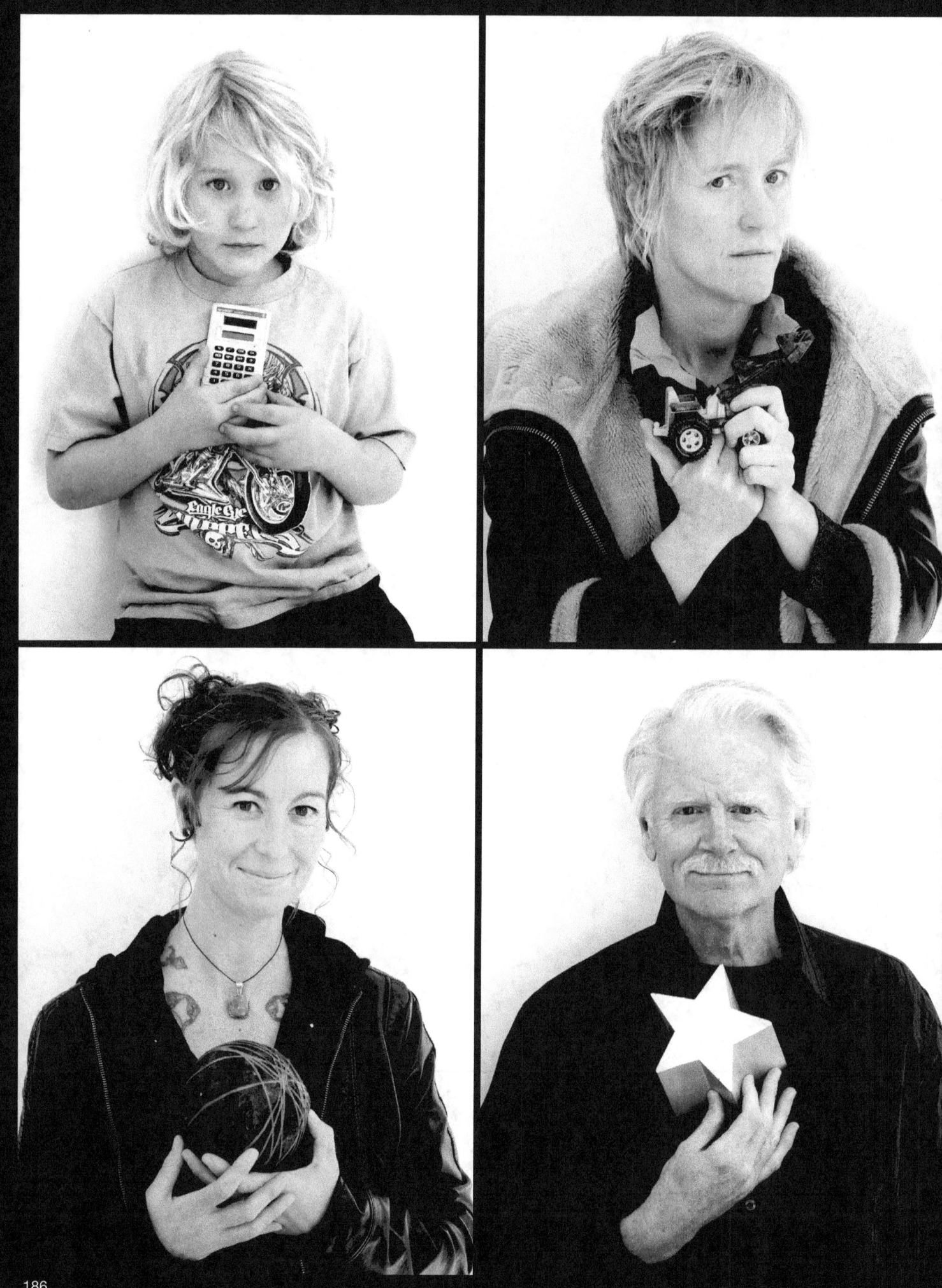

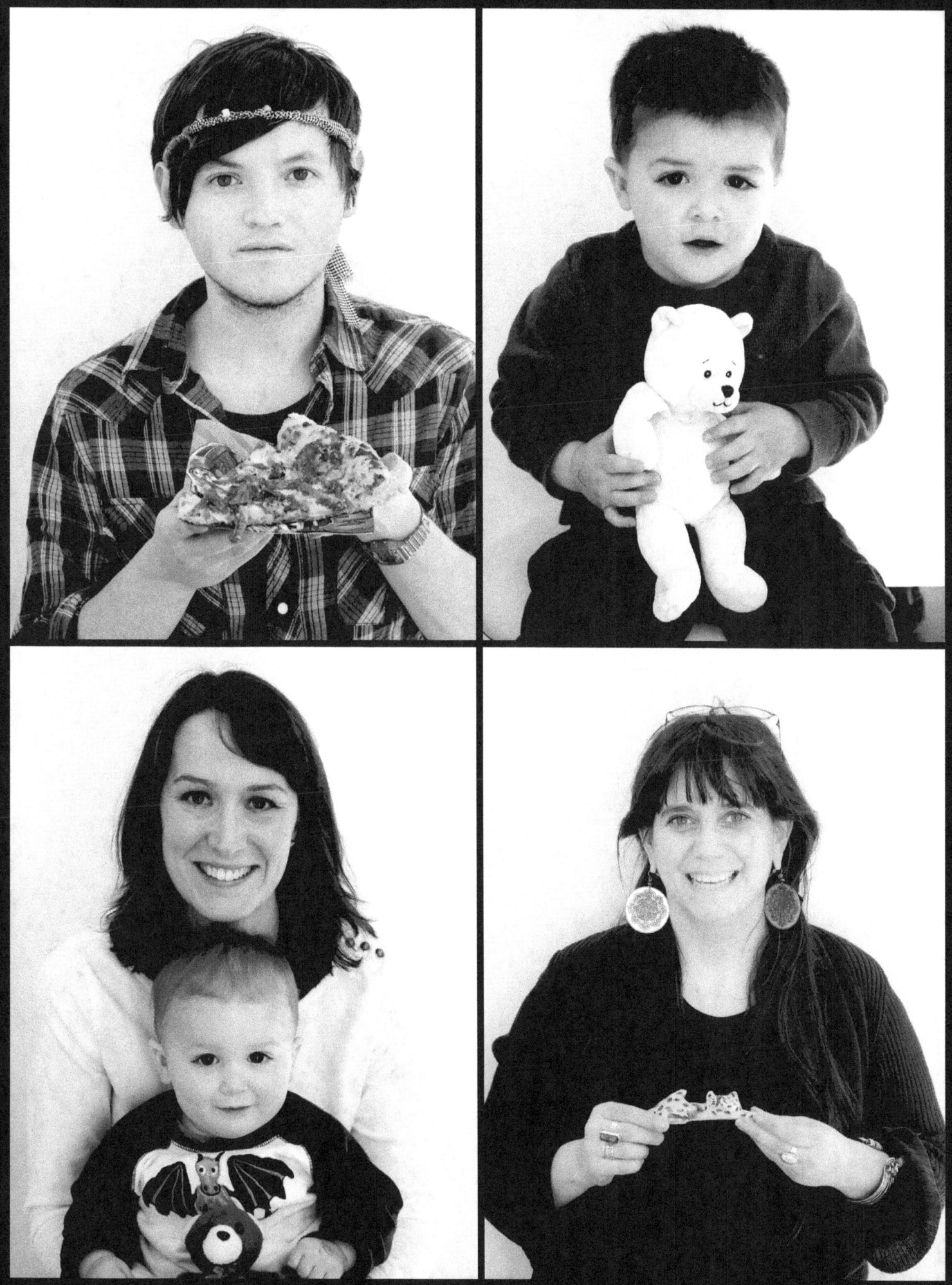

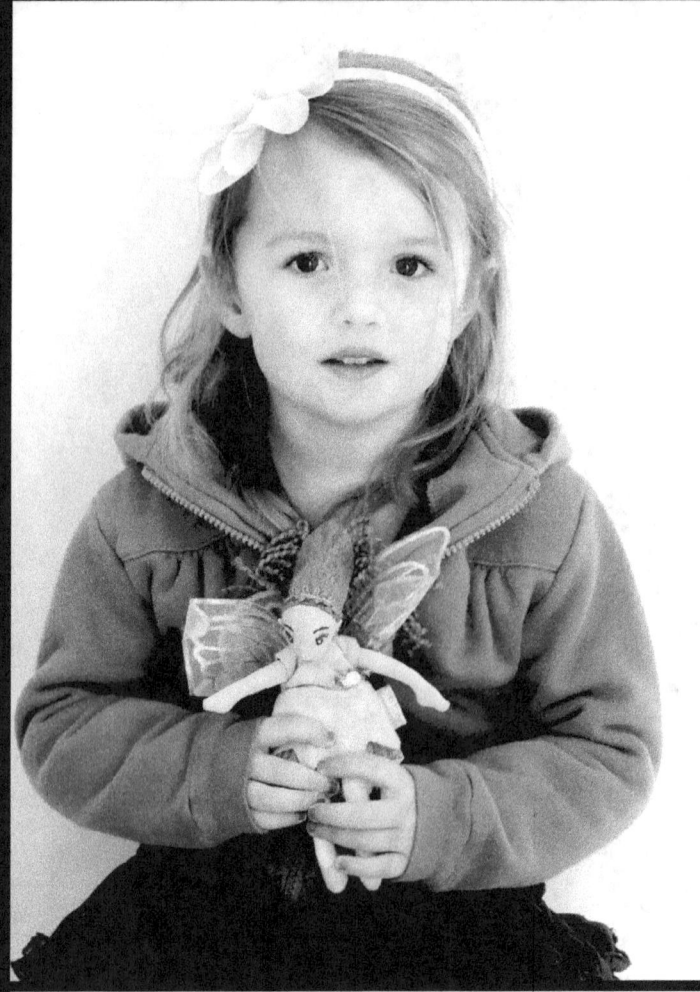
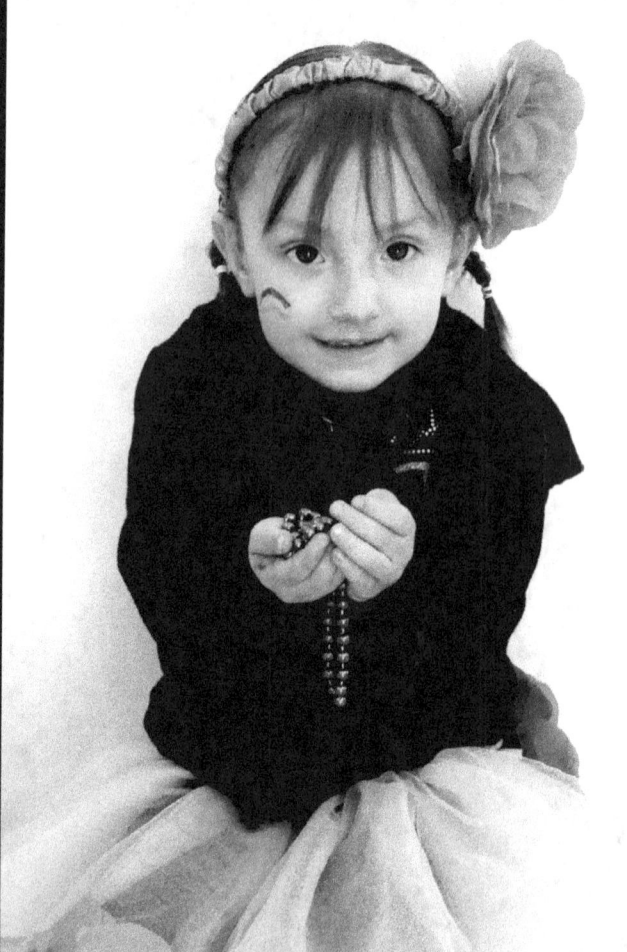
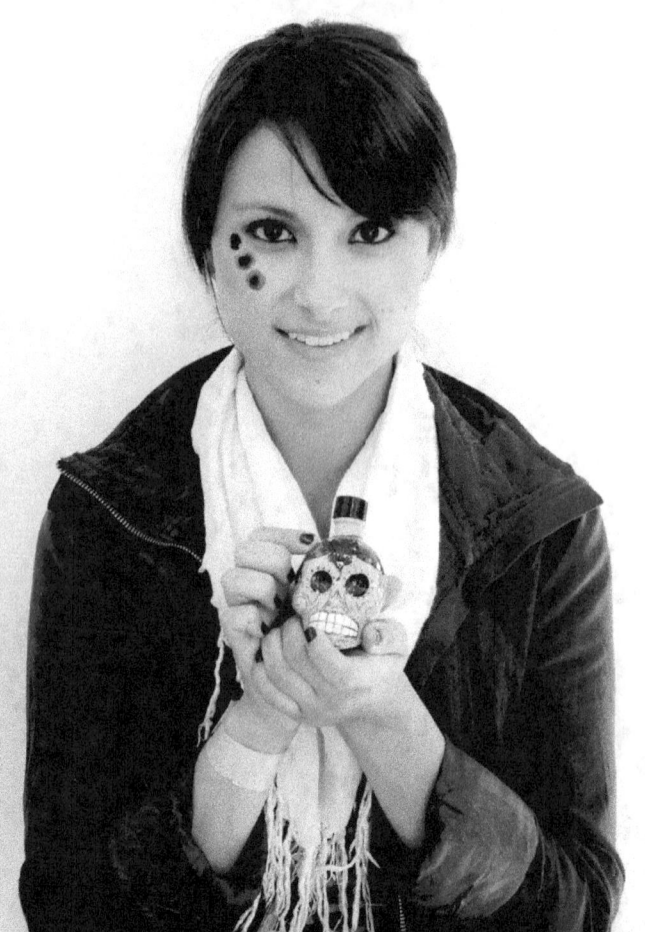
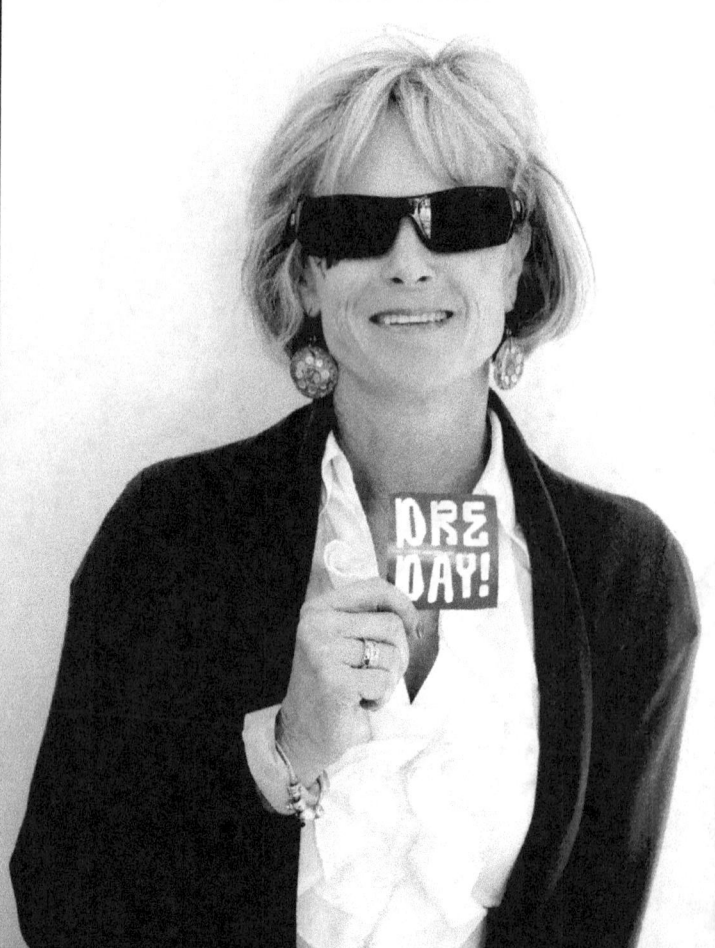

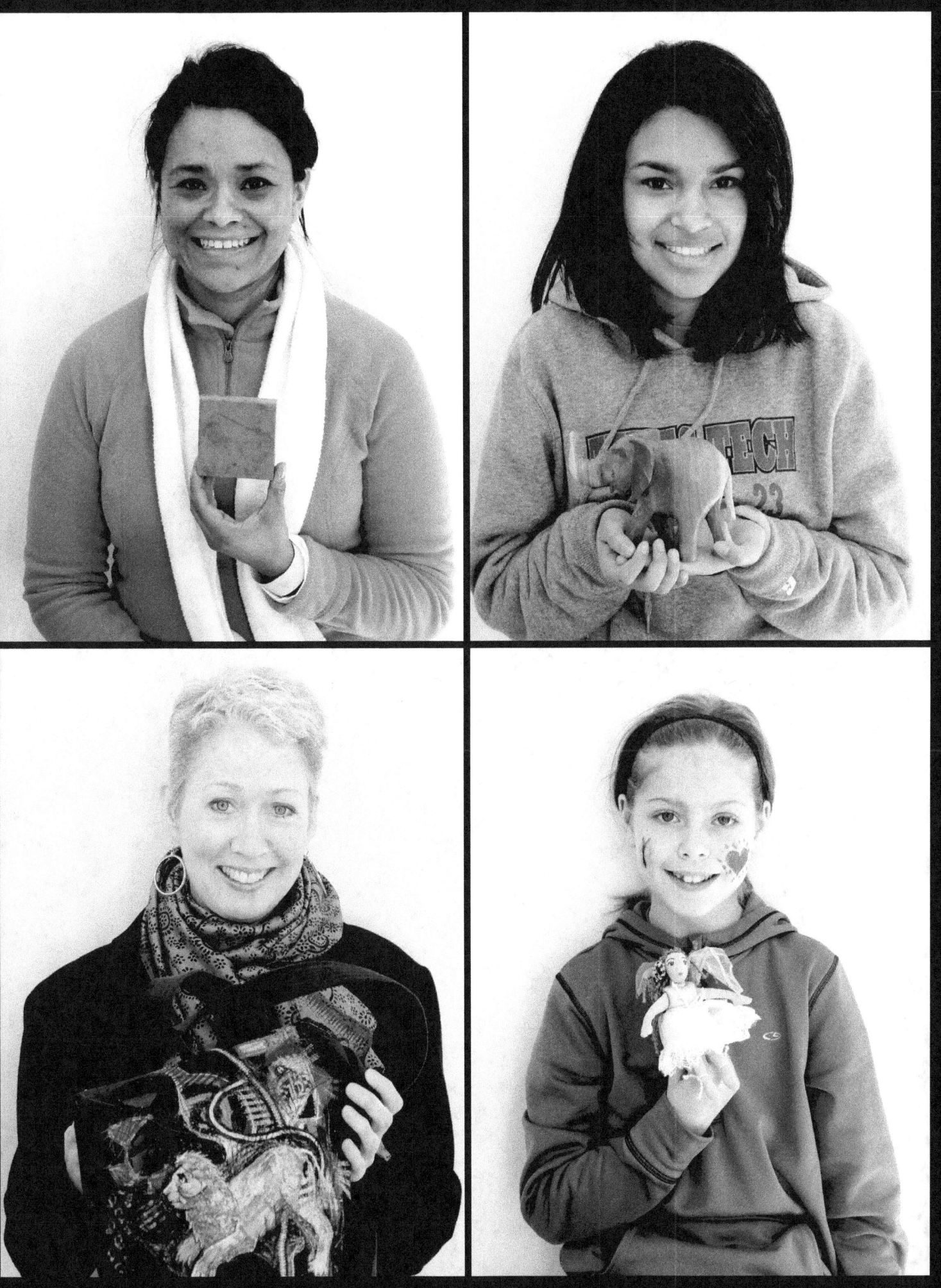

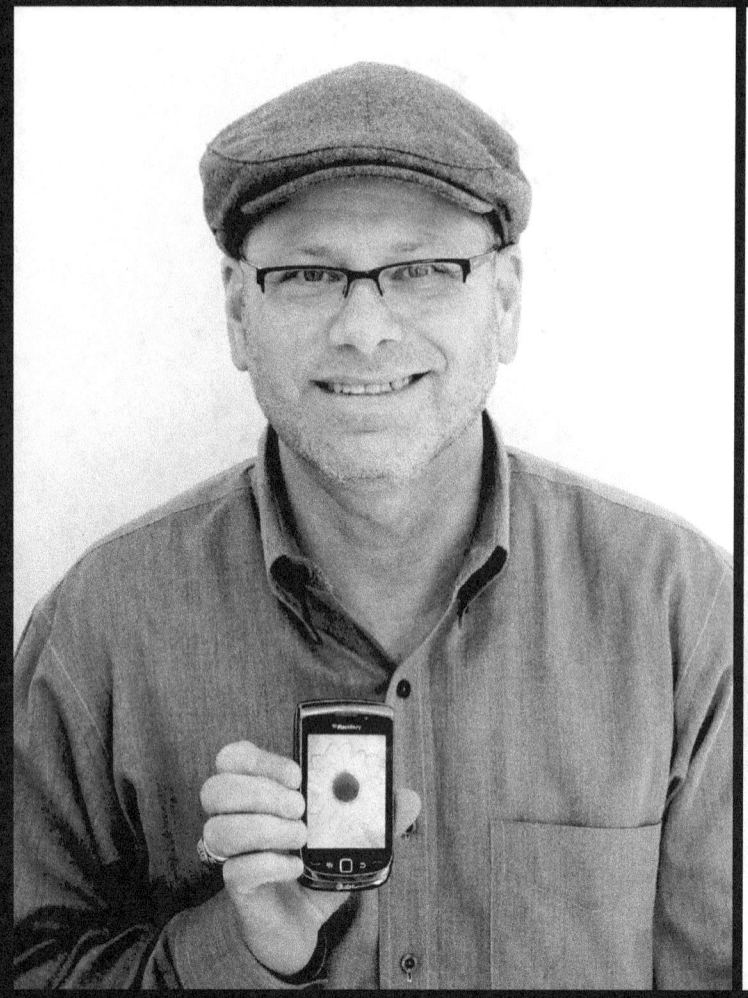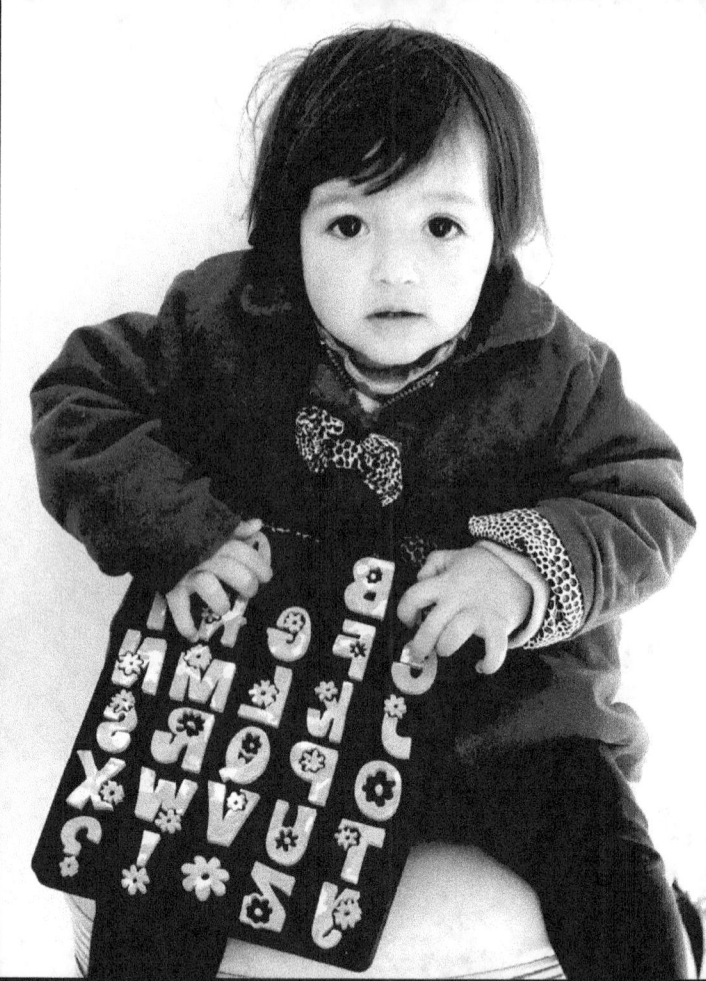

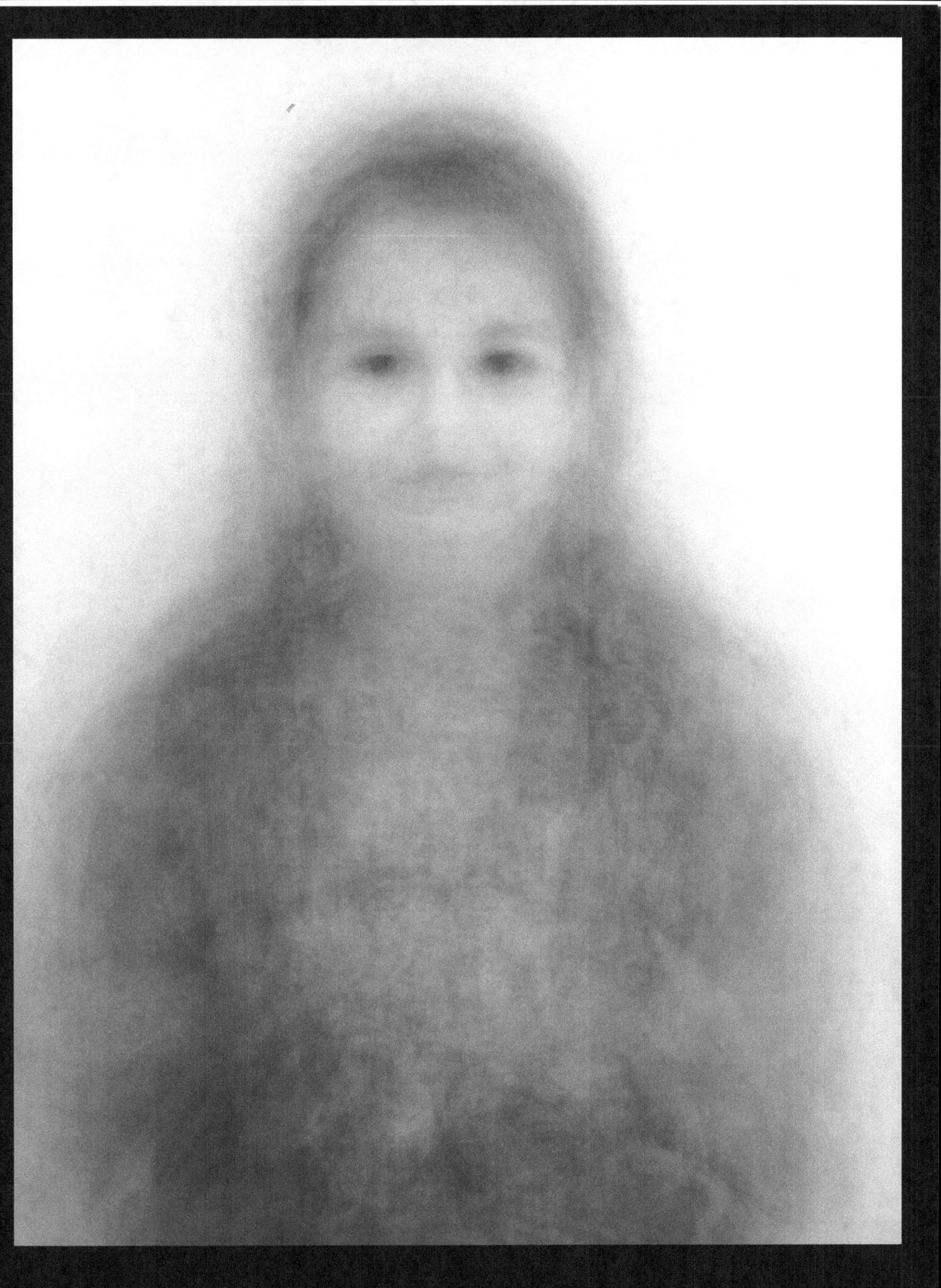

From Many One

March 2nd - 11th
2012

Santa Fe
New Mexico

www.ingramcontent.com/pod-product-compliance
Lightning Source LLC
Chambersburg PA
CBHW080009210526
45170CB00015B/1949